Practical Node.js

Building Real-World Scalable
Web Apps

Second Edition

Azat Mardan

Apress®

Practical Node.js

Azat Mardan
San Francisco, California, USA

ISBN-13 (pbk): 978-1-4842-3038-1
https://doi.org/10.1007/978-1-4842-3039-8

ISBN-13 (electronic): 978-1-4842-3039-8

Library of Congress Control Number: 2018958762

Managing Director, Apress Media LLC: Welmoed Spahr
Acquisitions Editor: Louise Corrigan
Development Editor: James Markham
Coordinating Editor: Nancy Chen

Cover designed by eStudioCalamar

Distributed to the book trade worldwide by Springer Science+Business Media New York, 233 Spring Street, 6th Floor, New York, NY 10013. Phone 1-800-SPRINGER, fax (201) 348-4505, e-mail orders-ny@springer-sbm.com, or visit www.springeronline.com. Apress Media, LLC is a California LLC and the sole member (owner) is Springer Science + Business Media Finance Inc (SSBM Finance Inc). SSBM Finance Inc is a **Delaware** corporation.

For information on translations, please e-mail rights@apress.com, or visit www.apress.com/rights-permissions.

Apress titles may be purchased in bulk for academic, corporate, or promotional use. eBook versions and licenses are also available for most titles. For more information, reference our Print and eBook Bulk Sales web page at www.apress.com/bulk-sales.

Any source code or other supplementary material referenced by the author in this book is available to readers on GitHub via the book's product page, located at www.apress.com/9781484230381. For more detailed information, please visit www.apress.com/source-code.

Printed on acid-free paper

To Vladimir Nabokov and The Defense

Table of Contents

About the Author

Azat Mardan works in technology leadership at Indeed.com, the world leader in job search. Azat is a JavaScript/Node.js expert with dozens of published online courses on Node University, edX, and Udemy, and books including much praised top-sellers *React Quickly* (Manning, 2017), *Full Stack JavaScript* (Apress, 2015), *Practical Node.js* (Apress, 2014), *Pro Express.js* (Apress, 2014) and many others.

Two of Azat's self-published books, *Rapid Prototyping with JS* and *Express.js Guide*, became bestsellers on Amazon in their categories before being revised and published by Apress.

In 2016 alone, Azat spoke at over a dozen tech conferences, including JSConf, Node Summit, NDC, Node Interactive, ConFoo, ForwardJS, All Things Open, GDG DevFest, Great Wide Open, and others. Over the years, Azat has shared a speaking platform with prominent software gurus such as Douglas Crockford, Christian Heilmann, Jeff Atwood, Dan Shaw, Mikeal Rogers, John Papa, Axel Rauschmayer, Kyle Simpso, Samer Buna, James Halliday, Maxwell Ogden, Rey Bango, and many others.

Azat is an ex-Technology Fellow at Capital One, a top U.S. bank. At various times, Azat has worked as software engineer and technology leader in different organizations, including U.S. federal government agencies, Fortune 200 companies, small startups, and medium-sized corporations. During his career, Azat has worked on teams with prominent tech people such as Raquel Vélez (first engineer at npm), Jim Jagielski (founder of Apache Foundation), Bobby Calderwood (contributor to ClojureScript), and Mitch Pirtle (co-founder of Joomla!).

Azat has taught in-person and face-to-face over a thousand software engineers at prominent U.S. and global corporations including Cisco, Walmart, Starbucks, Michael Kors, Salesforce, 20th Century Fox/Fox Studios, VMWare, CapitalOne, OnDeck, Northwestern Mutual, HubSpot, UC Davis, The University of Arizona, Intuit, DocuSign, Intuit, Macy's, Twillio, The Orchard, and Apple.

In his spare time, Azat enjoys a cup of Americano with ghee while recording videos for Node University (`https://node.university`), where thousands of developers sharpen and master their Node skills.

Acknowledgments

Thank you to the supporters of my Kickstarter campaign. Without you, I probably would have not worked on this release so hard, and maybe wouldn't have worked at all. You are *awesome* because you made this new edition a reality. Not only that but you have made this book available on GitHub for the entire world to read and learn Node, the greatest technology for building web applications ever.

In particular, a great many thanks to individual Kickstarter supporters (who will be getting the signed print edition books and other rewards): Matthew Amacker, Jordan Horiuchi, Tim Chen, Alexey Bushnev, Aleksey Maksimov, Maurice van Cooten, Ryan, Ng Yao Min, Kommana Karteek, Elias Yousef, Arhuman, Javier Armendariz, Dave Anderson, and Edithson Abelard. You guys are brilliant!

I can't not mention the biggest supporter, DevelopIntelligence, which is one of the best training companies, if not the best (`www.developintelligence.com`). If you need to train your software engineers in anything, e-mail them. Seriously, DevelopIntelligence has been around for more than 20 years and has great teachers and great technical classes. I was one of their instructors, so I know.

I convey my gratitude to all the wonderful people I've encountered in my software engineering career. These people supported, mentored, and trusted me with new challenges, helped me to find mistakes, and pushed my limits.

Of course, this book wouldn't be possible without the assistance, research, and championing done by my wonderful Apress editors. I especially thank Louise Corrigan, James Markham, Cat Ohala, and Peter Elst.

Also, appreciation and many thanks go to the readers who kindly provided feedback to the first edition of *Practical Node.js*, my Webapplog.com (`http://webapplog.com`) blog posts, and my prior books.

Introduction

More and more books and online resources are being published that cover Node.js basics (typically, how-to's of Hello World and simple apps). For the most part, these tutorials rely on core modules only or maybe one or two npm packages. This "sandbox" approach of tutorials is easy and doesn't require many dependencies, but it couldn't be further from the actual Node.js stack.

This is especially true with Node.js, the core of which—by design—is kept lean and minimal. At the same time, the vast "userland" (that is, npm) provides an ecosystem of packages/modules to serve specific granular purposes. Therefore, there is a need to show how Node.js is used in the industry and to have it all in one place—the all-encompassing practical resource that can be used as a learning tool, code cookbook, and reference.

What This Book Is and What It's Not

Practical Node.js: Building Real-World Scalable Web Apps is a hands-on manual for developing production-ready web applications and services by leveraging the rich ecosystem of Node.js packages. This is important because real applications require many components, such as security, deployment, code organization, database drivers, template engines, and more. That's why I include extensive 12-chapter coverage of third-party services, command-line tools, npm modules, frameworks, and libraries.

Just to give you some idea, *Practical Node.js* is a one-stop place for getting started with Express.js 4, Hapi.js, DerbyJS, Mongoskin, Mongoose, Everyauth, Mocha, Jade, Socket.IO, TravisCI, Heroku, Amazon Web Services (AWS), and many other technologies. Most of these are vital for any serious project.

In this book we'll create a few projects by building, step by step, a straightforward concept into a more complicated application. These projects can also serve as a boilerplate for jump-starting your own development efforts. The examples also show industry best practices to help you avoid costly mistakes. Last but not least, many topics and chapters serve as a reference to which you can always return later when you're faced with a challenging problem.

Practical Node.js aims to save you time and make you a more productive Node.js programmer. Although the first chapter is dedicated to installations and a few important differences between Node.js and browser JavaScript, I didn't want to dilute the core message of making production-ready apps, or make the book even larger and more convoluted. Therefore, **this book is not a beginner's guide**, and there is no extensive immersion into the inner workings of the Node.js platform and its core modules.

I also can't guarantee that I've explained each component and topic to the extent you need, because the nature of your project might be very specific. Most chapters in the book help you to get started with the stack. There is simply no realistic way to fit so many topics in one book and cover them comprehensively.

Another caveat of this book (and virtually any programming book) is that the versions of the packages we use will eventually become obsolete. Often, this isn't an issue because, in this book, versions are stated and locked explicitly. So, no matter what, the examples will continue to work with book's versions. Even if you decide to use the latest versions, in many cases that might not be an issue because essentials remain the same. However, if you go this off-path route, once in a while you might be faced with a breaking change introduced by the latest versions.

Who Can Benefit from This Book

Practical Node.js is an intermediate- to advanced-level book on programming with Node.js. Consequently, to get the most out of it, you need to have prior programming experience and some exposure to Node.js. I assume readers' prior knowledge of computer science, programming concepts, web development, Node.js core modules, and the inner workings of HTTP and the Internet.

However, depending on your programming level and ability to learn, you can fill in any knowledge gaps very quickly by visiting links to official online documentation and reading external resources referenced in this book. Also, if you have a strong programming background in some other programming language, it should be relatively easy for you to start Node.js development with *Practical Node.js*.

Written as it was for for intermediate and advanced software engineers, there are categories of programmers who can most benefit from it:

1. Generalist or full-stack developers including development operation (DevOps) and quality assurance (QA) automation engineers

2. Experienced front-end web developers with a strong background and understanding of browser JavaScript

3. Skilled back-end software engineers coming from other languages, such as Java, PHP, and Ruby, who don't mind doing some extra work getting up to speed with JavaScript.

What You'll Learn

Practical Node.js takes you from an overview of JavaScript and Node.js basics, through installing all the necessary modules, to writing and deploying web applications, and everything in between. It covers libraries including but not limited to Express.js 4 and Hapi.js frameworks, Mongoskin and the Mongoose object-relational mapping (ORM) library for the MongoDB database, Jade and Handlebars template engines, Auth and Everyauth libraries for OAuth integrations, the Mocha testing framework and Expect test-driven development/behavior-driven development language, and the Socket.IO and DerbyJS libraries for WebSocket real-time communication.

In the deployment chapters (Chapters 10 and 11), the book covers how to use Git and deploy to Heroku, and it provides examples of how to deploy to AWS, daemonize apps, and use NGINX, Varnish Cache, Upstart, init.d, and the forever module.

The hands-on approach of this book walks you through iterating on the Blog project we'll be building, in addition to many other smaller examples. You'll build database scripts, representational state transfer (RESTful) application programming interfaces (APIs), tests, and full-stack apps—all from scratch. You'll also discover how to write your own Node.js modules and publish them on npm.

Practical Node.js will show you how to do the following:

- Build web apps with Express.js 4, MongoDB, and the Jade template engine

- Use various features of Jade and Handlebars

- Manipulate data from the MongoDB console

- Use the Mongoskin and Mongoose ORM libraries for MongoDB

- Build REST API servers with Express.js 4 and Hapi.js

- Test Node.js web services with Mocha, Expect, and TravisCI

- Use token and session-based authentication

- Implement a third-party (Twitter) OAuth strategy with Everyauth

- Build WebSocket apps using Socket.IO and DerbyJS libraries

- Prepare code for production with Redis, Node.js domains, and the cluster library using tips and best practices

- Deploy apps to Heroku using Git

- Install necessary Node.js components on an AWS instance

- Configure NGINX, Upstart, Varnish, and other tools on an AWS instance

- Write your own Node.js module and publish it on npm

You already know what Node.js is. It's time to learn what you can do with it and see how far you can take it.

Why You Should Read This Book

Practical Node.js was designed to be one stop for going from Hello World examples to building apps in a professional manner. You get a taste of the most widely used Node.js libraries in one place, along with best practices and recommendations based on years of building and running Node.js apps in production. The libraries covered in the book greatly enhance the quality of code and make you more productive. Also, although the material in this book isn't groundbreaking, the convenience of the format will save you hours of frustration researching on the Internet. *Practical Node.js* is here to help you to jump-start your Node.js development.

Notation

The book and all its source code follow StandardJS (https://standardjs.com) coding style. When it comes to showing the code in the book, this book follows a few formatting conventions. Code is in monospace font. This is inline code, `var book = {name: 'Practical Node.js'};`, and this is a code listing:

```
server.on('stream', (stream, headers) => {
  // Stream is a Duplex
  stream.respond({
    'content-type': 'text/html',
    ':status': 200
  })
  stream.end('<h1>Hello World<h1>')
})
```

Unfortunately, book pages are narrower than expandable code editor windows. That's why some code formatting in books may be slightly different than StandardJS, because by necessity sometimes there are more line breaks.

For this reason, be especially careful in the code listings about maintaining proper syntax, avoiding typos, and not having extra line breaks. If in doubt, always refer to the GitHub source code instead of relying on the book because the GitHub source code will always have more proper formatting (StandardJS) and may even contain a bug fix that somehow sneaked into a code listing in the book.

If the code begins with $, that means it's meant to be executed in the terminal/command line. However, if the code line starts with >, the code is meant for the virtual environment (the console—either Node.js or MongoDB). If the Node.js module name is in code font, that means it's the npm name and you can use it with npm and the `require()` method, such as `superagent`.

Source Code

Learning is more effective when we apply our knowledge right away. For this reason, virtually every chapter in *Practical Node.js* ends with a hands-on exercise. For your convenience, and because the publisher and I believe in open source and transparency, all the book's examples are available publicly (free of charge) for exploration and execution on GitHub at `https://github.com/azat-co/practicalnode`.

Errata and Contacts

If you spot any mistakes or typos (and I'm sure you will), please open an issue—or, even better, make a pull request and fix it on the GitHub repository of the book's examples at `https://github.com/azat-co/practicalnode`. For all other updates and contact information, the canonical home of *Practical Node.js* on the Internet is `http://practicalnodebook.com`.

CHAPTER 1

Setting up Node.js and Other Essentials

In many technologies, it's vital to have the proper foundation set up first, before moving on to solving more complex problems. With Node.js, proper foundation is even more important because of all the bad syntax and quirks that JavaScript brings to Node. In this chapter, we cover the following:

- Node.js and npm (Node package manager) installation
- Node.js script launches
- Node.js syntax and basics
- Node.js integrated development environments (IDEs) and code editors
- Awareness of file changes
- Node.js program debugging

Installing Node.js and npm

Although your operating system (OS) might have Node.js installed on it already, you should update to at least version 8.x, which is the latest recommended long-term support (LTS) version as of this writing (July 2018). Version 8 is used in the examples and projects of this book. Version 8 is LTS and the recommended choice because it will be supported until October 2019 according to the Node official release schedule.

If you are reading the book after October 2019, please use the next LTS version for your real-life projects. You can still use Node.js version 8 for this book's projects to ensure

© Azat Mardan 2018
A. Mardan, *Practical Node.js*, https://doi.org/10.1007/978-1-4842-3039-8_1

smooth execution and lack of conflicts. In the following subsection, we examine a few different approaches to installing Node.js:

- *One-click installers*: Probably the easiest and fastest way to get started with the platform

- *Installing with HomeBrew or MacPorts*: Straightforward installation for macOS users

- *Installing from a tar file*: An alternative installation from an archive file

- *Installing without* `sudo`: The best way to avoid needing `sudo` (admin rights) when using the `node` and `npm` commands

- *Installing from a Git repo*: An option for advanced developers who need the latest version and/or contribute to the project

- *Multiversion setup with Nave*: a must-have for developers contributing to projects that use different Node.js versions

- *Multiversion setup with Node Version Manager* (*NVM*): alternative to Nave (see previous entry)

A note about Long-Term Support (LTS) and non-LTS versions: LTS versions have longer maintenance window. This means that LTS versions will have patches and updates longer than non-LTS versions. Thus LTS versions are recommended for most users and production deployment (not because non- LTS is not proven but simply because LTS has a longer support time).

LTS versions are even numbers, such as 4, 6, 8, 10, and so on. And non-LTS versions are odd numbers. Non-LTS versions have the latest features before they are rolled out to the next LTS version. We will be using LTS version 8.x. For more information and the current release schedule, please see `https://github.com/nodejs/LTS`.

One-Click Installers

First, let's go to `http://nodejs.org` and download a one-click installer for your OS (Figure 1-1) by clicking on the Install button. Don't choose binaries or source code unless you know what to do with them or your OS is not present there (i.e., not Windows or Mac).

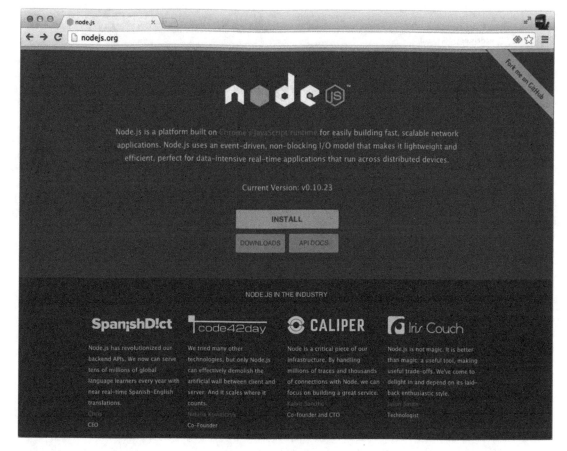

Figure 1-1. *One-click installers for Node.js*

The installers come with npm, Node package manager, which is an important tool for managing dependencies.

If there's no installer for your OS on the download page (page `https://nodejs.org/en/download`), you can get the source code and compile it yourself (Figure 1-2).

Figure 1-2. Multiple options for downloading

Note   For older macOS machines, you can pick 32-bit versions.

Installing with HomeBrew or MacPorts

If you already have HomeBrew (`brew`) installed, first update the brew itself, and run install commands:

```
$ brew update
$ brew install node
```

To install the latest Node version, run:

```
$ brew upgrade node
```

If your macOS does not have HomeBrew, go to `http://brew.sh` or install it with the following command:

```
$ ruby -e "$(curl -fsSL https://raw.github.com/Homebrew/homebrew/go/
install)"
```

Similarly, for MacPorts, run:

```
$ sudo port install nodejs
```

Installing from a Tar File

To install from a tar file (which is type of archive), set up a folder for the latest Node.js as follows:

```
$ echo 'export PATH=$HOME/local/bin:$PATH' >> ~/.bashrc
$ . ~/.bashrc
$ mkdir ~/local
$ mkdir ~/node-latest-install
$ cd ~/node-latest-install
```

Note   Advanced users who choose to make their own Node.js builds need to have certain compilers installed first. For more information about building Node from source, refer to the official documentation (`https://github.com/nodejs/node/blob/master/BUILDING.md`).

Download the tar file with CURL and unpack it:

```
$ curl http://nodejs.org/dist/node-latest.tar.gz | tar xz --strip-
components=1
$ ./configure --prefix=~/local
```

Build Node.js and install it:

```
$ make install
$ curl https://npmjs.org/install.sh | sh
```

Tip   If you find yourself getting errors when trying to install the module globally via npm (`$ npm install -g <packagename>`), reinstall Node.js and npm with the "Installing Without sudo" solution —discussed in the next section—to eliminate the need to use `sudo` with the installation command.

Installing Without sudo

Sometimes, depending on your configuration, npm asks users for `sudo` —root user permissions. To avoid using `sudo`, advanced developers can use the following:

```
$ sudo mkdir -p /usr/local/{share/man,bin,lib/node,include/node}
$ sudo chown -R $USER /usr/local/{share/man,bin,lib/node,
include/node}
```

Note   Please be sure you are comfortable with the functionality of the `chown` command before you run it.

Then, proceed with a normal installation:

```
$ mkdir node-install
$ curl http://nodejs.org/dist/node-v0.4.3.tar.gz | tar -xzf - -C
node-install
$ cd node-install/*
$ ./configure
$ make install
$ curl https://npmjs.org/install.sh | sh
```

Installing from Source Code

If you want to use the latest core Node.js code, and maybe even contribute to the Node.js and npm projects, your best choice is to use the installation from the source code that is in Node repository on GitHub. This will allow you to change the Node code itself, and then compile and run it.

This step requires Git. To install it, go to `http://git-scm.com` and click Download. For basic Git commands, refer to Chapter 11, which explores deployment.

For full, detailed instructions, go to `https://github.com/nodejs/node/blob/master/BUILDING.md`. Here is the short version of the instructions:

1. Make the folders and add the path:

```
$ mkdir ~/local
$ echo 'export PATH=$HOME/local/bin:$PATH' >> ~/.bashrc
$ . ~/.bashrc
```

   To clone the original Node.js repo from nodejs/node (alternatively, you can fork it and clone your own repository), do the following:

```
$ git clone git@github.com:nodejs/node.git
$ cd node
$ ./configure --prefix=~/local
```

2. Build Node with the make command:

```
$ make install
```

3. Repeat for npm:

```
$ git clone https://github.com/npm/npm
$ cd npm
$ make install
```

Multiversion Setup with NVM

If you plan to work on various Node projects, you might have to switch between multiple versions of Node.js. To make things easier, I recommend using a version manager that will allow you to install multiple versions and switch between them quickly and without a hassle.

One of the most trusted and battle-tested version managers is nvm (Node Version Manager): `https://github.com/creationix/nvm`. Install NVM as follows:

```
$ curl https://raw.github.com/creationix/nvm/master/install.sh | sh
```

or

```
$ wget -qO- https://raw.github.com/creationix/nvm/master/
install.sh | sh
```

Then you should be ready to start using NVM and its `install`. For example, to install Node v0.10, use this magic formula:

```
$ nvm install 0.10
```

After installing Node v0.10, to switch to the 0.10 version, apply the `use` command. For example:

```
$ nvm use 0.10
```

NVM won't move global npm modules from one version to another. If you are switching from y to x, then use `nvm install x --reinstall-packages-from=y` to reinstall all the global packages from "y" in the new "x". For example, to move packages to Node v8 from Node v6, use `nvm install 8.4.0 --reinstall-packages-from=6.11.2`.

Multiversion Setup with NVM for Windows

Node Version Manager (nvm) for Windows is a separate project from original nvm which is for macOS and Linux. nvm for Windows is (ironically) written in Go.

To download nvm for Windows, simply go to `https://github.com/coreybutler/nvm-windows` releases and select the latest version of the installer.

Alternative Multiversion Systems

The most popular and used alternatives to NVM include the following tools:

- *n* (`https://github.com/visionmedia/n`): The original and *simple* Node version manager without subshells (I still use it today on my personal computers)

- *nave* (`https://github.com/isaacs/nave`): The version manager written by the creator of npm Isaac Schelueter and that supports subshells

- *ndevn* (`https://github.com/riywo/ndenv`): Node.js version manager based on rbenv

Updating npm

You might have npm already, but due to big changes between npm versions 3 through 5, it's recommended to update npm to version 5, 6 or 7. Luckily, you can use npm to update npm!

```
npm i -g npm@latest
```

Checking the Installation

To test your installation, run the following commands in your Terminal or iTerm app (or in the command line cmd.exe for Windows):

```
$ node -v
$ npm -v
```

You should see the latest versions of Node.js and npm that you just downloaded and installed, as shown in Figure 1-3.

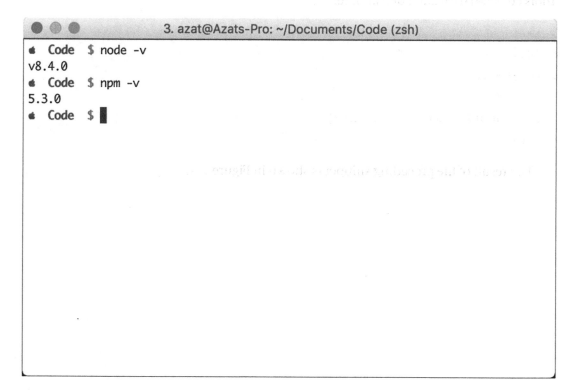

Figure 1-3. *Checking Node.js and npm installations*

That's it! Now you have Node.js and npm installed, and you should be ready to dig deeper into using the platform. The simplest way to run Node.js is through its virtual environment, which is often called *read–eval–print–loop*, or REPL.

Node.js Console (REPL)

Like most platforms/languages (e.g., Java, Python, Ruby, and PHP), Node.js comes with a virtual environment called read–eval–print loop (REPL). Using this shell program, we can execute pretty much any Node.js/JavaScript code. It's even possible to include modules and work with the file system! Other REPL use cases involve controlling drones nodecopters (`http://nodecopter.com`) and debugging remote servers (more about that in Chapter 10). To start the console, run the following command in your terminal:

```
$ node
```

The prompt should change from $ to > (or something else, depending on your shell). From this prompt, we can run any JavaScript/Node.js (akin to the Chrome Developer Tools console) we want. For example:

```
> 1+1
> "Hello"+" "+"World"
> a=1;b=2;a+b
> 17+29/2*7
> f = function(x) {return x*2}
> f(b)
```

The result of the preceding snippet is shown in Figure 1-4.

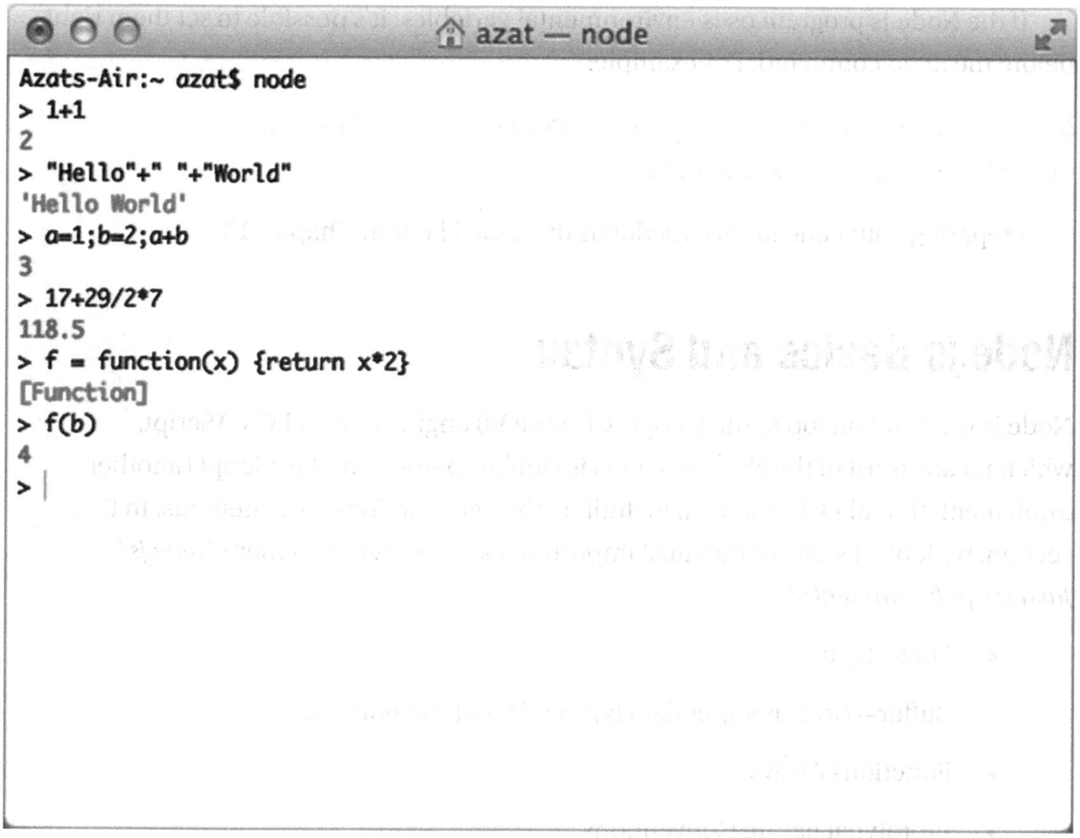

```
Azats-Air:~ azat$ node
> 1+1
2
> "Hello"+" "+"World"
'Hello World'
> a=1;b=2;a+b
3
> 17+29/2*7
118.5
> f = function(x) {return x*2}
[Function]
> f(b)
4
> |
```

Figure 1-4. *Executing JavaScript in Node.js REPL*

There are slight deviations in ECMAScript implementations between Node.js and browsers, such as the Chrome Developer Tools console. For example, `require()` is a valid method in Node.js REPL, whereas the same code produces `ReferenceError` in the Chrome DevTools console, because browsers don't support Node.js modules feature. However, for the most part, Node.js REPL and the Chrome/Firefox consoles are similar.

Launching Node.js Scripts

To start a Node.js script from a file, simply run $ `node filename` —for example, $ `node program.js`. If all we need is a quick set of statements, there's a `-e` option that allows us to run inline JavaScript/Node.js—for example, $ `node -e "console.log(new Date());"`.

If the Node.js program uses environmental variables, it's possible to set them right before the `node` command. For example:

```
$ NODE_ENV=production API_KEY=442CC1FE-4333-46CE-80EE
-6705A1896832 node server.js
```

Preparing your code for production is discussed later in Chapter 10.

Node.js Basics and Syntax

Node.js was built on top of the Google Chrome V8 engine and its ECMAScript, which means most of the Node.js syntax is similar to front-end JavaScript (another implementation of ECMAScript), including objects, functions, and methods. In this section, we look at some of the most important aspects—let's call them *Node.js/JavaScript fundamentals*:

- Loose typing

- Buffer—Node.js super data type Object literal notation

- Functions Arrays

- Prototypal nature Conventions

Loose Typing

Automatic typecasting works well most of the time. It's a great feature that saves a lot of time and mental energy! There are only a few types of primitives:

- String

- Number (both integer and real)

- Boolean

- Undefined

- Null

Everything else is an object. Class is an object. Function is an object. Array is an object. RegExp is an object. Objects are passed by reference whereas primitives are passed by values.

Also, in JavaScript, there are String, Number, and Boolean objects that contain helpers for the primitives, as follows:

```
'a' === new String('a') *// false*
```

but

```
'a' === new String('a').toString() *// true*
```

or

```
'a' == new String('a') *// true*
```

By the way, == performs automatic typecasting, whereas === does not.

Buffer—Node.js Super Data Type

Buffer is the data type. It is a Node.js addition to five primitives (boolean, string, number, undefined and null) and all-encompassing objects (arrays and functions are also objects) in front- end JavaScript. Think of buffers as extremely efficient data stores. In fact, Node.js tries to use buffers any time it can, such as when reading from a file system and when receiving packets over the network.

Buffer is functionally similar to JavaScript's ArrayBuffer. We use the class name Buffer to work with buffer objects.

To create a buffer object, use from. Buffer can be created from an array, another buffer, ArrayBuffer or a string:

```
const bufFromArray = Buffer.from([0x62, 0x75, 0x66, 0x66, 0x65, 0x72])
console.log(bufFromArray.toString()) // "buffer"

const arrayBuffer = new Uint16Array(2)
arrayBuffer[0] = 5
arrayBuffer[1] = 7000

// Shares memory with `arrayBuffer`
const bufFromArrayBuffer = Buffer.from(arrayBuffer.buffer)

// Prints: <Buffer 05 00 58 1b>
console.log(bufFromArrayBuffer)
```

```
// Changing the original Uint16Array changes the Buffer also
arrayBuffer[1] = 7001

// Prints: <Buffer 05 00 59 1b>
console.log(bufFromArrayBuffer)
```

As you saw in the preceding code, to convert Buffer to a string, you can use `toString()` method. By default, it will convert to UTF–8 encoding, but other encoding options are possible too, such as ASCII, HEX, or others:

```
const bufFromString = Buffer.from('¿Cómo está?')

console.log(bufFromString.toString('utf8')) // ¿Cómo está?
console.log(bufFromString.toString()) // ¿Cómo está?

console.log(bufFromString.toString('ascii')) // B?CC3mo estC!?

const bufFromHex = Buffer.from('c2bf43c3b36d6f20657374c3a13f', 'hex')

console.log(bufFromHex.toString()) // ¿Cómo está?
```

Object Literal Notation

Node object notation is the same as JavaScript, which means it is super readable and compact:

```
const car = {
  color: "green",
  type: "suv",
  owner: {
    ...
  },
  drive: function() {
    ...
  }
}
```

Node version 8 supports all the ES2015 (ES6) features, which allows developers to use new object literal syntax. This ES6 syntax makes defining objects so advanced that they resemble classes more than ES5 objects. For example, you can extend another object, define fields dynamically, invoke `super()` and use shorter syntax for functions:

```
const serviceBase = {
  port: 3000,
  url: 'azat.co'
}

const getAccounts = () => {
  return [1, 2, 3]
}

const accountService = {
  __proto__: serviceBase,
  getUrl() { // define method without "function"
    return "http://" + this.url + ':' + this.port
  },
  getAccounts() // define from an outer-scope function
  toString() { // overwrite proto method
    return JSON.stringify((super.valueOf()))
  },
  [ 'valueOf_' + getAccounts().join('_') ]: getAccounts()
}
console.log(accountService) // ready to be used
```

Functions

In Node.js (as well as in JavaScript), functions are *first-class citizens*, and we treat them as variables, because they are objects! Yes, functions can even have properties/attributes. First, let's learn how to define/create a function.

Define/Create a Function

The three most common ways to define/create a function are to use a named expression, an anonymous expression assigned to a variable, or both. The following is an example of a named expression:

```
function f() {
  console.log('Hi')
  return true
}
```

An anonymous function expression assigned to a variable looks as follows (note that it must precede the invocation, because the function is not hoisted, unlike the previous example):

```
const f = function() {
  console.log('Hi')
  return true
}
```

The new ES6 alternative of the anonymous function definition we just gave is a fat arrow function syntax. This new syntax has an added benefit of safer this due to its value always remaining an outer this:

```
// outer "this"
const f = () => {
  // still outer "this"
  console.log('Hi')
  return true
}
```

The following is an example of both approaches, anonymous and named:

```
const f = function f() {
  console.log('Hi')
  return true
}
```

A function with a property (remember, functions are just objects that can be invoked/initialized) is as follows:

```
const f = function() {console.log('Boo')}
f.boo = 1
f() *//outputs Boo*
console.log(f.boo) *//outputs 1*
```

Note   The `return` keyword is optional. When it is omitted, the function returns `undefined` on invocation. I like to call functions with `return`, expressions (see upcoming section "Function Invocation vs. Expression").

Pass Functions as Parameters

JavaScript treats functions like any other objects, so we can pass them to other functions as parameters (usually, callbacks in Node.js):

```
const convertNum = function(num) {
  return num + 10
}
const processNum = function(num, fn) {
  return fn(num)
}
processNum(10, convertNum)
```

Function Invocation vs. Expression

The function definition is as follows:

```
function f() {

}
```

On the other hand, the function invocation looks like the following:

```
f()
```

Expression, because it resolves to some value (which could be a number, string, object, or boolean), is as follows:

```
function f() {
  return false
}
f()
```

A statement looks like this:

```
function f(a) {
  console.log(a)
}
```

There's also an implicit `return` when you are using the fat arrow function. It works when there's just one statement in a function:

```
const fWithImplicitReturn = (a,b) => a+b
```

Arrays

Arrays are also objects that have some special methods inherited from the Array. prototype (`https://developer.mozilla.org/en-US/docs/Web/JavaScript/Reference/Global_Objects/Array/prototype#Properties`) global object. Nevertheless, JavaScript arrays are *not* real arrays; instead, they are objects with unique integer (usually 0-based) keys:

```
let arr = []
let arr2 = [1, "Hi", {a:2}, () => {console.log('boo')}]
let arr3 = new Array()
let arr4 = new Array(1,"Hi", {a:2}, () => {console.log('boo')})
arr4[3]() // boo
```

Prototypal Nature

There are *no classes* in JavaScript because objects inherit directly from other objects, which is called *prototypal inheritance*. There are a few types of inheritance patterns in JavaScript:

- Classical

- Pseudoclassical

- Functional

This is an example of the functional inheritance pattern in which two function factories create objects user and agent:

```
let user = function (ops) {
  return { firstName: ops.firstName || 'John',
    lastName: ops.lastName || 'Doe',
    email: ops.email || 'test@test.com',
    name: function() { return this.firstName + this.lastName}
  }
}

let agency = function(ops) {
  ops = ops || {}
  var agency = user(ops)
  agency.customers = ops.customers || 0
  agency.isAgency = true
  return agency
}
```

With class introduced in ES2015 (ES6), things are somewhat easier, especially for object-oriented programmers. A class can be extended, defined, and instantiated with extends, class, and new.

For example, this base class has constructor and a method:

```
class baseModel {
  constructor(options = {}, data = []) { // class constructor
    this.name = 'Base'
```

```
    this.url = 'http://azat.co/api'
    this.data = data
    this.options = options
  }
  getName() { // class method
    console.log(`Class name: ${this.name}`)
  }
}
```

Then we can create a new class using the base class. The new class will have all the functionality of a base class from which it inherits and then some more:

```
class AccountModel extends baseModel {
  constructor(options, data) {
    super({private: true}, ['32113123123', '524214691'])
// call the parent method with super
    this.name = 'Account Model'
    this.url +='/accounts/'
  }
  get accountsData() { // calculated attribute getter
    // ... make XHR
    return this.data
  }
}

let accounts = new AccountModel(5)
accounts.getName()
console.log('Data is %s', accounts.accountsData)
```

The results will be:

```
Class name: Account Model
Data is %s 32113123123,524214691
```

Conventions

It's important to follow the most common language conventions. Some of them are listed here:

- Semicolons

- camelCase

- Naming

- Commas

- Indentations

- Whitespace

These JavaScript/Node.js conventions (with semicolons being an exception) are stylistic and highly preferential. They don't impact the execution; however, it's strongly suggested that you follow one style consistently, especially if you are a developer working in teams and/or on open-source projects. Some open-source projects might not accept pull requests if they contain semicolons (e.g., npm) or if they don't use comma-first style (e.g., `request`).

Semicolons

Almost all statements in JavaScript and thus Node.js must be terminated with a semicolon. However, JavaScript engines have an automatic semicolon insertion feature. It inserts semicolons for developers by following a set of language rules. As with any programming language, developers should learn the syntax rules. Typing extra symbols is counterproductive. Hence, the use of semicolons is optional and counter-productive.

Learn the rules of ASI and you'll be more productive. Here's my very short and probably not complete version of the rules. Do not use semicolons, except for these cases:

1. In loop constructions such as `for (var i=0; i++; i<n)`

2. When a new line starts with parentheses or square brace or regular expression, such as when using an immediately invoked function expression (IIFE): `;(function(){...}())`

3. When doing something weird like empty statements (see Automatic semicolon insertion in JavaScript)

In this, as well as in my other best-selling books such as React Quickly, or Full Stack JavaScript, I don't use semicolons. There are a few reasons why. If you use semicolons and forget or omit one, then your code will still work, but you'll end up with inconsistency, which will require a linter or a similar tool to check for your syntax. Let's say you spotted a missing semicolon or saw a warning from a linter, then you need to go to your code and fix it. Why go through all this trouble?

Semicolon-less code works perfectly fine except for two cases shown prior and when you try to write multiple statements on one line. But developers should NOT write multiple statements in one line. That's a job for a bundler/minimizer. The bottom line: I recommend that developers focus on their work and not on looking for missing semicolons when the language has a feature (Automatic Semicolon Insertion) to make semicolons redundant.

camelCase

camelCase is the main naming pattern in JavaScript, except for class names, which are CapitalCamelCase. An example follows:

```
let MainView = Backbone.View.extend({...})
let mainView = new MainView()
```

Naming

_ and $ are perfectly legitimate characters for literals (jQuery and Underscore libraries use them a lot). Private methods and attributes start with _ (it does nothing by itself because it's just a code convention and not something enforced by the language).

Commas

One in a while you might see comma-first style. An example of a comma-first style is as follows:

```
const obj = { firstName: "John"
  , lastName: "Smith"
  , email: "johnsmith@gmail.com"
}
```

I recommend avoiding comma-first style. The *erroneous* (in my view) reason for using comma-first style is that it can make a developer's work easier. But although it simplifies the removal of the last line, it complicates the removal of the first line.

Moreover, with ES2017/ES8 developers can use trailing commas in function calls (for arguments) in addition to object literals and arrays. I recommend using traditional style (with or without the trailing comma). This shows a trailing comma:

```
const obj = { firstName: "John",
  lastName: "Smith",
  email: "johnsmith@gmail.com", // trailing comma - okay
}
```

Indentation

Indentation is usually done using either a tab, four- or two-space indentation, with supporting camps split almost religiously between the two options. I recommend using two spaces because it leaves more room on the screen and believe me, you'll need all the width of your code editor due to nested promises and callbacks.

I recommend having the closing curly brackets on the same indentation level as the opening statement. It'll be easier to find the matching brackets. For example, like this:

```
if (error) {
  console.error(error)
  process.exit(1)
}
```

Whitespace

Usually, there is a space before and after the =, +, {, and } symbols. There is no space on invocation (e.g., `arr.push(1);`). And there's no space when we define an anonymous function: `function() {}`.

For example, these function definition and invocation do not have space after word `function` but there's space before and after = and +. This example puts the closing curly brace at the same level as the beginning of the logical block `const`.

```
const f = function(a, b) {
  return a + b
}

f(1, 2)
```

Node.js Globals and Reserved Keywords

Despite being modeled after one standard, Node.js and browser JavaScript differ when it comes to globals. As you may know, in browser JavaScript we have a `window` object. However, in Node.js it is absent (obviously we don't deal with a browser window), but developers are provided with new objects/keywords:

- `process`
- `global`
- `module.exports` and `exports`

So, let's take a look at the main differences between Node.js and JavaScript.

Node.js Process Information

Each Node.js script that runs is, in essence, a system process. For example, a POSIX (Linux, macOS, etc.) command `ps aux | grep 'node'` outputs all Node.js programs running on a machine. Conveniently, developers can access useful process information in code with the `process` object (e.g., `node -e "console.log(process.pid)"`), as shown in Figure 1-5.

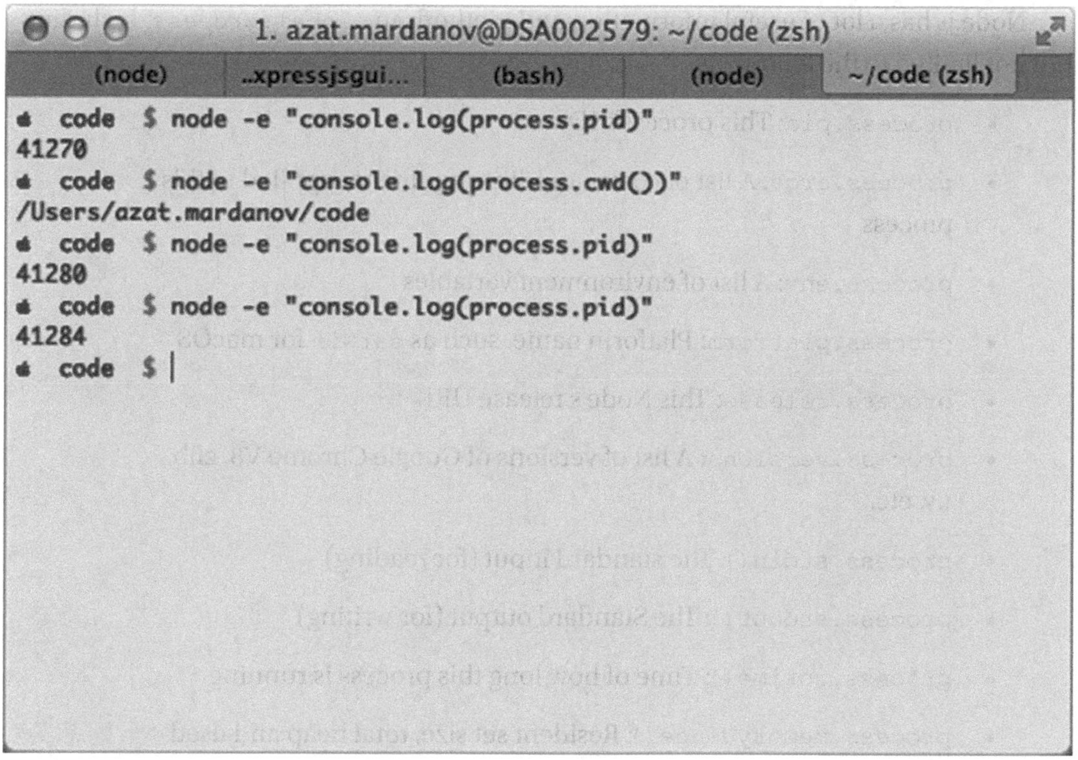

```
● ● ●                1. azat.mardanov@DSA002579: ~/code (zsh)
    (node)      ..xpressjsgui...      (bash)         (node)       ~/code (zsh)
⬢  code  $ node -e "console.log(process.pid)"
41270
⬢  code  $ node -e "console.log(process.cwd())"
/Users/azat.mardanov/code
⬢  code  $ node -e "console.log(process.pid)"
41280
⬢  code  $ node -e "console.log(process.pid)"
41284
⬢  code  $ |
```

Figure 1-5. *Node.js process examples using* `pid` *(process ID) and* `cwd` *(current working directory)*

Accessing Global Scope in Node.js

Node.js is JavaScript, which is a good news for front-end developers who are already familiar with JavaScript. You'll learn Node quickly. But there are huge differences when it comes to global objects. In a sense, the `window` object from front-end/browser JavaScript metamorphosed into a combination of `global` and `process` objects. Needless to say, the `document` object, which represents the DOM (Document Object Model) of the web page, is nonexistent in Node.js.

`global` can be accessed from anywhere. It has special methods, including the familiar to you `console`, `setTimeout()`, as well as new to you Node-specific `global.process`, `global.require()` and `global.module`.

Node.js has a lot of useful information and methods in `global.process`, including but not limited to the following:

- `process.pid`: This process's ID

- `process.argv`: A list of command-line argument supplied to this process

- `process.env`: A list of environment variables

- `process.platform`: Platform name, such as `darwin` for macOS

- `process.release`: This Node's release URL

- `process.versions`: A list of versions of Google Chrome V8, zlib, uv, etc.

- `process.stdin()`: The standard input (for reading)

- `process.stdout()`: The Standard output (for writing)

- `process.uptime()`: Time of how long this process is running

- `process.memoryUsage()`: Resident set size, total heap and used heap memory usage

- `process.exit()`: Terminating this process

- `process.kill()`: Termination of another process

Exporting and Importing Modules

One of the bad parts of browser JavaScript is that there is no easy way to include other JavaScript files (modules), at least not until ES Modules become widely supported. Browser JavaScript files are supposed to be linked together using a different language (HTML), but everything from an included file is just run without name spacing and dependency management is hard because managing a lot of `<script>` tags and files is not fun.

CommonJS (`http://www.commonjs.org`) and RequireJS (`http://requirejs.org`) solve this problem with the AJAX-y approach. ES6 solved the issue on the standard level, but lacks implementations. Node.js offers modules natively. No tools or hacks are needed. Node.js borrowed many things from the browser CommonJS concept but took the implementation steps further than CommonJS.

Node.js modules are simple to learn and use. They allow of import/export only specific targeted functionality, making name spacing easier, unlike when you include a browser JavaScript file with a `<script>` tag.

To export an object in Node.js, use `exports.name = object;`. An example follows:

```
const messages = {
  find: function(req, res, next) {
  ...
  },
  add: function(req, res, next) {
  ...
  },
  format: 'title | date | author'
}
exports.messages = messages
```

You can use `let` or `var` for `messages` in the module above, but `const` makes more sense since we are not updating this object, and can use an extra safety of `const`, which respects the logical scope and prevents re-declaration. `const` will still allow you to modify object properties.

While in the file where we import the aforementioned script (assuming the path and the file name is `route/messages.js`), write the following:

```
const messages = require('./routes/messages.js')
```

However, sometimes it's more fitting to invoke a constructor, such as when we attach properties to the Express.js app (which is explained in detail in a blog post *Express. js FUNdamentals: An Essential Overview of Express.js* (`http://webapplog.com/ express-js-fundamentals`) *[2013]*). In this case, `module.exports` is needed:

```
module.exports = (app) => {
  app.set('port', process.env.PORT || 3000)
  app.set('views', __dirname + '/views')
  app.set('view engine', 'jade')
  return app
}
```

In the file that includes the previous sample module, write:

```
...
let app = express()
const config = require('./config/index.js')
app = config(app)
...
```

The more succinct code is to skip the `config` variable declaration:

```
const express = require('express')
let app = express()
require('./config/index.js')(app)
```

The most common mistake when including modules is creating a wrong path to the file. For core Node.js modules, use the name without any path—for example, `require('name')`. The same goes for modules in the `node_modules` folder (more on this when we examine npm later in the chapter).

For all other files (i.e., not modules), use `.` with or without a file extension. An example follows:

```
const keys = require('./keys.js'),
  messages = require('./routes/messages.js')
```

In addition, for including files it's advisable to use statements with `__dirname` and `path.join()` to insure the paths work across platforms. For example, to include a file `messages.js` in a `routes` folder, which itself is inside a folder where the currently running script is, use:

```
const messages = require(path.join(__dirname, 'routes',
'messages.js'))
```

Using `path.join()` is a recommended approach, because `path.join()` will produce a path with valid slashes (forward or backward depending on your OS). You'll also use absolute path, which will make `require()` behave in a more robust and predictable manner.

Oh yeah, if `require()` points to a folder, Node.js attempts to read the `index.js` file in that folder. For example, the following statement will import file `index.js` in the folder `routes/messages` *if* there's no file `messages.js` in `routes`:

```
const messages = require(path.join(__dirname, 'routes', 'messages'))
```

That's not it. There's another special Node variable related to paths.

__dirname vs. process.cwd

`__dirname` is an absolute path to the folder with the source code script (a file in which the global variable is called), whereas `process.cwd` is an absolute path to the folder from which the process that runs the script was launched. They are the same in the example of `node program.js`.

The `cwd` value will be different from `__dirname`, if we started the program from a different folder. For example, for the process `$ node ./code/program.js`, `__dirname` will have `code` but `cwd` wont' because it'll be one folder above in the directory tree.

On POSIX systems (macOS, Linux, and its distributions), Node developers can also use `process.env.PWD`, which works similarly to `process.cwd`.

Browser Application Programming Interface Helpers

There are myriad helper functions in Node.js from the browser JavaScript application programming interface (API). The most useful come from `String`, `Array`, and `Math` objects. To make you aware of their existence, or to remind you, here is a list of the most common functions and their meanings:

- **Array**

  - `some()` and `every()`: Assertions for array items

  - `join()` and `concat()`: Conversion to a string

  - `pop()`, `push()`, `shift()`, and `unshift()`: Working with stacks and queues

  - `map()`: Model mapping for array items

- `filter()`: Querying array items

- `sort()`: Ordering items

- `reduce()`, `reduceRight()`: Computing

- `slice()`: Copying

- `splice()`: Removing

- `indexOf()`: Lookups of finding the value in the array

- `reverse()`: Reversing the order

- *The* `in` *operator*: Iteration over array items

- **Math**

  - `random()`: random real number less than one

- **String**

  - `substr()` and `substring()`: extracting substrings

  - `length`: length of the string

  - `indexOf()`: index of finding the value in the string

  - `split()`: converting the string to an array

In addition, we have `setInterval()`, `setTimeout()`, `forEach()`, and `console` methods in Node.js. For the complete list of methods and examples of the `String`, `Array` and `Math` Node.js classes (really objects), visit the following Mozilla Developer Network documentation pages:

- *String*: https://developer.mozilla.org/en-US/docs/Web/JavaScript/Reference/Global_Objects/String

- *Array*: https://developer.mozilla.org/en-US/docs/Web/JavaScript/Reference/Global_Objects/Array

- *Math*: https://developer.mozilla.org/en-US/docs/Web/JavaScript/Reference/Global_Objects/Math

Node.js Core Modules

Unlike other programming technologies, Node.js doesn't come with a heavy standard library. The core modules of Node.js are a bare minimum, and the rest can be cherry-picked via the npm registry. The core is small but it has enough modules to build almost any networking application. Networking is at the core of Node.js!

The main (though not all) core modules, classes, methods, and events include the following:

- `http` (http://nodejs.org/api/http.html#http_http): **Allows to create HTTP clients and servers**

- `util` (http://nodejs.org/api/util.html): **Has a set of utilities**

- `querystring` (http://nodejs.org/api/querystring.html): **Parses query-string formatted data**

- `url` (http://nodejs.org/api/url.html): **Parses URL data**

- `fs` (http://nodejs.org/api/fs.html): **Works with a file system (write, read)**

Let's dive deeper into each of these core modules.

http (http://nodejs.org/api/http.html)

`http` is the main module responsible for the Node.js HTTP server. The main methods are as follows:

- `http.createServer()`: **Returns a new web server object**

- `http.listen()`: **Begins accepting connections on the specified port and hostname**

- `http.createClient()`: **Creates a client and makes requests to other servers**

- `http.ServerRequest()`: **Passes incoming requests to request handlers**

- **data**: Emitted when a part of the message body is received

- **end**: Emitted exactly once for each request

- `request.method()`: Returns the request method as a string

- `request.url()`: Returns the request URL string

- `http.ServerResponse()`: Creates this object internally by an HTTP server—not by the user —and is used as an output of request handlers

  - `response.writeHead()`: Sends a response header to the request

  - `response.write()`: Sends a response body

  - `response.end()`: Sends and ends a response body

util (http://nodejs.org/api/util.html)

The `util` module provides utilities for debugging. One method is as follows:

- `util.inspect()`: Returns a string representation of an object, which is useful for debugging

querystring (http://nodejs.org/api/querystring.html)

The `querystring` module provides utilities for dealing with query strings. Some of the methods include the following:

- `querystring.stringify()`: Serializes an object to a query string

- `querystring.parse()`: Deserializes a query string to an object

url (http://nodejs.org/api/url.html)

The `url` module has utilities for URL resolution and parsing. One method is as follows:

- `parse()`: Takes a URL string and returns an object

fs (http://nodejs.org/api/fs.html)

`fs` handles file system operations such as reading to and writing from files. There are synchronous and asynchronous methods in the library. Some of the methods include the following:

- `fs.readFile()`: Reads files asynchronously

- `fs.writeFile()`: Writes data to files asynchronously

There is no need to install or download core modules. To include them in your application, all you need is to use the following syntax:

```
const http = require('http')
```

Node comes with core modules, but most developers rely on the vast ecosystem of community- created FOSS (free and open-source) modules. These modules often allow developers to not write code because a module has all the functionality needed. With large number of modules, it's important to find just the right one for the job. The best place to start your search for a module is your favorite search engine such as Google, Bing, or DuckDuckGo. A list of noncore modules is found at the following locations:

- npm search: `https://www.npmjs.com/browse/keyword/search`: The main npm search by npm itself

- node-modules.com (`http://node-modules.com`): Search for npm

- npms.io (`https://npms.io`): Another search for npm

Handy Node.js Utilities

Although the core of the Node.js platform was, intentionally, kept small, it has some essential utilities, including the following:

- *Crypto* (`http://nodejs.org/api/crypto.html`): Has randomizer, MD5, HMAC-SHA1, and other algorithms

- *Path* (`http://nodejs.org/api/path.html`): Handles system paths

- *String decoder* (`http://nodejs.org/api/string_decoder.html`): Decodes to and from `Buffer` and `String` types

The method we use throughout is `path.join` and it concatenates the path using an appropriate folder separator (/ or \\ ).

Reading to and Writing from the File System in Node.js

Reading from files is done via the core `fs` module (http://nodejs.org/api/fs.html). There are two sets of reading methods: async and sync. In most cases, developers should use async methods, such as `fs.readFile` (http://nodejs.org/api/fs.html#fs_fs_readfile_filename_options_callback):

```
const fs = require('fs')
const path = require('path')
fs.readFile(path.join(__dirname,
  '/data/customers.csv'),
  {encoding: 'utf-8'}, (err, data) => {
  if (err) {
    console.error(err)
    process.exit(1)
  } else {
    console.log(data)
  }
})
```

To write to the file, execute the following:

```
const fs = require('fs')
fs.writeFile('message.txt',
  'Hello World!', (err) => {
  if (err) {
    console.error(err)
    process.exit(1)
  } else {
    console.log('Writing is done.')
  }
})
```

Streaming Data in Node.js

Streaming Data in Node.js means processing data by Node.js application while transmission is in progress. Node supports streams. This feature is useful for extra large datasets, such as video or database migrations.

Here's a basic example of using streams that reads a file as a stream and outputs the binary file content back to the standard output:

```
const fs = require('fs')
fs.createReadStream('./data/customers.csv').pipe(process.stdout)
```

By default, Node.js uses buffers for streams. For more immersive instruction, take a look at `stream-adventure` (`http://npmjs.org/stream-adventure`) and Stream Handbook (`https://github.com/substack/stream-handbook`).

Installing Node.js Modules with npm

npm comes with the Node.js platform and allows for seamless Node.js package management. The way `npm install` works is similar to Git in the way it traverses the working tree to find a current project (`https://npmjs.org/doc/files/npm-folders.html`). For starters, keep in mind that we need either the `package.json` file or the `node_modules` folder to install modules locally with `$ npm install name`. For example, to import `superagent` first install it with `$ npm install superagent` and then in the `program.js` write: `const superagent = require('superagent')` to import the `superagent` module.

The best thing about npm is that it keeps all the dependencies local, so if module A uses module B v1.3, and module C uses module B v2.0 (with breaking changes compared with v1.3), both A and C will have their own localized copies of different versions of B. This proves to be a more superior strategy than that of Ruby and other platforms that use global installations by default.

The best practice is *not to include* a `node_modules` folder in the Git repository when the project is a module that is supposed to be used in other applications. However, it's recommended *to include* `node_modules` for deployable applications to prevent breakage caused by unfortunate dependency updates.

Note   The npm creator likes to call it `npm` lowercase (`http://bit.`
`ly/2MRRakD`).

Taming Callbacks in Node.js

Callbacks (`https://github.com/maxogden/art-of-node#callbacks`) are able to
make Node.js code asynchronous, yet programmers unfamiliar with JavaScript, who
work with Java or PHP, might be surprised when they see Node.js code described on
Callback Hell (`http://callbackhell.com`):

```
fs.readdir(source, (err, files) => {
  if (err) {
    console.log('Error finding files: ' + err)
  } else {
    files.forEach((filename, fileIndex) => {
      console.log(filename)
      gm(source + filename).size((err, values) => {
        if (err) {
          console.log('Error identifying file size: ' + err)
        } else {
          console.log(filename + ' : ' + values)
          aspect = (values.width / values.height)
          widths.forEach((width, widthIndex) => {
            height = Math.round(width / aspect)
            console.log('resizing ' + filename + 'to ' + height + 'x'
+ height)
            this.resize(width, height).write(destination + 'w' +
width + '_' + filename, (err) => {
              if (err) console.log('Error writing file: ' + err)
            })
          }.bind(this))
        }
      })
    })
```

```
    })
  }
})
```

There's nothing to be afraid of here as long as two-space indentation is used. ;-) However, callback code can be rewritten with using event emitters or promises, or using the `async` library (see Chapter 14).

Hello World Server with HTTP Node.js Module

Although Node.js can be used for a wide variety of tasks, it's used primarily for building networking applications including web apps. Node.js thrives in networks as a result of its asynchronous nature and built-in modules such as `net` and `http`.

Here's a quintessential Hello World example in which we create a server object, define the request handler (function with `req` and `res` arguments), pass some data back to the recipient, and start up the whole thing (`hello.js`):

```
const http = require('http')
const port = 3000
http.createServer((req, res) => {
  res.writeHead(200, {'Content-Type': 'text/plain'})
  res.end('Hello World\n')
}).listen(port, () => {
  console.log(`Server running at http://localhost:${port}`)
})
```

Let's break it down a bit (if you know this already, skip to the next section). The following loads the core `http` module for the server (more on the modules later):

```
const http = require('http')
const port = 3000
```

This snippet below creates a server with a callback function that contains the response handler code:

```
const server = http.createServer((req, res) => {
```

To set the right header and status code, use the following:

```
res.writeHead(200, {'Content-Type': 'text/plain'})
```

To output Hello World with the line end symbol, use

```
res.end('Hello World\n')
})
```

The `req` and `res` arguments have all the information about a given HTTP request and response correspondingly. In addition, `req` and `res` can be used as streams (see the previous section).

To make the server accept requests, use the following:

```
}).listen(port, () => {
  console.log(`Server running at http://localhost:${port}`)
})
```

From the folder in which you have `server.js`, launch in your terminal the following command:

```
$ node server.js
```

Open `localhost:3000` (http://localhost:3000) or `127.0.0.1:3000` (http://127.0.0.1:3000) or any other address you see in the terminal as a result of the `console.log()` function, and you should see Hello World in a browser. To shut down the server, press Control+C (on macOS X).

Note   The name of the main file could be different from `server.js` (e.g., `index.js` or `app.js`). In case you need to launch the `app.js` file, just use `$ node app.js`.

Debugging Node.js Programs

Modern-day software developers, especially those who use compiled languages such as Java, have gotten accustomed to rich tool sets for debugging purposes. Back in the day, before JavaScript and AJAX apps were starting to gain momentum (~2005–2007), the only way to debug was to put a bunch of `alert()` statements everywhere.

Now, there are amazing environments such as Chrome Developer Tools and Firefox Firebug, and because Node.js has a lot of things in common with the browser JavaScript environment, we have plenty of options for debugging in Node.js, including the following:

- *Core Node.js Debugger*: A non-graphic user interface (non-GUI) minimalistic tool that works everywhere

- *Node Inspector*: Port of Google Chrome Developer Tools

- *IDEs*: WebStorm, VS Code and other IDEs (covered in the next section)

Core Node.js Debugger

The best debugger is `console.log()`, because it doesn't break/interrupt the flow, and it is fast and informative. However, to use it, we first need to know where to put it. Sometimes, we just don't know where to put the logs! Other times, we need to see the call stack and orient ourselves in the async code a bit more. To do this, put `debugger` statements in your code and use `$ node inspect program.js` to start the debugging process (`http://nodejs.org/api/debugger.html`).

For example, the Hello World from the previous section can be enhanced with `debugger` in two places: when an instance is created and when a request is made (`hello-debug.js`):

```
const http = require('http')
const port = 3000
debugger
http.createServer((req, res) => {
  res.writeHead(200, {'Content-Type': 'text/plain'})
  debugger
  res.end('Hello World\n')
}).listen(3000, () => {
  console.log(`Server running at http://localhost:${port}`)
})
```

Now, if we run the previous snippet (`hello-debug.js`), just like we did earlier (`$ node hello-debug.js`), nothing changes, because we need to use `$ node inspect hello-debug.js`. And only then the execution will halt at the first line, and then again on the next `debugger` statement if we use the `cont` command.

The main node debug commands are as follows:

- `next`, `n`: step to the next statement

- `cont`, `c`: continue until the next debugger/break point

- `step`, `s`: step inside the function call

- `out`, `o`: step outside the function call

- `watch(expression)`: watch the expression

The full list of commands is available through the `help` command or on the official web site (`http://nodejs.org/api/debugger.html`).

So, in our example (`hello-debug.js`), after we start the debugger client and execute `cont` or `c` twice (first for the first line, and second for our debugger on the second line), the server will be up and running. After that, we can open the browser at `http://localhost:3000` or execute `$ curl "http://localhost:3000/"` in the Terminal/Command line, and the debugger client stops inside the request handler (line 5). Now we can type `repl` and `console.log(req)` to inspect the HTTP response object dynamically.

Debugging with Node Inspector

The built-in Node.js debugger client is extensive, but it's not intuitive because of the lack of a GUI. Therefore, for a more developer-friendly interface than the core Node.js debugger provides, Node Inspector comes to the rescue! Node Inspector is the node-inspector npm module (`https://github.com/node-inspector/node-inspector`).

To download and install Node Inspector, we use our beloved npm in the global mode (`-g` or `-global`):

```
$ npm install -g node-inspector
```

Then, we start Node Inspector with the following (Figure 1-6):

```
$ node-inspector
```

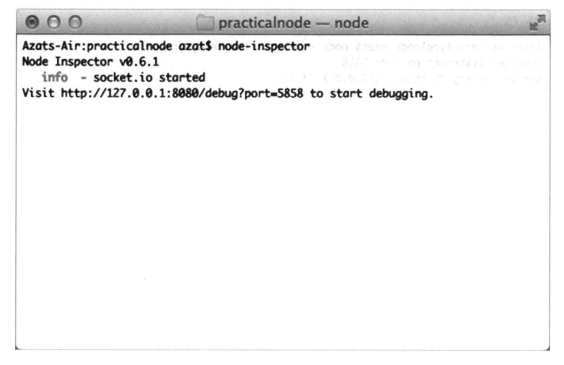

Figure 1-6. *Running the Node Inspector tool*

Now start the program in a new terminal window/tab/session with --debug or --debug-brk flags (not just debug; see Figure 1-7). For example:

```
$ node --debug-brk hello-debug.js
```

or

```
$ node --debug hello-debug.js
```

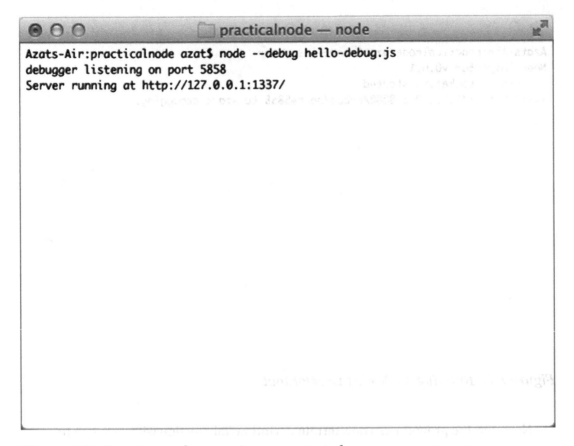

Figure 1-7. *Running node server in* `--debug` *mode*

Open `http://127.0.0.1:8080/debug?port=5858` (or `http://localhost:8080/debug?port=5858`) in Chrome (it must be Chrome and not another browser because Node Inspector uses the Web Developer Tools interface). You should be able to see the program halted at a breakpoint. Clicking the blue play button resumes the execution, as shown in Figure 1-8.

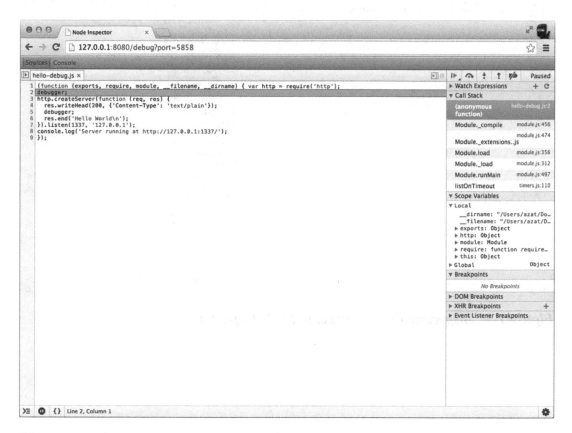

Figure 1-8. *Resuming execution in Node Inspector*

If we let the server run and open `http://localhost:1337/` in a new browser tab, this action pauses the execution on the second breakpoint, which is inside the request handler. From here, we can use Node Inspector's right GUI and add a `res` watcher (Figure 1-9), which is way better than the terminal window output!

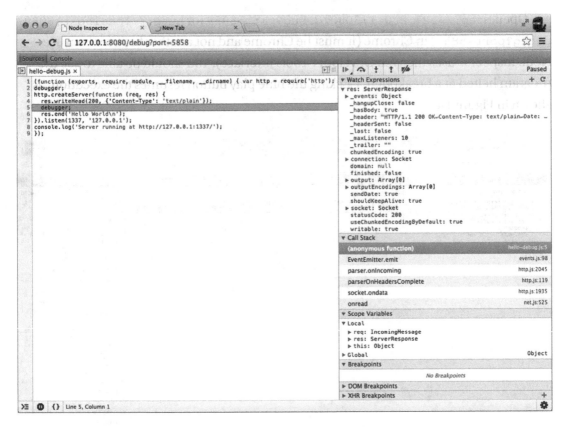

Figure 1-9. *Inspecting the* `res` *object in Node Inspector*

In addition, we can follow the call stack, explore scope variables, and execute any Node.js command in the console tab (see Figure 1-10)!

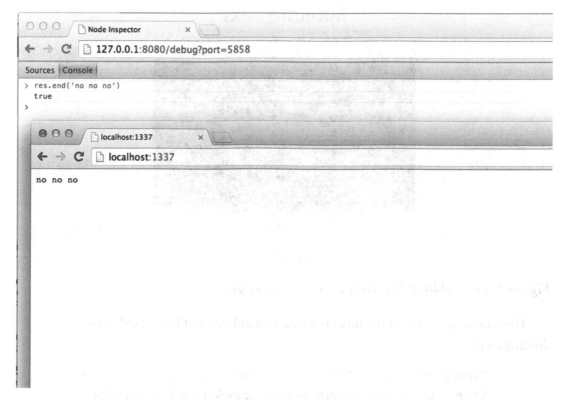

Figure 1-10. *Writing to response (i.e., the* `res` *object) from the Node Inspector console*

Node.js IDEs and Code Editors

One of the best things about Node.js is that you don't need to compile the code, because it's loaded into memory and interpreted by the platform! Therefore, a lightweight text editor is highly recommended, such as Sublime Text (Figure 1-11), vs. a full-blown IDE. However, if you are already familiar and comfortable with the IDE of your choice, such as Eclipse (`http://www.eclipse.org`), NetBeans (`http://netbeans.org`), or Aptana (`http://aptana.com`), feel free to stick with it.

Figure 1-11. *Sublime Text code editor home page*

The following is a list of the most popular text editors and IDEs used in web development:

- *Visual Studio Code (https://code.visualstudio.com/nodejs)*: A free, cross-platform, feature-rich editor by Microsoft powered by Node.js. It includes a built-in terminal, Node.js debugging, and lots of handy extensions (Figure 1-12). *I highly recommend using this editor! (At least until something new comes out in the next few years.)*

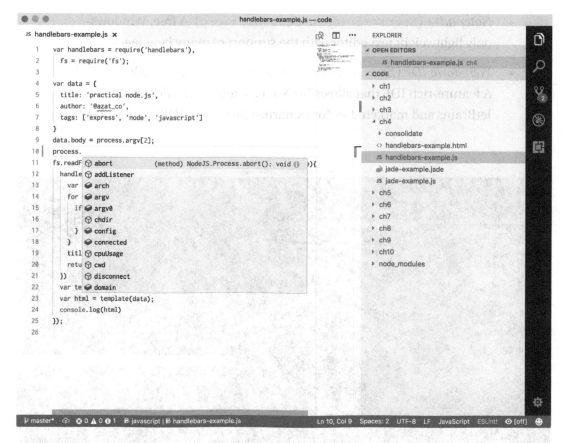

Figure 1-12. *VS Code has intelligent autocomplete based on the object type/class/library as well as many other features*

- *Atom* (`https://atom.io`): A free, cross-platform editor by GitHub (also powered by Node.js) comparable to Visual Studio Code.

- *TextMate* (`http://macromates.com`): Editor for macOS, free 30-day trial for v1.5, dubbed *The Missing Editor for macOS*.

- *Sublime Text* (`http://www.sublimetext.com`): Editor for macOS and Windows, an even better alternative to TextMate, with an unlimited evaluation period

- *Coda* (`http://panic.com/coda`): An all-in-one editor with an FTP browser and preview, has support for development with an iPad

- *Aptana Studio* (`http://aptana.com`): A full-size IDE with a built-in terminal and many other tools

- *Notepad++* (`http://notepad-plus-plus.org`): A free, Windows-only lightweight text editor with the support of many languages

- *WebStorm IDE* (`http://www.jetbrains.com/webstorm`):
  A feature-rich IDE that allows for Node.js debugging, developed by JetBrains and marketed as "the smartest JavaScript IDE" (Figure 1-13)

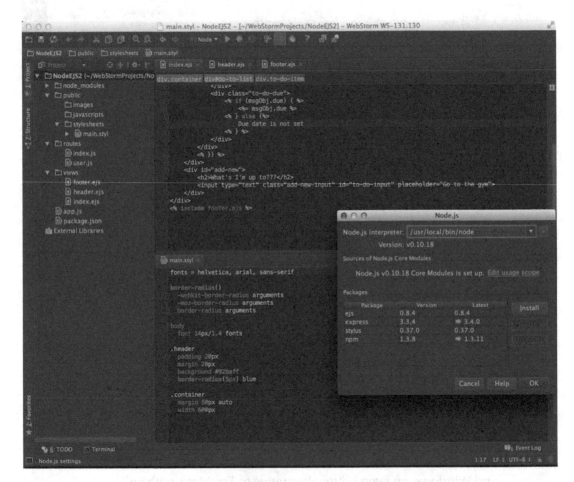

Figure 1-13. *WebStorm IDE work space*

For most developers, a simple code editor such as Sublime Text 2, TextMate, or Emacs is good enough. However, for programmers who are used to working in IDEs, there's WebStorm by JetBrains (`http://www.jetbrains.com/webstorm`). For an example of the WebStorm work space, see Figure 1-13.

Watching for File Changes

If you are familiar with tools that are watching for file changes and restarting Node apps, or if it's not an issue for you, feel free to skip this section. All other developers must pay attention.

Node.js applications are stored in memory, and if we make changes to the source code, we need to restart the process (i.e., node). We do this manually by killing the process and starting a new one (Control+C on macOS and Ctrl+C on Windows).

However, it's faster for development if this constant sequence of restarts is automated. There are brilliant tools that leverage the `watch` method (`http://bit.ly/2xPKCgr`) from the core Node.js `fs` module and restart servers when we save changes from an editor:

- *node-dev* (`https://npmjs.org/package/node-dev`):
  A development tool to restart your Node servers

- *nodemon* (`https://npmjs.org/package/nodemon`): Another
  development tool to restart your Node servers

- *supervisor* (`https://npmjs.org/package/supervisor`):
  A tool which was used in production to restart your Node servers, but which can be used in development as well

- *pm2-dev* (`http://npmjs.org/pm2`): A development version of the production-level pm2 tool

- *forever* (`http://npmjs.org/forever`): A production tool similar to pm2 but older (we examine this topic in Chapter 11)

Any one of these tools is as easy to use as installing globally with `$ npm install -g node-dev`, then running the Node.js script with `$ node-dev program.js`. Just replace `node-dev` with another module name.

For a comparison between these tools, refer to Comparison: Tools to Automate Restarting Node.js Server After Code Changes (`http://bit.ly/2QSEDAm`).

Tip   It's good to know that Express.js reloads a template file for every new request by default. So, no server restart is necessary. However, we can cache templates by enabling the `view cache` setting. For more on Express.js setting, take a look at one of the best books I ever wrote Pro Express.js 4 (Apress, 2014) at `http://amzn.to/1D6qiqk`.

Summary

In this chapter, we explored Installing Node.js and npm, and launching Node.js scripts from the command line. We also looked at the essential concepts of Node.js syntax and the platform. Lastly, I provided the lists of Node.js IDEs and libraries for development were provided.

In the next chapter, we dive deep into using the most popular Node.js framework for creating web apps.

CHAPTER 2

Using Express.js to Create Node.js Web Apps

It's only logical that, by using frameworks, software engineers become more productive and can achieve results faster. Often, the results are of a better quality because the frameworks are used and maintained by many other developers and contributors. Even if developers build everything from scratch, they end up with *their own framework* in the end. It's just a very customized one!

Node.js is a relatively young platform when it comes to frameworks (unlike Ruby or Java), but there's already a leader that has become a de facto standard used in the majority of Node.js projects: Express.js.

Express.js is an amazing framework for Node.js projects, and it's used in the majority of web apps, which is why this second chapter is dedicated to getting started with this framework.

In this chapter we cover the following topics, which serve as an introduction to Express.js:

- What Express.js is

- How Express.js works

- Express.js Installation

- Express.js scaffolding (command-line tool)

- The Blog Project overview

- Express.js Hello World example

© Azat Mardan 2018
A. Mardan, *Practical Node.js*, https://doi.org/10.1007/978-1-4842-3039-8_2

What Is Express.js?

Express.js is a web framework based on the core Node.js `http` module and Connect (`http://www.senchalabs.org/connect`) components. The components are called *middleware* and they are the cornerstones of the framework philosophy, which is *configuration over convention*. In other words, Express.js systems are highly configurable, which allows developers to freely pick whatever libraries they need for a particular project. For these reasons, the Express.js framework leads to flexibility and high customization in the development of web applications.

If you write serious Node web apps using only core Node.js modules (refer to the following snippet for an example), you most likely find yourself reinventing the wheel by writing the same code continually over and over for similar boring mundane tasks, such as the following:

- Parsing of HTTP request bodies Parsing of cookies

- Getting information from URL

- Reading query string data from URLs or request bodies (payloads) Managing web sessions

- Organizing routes with a chain of `if` conditions based on URL paths and HTTP methods of the requests

- Determining proper response headers based on data types

The list could go on and on, but a good example is worth hundreds of words. To illustrate my point, here is an example of a two-route representational state transfer (REST) API server, i.e., we have only two endpoints and they are also called *routes*. In this application, we use only core Node.js modules for server functions. A single "userland"/ external module native MongoDB driver is used for persistence. This example is taken from my another best selling book on Node, beginner-friendly Full Stack JavaScript, 2nd Edition (`https://github.com/azat-co/fullstack-javascript`) (Apress, 2018). Pay attention to how I had to use if/else and parse the incoming data.

```
const http = require('http')
const util = require('util')
const querystring = require('querystring')
const mongo = require('mongodb')
```

```javascript
const host = process.env.MONGOHQ_URL ||
    'mongodb://@127.0.0.1:27017'
// MONGOHQ_URL=mongodb://user:pass@server.mongohq.com/db_name
mongo.Db.connect(host, (error, client) => {
  if (error) throw error;
  let collection = new mongo.Collection(
    client,
    'test_collection'
  );
  let app = http.createServer(
    (request, response) => {
      if (
        request.method === 'GET' &&
        request.url === '/messages/list.json'
      ) {
        collection.find().toArray((error, results) => {
          response.writeHead(
            200,
            {'Content-Type': 'text/plain'}
          );
          console.dir(results);
        response.end(JSON.stringify(results));
        });
      };
      if (request.method === "POST" &&
        request.url === "/messages/create.json"
      ) {
        request.on('data', (data) => {
          collection.insert(
            querystring.parse(data.toString('utf-8')),
            {safe: true},
            (error, obj) => {
            if (error) throw error;
            response.end(JSON.stringify(obj));
            }
```

```
        );
      });
    };
  }
);
const port = process.env.PORT || 5000
app.listen(port)
})
```

As you can see, developers have to do *a lot* of manual work themselves, such as interpreting HTTP methods and URLs into routes, and parsing input and output data. And I didn't even use URL parameters such as `/message/ID`. Not nice!

Express.js solves these and many other problems as abstraction and code organization. The framework provides a model-view-controller-like (MVC-like) structure for your web apps with a clear separation of concerns (views, routes, models).

For the models (the M in MVC), we can use Mongoose (`http://mongoosejs.com`) or Sequelize (`http://sequelizejs.com`) libraries in *addition* to Express.js—more on this later in the book in Chapter 7. In this chapter we'll cover just the basics of Express.js. This will be enough for you to start building your own small Express apps.

Built on top this framework, Express.js applications can vary from bare-bones, back-end-only REST APIs to full-blown, highly scalable, full-stack (with jade-browser (`https://npmjs.org/package/jade-browser`) and Socket.IO (`http://socket.io`)) real-time web apps. To give some analogies to developers who are familiar with Ruby and Ruby on Rails, Ruby on Rails is convention over configuration. Other frameworks like Sails and Loopback are more like Ruby's Ruby on Rails framework. Express.js on the other hand is often seen as another Ruby framework Sinatra, which has a very different approach to the Ruby on Rails framework. Express.js and Sinatra promote configurability, whereas Ruby on Rails promotes *convention over configuration.*

Although Express.js is one of the most popular libraries on npm (16 million downloads only for June 2018), and is the most mature and most used Node.js framework, the playing field is still relatively level with many different frameworks, and new ones are released every month. Some of them, such as Meteor (`http://meteor.com`) and Hapi (`https://www.npmjs.com/package/hapi`), show an interesting trend in attempts to merge front-end and back-end code bases. For a hand-picked list of Node.js frameworks, refer to the Node Framework (`http://nodeframework.com`) resource.

When evaluating a Node.js framework for your project, use these easy steps to guide you:

- Build a sample app, which is usually provided by the creators of frameworks on GitHub or official web sites. See how the app feels in terms of styles and patterns.

- Consider the type of application you're building: prototype, production app, minimum viable product (MVP), small scale, large scale, and so on.

- Consider the libraries already familiar to you and determine whether you can or plan to reuse them, and whether your framework plays nicely with them. Provide out-of-the-box solutions: template engines, database object-relational mapping (`http://en.wikipedia.org/wiki/Object-relational_mapping`) libraries (ORMs)/drivers, Cascading Style Sheets (`http://en.wikipedia.org/wiki/Cascading_Style_Sheets`) (CSS) frameworks.

- Consider the nature of your application: REST API (with a separate front-end client), a traditional web app, or a traditional web app with REST API endpoints (such as Blog).

- Consider whether you need the support of reactive templates with WebSocket from the get-go (or use the Meteor framework).

- Evaluate the number of stars and follows on npm and GitHub to judge the popularity of the framework. More popular typically means more blog posts, books, screencasts, tutorials, and programmers exist; less popular means it's a newer framework, a niche/custom choice, or a poor choice. With newer frameworks, there is a greater chance that contributing back to them will be valued, so pick your comfortable spot.

- Evaluate npm, GitHub pages, and a framework's website for the presence of good API documentation with examples or open issues/bugs. If there are more than a few hundred, depending on popularity, this may not be a good sign. Also, determine the date of the last commit on the GitHub repository. Anything older than six months is not a good sign.

How Express.js Works

Express.js usually has an entry point, a.k.a., the main file. The names of this file typically are `server.js`, `app.js` or `index.js`. Most of the time, this is the file that we start with the `node` command, or export it as a module, in some cases. And in this file, we do the following:

1. Include third-party dependencies as well as our own modules, such as controllers, utilities, helpers, and models

2. Configure Express.js app settings, such as template engine and its file extensions

3. Connect to databases such as MongoDB, Redis, or MySQL (optional)

4. Define middleware such as error handlers, static file folder, cookies, and other parsers

5. Define routes

6. Start the app

7. Export the app as a module (optional)

When the Express.js app is running, it's listening to requests. Each incoming request is processed according to a defined chain of middleware and routes, starting from top to bottom. This aspect is important in controlling the execution flow. For example, routes/middleware that are higher in the file have precedence over the lower definitions.

Because we can have multiple middleware functions processing each HTTP request, some of the functions are in the middle (hence the name *middleware*). Here are some examples of middleware purposes:

1. Parse cookie information and put it in `request` object for following middleware/routes.

2. Parse parameters from the URL and put it in `request` object for following middleware/routes.

3. Get the information from the database based on the value of the parameter, if the user is authorized (cookie/session), and put it in `request` object for following middleware/routes.

4. Authorize users/requests (or not).

5. Display the data and end the response.

Express.js Installation

The Express.js app can be created using two methods:

1. `express-generator`: A global npm package that provides the command-line tool for rapid app creation (scaffolding)— recommended for quick prototyping and server-side rendering (thick server) apps.

2. `express`: A local package module in your Node.js app's `node_modules` folder— recommended for any project which needs to import `express` with `require()` or `import`.

Express.js Generator Version

Before we proceed with installations, let's check the Express.js versions. We'll use an exact version 4.15.4 to avoid confusion resulting from potential future changes to the Express.js skeleton-generating mechanism and the module API.

For the Express.js Generator, which is a separate module, we'll use version 4.15.5, which is compatible with Express.js 4.15.5 and most likely with any other Express version which starts with number 4. Luckily, Express Generator will write the version of `express` it needs in `package.json` so we, developers, don't have to preoccupy ourselves too much with keeping versions compatible.

If you already have Express Generator, then check the version with `$ express -V`. Yes, the actual command for Express Generator is confusingly enough is not `express-generator` like its npm name but just `express`. WHAT?! Go figure... Subsequently, any Express Generator commands are invoked with `express NAME`.

You can uninstall generator using `$ sudo npm uninstall -g express-generator`. Or `$ sudo npm uninstall -g express` for Express.js 2.x and 3.x because before, version 4.x, Express.js Generator was a part of the Express.js module itself. After you've uninstalled the older versions, install the proper version with the next section's commands.

Alternatively, you can just install a new version, and it should overwrite any prior installations. Here's the command to install the latest version:

```
npm i -g express-generator@latest
```

Let's see some other ways to install Express Generator.

Express.js Generator Installation

To install the Express.js Generator as global package, run `$ npm install -g express-generator@4.15.5` from anywhere on your computer. This downloads and links the `$ express` terminal command to the proper path, so that later we can access its command-line interface (CLI) for the creation of new apps.

Note   For macOS and Linux users, if there is an error installing globally, most likely your system requires root/administrator rights to write to the folder. In this case, `$ sudo npm install -g express-generator@4.15.0` might be needed. Refer to Chapter 1 for more information on changing npm ownership.

Of course, we can be more vague and tell npm to install the latest version of `express-generator`:

`$ npm i -g express-generator@4.15.5`. But in this case your results might be inconsistent with the book's examples.

Here are the results of running the aforementioned command:

```
/usr/local/bin/express -> /usr/local/lib/node_modules/express-
generator/bin/express-cli.js
+ express-generator@4.15.5
updated 1 package in 1.793s
```

Please notice the path: `/usr/local/lib/node_modules/express-generator`. This is where, on macOS/Linux systems, npm puts global modules by default. We verify the availability of Express.js CLI by running this:

```
$ express --version
```

Express is used with `require()`, and it's a local project dependency. Let's built a quick Hello World with Express.

Local Express.js

For the local Express.js 4.15.5 module installation, let's create a new folder `hello-simple` somewhere on your computer: `$ mkdir hello-simple`. This will be our project folder for the chapter. Now we can open it with `$ cd hello-simple`. When we are inside the project folder, we can create `package.json` manually in a text editor or with the `$ npm init` terminal command.

The following is an example of the `package.json` file with vanilla `$ npm init` options (the license and author are configured by defaults in `npm config`):

```
{
  "name": "hello-simple",
  "version": "1.0.0",
  "description": "",
  "main": "index.js",
  "scripts": {
    "test": "echo \"Error: no test specified\" && exit 1"
  },
  "keywords": [],
  "author": "Azat Mardan (http://azat.co/)",
  "license": "MIT"
}
```

Lastly, we install the module using npm (no need for `--save` in npm v5+):

```
$ npm install express@4.15.4 --save --exact
```

Or, if we want to be less specific, which is not recommended for this example, use:

```
$ npm i express -E
```

Note Depending on your npm version, if you attempt to run the aforementioned `$ npm install express` command without the `package.json` file or the `node_modules` folder, the *smart* npm will traverse up the directory tree to the folder that has either of these two things. This behavior mimics

---

Git's logic somewhat. For more information on the npm installation algorithm, please refer to the official documentation (`https://npmjs.org/doc/folders.html`).

Alternatively, we can update the `package.json` file by specifying the dependency (`"express": "4.15.4"` or `"express": "4.x"`) and run `$ npm install`.

The following is the `package.json` file with an added Express.js v4.15.4 dependency:

```json
{
  "name": "hello-simple",
  "version": "1.0.0",
  "description": "",
  "main": "index.js",
  "scripts": {
    "test": "echo \"Error: no test specified\" && exit 1"
  },
  "keywords": [],
  "author": "Azat Mardan (http://azat.co/)",
  "license": "MIT",
  "dependencies": {
    "express": "4.15.4"
  }
}
```

Now when someone downloads this project, they can install all dependencies from `package.json` with either of the following two commands:

```
$ npm install
$ npm i
```

Here are the result of installing Express.js v4.15.4 locally into the `node_modules` folder. Please notice the `package-lock.json` file created in the project root. It helps to lock versions to avoid breaking your code with new versions of dependencies.

```
$ npm i express -E
npm notice created a lockfile as package-lock.json. You should commit
this file.
npm WARN hello-simple@1.0.0 No description
npm WARN hello-simple@1.0.0 No repository field.

+ express@4.15.4
added 43 packages in 4.686s
```

If you want to install Express.js to an existing project and save the dependency (a smart thing to do!) into the `package.json` file, which is already present in that project's folder, run `$ npm install express@4.15.5 --save`.

Create a `server.js` file in the `hello-simple` folder:

```js
const express = require('express')
let app = express()

app.all('*', (req, res) => {
  res.send('Welcome to Practical Node.js!')
})

app.listen(3000,
  () => {console.log('Open at localhost:3000')}
)
```

Then launch it with `node server.js` to see "Welcome to Practical Node.js!" in a browser at `http://localhost:3000`. You first Express app is working!

Now let's actually see how to use the generator cause let's admit it because who doesn't like to have software to write our software?

Express.js Scaffolding

So far, we've covered Express.js installation and a simple Express server. When it comes to prototyping, it's vital to be able to get started quickly with the solid app skeleton, which is why many modern frameworks provide some type of scaffolding. Now is the time to explore its rapid app-creation mechanism, Express.js Generator!

Comparable with Ruby on Rails and many other web frameworks, Express.js comes with a CLI for jump-starting your development process. The CLI generates a basic foundation for the most common cases.

If you followed the global installation instructions in the installation section, you should be able to see the version number 4.15.0 if you run $ `express -V` from anywhere on your machine. If we type $ `express -h` or $ `express --help`, we should get a list of available options and their usage. The list of options is broken down below in this section to serve you, my dear readers, as a reference.

To generate a skeleton Express.js app, we need to run a terminal command— `express [options] [dir|appname]` —the options for which are the following:

- `-v, --view <engine>`: Add view support (dust|ejs|hbs|hjs|jade|pug|t wig|vash) (defaults to pug)

- `-c <engine>, --css <engine>`: Add stylesheet `<engine>` support, such as LESS (`http://lesscss.org`), Stylus (`http://learnboost.github.io/stylus`) or Compass (`http://compass-style.org`) (by default, plain CSS is used)

- `--git`: Add .gitignore

- `-f, --force`: Force app generation on a nonempty directory

If the dir/appname option is omitted, Express.js creates files using the current folder as the base for the project. Otherwise, the application is in the folder with the name provided.

Now that we're clear on the `express` Express Generator command and its options, let's go step by step to create an app with the scaffolding:

1. Check the Express.js version, because the app-generating code is prone to changes.

2. Execute the scaffolding command with options.

3. Run the application locally.

4. Understand the different sections, such as routes, middleware, and configuration.

5. Peek into the Pug template (more on this in Chapter 3).

Express.js Command-Line Interface

Now we can use the CLI to spawn new Express.js apps. For example, to create an app with Stylus support, type the following:

```
$ express -c styl express-styl
```

Then, as the instructions in the terminal tell us (Figure 2-1), type:

```
$ cd express-styl && npm install
$ DEBUG=my-application ./bin/www
```

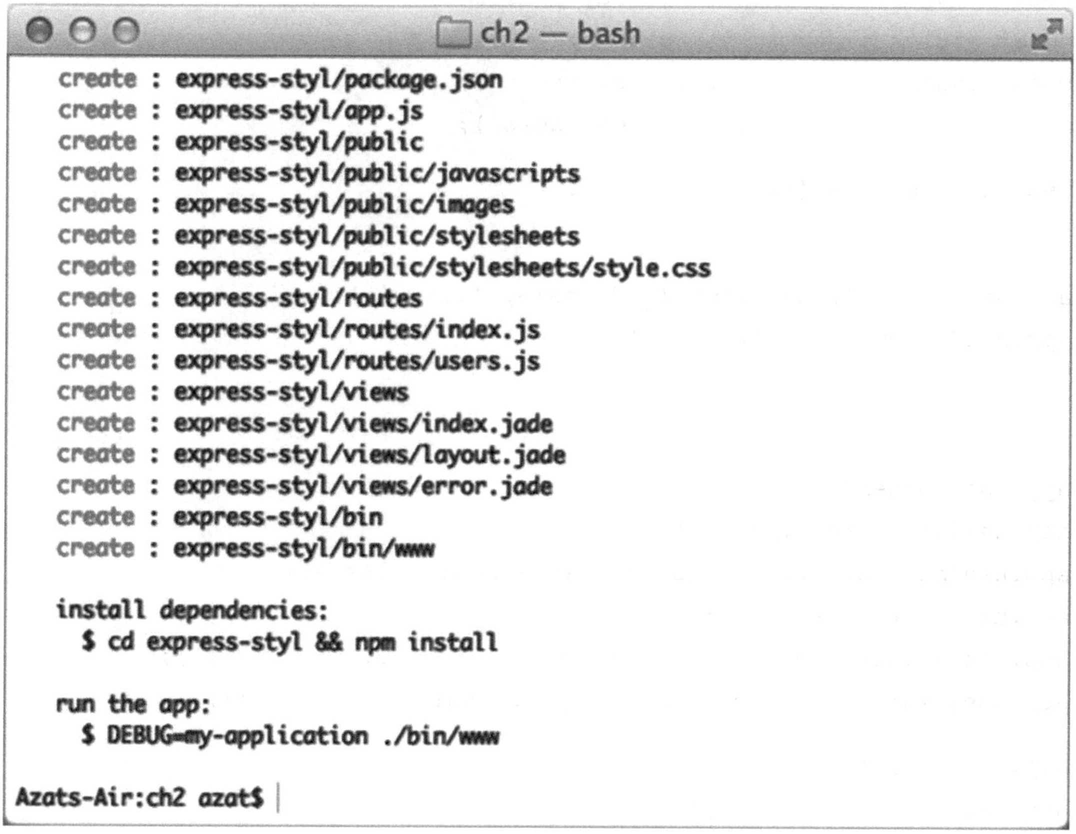

Figure 2-1. *The result of using Express.js Generator*

Open the browser of your choice at `http://localhost:3000` and you'll see "Express Welcome to Express" styled with a CSS which is coming from a Stylus file (`.styl`). If you go to `http://localhost:3000/users`, then you'll see "respond with a resource". If everything is working, then kudos, you've created an Express app with the Stylus support.

If you don't have computer in front of you right now, here's the full code of `express-styl/app.js` using Express.js Generator v4.15.0. The server file has routes from the `routes` folder, Stylus, and a rudimentary error handler. You know I don't like semicolons. The `;` and `var` style are preserved from the code generated by the tool.

```
const express = require('express');
const path = require('path');
const favicon = require('serve-favicon');
const logger = require('morgan');
const cookieParser = require('cookie-parser');
const bodyParser = require('body-parser');
const stylus = require('stylus');
const index = require('./routes/index');
const users = require('./routes/users');

let app = express();

// view engine setup
app.set('views', path.join(__dirname, 'views'));
app.set('view engine', 'jade');

// uncomment after placing your favicon in /public
//app.use(favicon(path.join(__dirname, 'public', 'favicon.ico')));
app.use(logger('dev'));
app.use(bodyParser.json());
app.use(bodyParser.urlencoded({ extended: false }));
app.use(cookieParser());
app.use(stylus.middleware(path.join(__dirname, 'public')));
app.use(express.static(path.join(__dirname, 'public')));

app.use('/', index);
app.use('/users', users);
// catch 404 and forward to error handler
app.use(function(req, res, next) {
  var err = new Error('Not Found');
  err.status = 404;
  next(err);
});
```

```
// error handler
app.use(function(err, req, res, next) {
  // set locals, only providing error in development
  res.locals.message = err.message;
  res.locals.error = req.app.get('env') === 'development' ? err : {};

  // render the error page
  res.status(err.status || 500);
  res.render('error');
});

module.exports = app;
```

The Express app is exported with `module.exports` and is launched with `listen()`
in the `bin/www` file. Let's see the main parts of the server file `app.js` that was created by
the Express Generator.

Routes in Express.js

When you open `express-styl/app.js`, you see two routes in the middle:

```
const index = require('./routes/index');
const users = require('./routes/users');
...
app.use('/', routes);
app.use('/users', users);
```

The first one basically takes care of all the requests to the home page, such as
`http://localhost:3000/`. The second takes care of requests to `/users`, such as
`http://localhost:3000/users`. Both of the routes process URLs in a case-insensitive
manner and in a same way as with trailing slashes.

By default, Express.js doesn't allow developers to route by query string arguments,
such as the following:

```
GET: www.webapplog.com/?id=10233
GET: www.webapplog.com/about/?author=10239
GET: www.webapplog.com/books/?id=10&ref=201
```

However, it's trivial to write your own middleware. It might look like this:

```
app.use((req, res, next) => {

})
```

That's right. The middleware is just a function with three argument. Two of which are good old friends: request and response. Then third argument is a callback that is invoked when all is done:

```
app.use((req, res, next) => {
  next()
})
```

Developers can also finish the response with `send()`, `end()`, `render()` or any other Express method, or pass an error object to the `next()` callback:

```
app.use((req, res, next) => {
  if (!req.session.loggedIn) // User didn't log in
    return next(new Error('Not enough permissions'))
  if (req.session.credits === 0) // User has not credit to play
    return res.render('not-enough-credits.pug')
  next()
})
```

Let's take a look at another example that has some logic to deal with a query string data using the `req.query` object:

```
app.use((req, res, next) => {
  if (req.query.id) {
  // Process the id, then call next() when done
  else if (req.query.author) {
  // Same approach as with id
  else if (req.query.id && req.query.ref) {
    // Process when id and ref present
  } else {
    next();
  }
});
```

```
app.get('/about', (req, res, next) => {
    // This code is executed after the query string middleware
});
```

What's useful is that each `req` or `request` object in the *subsequent* middleware functions or request handler functions (i.e., routes) is the same object for the same request. This allows developers to decorate a reference or a value. For example, by having this middleware we can ensure that all subsequent middleware and routes *have access to*:

```
app.use((req, res, next) => {
  req.db = const db = mongoskin.db('mongodb://@localhost:27017/test')
})

app.use((req, res, next) => {
  req.articles = req.db.collection('articles')
})

app.post('/users', (req, res, next) => { // use req.db or req.articles
  req.db.collection('users').insert({}, {}, (error, results)=>{
    req.articles.insert({}, {}, (error, results)=>{
      res.send()
    })
  })
})
```

Back to the `app.js` file. The request handler for the root route, that is `/`, is straightforward (`routes/index.js`, in this case). Everything from the HTTP request is in `req` and it writes results to the response in `res`. Here's `routes/index.js`:

```
var express = require('express');
var router = express.Router();
/* GET home page. */
router.get('/', function(req, res, next) {
  res.render('index', { title: 'Express' });
});

module.exports = router;
```

Here's `routes/users.js` in which we define and export a route:

```
var express = require('express');
var router = express.Router();

/* GET users listing. */
router.get('/', function(req, res, next) {
  res.send('respond with a resource');
});

module.exports = router;
```

Middleware as the Backbone of Express.js

Each line/statement above the routes in `express-styl/app.js` is middleware:

```
const express = require('express');
const path = require('path');
const favicon = require('serve-favicon');
const logger = require('morgan');
const cookieParser = require('cookie-parser');
const bodyParser = require('body-parser');
const stylus = require('stylus');
//...
app.use(favicon(path.join(__dirname, 'public', 'favicon.ico')));
app.use(logger('dev'));
app.use(bodyParser.json());
app.use(bodyParser.urlencoded());
app.use(cookieParser());
app.use(express.static(path.join(__dirname, 'public')));
```

The middleware includes pass-through functions that either do something useful or add something helpful to the request as it travels along each of them. For example, `bodyParser()` and `cookieParser()` add HTTP request payload (`req.body`) and parsed cookie data (`req.cookie`), respectively. And in our `app.js`, `app.use(logger('dev'));` is tirelessly printing in the terminal pretty logs for each request. In Express.js 3.x, many of these middleware modules were part of the Express.js module, but not in version 4.x. For this reason, Express Generator declared and included in `app.js` and `package.json`, and we installed with npm additional modules like `static-favicon`, `morgan`, `cookie-parser` and `body-parser`.

Configuring an Express.js App

Here is how we define configuration statements in a typical Express.js app (the `app.js` file) with the use of `app.set()` methods, which take the name as a first argument and the value as the second:

```
app.set('views', path.join(__dirname, 'views'));
app.set('view engine', 'pug');
```

And then in the `bin/www` file, you will see the statement that saves the value of the port, which will be used later during the server bootup. The value is coming either from the environment variable or the hard-coded value of 3000 as a fallback when the environment variable `PORT` is undefined:

```
app.set('port', process.env.PORT || 3000);
```

An ordinary setting involves a name, such as `views`, and a value, such as `path.join(dirname, 'views')`, the path to the folder where templates/views live.

Sometimes there is more than one way to define a certain setting. For example, `app.enable('trust proxy')` for Boolean flags is identical (a.k.a., *sugar-coating*) to `app.set('trust proxy', true)`. Chapter 11 explains why we might need to trust proxy.

Pug Is Haml for Express.js/Node.js

The Pug template engine is akin to the Ruby on Rails' Haml in the way it uses whitespace and indentation, such as `layout.pug`:

```
doctype html
html
  head
    title= title
    link(rel='stylesheet', href='/stylesheets/style.css')
  body
    block content
```

Yes, it might look weird, and yes, you might hate it (`https://webapplog.com/jade`) in the beginning because of a missing white space that breaks your app, but believe me: **Pug is awesome...** when you know it. Luckily, there's a whole chapter (Chapter 4) dedicated to templates, and you can learn Pug in there.

Final Thoughts Scaffolding

As you've seen, it's effortless to create web apps with Express.js. The framework is splendid for REST APIs as well. If you feel like the settings and other methods mentioned in this chapter just flew over your head, don't despair! *Pro Express.js: Master Express.js: The Node.js Framework For Your Web Development* (Apress, 2014) is dedicated solely to the Express.js, and its interface and can server as a good reference. This book published in 2014 is still relevant in 2018 and will be in 2019 because the book covers Express version 4 and its still the latest version because this version is very mature and "complete". Get the book on Amazon: `https://amzn.to/2tlSwNw`. For now, the next step is to create a foundation for our project: the Blog app.

The Blog Project Overview

Our Blog app consists of five main parts from the user perspective:

- A home page with a list of articles (Figure 2-2)

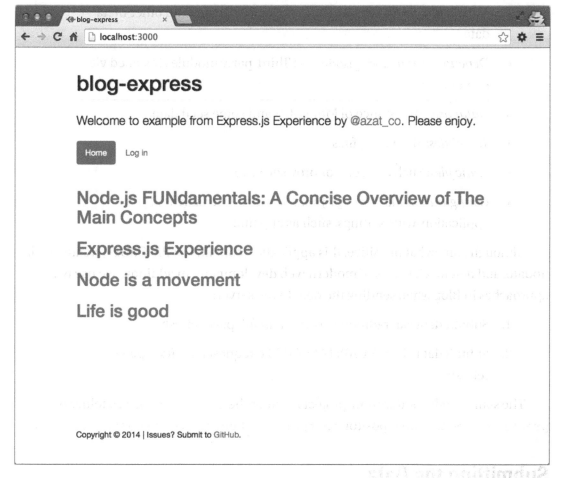

Figure 2-2. The home page of the Blog app

- An individual article page with the full-text article

- An admin page for publishing and removing content

- A login page for accessing the aforementioned admin page

- A post article page for adding new content

From a developer's point of view, the app has the following elements:

- *Main file* app.js: Settings, inclusions of routes, and other important logic. This is the file we typically run with node to start the server.

- *Routes*: All the logic related to pages and abstracted from app.js based on functional meaning, such as getting the data from the database and compiling the data into HTML

- *Node.js project file* `package.json`: Dependencies and other meta data

- *Dependencies in* `node_modules`: Third-party modules installed via `package.json`

- *Database*: An instance of MongoDB and some seed data

- *Templates*: The `*.pug` files

- *Static files*: Such as `*.css` or browser `*.js`

- *Configuration file* `config.json`: Security-insensitive application-wide settings, such as app title

Although somewhat primitive, this application contains all the CRUD (create, read, update, and delete) elements of modern web development. In addition, we use two approaches in Blog when sending the data to the server:

1. Submit data via traditional forms *with* full page refresh

2. Submit data via REST API (AJAX HTTP requests) *without* page refresh

The source code for this mini-project is under the `ch2/hello-world` folder of `practicalnode` GitHub repository: `https://github.com/azat-co/practicalnode`.

Submitting the Data

The first approach, which is depicted in Figure 2-3, is called traditional or thick server, and is more SEO (search engine optimization) friendly. With this approach, all HTML is rendered on the server. Almost all of the logic is on the server as well. This is how web was designed to work. This is how all web apps worked in late 1990s.

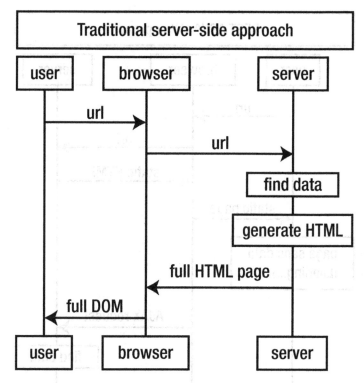

Figure 2-3. *Traditional server-side approach*

However, this traditional approach requires the reloading of the entire webpage. Thus it takes longer for users (especially on mobile) and is not as smooth and snappy as working with desktop apps. For this reason, developers started to move rendering and other logic to clients (browser). This is the second approach called thick client or client-side rendering and depicted in Figure 2-4.

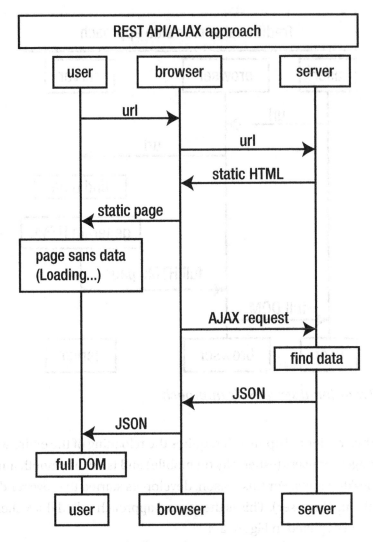

Figure 2-4. *REST API approach diagram*

Sending and receiving data via REST API/HTTP requests and rendering HTML on the client side is used with front-end frameworks such as React, Backbone.js, Angular, Ember, and many others (`http://todomvc.com`) (Figure 2-4). The use of these frameworks is becoming more and more common nowadays because it allows for more efficiency (HTML is rendered on the client side, and only the data is transmitted) and better code organization.

Under the hood, virtually all front-end frameworks use jQuery's `ajax()` method. So, to give you a realistic example, the admin page uses REST API endpoints via jQuery `$.ajax()` calls to manipulate the articles, including publish, unpublish, and remove (Figure 2-5).

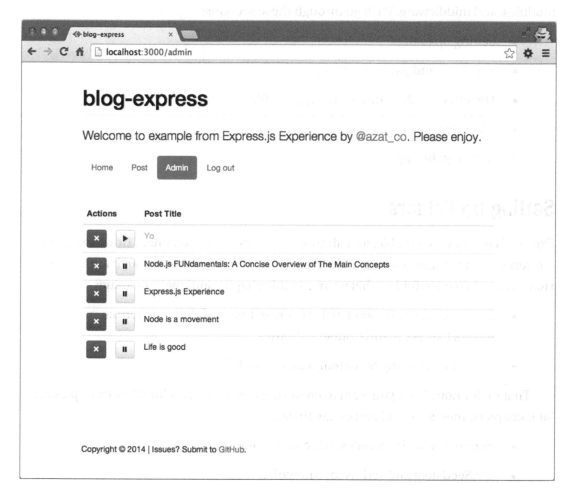

Figure 2-5. *The admin page of Blog*

Unlike the previous sections of this chapter, which dealt with scaffolding with CLI, in this practical exercise I intentionally wanted to show how to create an Express.js app manually, because it will give you a better understanding of how things really work together in the framework.

Let's wait no more, and start by creating our project folders.

Express.js Hello World Example

This is the second and the last Hello World example in this book! :-) The goal is to show readers how easy is it to create Express.js apps from scratch without generators, fancy modules, and middleware. We'll go through these sections:

- Setting up folders

- `npm init` and `package.json`

- Dependency declaration The `app.js` file

- Meet Pug

- Running the app

Setting Up Folders

Express.js is very configurable, and almost all folders can be renamed. However, there are certain conventions that may help beginners to find their way through many files. Here are the two main folders that we use in this chapter, and their meaning:

- `node_modules`: Dependencies (third-party modules) live here as well as Express.js and Connect libraries

- `views`: Pug (or any other template engine) files

That's it for now, but if you want to create a few more folders for other examples for later chapters, then go ahead and create these:

- `routes`: Node.js modules that contain request handlers

- `db`: Seed data and scripts for MongoDB

- `public`: All the static (front-end) files, including HTML, CSS, JavaScript (browser), and Stylus (or any other CSS-language framework files)

Let's choose a project folder called `hello-world`, and create these directories with the Finder macOS app or with the following terminal command, which works on macOS and Linux (Figure 2-6):

```
$ mkdir {public,public/css,public/img,public/js,db,views,views/
includes,routes}
```

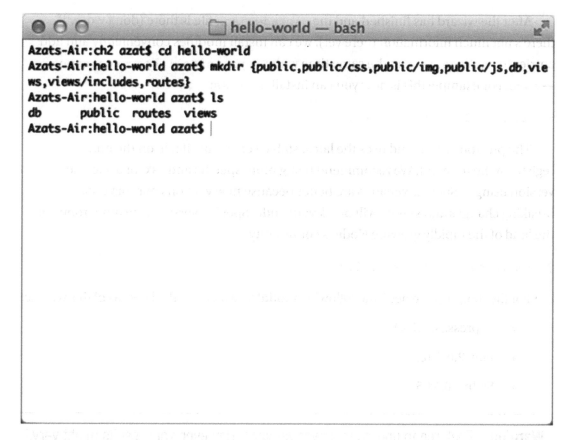

```
● ● ●                     📁 hello-world — bash                        ⬏
Azats-Air:ch2 azat$ cd hello-world
Azats-Air:hello-world azat$ mkdir {public,public/css,public/img,public/js,db,vie
ws,views/includes,routes}
Azats-Air:hello-world azat$ ls
db        public  routes  views
Azats-Air:hello-world azat$ |
```

Figure 2-6. *Setting up folders*

Now we're all set to add project metadata with npm.

npm init and package.json

For this example we will be creating the Express.js app from scratch, i.e., without Express. js Generator. We'll start with defining dependencies with `package.json` and npm.

npm is used not only as a registry, but also as a dependency management tool. Therefore, it's essential to set up the project file, `package.json`. Although it's possible to create the `package.json` file manually in a text editor, we can use the $ `npm init` command. Run this command in your project folder and answer all the questions (or leave them blank):

```
$ npm init
```

After the wizard has finished and the `package.json` file is there (don't worry if there's not much information there yet), we can install modules conveniently and add entries to `package.json` at the same time with `$ npm install <package-name>` `--save`. For example this is how you can install `express`:

```
$ npm install express --save
```

The previous command uses the latest stable version available on the npm registry at the moment. We recommend being more specific and ask for a specific version using `@`. Specific versions are better because new versions may have some breaking changes and simply will break your code. Specific versions are more robust in the land of the rapidly growing Node.js community.

```
$ npm install express@4.15.4 --save
```

For the Blog app, we need the following modules, which are the latest as of this writing:

- Express.js: 4.15.4

- Pug: 2.0.0-rc.4

- Stylus: 0.54.5

Warning   Feel free to update to newer versions. However, your results might vary, because it's very common in the Node.js ecosystem ("userland") to see breaking changes introduced by new versions. This usually happens unintentionally by the dependency of a dependency.

For example, even if we include a specific version of Express.js, such as 3.4.5, that module includes Pug with a wildcard `*`. This means after every `npm i` the latest version of Pug will be downloaded. One sunny wonderful day a new version of Pug will have some breaking update like a removal of a method which your app uses. Boom! Your app will suffer a great damage and will be broken.

There are several strategies to mitigate such breaking behavior. Most of them involve locking the versions. And one cure is to just commit your `node_modules` folder along with the rest of the source code to a Git repository and use that instead of fetching modules according to `package.json` each time on deployment. That's what we did at DocuSign. We just committed entire `node_modules`. It worked well. Or use npm's shrinkwrap or package-lock features. Read more about this issue in Chapter 12.

Dependency Declaration: npm install

Another way to create a `package.json` file (without using `$ npm init`) is to type or copy and paste `package.json` and run `$ npm install`:

```
{{
  "name": "hello-advanced",
  "version": "0.0.1",
  "private": true,
  "scripts": {
    "start": "node app.js"
  },
  "dependencies": {
    "express": "4.15.4",
    "pug": "2.0.0-rc.4"
  }
}
```

In the end, the `node_modules` folder should be filled with the corresponding libraries.

If you noticed, one of the questions `npm init` asked was about the so-called entry point. In our case, it's the `app.js` file, and it's the home for most of the application's logic. To run it, simply use one of the following commands:

- `$ node app.js`
- `$ node app`
- `$ npm start`

Another approach is to name the entry point `index.js`. In this case, we get the benefit of running the script with the `$ node.` command.

Let's create the first iteration of `app.js`.

The App.js File

The `app.js` file is the main file for this example. A typical structure of the main Express. js file `app.js` consists of the following areas (this may be a partial repeat from an earlier section, but this is important, so bear with me):

1. Require dependencies

2. Configure settings

3. Connect to database (*optional*)

4. Define middleware

5. Define routes

6. Start the server on a particular port

7. Start workers with clusters to scale (a term *spawn workers* is also used for this) (*optional*)

The order here is important, because requests travel from top to bottom in the chain of middleware.

Let's perform a quintessential programming exercise: writing the Hello World application. This app transitions smoothly into the Blog example project, so no effort is wasted!

Open `app.js` in a code editor of your choice and start writing (or just copy code from GitHub (`http://github.com/azat-co/blog-express`)).

First, all the dependencies need to be included with `require()`:

```
const express = require('express');
const http = require('http');
const path = require('path');
```

Then, the Express.js object is instantiated (Express.js uses a functional pattern):

```
let app = express();
```

One of the ways to configure Express.js settings is to use `app.set()`, with the name of the setting and the value. For example:

```
app.set('appName', 'hello-advanced');
```

Let's define a few such configurations in `app.js`:

- `port`: A number on which our server should listen to requests

- `views`: Absolute path to the folder with template (`views` in our example)

- `view engine`: File extension for the template files (for example, `pug`, `html`)

If we want to use the port number provided in the environmental variables (*env vars* for short), this is how to access it: `process.env.PORT`.

So let's write the code for the settings we listed earlier:

```
app.set('port', process.env.PORT || 3000);
app.set('views', path.join(__dirname, 'views'));
app.set('view engine', 'pug');
```

Next comes the middleware section of the application. Middleware is the backbone of the Express.js framework, and it comes in two flavors:

- Defined in external (third-party) modules, e.g., `app.use(bodyParser.json());` with `bodyParser.json` being imported from `body-parser`

- Defined in the app or its modules, e.g., `app.use(function(req, res, next){...});`

Middleware is a way to organize and reuse code and, essentially, **middleware is nothing more than a function with three parameters**: `request`, `response`, and `next`. We'll use more middleware (for example, for authorization and for persistence) in Chapter 6, but for now, its use will be minimal.

The next components in the `app.js` file are routes. Routes process requests. An illustration in Figure 2-7 shows how an HTTP request is processed. So the next section of `app.js` is where we define routes themselves (the order in `app.js` matters). The way routes are defined in Express.js is with helpers `app.VERB(url, fn1, fn2, ..., fn)`, where `fnNs` are request handlers, `url` is on a URL pattern in RegExp, and `VERB` values are as follows:

- `all`: Catch any requests, i.e., all HTTP methods

- `get`: Catch GET requests

- `post`: Catch POST requests

- `put`: Catch PUT requests

- `patch`: Catch PATCH requests

- `del`: Catch DELETE requests

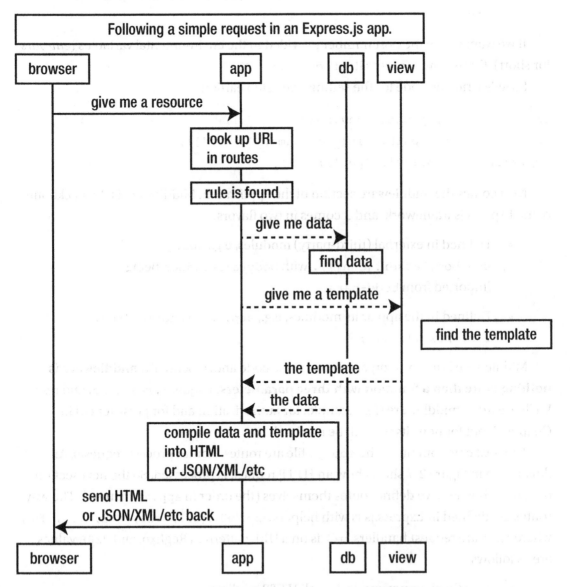

Figure 2-7. *Following a simple request in an Express.js app*

Note   `del` and `delete` methods are aliases in older versions of Express. Just remember that `delete` is a valid operator in JavaScript/ECMAScript, and therefore in Node.js. The operator removes a property from an object, e.g., `delete books.nodeInAction`.

Routes are processed in the order in which they are defined. Usually, routes are put after middleware, but some middleware may be placed following the routes. A good example of such middleware, found after routes, is an error handler.

Figure 2-7 shows how a trivial request might travel across the web and the Express.js app, with the dotted lines being the connection inside it.

In this Hello World example, a single route is used to catch requests of all methods on all URLs (`*` wildcard):

```
app.all('*', (req, res) => {
  ...
})
```

Inside the request handler, a template is rendered with the `res.render()` function using name of the template `index` as the first argument and the data object as a second argument. The data has a message `msg` as the property of the second argument:

```
app.all('*', function(req, res) {
  res.render('index', {msg: 'Welcome to Practical Node.js!'})
})
```

For reference, in `res.render(viewName, data, callback(error, html))` where parameters mean the following:

- `viewName`: A template name with filename extension or if `view engine` is set without the extension

- `data`: An optional object that is passed as `locals`; for example, to use `msg` in Pug, we need to have `{msg: "..."}`

- `callback`: An optional function that is called with an error and HTML when the compilation is complete res.render() is not in the Node.js core and is purely an Express.js addition that, if invoked, calls core res.end(), which ends/completes the response. In other words, the middleware chain doesn't proceed after res.render(). res.render is highlighted in Chapter 4.

Last but not least are the instructions to start the server. In the previous Hello World app, you saw app.listen(), but http.createServer(app).listen() will work too. It consists of the core http module and its createServer method. In this method, the system passes the Express.js app object with all the settings and routes:

```
http.createServer(app).listen(app.get('port'), () => {
  console.log(`Express server listening on port ${app.get('port')}`)
})
```

You can also use https.createServer(app).listen() for the HTTPS support when you are ready to deploy your server to production.

Here's the full source code of the app.js file for your reference:

```
const express = require('express')
const http = require('http')
const path = require('path')

let app = express()

app.set('port', process.env.PORT || 3000)
app.set('views', path.join(__dirname, 'views'))
app.set('view engine', 'pug')

app.all('*', (req, res) => {
  res.render(
    'index',
    {msg: 'Welcome to Practical Node.js!'}
  )
})

http
  .createServer(app)
  .listen(
    app.get('port'),
```

```
  () => {
    console.log(`Express.js server is listening on port ${app.
get('port')}`)
  }
)
```

Before we can run this server, we need to create the `index.pug` file in the `views` folder.

Meet Pug: One Template to Rule Them All

Pug is an absolutely amazing template engine that allows developers to type less code and to execute powerfully almost all JavaScript functions. It also supports top-to-bottom and bottom-to-top inclusion and other useful things. Like its brother from the Ruby world, Haml, Pug uses whitespace/indentation as a part of its language. It's a convention to use two-space indentation.

The Pug syntax and its features are covered more extensively in Chapter 4. For now, just keep in mind that the way Pug works is that the first word is used as an HTML tag (HTML element), and the text that follows, which is inner text or inner content, is put inside this element. For example, here are two sibling elements <h1> and <p> with text inside of them. The space after the Pug elements h1 and p is super important!

```
h1 hello
p Welcome to the Practical Node.js!
```

That produces the following HTML code:

```
<h1>hello</h1>
<p>Welcome to the Practical Node.js!</p>
```

If we want to output a value of a variable (called `locals`), we use =. For example:

```
p= msg
```

For this example, create `index.pug` in the `views` folder that outputs a header and a paragraph with the value `msg` variable inside of that paragraph (i.e., inner text):

```
h1 hello
p= msg
```

I included more advanced examples of Pug later in this book. For now, everything is set for the first demo!

Running the Hello World App

Run the $ node app command from the project root. When your app is running you can open a browser at http://localhost:3000. Now you should see the Hello World text as it appears in Figure 2-8.

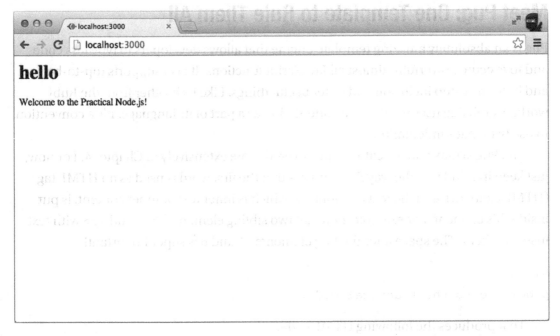

Figure 2-8.   *The Hello World app in action*

Nothing fancy so far, but it's worth pointing out that it took us just a few lines (the app.js file) to write a fully functional HTTP server! In the next chapter, we add more new and exciting pages using Pug instructions.

Summary

In this chapter we learned what Express.js is and how it works. We also explored different ways to install it and use its scaffolding (command-line tool) to generate apps. We went through the Blog example with a high-level overview (traditional vs. REST API approaches), and proceeded with creating the project file, folders, and the simple Hello World example, which serves as a foundation for the book's main project: the Blog app. And then lastly, we touched on a few topics such as settings, a typical request process, routes, AJAX versus server side, Pug, templates, and middleware.

In the next chapter we'll examine an important aspect of modern web development and software engineering: test-driven development. We look at the Mocha module and write some tests for Blog in true TDD/BDD style. In addition, the next chapter deals with adding a database to Blog routes to populate these templates, and shows you how to turn them into working HTML pages!

CHAPTER 3

TDD and BDD for Node.js with Mocha

Test-driven development (TDD), as many of you may know, is one of the main agile development techniques. The genius of TDD lies in increased quality of code, faster development resulting from greater programmer confidence, and improved bug detection (duh!).

Historically, web apps have been hard to autotest, and developers relied heavily on manual testing. But certain parts such as standalone services and REST APIs can be *and should be* tested thoroughly by the TDD. At the same time, rich user interface (UI)/user experience (UX) can be tested with headless browsers such as Selenium or Puppeteer.

And before you start yawning and thinking about skipping this chapter because—well, I won't be far off in saying that a lot of developers like testing as much as they might like a warm can of beer on a hot Sunday afternoon at the beach, please think about testing as the **time saver**. With proper tests in place and a bit of time spent on writing them, developers save time in the long term. The longer the long term, the more the payoff. It's not uncommon for *a good module* to have two to three times (2–3x) more tests than the code itself. Crazy? No. It's not an overkill but a smart and pragmatic strategy!

But what is BDD then? The behavior-driven development (BDD) concept is based on TDD. It differs from TDD in language/interface, which is more natural. Thus, BDD is the preferred way of writing tests. An example of a BDD interface is `expect` such as in `expect(response.status).to.equal(200)`. Compare that to the dryness of TDD with `assert`, such as in `assert.equal(response.status, 200)`

© Azat Mardan 2018
A. Mardan, *Practical Node.js*, https://doi.org/10.1007/978-1-4842-3039-8_3

Similar to building apps themselves, most of the time software engineers should use a testing framework. To get you started with the Node.js testing framework, Mocha, in this chapter, we cover the following:

- Installing and understanding Mocha TDD with the assert

- BDD with Expect.js

- Project: Writing the first BDD test for Blog

The source code for this chapter is in the `code/ch3` folder of the `azat-co/practicalnode` GitHub repository, which is located at `https://github.com/azat-co/practicalnode`.

Installing and Understanding Mocha

Mocha is a mature and powerful testing framework for Node.js. To install it globally, simply run the following shell command:

```
$ npm i -g mocha@4.0.1
```

Note   We use a specific version (the latest as of this writing is 4.0.1) to prevent inconsistency in this book's examples caused by potential breaking changes in future versions of Mocha.

If you encounter the lack-of-permissions issue discussed in Chapters 1 and 2, run the following "super user" shell command:

```
$ sudo npm i -g mocha@4.0.1
```

To avoid using `sudo`, follow the instructions in Chapter 1 on how to install Node.js correctly... or just install Mocha locally.

Tip   It's possible to have a separate version of Mocha for each project by simply pointing to the local version of Mocha, which you install like any other npm module into `node_modules`. The command for macOS/Linux will be:

```
$ ./node_modules/.bin/mocha test_name
```

For a more advanced example, refer to "Putting Configs into a Makefile" later in this chapter. For my Windows users, who cannot use . or /, modify to this command:

```
$ node_modules\.bin\mocha test_name
```

Most of you have heard about TDD and why it's a good thing to follow. Do you have an idea how it works? The main process of TDD can be summed up in the three following steps:

1. Implement a test

2. Implement the code to make the test pass

3. Verify that the test passes and repeat the cycle

BDD is a specialized version of TDD that specifies what needs to be unit-tested from the perspective of business requirements. It's possible to just write tests with the good old plain core Node.js module `assert`. However, as in many other situations, using a special testing library is more preferable. You might also want to use a test runner (sometimes also called a testing framework). For both TDD and BDD, we'll be using the Mocha testing framework because by doing so we gain many things for "free." Among them are the following:

- Reporting

- Asynchronous support

- Rich configurability

- Notifications

- Debugger support

- Common interface with `before, after`

- hooks File watcher support

There are many more features and benefits to using Mocha. Here is a list of some of the optional parameters (options) that the `$ mocha [options]` command takes (the full list is obtainable with `mocha -h`):

- `-h` or `--help`: Print help information for the Mocha command

- `-V` or `--version`: print the version number that's being used

- `-r` or `--require <name>`: Require a module with the name provided

- `-R` or `--reporter` `<name>`: Use a reporter with the name provided

- `-u` or `--ui` `<name>`: Use the stipulated reporting user interface (such as `bdd`, `tdd`)

- `-g` or `--grep` `<pattern>`: Run tests exclusively with a matching pattern

- `-i` or `--invert`: Invert the `--grep` match pattern

- `-t` or `--timeout` `<ms>`: Set the test case time out in milliseconds (for example, 5000)

- `-s` or `--slow` `<ms>`: Set the test threshold in milliseconds (for example, 100)

- `-w` or `--watch`: Watch test files for changes while hanging on the terminal

- `-c` or `--colors`: Enable colors

- `-C` or `--no-colors`: Disable colors

- `-G` or `--growl`: Enable macOS Growl notifications

- `-d` or `--debug`: Enable the Node.js debugger—`$ node --debug`

- `--debug-brk`: Enable the Node.js debugger breaking on the first line—`$ node --debug-brk`

- `-b` or `--bail`: Exit after the first test failure

- `-A` or `--async-only`: Set all tests in asynchronous mode

- `--recursive`: Use tests in subfolders

- `--globals` `<names>`: Provide comma-delimited global names

- `--check-leaks`: Check for leaks in global variables

- `--interfaces`: Print available interfaces

- `--reporters`: Print available reporters

- `--compilers` `<ext>:<module>, ...`: Provide compiler to use

Figure 3-1 shows an example of Nyan cat reporter with the command $ `mocha test-expect.js - R nyan`. I mean, Nyan cat is important in a testing framework, right?! Right?

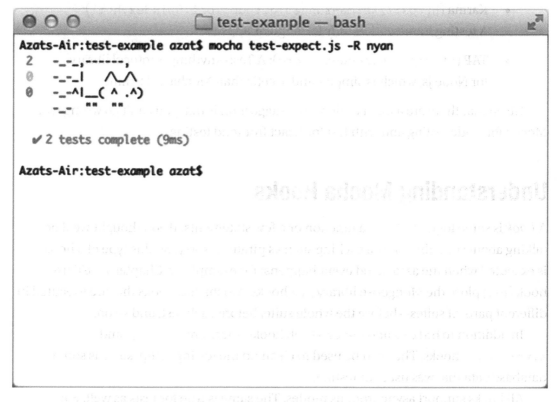

Figure 3-1. *Mocha Nyan reporter hints that Mocha has a lot of reporters to choose from*

Usually, when it comes to choosing a type of framework, there are a few options. Mocha is one of the more robust and widely used. However, the following alternatives to Mocha are worth considering:

- Jest (`https://facebook.github.io/jest`): A framework for *mostly* React and browser testing, which is built on Jasmine and has a lot of things included

- Jasmine: (`https://jasmine.github.io`): A BDD framework for Node and browser testing, which follows Mocha notation

- Vows (`http://vowsjs.org`): A BDD framework for asynchronous testing

- Encyme (`http://airbnb.io/enzyme`): A language *mostly* for React apps, which has a jQuery-like syntax and is used with Mocha, Jasmine, or other test frameworks

- Karma (`https://karma-runner.github.io/1.0/index.html`): A testing framework *mostly* for Angular apps

- TAP (`http://www.node-tap.org`): A Test-Anything-Protocol library for Node.js, which is simpler and ascetic than Mocha or Jasmine

Given that there are a lot of options, my suggestion is that you can't go wrong with Mocha for Node testing and with Jest for React frontend testing.

Understanding Mocha Hooks

A *hook* is some logic, typically a function or a few statements. If you thought we'll be talking about something more exciting such as pirates... sorry. So this type of a hook is executed when the associated event happens; for example, in Chapter 7 we'll use hooks to explore the Mongoose library `pre` hooks. Mocha has hooks that are executed in different parts of suites—before the whole suite, before each test, and so on.

In addition to `before` and `beforeEach` hooks, there are `after()`, and `afterEach()` hooks. They can be used to clean up the testing setup, such as some database data that was used for testing.

All hooks support asynchronous modes. The same is true for tests as well. For example, the following test suite is synchronous and won't wait for the response to finish:

```
describe('homepage', () => {
  it('should respond to GET', () => {
    superagent
      .get(`http://localhost:${port}`)
      .end((error, response) => {
        expect(response.status).to.equal(200)
        // This will never happen
    })
  })
})
```

But as soon as we add a `done` parameter to the test's function, our test case waits for the HTTP request to come back. We call `done()` to let Mocha (or Jasmine or Jest, since they share this syntax) know that "Hey, you can move on, nothing else to assert here." If this `done()` is omitted, then the test will time out because no one will let the test runner/ framework know about the finish.

```
describe('homepage', () => {
  it('should respond to GET', (done) => {
    superagent
      .get(`http://localhost:${port}`)
      .end((error, response) => {
        expect(response.status).to.equal(200)
        done()
      })
  })
})
```

Test cases (`describe`) can be nested inside other test cases, and hooks such as `before` and `beforeEach` can be mixed in with different test cases on different levels. Nesting of `describe` constructions is a good idea in large test files.

Sometimes developers may want to skip a test case/suite (`describe.skip()` or `it.skip()`) or make them exclusive (`describe.only()` or `describe.only()`). Exclusivity means that only that particular test runs (the opposite of `skip`).

As an alternative to the BDD interface's `describe`, `it`, `before`, and others, Mocha supports more traditional TDD interfaces:

- `suite`: Analogous to `describe`

- `test`: Analogous to `it`

- `setup`: Analogous to `before`

- `teardown`: **Analogous to** `after`

- `suiteSetup`: **Analogous to** `beforeEach`

- `suiteTeardown`: **Analogous to** `afterEach`

TDD with the Assert

Let's write our first tests with the assert library. This library is part of the Node.js core, which makes it easy to access. It has minimal set of methods, but it may be enough for some cases, such as unit tests... and less is more in some cases, right?

Again, as in the previous project, developers can install Mocha globally or locally. After the Mocha installation is finished, a test file can be created in a `test-example` folder:

```
$ code test-example/test-assert.js
```

Note   `code` is a VS Code alias command that allows developers to open a folder in a code editor by executing this command in a terminal. You can use any other editor, such as Sublime Text 3 (`subl`), Vi (`vi`), or TextMate (`mate`), assuming you have these commands configured in your PATH variable or `bash_profile`.

Let's try a simple test in `test.js` with the following content, to test an array method `split()`, which creates an array out of a string:

```
const assert = require('assert')
describe('String#split', () => {
  it('should return an array', () => {
    assert(Array.isArray('a,b,c'.split(',')))
  })
})
```

We can run this simple `test.js`, which is inside the `code/ch3/test-example` folder, to test

`String.split()` with just the folder name:

```
$ mocha test-assert
```

or, we can navigate inside the folder and run the test from there

```
$ cd test-example
$ mocha test.js
```

The two commands above is only if you installed Mocha globally or if you expose the local `.bin` path to the `PATH` environment variable. If you installed Mocha locally (see your `package.json` and `node_modules`), then you *may* need to specify the path directly to the local installation because the local installation is not exposed in PATH automatically. This is the command for Linux, macOS, and other POSIX systems:

```
$ ./node_modules/.bin/mocha test.js
```

And this is the command for Windows:

```
$ node_modules\.bin\mocha test.js
```

The results of these Mocha commands are shown in Figure 3-2.

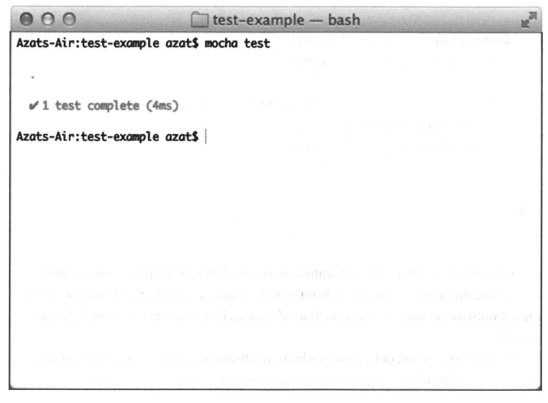

Figure 3-2. *Running to test*

We can add to our example another test case (`it`) that asserts equality of array values (`code/ch3/test-example/test.js`) using a `for` loop and `assert.equal` on individual array items:

```js
const assert = require('assert')
const testArray = ['a','b','c']
const testString = 'a,b,c'

describe('String#split', () => {

  it('should return an array', () => {
    assert(Array.isArray('a,b,c'.split(',')))
  })

  it('should return the same array', () => {
    assert.equal(testArray.length,
      testString.split(',').length,
      `arrays have equal length`)
    for (let i = 0; i < testArray.length; i++) {
      assert.equal(testArray[i],
        testString.split(',')[i],
        `i element is equal`)
    }
  })

})
```

As you can see, some code is repeated, so we can abstract it into `beforeEach` and `before` constructions. A little bit of abstraction is always a good thing! (Abstraction is just a fancy word for cut and paste, a term that software architects like to use to justify higher wages.)

Here's a new version of the test in which we abstracted away the seed data of the `current` variable. It's in `code/ch3/test-example/test-assert-v2.js`:

```js
var assert = require('assert')
var expected, current

before(() => {
  expected = ['a', 'b', 'c']
})
```

```
describe('String#split', () => {

  beforeEach(() => {
    current = 'a,b,c'.split(',')
  })

  it('should return an array', () => {
    assert(Array.isArray(current))
  })

  it('should return the same array', () => {
    assert.equal(expected.length,
      current.length,
      'arrays have equal length')
    for (let i = 0; i < expected.length; i++) {
      assert.equal(expected[i],
        current[i],
        `i element is equal`)
    }
  })

})
```

Chai Assert

In the previous example with `test.js` and assert, we used the Node.js core module
assert. At the same time, there's also a `chai` library that has assert module (and an
`expect` module, and `should` module). Developers prefer to use chai assert over core
assert because chai assert has more features.

To get started with chai assert, simply replace

```
const assert = require('assert')
```

with

```
const assert = require('chai').assert
```

Ergo, we can modify our previous example to use `chai assert`, but first of all, we MUST INSTALL `chai`:

```
$ npm install chai@4.1.2
```

And then import the chai assert with following code that goes into `test-example/test.js`:

```
const assert = require('chai').assert
```

Or use the code that uses destructuring:

```
const {assert} = require('chai')
```

I mentioned that chai assert has more method than the Node's core assert. That's true. And the following are just some of the methods from the chai assert library:

- `assert(expressions, message)`: Throws an error if the expression is false

- `assert.fail(actual, expected, [message], [operator])`: Throws an error with values of `actual, expected, and operator`

- `assert.ok(object, [message])`: Throws an error when the object is not double equal (==) to true—a.k.a., truthy (0, and an empty string is false in JavaScript/Node.js)

- `assert.notOk(object, [message])`: Throws an error when the object is falsy, i.e., false, 0 (zero), "" (empty string), null, undefined, or NaN

- `assert.equal(actual, expected, [message])`: Throws an error when `actual` is not double equal (==) to expected

- `assert.notEqual(actual, expected, [message])`: Throws an error when `actual` is double equal (==)—in other words, not unequal (!=)—to expected

- `.strictEqual(actual, expected, [message])`: Throws an error when objects are not triple equal (===)

Of course there's no need to duplicate the documentation here, so for the full chai assert API, refer to the official documentation (`http://chaijs.com/api/assert`).

Note   The chai assert (`chai.assert`) and the Node.js core assert (`assert`) modules are *not 100% compatible*, because the former has more methods. The same is true for `chai.expect` and a standalone `expect.js`. We will use `expect` from `chai`.

BDD with Expect

Expect is one of the BDD languages. It's very popular because its syntax allows for chaining. It is richer in features than core module `assert`. Yes, the syntax is very natural to read and understand... by software developers, quality assurance engineers and even program managers. And again, there are at least two flavors of Expect for you to use choose from:

- Standalone: Install as a `expect.js` module

- Chai: Install as a part of the `chai` library (recommended)

For the former, simply execute the following in an *existing* Node project (you must have `package.json` already there, which you can create with `npm init -y`):

```
$ npm install chai@4.1.2 --save-exact
```

Tip   While `install` and `i` are the same, `--save-exact` or `-E` will add a precise version of the library to `package.json`, and not a version with ^, which means install latest up to major release (first digit in semantic versioning)—a behavior responsible for sleepless nights trying to fix a breaking change in a newer version.

And, then after you install `chai`, import it inside a Node.js test file using:

```
const expect = require('chai').expect
```

Hey, you can use ES6 destructuring assignment as well. Check this out:

```
const {expect} = require('chai')
```

And what about the actual usage of Expect? How to write Expect assertions? Each assert assertion can be rewritten with Expect. The idea is to use `expect()` and pass an object we are testing to it as an argument, e.g., `expect(current.length)`.

Then use the properties and methods by chaining them in some resemblance to the English language: `expect(current.length).to.equal(3)`.

For example, the previous test can be rewritten in `chai.expect` BDD style using `to.be.true`, `equal` and `to.equal`:

```
const {expect} = require('chai')
let expected
let current

before(() => {
  expected = ['a', 'b', 'c']
})

describe('String#split', () => {

  beforeEach(() => {
    current = 'a,b,c'.split(',')
  })

  it('should return an array', () => {
    expect(Array.isArray(current)).to.be.true
  })

  it('should return the same array', () => {
    expect(expected.length).to.equal(current.length)
    for (let i = 0; i < expected.length; i++) {
      expect(expected[i]).equal(current[i])
    }
  })

})

})
```

I cover more of the `expect` syntax and methods later. Now, I'll show you another library—standalone `expect.js`. For the standalone `expect.js` (not 100% compatible with `chai.expect`) approach, import another module called `expect.js` with the following command:

```
$ npm install expect.js
```

And, replace the chai expect `const {expect} = require('chai')` inside a Node.js test file with the `expect.js` module:

```
const expect = require('expect.js')
```

Note   `$ npm i expect.js` or any other `$ npm i name` needs to be in the project's root (topmost) folder, which must contain either the `node_modules` directory already or a `package.json` file (recommended because you can save the version number in there). For more information on module installations and the ways of npm, please refer to Chapter 1.

Expect Syntax

The `expect.js` library is very extensive. Part of its appeal is that it has nice methods that mimic natural language. Often there are a few ways to write the same assertion, such as `expect(response).to.be(true)` and `expect(response).equal(true)`. The following lists some of the main `expect.js` methods and properties:

- `ok`: Checks for truthyness

- `true`: Checks whether the object is truthy

- `to.be, to`: Chains methods as in linking two methods

- `not`: Chains with a not connotation, such as `expect(false).not. to.be(true)`

- `a/an`: Checks type (works with `array` as well)

- `include/contain`: Checks whether an array or string contains an element

- `below/above`: Checks for the upper and lower limits

Note   Again, there is a slight deviation between the standalone `expect.js` module and its Chai counterpart.

I bet you didn't buy this book to read the documentation, did you? So we will save you time and not list every single method in the book because the documentation is easily available online. And hey, most likely you can get by with just a handful of them, such as `equal` and `ok` and `true`. I do. I rarely use more than several methods. But in case you need the whole list of methods, go to the full documentation on `chai.expect`, refer to `http://chaijs.com/api/bdd`. And for the standalone `expect.js`, see `https://github.com/LearnBoost/expect.js`.

Project: Writing the First BDD Test for Blog

The goal of this mini-project is to add a few tests for Blog (this book's primary project). I won't get into headless browsers and UI testing, because that's an extensive topic in and of itself. But we can send a few HTTP requests and parse their responses from the app's REST endpoints (see Chapter 2 for a description of the Blog app).

The source code for this chapter is in the `code/ch3/blog-express` folder of the practicalnode GitHub repository (`https://github.com/azat-co/practicalnode`).

First, let's copy the Hello World project. It will serve as a foundation for Blog. Then, install Mocha in the Blog project folder, and add it to the `package.json` file at the same time with `$ npm install` **mocha@4.0.1** `--save-dev`. The `--save-dev` flag will categorize this module as a development dependency (`devDependencies`). Modify this command by replacing package name and version number for expect.js (0.3.1) and superagent (`https://npmjs.org/package/superagent`) (3.8.0). The latter is a library to streamline the making of HTTP requests. Alternatives to `superagent` include the following:

- `axios` (`https://npmjs.org/package/axios`): A promise and async/await-based library, which works both in Node and browsers (recommended)

- `node-fetch` (`https://npmjs.org/package/node-fetch`): A port of a native Fetch API from ECMAScript and browsers, which works universally in Node and browsers

- `request` (`https://npmjs.org/package/request`): A versatile HTTP agent and one of the most downloaded and dependents upon npm module

- http: A core module, which clunky and very low level

- supertest (https://npmjs.org/package/supertest):
  A superagent-based assertions library

Here's the updated package.json:

```
{
  "name": "blog-express",
  "version": "0.0.2",
  "private": true,
  "scripts": {
    "start": "node app.js",
    "test": "mocha tests"
  },
  "dependencies": {
    "express": "4.16.2",
    "pug": "2.0.0-rc.4",
    "stylus": "0.54.5"
  },
  "devDependencies": {
    "expect.js": "0.3.1",
    "mocha": "4.0.1",
    "superagent": "3.8.0"
  }
}
```

Now, create a test folder with $ mkdir tests and open tests/index.js in your editor. The test needs to start the server. We will use two methods, boot() and shutdown(), which are imported from the yet-to-be-created app.js. The test is straightforward. It makes a single GET request to a home page and checks that the response has status code 200 (OK):

```
const boot = require('../app').boot
const shutdown = require('../app').shutdown
const port = require('../app').port
const superagent = require('superagent')
const expect = require('expect.js')
```

```
describe('server', () => {
  before(() => {
    boot()
  })

  describe('homepage', () => {
    it('should respond to GET', (done) => {
      superagent
        .get(`http://localhost:${port}`)
        .end((error, response) => {
          expect(response.status).to.equal(200)
          done()
        })
    })
  })

  after(() => {
    shutdown()
  })
})
```

Now we will get to the actual meat and potatoes (or rice and tofu bacon for my vegetarian readers) of the Blog project: the Express server in app.js.

Remember, in the test we are using boot and shutdown. Thus, we expose those two methods, boot and shutdown, in app.js when the file app.js is imported by some other file. In our case, the importation will be done by the test, i.e., tests/index.js. This is to make the system more flexible. The goal is to allow the test to boot the server, and to be able to start the server without tests.

So, instead of just using listen() straight up to launch the server right in the app.js like we did before:

```
http.createServer(app).listen(app.get('port'), () => {
  console.log(`Express server listening on port ${app.get('port')}`)
})
```

Let's refactor this into using an if/else condition with `require.main === module`, which would either export the server Express app object (false) for usage in the Mocha test file (`tests/index.js`) or boot up the server right away (true). We would move the `listen()` into the new `boot()` function, which is either called directly or exported to be called by another file:

```
const server = http.createServer(app)
const boot = () => {
  server.listen(app.get('port'), () => {
    console.info(`Express server listening on port ${app.get('port')}`)
  })
}
const shutdown = () => {
  server.close()
}
if (require.main === module) {
  boot() // "node app.js" command
} else {
  console.info('Running app as a module')
  exports.boot = boot
  exports.shutdown = shutdown
  exports.port = app.get('port')
}
```

To launch the test, simply run $ `mocha tests`. The `tests` is a folder. The file name `index.js` is optional.

If that fails, then run a more exact POSIX command with the path:

```
$ ./node_modules/.bin/mocha tests
```

Or run this Windows command:

```
$ node_modules\.bin\mocha tests
```

If you have more than one file in the `tests` folder, then all of them would be run by the Mocha test runner. When you run the tests, the server should boot and respond to the home page request (/ route), as shown in Figure 3-3.

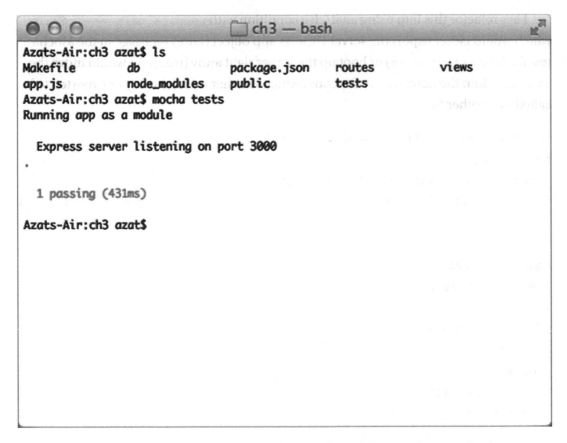

Figure 3-3. *The result of running shows the number of executed tests, which is 1*

So having tests boot up your server is convenient. You don't need to keep remembering to boot up the server separately before running the tests. Can we make the test report prettier? Sure!

Putting Configs into a Makefile

The mocha command accepts many, many, many options. It's often a good idea to have these options gathered in one place, which could be a Makefile. For example, we can have test, test-w, which tests all files in the test folder, and have separate commands for just the module-a.js and module-b.js files to test them separately. We can add

any extra flags/options, such as reporter, timeout time, file watching, macOS growl
notification, and so on:

```
REPORTER = list
MOCHA_OPTS = --ui tdd --ignore-leaks

test:
        clear
        echo Starting test ******************************
        ./node_modules/mocha/bin/mocha \
        --reporter $(REPORTER) \
        $(MOCHA_OPTS) \

tests/*.js
        echo Ending test
        test-w:
        ./node_modules/mocha/bin/mocha \
        --reporter $(REPORTER) \
        --growl \
        --watch \
        $(MOCHA_OPTS) \
        tests/*.js

test-module-a:
        mocha tests/module-a.js --ui tdd --reporter list --ignore-
        leaks

test-module-b:
        clear
        echo Starting test ******************************
        ./node_modules/mocha/bin/mocha \
        --reporter $(REPORTER) \
        $(MOCHA_OPTS) \
        tests/module-b.js
        echo Ending test

.PHONY: test test-w test-module-a test-module-b
```

To launch this Makefile, run $ `make <mode>`. For example, $ `make test`, where the `test` command is one of the commands in the Makefile. Other commands are `test-w`, `test-module-a`, and `test- module-b`.

Of course, developers aren't limited only to testing in Makefiles. Anything can be there: building, compilation, linting, configuration and maybe even deployment! For more information on a Makefile please refer to "Understanding Make" at `http://www.cprogramming.com/tutorial/makefiles.html` and "Using Make and Writing Makefiles" at `http://www.cs.swarthmore.edu/~newhall/unixhelp/howto_makefiles.html`.

For our Blog app, we can keep the Makefile simple:

```
REPORTER = list
MOCHA_OPTS = --ui bdd -c

test:
    clear
    echo Starting test ********************************
    ./node_modules/mocha/bin/mocha \
    --reporter $(REPORTER) \
    $(MOCHA_OPTS) \
    tests/*.js
    echo Ending test

.PHONY: test
```

Note   In this Makefile, we point to the local Mocha in the Makefile, so the dependency needs to be added to `package.json` and installed in the `node_modules` folder using `npm i` or `npm i mocha` commands.

Now we can run tests with the $ `make test` command, which allows for more configuration compared with the simple $ `mocha tests` (Figure 3-4).

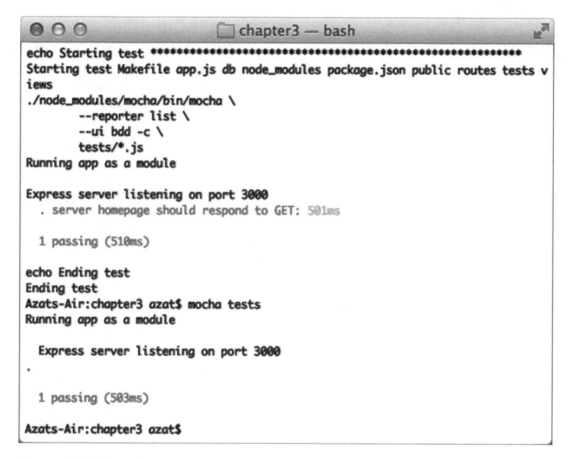

```
echo Starting test ••••••••••••••••••••••••••••••••••••••••••••••••••••••••••••••••
Starting test Makefile app.js db node_modules package.json public routes tests v
iews
./node_modules/mocha/bin/mocha \
        --reporter list \
        --ui bdd -c \
        tests/*.js
Running app as a module

Express server listening on port 3000
  . server homepage should respond to GET: 501ms

  1 passing (510ms)

echo Ending test
Ending test
Azats-Air:chapter3 azat$ mocha tests
Running app as a module

  Express server listening on port 3000

  .

  1 passing (503ms)

Azats-Air:chapter3 azat$
```

Figure 3-4. *Running*

Don't forget that make test uses singular and mocha tests uses a plural word in the command. :-)

Summary

In this chapter, we installed Mocha as a command-line tool and learned its options, we wrote simple tests with assert, the chai.expect and expect.js libraries, and we created the first test for the Blog app by modifying app.js to work as a module.

There's more to testing. In Chapter 10, I will teach how to utilize the continuous integration service TravisCI and use GitHub to trigger continuous multiple tests in virtual cloud environments.

For now in the next chapter, we proceed with the essence of a web app that outputs HTML—template engine. We'll dive deep into Pug and Handlebars, and add pages to Blog.

111

CHAPTER 4

Template Engines: Pug and Handlebars

A *template engine* is a library or a framework that uses some rules/languages to interpret data and render views. In the case of web applications, *views* are HTML pages (or parts of them), but they can be JSON or XML files, or GUIs in the case of desktop programs. For those of you familiar with the model–view–controller concept, templates belong to the view.

In web apps, it's beneficial to use templates because we can generate an infinite number of pages dynamically with a single template! Another side benefit is when we need to change something; we can do it in one place only.

If we go back to the diagrams in the previous chapter (traditional vs. REST API approaches), we can deduce that templates can be compiled into HTML either server-side (traditional approach) or client- side (REST API approach). No matter which approach we take, the syntax of the libraries themselves remains intact.

In this chapter we cover the following:

- Pug syntax and features

- Pug standalone usage

- Handlebars syntax

- Handlebars standalone usage

- Pug and Handlebars usage in Express.js

- Project: adding Pug templates to Blog

© Azat Mardan 2018
A. Mardan, *Practical Node.js*, https://doi.org/10.1007/978-1-4842-3039-8_4

Pug Syntax and Features

Pug is a Node.js brother of Haml, in the sense that it uses whitespace and indentation as part of its language. As with a real pugs, this Pug can either be cute and friendly or can chew your butt off if you don't know how to use it. Therefore, we need to be careful to follow the proper syntax.

You can follow the Pug syntax examples in this section online, at the official web site's demo page (`https://pugjs.org/api/reference.html`) or by writing standalone Node.js scripts (examples are presented in the section "Pug Standalone Usage," which appears later in this chapter).

Tags

Any text at the beginning of a line—by default—is interpreted as an HTML tag. The main advantage of Pug is that this text renders both closing and opening tags for the HTML element, as well as the `<></>` symbols. Therefore, we save many keystrokes as developers writing in Pug! It's very important to type as little as possible. It will allow you not only to avoid silly typos but also to avoid having a repetitive stress injury done to your hands.

The text following a tag and a space (e.g., `tag <text>`) is parsed as the inner HTML (i.e., content inside the element). For example, if we have the following Pug code with `h1` and `p` tags (elements). After the tag/element name, there's a space, then text:

```
body
  div
    h1 Practical Node.js
    p The only book most people will ever need.
  div
    footer &copy; Apress
```

The text after the first space becomes the content of those elements. The output of the template above will be `<h1>`, `<p>`, and other elements with the corresponding text inside of them:

```
<body>
  <div>
    <h1> Practical Node.js </h1>
    <p> The only book most people will ever need. </p>
  </div>
```

```
<div>
  <footer> &copy; Apress </footer>
</div>
</body>
```

The preceding code above is an HTML <body> element. How about some more interesting HTML elements to generate the entire web page with the <head> and other tags? Sure. You can do that too (eat that, React!). Here's an example of how to define DOCTYPE, and element attributes such as lang (for html), type (for script), and id and class for div:

```
doctype html
html(lang="en")
  head
    title Why JavaScript is Awesome | CodingFear: programming and
    human circumstances
    script(type='text/javascript').
      const a = 1
      console.log(`Some JavaScript code here and the value of a is
      ${a}`)
  body
    h1 Why JavaScript is Awesome
    div(id="container", class="col")
      p You are amazing
      p Get on it!
      p.
        JavaScript is fun. Almost everything
        can be written in JavaScript. It is huge.
```

The output will contain attributes defined with parenthesis (key=value), such as id, class, type and lang. The output will also have JavaScript code that will be executed when the page is viewed in the browsers. The output will also have text in <p>. A dot . after the element name or parenthesis allows to define text on a new line and to use multiple lines as show in the last p element.

The # means it's an `id` attribute, whereas the dot in the element means a `class` attribute. Thus, omitting the element name like we did with the `#container.col` will produce `<div>` with the id `container` and class `col`. See for yourself:

```html
<!DOCTYPE html>
<html lang="en">
  <head>
    <title>Why JavaScript is Awesome | CodingFear: programming and
    human circumstances</title>
    <script type="text/javascript">
      const a = 1
      console.log(`Some JavaScript code here and the value of a is
      ${a}`)
    </script>
  </head>
  <body>
    <h1>Why JavaScript is Awesome</h1>
    <div class="col" id="container">
      <p>You are amazing</p>
      <p>Get on it!</p>
      <p>
        JavaScript is fun. Almost everything
        can be written in JavaScript. It is huge.
      </p>
    </div>
  </body>
</html>
```

Check out the code bellow *without* the tag/element name... nothing?! Huh. You see, when you omit the tag name like in the `#contaner.col`, Pug will use `div`, so the code below:

```pug
#container.col
  p You are amazing
  p Get on it!
```

becomes a <div with the id container and the class col:

```
<div class="col" id="container">
  <p>You are amazing</p>
  <p>Get on it!</p>
</div>
```

You can play with these example using the code, which is in the code/ch4/ pug-example/pug- method-example.js. The code uses the pug npm modules and its render() method. For example, this is a Node file and it generates HTML:

```
const pug = require('pug')
const pugTemplate = `body
  div
    h1 Practical Node.js
    p The only book most people will ever need.
  div
    footer &copy; Apress`
const htmlString = pug.render(pugTemplate, {pretty: true})
console.log(htmlString)
```

So far, we've just outputted some pre-programmed code that is not modifiable by the application. This is static and not much fun. Most of the time we want to have some dynamism in the form of variables that will allow the application itself to modify the output, that is HTML.

Variables/Locals

Pug, Express and Node developers call the data that is passed to the Pug template *local*. This data is available within the template as a regular Node variable. To output the value of a local/variable, use =. Let's look at some examples to make the lesson stick.

This Pug code prints values of variables title and body using the equal = symbol:

```
h1= title
p= body
```

The variables `title` and `body` are called locals. They are the data to supply to the Pug template to generate HTML. The data comes in the form of an object. It must have properties and the properties *must* be the same as the names of the locals that you want to use, i.e., `title` and `body`:

```
{
  title: "Express.js Guide",
  body: "The Comprehensive Book on Express.js"
}
```

The HTML output generated from the Pug template and locals shows the values of the variables `title` and `body`:

```
<h1>Express.js Guide</h1>
<p>The Comprehensive Book on Express.js</p>
```

What about HTML element attributes such as `href` or `class`? You saw some of these, already but, let's dive deeper.

Attributes

Attributes are added by putting them into parentheses right after the tag name. They follow the `tagName(name=value)` format. In addition, multiple attributes *need* to be separated by a comma. For example, this Pug code has various attributes on `div`, `a`, and other elements:

```
div(id="content", class="main")
  a(href="http://expressjsguide.com", title="Express.js Guide",
  target="_blank") Express.js Guide
  form(action="/login")
    button(type="submit", value="save")
  div(class="hero-unit") Lean Node.js!
```

The preceding Pug template code above turns into the following HTML with attributes rendered inside of the HTML elements:

```
<div class="main" id="content"><a href="http://expressjsguide.com"
title="Express.js Guide" target="_blank">Express.js Guide</a>
```

```
<form action="/login"><button type="submit" value="save">
</button></form>
<div class="hero-unit">Lean Node.js!</div>
</div>
```

Yes, the <a> element is right on the same line as <div>. It's a mystery to me too.

Sometimes, the value of an attribute needs to be dynamic. It's more fun this way! In this case, just use the variable name without double quotes as the value of the attribute.

Another trick is to use the pipe, or |. It allows us to define text DOM node. In other words, the line with the pipe becomes raw text. This is useful when defining multiple lines of text.

An example uses attribute values from locals/variables and defines the <input> content text yes/no on a new line:

```
a(href=url, data-active=isActive)
label
  input(type="checkbox", checked=isChecked)
  | yes / no
```

If the template above is provided with these locals, some of which are boolean and url is a string:

```
{
  url: "/logout",
  isActive: true,
  isChecked: false
}
```

then they both—meaning template and locals data—produce the following HTML output, which doesn't have checked (false) and has yes/no as text.

```
<a href="/logout" data-active="data-active"></a>
<label>
  <input type="checkbox"/> yes / no
</label>
```

Note that the attribute with the value `false` is omitted from the HTML output. However, when no value is passed, `true` is assumed. For example, this is a Pug template with boolean attributes `checked`:

```
input(type='radio', checked)
input(type='radio', checked=true)
input(type='radio', checked=false)
```

The attributes checked will be omitted when the value is false. When the value is true in Pug, then the value is "checked" in HTML. This is the resulting HTML:

```
<input type="radio" checked="checked"/>
<input type="radio" checked="checked"/>
<input type="radio"/>
```

Next we will study literals.

Literals

For convenience, we can write classes and ids right after tag names. For example, we can then apply `lead` and `center` classes to a paragraph, and create a `div` element with the `side-bar` id and `pull- right` class (again, the pipe signifies an inner text):

```
div#content
  p.lead.center
    | webapplog: where code lives
    #side-bar.pull-right
    span.contact.span4
      a(href="/contact") contact us
```

Note that if the tag name is omitted, `div` is used instead. See the `<div id="side-bar" class="pull-right"></div>` in the generated HTML below. This `<div>` was created by Pug when no element name was provided, and only a an id of `side-bar`:

```
<div id="content">
  <p class="lead center">
    webapplog: where code lives
    <div id="side-bar" class="pull-right"></div>
```

```
    <span class="contact span4">
      <a href="/contact">contact us</a>
    </span>
  </p>
</div>
```

Pug is all about eloquence, compactness, and convenience. `<div>` elements are very popular for layouts. Therefore, Pug defaults to rendering `<div>` when there's no element name and there is a class or an id. Nice!

Our next feature is rendering text.

Text

Outputting raw text is done via |. For example, this template produces one `<div>` with inner text:

```
div
  | Pug is a template engine.
  | It can be used in Node.js and in the browser JavaScript.
```

If you move the | to the left, then the result will be one empty `<div>` with sibling text nodes.

To avoid using pipes on multiple lines, there's a dot . syntax. Thus, if you want to render all nested (indented) lines as inner text, then use dot . right after the element name. For example, this template is analogous to the preceding code in that it produces one `<div>` with inner text of two lines:

```
div.
  Pug is a template engine.
  It can be used in Node.js and in the browser JavaScript.
```

The result in both cases is HTML with `<div>` and text inside:

```
<div>Pug is a template engine. It can be used in Node.js and in the
browser JavaScript.</div>
```

The dot comes in handy for writing JavaScript that executes at run time, which is the topic of the next section.

Script and Style Blocks

Sometimes, developers want to write chunks of content for `script` or `style` tags in the HTML! This is possible with a dot.

For example, we can write inline front-end JavaScript like this:

```
script.
  console.log('Hello Pug!')
  setTimeout(function(){
    window.location.href='http://rpjs.co'
  },200))
  console.log('Good bye!')
```

And the HTML output will have the `<script>` tag with all of our code:

```
<script>
  console.log('Hello Pug!')
  setTimeout(function() {
  window.location.href = 'http://rpjs.co'
  }, 200))
  console.log('Good bye!')
</script>
```

Did you like this little trick with the dot and JavaScript? Of course! But this code is not executed until the page loads. In other words, it's runtime but not compile.

JavaScript Code

Contrary to the previous example, if we want to use *any* JavaScript at template compilation time—in other words, to write executable JavaScript code that manipulates the output of the Pug (i.e., HTML)— we can use the -, =, or != symbols. This may come in handy when we output HTML elements and inject JavaScript.

Obviously, these types of things should be done carefully to avoid cross-site scripting (XSS) attacks. For example, if we want to define an array and output <> symbols, we can use !=.

```
- var arr = ['<a>','<b>','<c>']
ul
  - for (var i = 0; i< arr.length; i++)
    li
      span= i
      span!="unescaped: " + arr[i] + " vs. "
      span= "escaped: " + arr[i]
```

The Pug above produces the following HTML which *does NOT include* JavaScript but the result of the JavaScript code, because this JS is a compile-time JS for Pug. This is not run-time JS for a browser as was defined with `script`. earlier. The resulting HTML has `<ul>` and three `<li>` elements:

```
<ul>
  <li><span>0</span><span>unescaped: <a> vs.
  </span><span>escaped: &lt;a&gt;</span></li>
  <li><span>1</span><span>unescaped: <b> vs.
  </span><span>escaped: &lt;b&gt;</span></li>
  <li><span>2</span><span>unescaped: <c> vs.
  </span><span>escaped: &lt;b&gt;</span></li>
</ul>
```

Tip   One of the main differences between Pug and Handlebars is that the former allows pretty much any JavaScript in its code, whereas the latter restricts programmers to only a handful of built-in and custom-registered helpers.

Comments

When it comes to comments, we have a choice to render/output them into HTML or not. To render/output them into HTML, use JavaScript style `//`; to not render them, use `//-`. For example, here are two comments:

```
// content goes here
p Node.js is a non-blocking I/O for scalable apps.
//- @todo change this to a class
p(id="footer") Copyright 2014 Azat
```

The Pug above with comments outputs the HTML style comments with `//` but hides them with `//-`. Thus, the resulting HTML has only `content goes here` without `@todo change this to a class`:

```
<!-- content goes here-->
<p>Node.js is a non-blocking I/O for scalable apps.</p>
<p id="footer">Copyright 2014 Azat</p>
```

Of course, views (i.e., templates) benefit greatly from an if/else condition. Let's cover them next.

Conditions (if)

Interestingly enough, in addition to the standard JavaScript code, where the `if` statement can be used by prefixing it with `-`, we can use an even shorter Pug alternative with no prefix and no parentheses. For example, this if/else works fine:

```
- var user = {}
- user.admin = Math.random()>0.5
if user.admin
    button(class="launch") Launch Spacecraft
else
    button(class="login") Log in
```

There's also `unless`, which is equivalent to `not` or `!`.

Iterations (each loops)

Similar to conditions, *iterators* in Pug can be written simply with `each`. For example, this is code to iterate over an array of programming languages and create paragraphs for each of them:

```
- var languages = ['php', 'node', 'ruby']
div
  each value, index in languages
    p= index + ". " + value
```

The HTML output with three <p> elements is as follows:

```
<div>
  <p>0. php</p>
  <p>1. node</p>
  <p>2. ruby</p>
</div>
```

The same iterative `each` construction works with objects as well. Developers even can access a `key` value. Take a look at this object with languages as keys and their importance as values:

```
- var languages = {'php': -1, 'node': 2, 'ruby':1}
div
  each value, key in languages
    p= key + ": " + value
```

The Pug above is compiled into the HTML output in which each iteration over the array values produces a paragraph <p> element for each language:

```
<div>
  <p>php: -1</p>
  <p>node: 2</p>
  <p>ruby: 1</p>
</div>
```

Next are filters!

Filters

Filters are used when there are blocks of texts written in a different language. For example, the filter for Markdown looks like this:

```
p
  :markdown
    # Practical Node.js
```

Note   The Markdown modules still need to be installed. The `marked` and markdown npm packages are often used for this. There's no need for an additional configuration; just install them in the project's local `node_modules` folder.

Interpolation

Interpolation is mixing of strings and dynamic values from variables. That's another term that will make you look at least five (5) IQ points smarter. You are welcome.

In Pug, interpolation is achieved via the syntax with curly braces and a hashtag: `#{name}`, where `name` is the name of a variable. For example, to output `title` in a paragraph, simply use `#{title}` *in the text*, as in the following code:

```
- var title = "React Quickly: Painless web apps with React, JSX,
Redux, and GraphQL"
p Read the #{title} in PDF, MOBI and EPUB
```

The interpolation is processed at the template compilation. Therefore, don't use interpolation in executable JavaScript, that is, JS with –. For the – JS, use standard ES6 string interpolation with `${name}`.

Case

Case allows Node developers to avoid a chain of if/else conditions. You probably used something similar. In other languages, case implemented with `switch`. Here's an example of the `case` statement in Pug:

```
- var coins = Math.round(Math.random()*10)
case coins
  when 0
    p You have no money
  when 1
    p You have a coin
  default
    p You have #{coins} coins!
```

Mixins

Mixins are functions that take parameters and produce some HTML. They are super cool because they allow you reuse boatloads of code if used correctly. The declaration syntax is `mixin name(param, param2,...)`, and the usage is `+name(data)`. For example, here I define `row` and `table` mixins, which I use later with real data from arrays:

```
mixin row(items)
  tr
    each item, index in items
      td= item

mixin table(tableData)
  table
    each row, index in tableData
      +row(row)
- var node = [{name: "express"}, {name: "hapi"}, {name: "derby"}]
+table(node)
- var js = [{name: "backbone"}, {name: "angular"}, {name: "ember"}]
+table(js)
```

The preceding Pug code, above when used in Express or elsewhere, produces the following output by "invoking" the mixins `table` and `row` just as a function would be invoked with arguments (bonus: developers can use `table` and `row` mixins over and over for other data!):

```
<table>
  <tr>
    <td>express</td>
  </tr>
  <tr>
    <td>hapi</td>
  </tr>
  <tr>
    <td>derby</td>
  </tr>
</table>
```

```
<table>
  <tr>
    <td>backbone</td>
  </tr>
  <tr>
    <td>angular</td>
  </tr>
  <tr>
    <td>ember</td>
  </tr>
</table>
```

Include

`include` is a way to split logic into a separate file for the purpose of reusing it across multiple files. Don't confuse this with ES6 `include`. That's JavaScript, but we are talking about Pug here.

This `include` is a *top-to-bottom* approach, meaning we dictate what to use in the file that includes another file. The file that includes is processed first (we can define locals there), and then the included file is processed (we can use earlier defined locals).

To include a Pug template, use `include /path/filename`. No need for double quotes " or single quotes '. I like it! For example, in a layout file you can import a header:

```
include ./includes/header
```

Notice there's no need for double or single quotes for the template name and its path. And it's possible to traverse up the folder tree. This footer can be in a parent folder's includes folder:

```
include ../includes/footer
```

But, there's no way to use a dynamic value for the file and path (use a variable), because includes/partials are handled at compilation (not at runtime).

Extend

extend is a *bottom-to-top* approach (as oppose to include), in the sense that the included file commands which parts of the main file it wants to replace. The way it works is with extend filename and block blockname statements.

In file_a, which is like a layout you define blocks, define block elements with some default content:

```
block header
  p some default text
block content
  p Loading ...
block footer
  p copyright
```

In file_b, which is like a subview, you define what layout to use and what blocks to overwrite (and what not to, by omission).

For example, in this file_b file, the header and content blocks will have new content, but footer will stay as in file_a. Here's the file_b example:

```
extend file_a
block header
  p very specific text
block content
  .main-content
```

The bottom line is that extend and block implement inverted inheritance pattern.

Standalone Pug Usage

Template engines (Pug) and web frameworks (Express) go together like ketchup and hotdogs—but not always. Template engines are not not always used with Node.js frameworks like Express.js. Sometimes, we might just want to use Pug in a standalone manner. The use cases include generating an e-mail template, precompiling Pug before deployment, and debugging. In this section, we do the following:

- Install a Pug module
- Create our first Pug file

- Create a Node.js program that uses the Pug file

- Compare `pug.compile`, `pug.render`, and `pug.renderFile`

To add a `pug` dependency to your project, or if you're starting from scratch from an empty project folder, do the following:

1. Create a `package.json` file manually or with `$ npm init -y`.

2. Install and add `pug` to `package.json` with `$ npm i pug -save`. See the results in Figure 4-1.

3. Create a Node file.

4. Import `pug` in the Node file.

5. Invoke a method from `pug` module in your Node file.

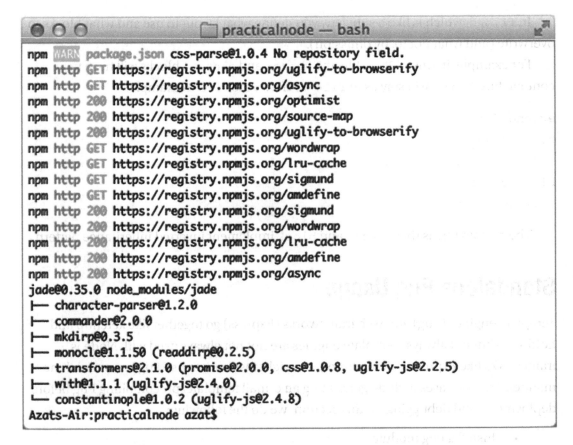

Figure 4-1. *Installing Pug*

Tip   Add `{pretty: true}` to `pug.render()`, as in `pug.`
`render(pugTemplate, {pretty: true})`, in order to have properly
formatted, *pretty* HTML.

Let's say we have some Node.js script that sends an e-mail and we need to use a
template to generate HTML dynamically for the e-mail. This is how it might look (file
`pug-example.pug`):

```
.header
  h1= title
  p
.body
  p= body
.footer
  div= By
    a(href="http://twitter.com/#{author.twitter}")= author.name
  ul
    each tag, index in tags
      li= tag
```

In this case, our Node.js script needs to *hydrate*, or populate, this template with the
following data:

- `title`: String

- `tags`: Array

- `body`: String

- `author`: String

We can extract these variables from multiple sources (databases, file systems, user
input, tassology, and so on). For example, in the `pug-example.js` file, we use hard-
coded values for `title`, `author`, `tags`, but pass through a command-line argument for
`body` using `process.argv[2]`:

```
const pug = require('pug'),
  fs = require('fs')
```

```
let data = {
  title: 'Practical Node.js',
  author: {
    twitter: '@azatmardan',
    name: 'Azat'
  },
  tags: ['express', 'node', 'javascript']
}
data.body = process.argv[2]

fs.readFile('pug-example.pug', 'utf-8', (error, source) => {
  let template = pug.compile(source)
  let html = template(data)
  console.log(html)
})
```

In this way, when we run $ node pug-example.js 'email body', we get the HTML output printed in the terminal as shown in Figure 4-2.

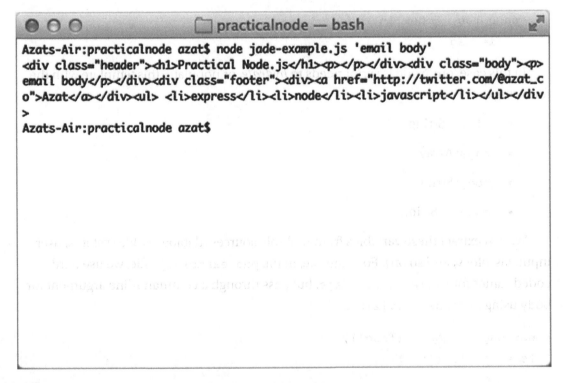

Figure 4-2. *The result of a standalone Pug rendering*

The "prettified" HTML output with proper spaces and indentation that I took from the terminal looks as follows:

```html
<div class="header">
    <h1>Practical Node.js</h1>
    <p></p>
</div>
<div class="body">
    <p>email body</p>
</div>
<div class="footer">
    <div><a href="http://twitter.com/@azatmardan">Azat</a>
    </div>
    <ul>
        <li>express</li>
        <li>node</li>
        <li>javascript</li>
    </ul>
</div>
```

In addition to `pug.compile()`, the Pug API has the functions `pug.render()` and `pug.renderFile()`. For example, the previous file can be rewritten with `pug.render()`:

```js
fs.readFile('pug-example.pug', 'utf-8', (error, source) => {
  const html = pug.render(source, data)
  console.log(html)
})
```

Furthermore, with `pug.renderFile()`, the `pug-example.js` file is even more compact because it will do two things at the same time: read a file and render it:

```js
pug.renderFile('pug-example.pug', data, (error, html) => {
  console.log(html)
})
```

Note   Pug can also be used as a command-line tool after installing it with the `-g` or `--global` option via npm. For more information, run `pug -h` or see the official documentation (`http://pug-lang.com/command-line`).

To use Pug in a browser, you can use `browserify` (`https://github.com/substack/node-browserify`) and its `pugify` (`https://www.npmjs.org/package/pug-browser`) middleware.

Note   To use the same Pug templates on front-end (browser) and server sides, I recommend `jade-browser` (`https://www.npmjs.org/package/jade-browser`) by Storify, for which I was the maintainer for a time during my work there. `jade-browser` acts as an Express.js middleware, and exposes server- side templates to the browser along with helpful utility functions.

Handlebars Syntax

The Handlebars library is another template engine. It inherits from Mustache and, for the most part, is compatible with Mustache's syntax. However, Handlebars adds more features. In other words, Handlebars is a superset of Mustache.

Unlike Pug, Handlebars by design was made so that developers *can't write* a lot of JavaScript logic inside the templates. This helps to keep templates lean and related strictly to the representation of the data (no business logic).

Another drastic difference between Pug and Handlebars is that the latter requires full HTML code (<, >, closing </> tags, and so on). For this reason it could care less about whitespace and indentation, which means that it's easy to copypasta your existing HTML and make it Handlebars, and that developers have to type *more* code when writing templates from scratch.

Variables

A Handlebars expression is {{, some content, followed by }}, hence the name of the library (see the resemblance to handlebars on a bicycle?). For example, this Handlebars code:

```
<h1>{{title}}</h1>
<p>{{body}}</p>
```

with data that has `title` and body properties:

```
{
  title: "Express.js Guide",
  body: "The Comprehensive Book on Express.js"
}
```

renders the elements with values from `title` and body:

```
<h1>Express.js Guide</h1>
<p>The Comprehensive Book on Express.js</p>
```

Iteration (each)

In Handlebars, `each` is one of the built-in helpers; it allows you to iterate through objects and arrays. Inside the block, we can use `@key` for the former (objects), and `@index` for the later (arrays). In addition, each item is referred to as `this`. When an item is an object itself, `this` can be omitted, and just the property name is used to reference the value of that property.

The following are examples of the `each` helper block in Handlebars:

```
<div>
{{#each languages}}
  <p>{{@index}}. {{this}}</p>
{{/each}}
</div>
```

The template above is supplied with this data that has array of strings:

```
{languages: ['php', 'node', 'ruby']}
```

and output this HTML upon compilation, which has `<p>` for each array element:

```
<div>
  <p>0. php</p>
  <p>1. node</p>
  <p>2. ruby</p>
</div>
```

Unescaped Output

By default, Handlebars escapes values. If you don't want Handlebars to escape a value, use triple curly braces: {{{ and }}}.

As data, let's use this object that has an array with some HTML tags (angle braces):

```
{
  arr: [
    '<a>a</a>',
    '<i>italic</i>',
    '<strong>bold</strong>'
  ]
}
```

To apply this Handlebars template to our data above (i.e., hydration) use an iterator each with {{{this}}} for the unescaped value of an individual array item, which is HTML and hence *needs* to be unescaped:

```
<ul>
    {{#each arr}}
    <li>
      <span>{{@index}}</span>
      <span>unescaped: {{{this}}} vs. </span>
      <span>escaped: {{this}}</span>
    </li>
  {{/each}}
</ul>
```

The hydrated template produces the following HTML by printing array indices ({{@index}}), unescaped HTML ({{{this}}}) and escaped HTML ({{this}}):

```
<ul>
  <li>
    <span>0</span>
    <span>unescaped: <a>a</a> vs. </span>
    <span>escaped: &lt;a&amp;gt;a&lt;/a&gt;</span>
  </li>
```

```
<li>
  <span>1</span>
  <span>unescaped: <i>italic</i> vs. </span>
  <span>escaped: &lt;i&gt;italic&lt;/i&gt;</span>
</li>
<li>
  <span>2</span>
  <span>unescaped: <strong>bold</strong> vs. </span>
  <span>escaped: &lt;strong&gt;bold&lt;/strong&gt;
  </span>
</li>
</ul>
```

Conditions (if)

if is another built-in helper invoked via #. For example, this Handlebars code uses an if/else condition to check for a user.admin value (if a user is an administrator):

```
{{#if user.admin}}
  <button class="launch"> Launch Spacecraft</button>
{{else}}
  <button class="login"> Log in</button>
{{/if}}
```

The template is populated with data that will make the if/else condition true:

```
{
  user: {
    admin: true
  }
}
```

Everything turns into this HTML output, which has a launch element rendered due to the value of user.admin being true:

```
<button class="launch">Launch Spacecraft</button>
```

Unless

To inverse an if not ... (if ! ...) statement (convert negative to positive), we can harness the unless built-in helper block. For example, the previous code snippet can be rewritten with unless.

The Handlebars code that checks the truthiness of the admin flag (property user. admin). If the value is true, then else will be applied. Notice the change in Log in and Launch Spacecraft. They are flipped now compared to if/else:

```
{{#unless user.admin}}
  <button class="login"> Log in</button>
{{else}}
  <button class="launch">Launch Spacecraft</button>
{{/unless}}
```

We supply our template with the data that makes the user an administrator:

```
{
  user: {
    admin: true
  }
}
```

The HTML output renders the launch button, which is available only to admins because this button was in else, we used unless, and the value is true.

```
<button class="launch">Launch Spacecraft</button>
```

With

In case there's an object with nested properties, and there are a lot of them, it's possible to use with to pass the context.

We have this Handlebars code that is handling a user's contact and address information:

```
{{#with user}}
  <p>{{name}}</p>
  {{#with contact}}
    <span>Twitter: @{{twitter}}</span>
```

```
  {{/with}}
  <span>Address: {{address.city}},
{{/with}}
{{user.address.state}}</span>
```

Then we merge the template with this data. Notice the properties' names are the same as in the Handlebars template, there's only one reference to the user object:

```
{user: {
  contact: {
    email: 'hi@node.university',
    twitter: 'azatmardan'
  },
  address: {
    city: 'San Francisco',
    state: 'California'
  },
  name: 'Azat'
}}
```

The snippets above, when compiled, produce HTML that prints values using the object name for every property:

```
<p>Azat</p>
<span>Twitter: @azatmardan</span>
<span>Address: San Francisco, California
</span>
```

Comments

To output comments, use regular HTML <!-- and -->. To hide comments in the final output, use {{! and }} or {{!-- and --}}. For example, the following code below has two types of comments:

```
<!-- content goes here -->
<p>Node.js is a non-blocking I/O for scalable apps.</p>
{{! @todo change this to a class}}
{{!-- add the example on {{#if}} --}}
<p id="footer">Copyright 2019 Azat</p>
```

The preceding code outputs the comments with <!-- ... --> but omits comments with {{! ... }} so the result is this:

```
<!-- content goes here -->
<p>Node.js is a non-blocking I/O for scalable apps.</p>
<p id="footer">Copyright 2019 Azat</p>
```

Custom Helpers

Custom Handlebars helpers are similar to built-in helper blocks and Pug mixins. To use custom helpers, we need to create them as a JavaScript function and register them with the Handlebars instance.

For example, let's assume we have a custom helper `table` which we'll register (i.e., define) later in the JavaScript/Node.js code, then this Handlebars template uses our `table`:

```
{{table node}}
```

Here goes the JavaScript/Node.js that *registers* or tells the Handlebars compiler what to do when it encounters the custom `table` function (i.e., print an HTML table out of the provided array):

```
handlebars.registerHelper('table', (data) => {
  let str = '<table>'
  for (let i = 0; i < data.length; i++ ) {
    str += '<tr>'
    for (var key in data[i]) {
      str += '<td>' + data[i][key] + '</td>'
    }
    str += '</tr>'
  }
  str += '</table>'
  return new handlebars.SafeString (str)
})
```

The following is our array for the table data. It has an array of object. Each object has name and URL:

```
[
  {name: 'express', url: 'http://expressjs.com/'},
  {name: 'hapi', url: 'http://spumko.github.io/'},
  {name: 'compound', url: 'http://compoundjs.com/'},
  {name: 'derby', url: 'http://derbyjs.com/'}
]
```

The resulting HTML from iterating over the name and URL objects within the table function looks like this:

```
<table>
    <tr>
        <td>express</td>
        <td>http://expressjs.com/</td>
    </tr>
    <tr>
        <td>hapi</td>
        <td>http://spumko.github.io/</td>
    </tr>
    <tr>
        <td>compound</td>
        <td>http://compoundjs.com/</td>
    </tr>
    <tr>
        <td>derby</td>
        <td>http://derbyjs.com/</td>
    </tr>
</table>
```

Thus, helpers are good for reusing the code. Another way to reuse code is includes or partials.

Includes (Partials)

In Handlebars, *includes* or *partials* templates are interpreted by the `{{> partial_ name}}` expression. Partials are akin to helpers and are registered with `Handlebars. registerPartial(name, source)`, where `name` is a string and `source` is a Handlebars template code for the partial (JS/Node code, not template):

```
Handlebars.registerPartial('myPartial', '{{name}}')
```

Calling the partial is done with the following syntax (written in the Handlebars template, not JS/Node code):

```
{{> myPartial }}
```

For more on includes and partials, see the documentation at `http:// handlebarsjs.com/partials.html`.

Standalone Handlebars Usage

Developers can install Handlebars via npm with `$ npm install handlebars` or `$ npm install handlebars --save`, assuming either `node_modules` or `package.json` is in the current working directory (see the results of a sample installation in Figure 4-3).

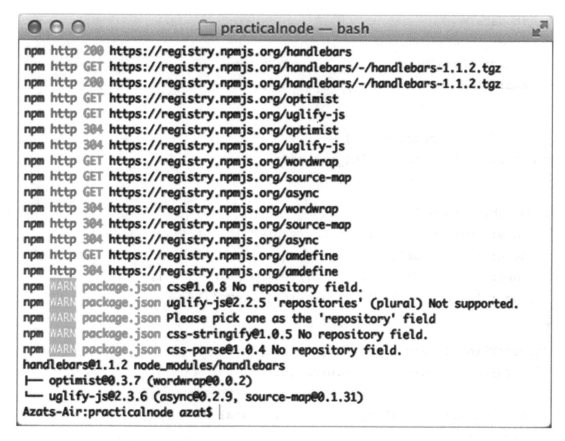

```
● ● ●                    📁 practicalnode — bash                         ⤢
npm http 200 https://registry.npmjs.org/handlebars
npm http GET https://registry.npmjs.org/handlebars/-/handlebars-1.1.2.tgz
npm http 200 https://registry.npmjs.org/handlebars/-/handlebars-1.1.2.tgz
npm http GET https://registry.npmjs.org/optimist
npm http GET https://registry.npmjs.org/uglify-js
npm http 304 https://registry.npmjs.org/optimist
npm http 304 https://registry.npmjs.org/uglify-js
npm http GET https://registry.npmjs.org/wordwrap
npm http GET https://registry.npmjs.org/source-map
npm http GET https://registry.npmjs.org/async
npm http 304 https://registry.npmjs.org/wordwrap
npm http 304 https://registry.npmjs.org/source-map
npm http 304 https://registry.npmjs.org/async
npm http GET https://registry.npmjs.org/amdefine
npm http 304 https://registry.npmjs.org/amdefine
npm WARN package.json css@1.0.8 No repository field.
npm WARN package.json uglify-js@2.2.5 'repositories' (plural) Not supported.
npm WARN package.json Please pick one as the 'repository' field
npm WARN package.json css-stringify@1.0.5 No repository field.
npm WARN package.json css-parse@1.0.4 No repository field.
handlebars@1.1.2 node_modules/handlebars
├── optimist@0.3.7 (wordwrap@0.0.2)
└── uglify-js@2.3.6 (async@0.2.9, source-map@0.1.31)
Azats-Air:practicalnode azat$ |
```

Figure 4-3. *Installing Handlebars*

Note   Handlebars can be installed via npm as a command-line tool with the `-g` or `--global` options. For more information on how to use Handlebars in this mode, refer to the `$ handlebar` command or the official documentation (`https://github.com/wycats/handlebars.js/#usage-1`).

Here's an example of standalone Node.js Handlebars usage from `handlebars-example.js` in which we import modules, then define `data` object (with book info), and then register a few helpers and generate HTML:

```
const handlebars = require('handlebars')
const fs = require('fs')
const path = require('path')
```

```
const data = {
  title: 'practical node.js',
  author: '@azatmardan',
  tags: ['express', 'node', 'javascript']
}

data.body = process.argv[2]
const filePath = path.join(__dirname,
  'handlebars-example.html')

data.tableData = [
  {name: 'express', url: 'http://expressjs.com/'},
  {name: 'hapi', url: 'http://spumko.github.io/'},
  {name: 'compound', url: 'http://compoundjs.com/'},
  {name: 'derby', url: 'http://derbyjs.com/'}
]

fs.readFile(filePath, 'utf-8', (error, source) => {
  if (error) return console.error(error)
  // Register helper to generate table HTML from data (array)
  handlebars.registerHelper('table', (data) => {
    let str = '<table>'
    for (let i = 0; i < data.length; i++) {
      str += '<tr>'
      for (var key in data[i]) {
        str += '<td>' + data[i][key] + '</td>'
      }
      str += '</tr>'
    }
    str += '</table>'
    return new handlebars.SafeString(str)
  })
  // Register helper to create capitalize a string
  handlebars.registerHelper('custom_title', (title) => {
    let words = title.split(' ')
    for (let i = 0; i < words.length; i++) {
```

```
    if (words[i].length > 4) {
      words[i] = words[i][0].toUpperCase() + words[i].substr(1)
    }
  }
  title = words.join(' ')
  return title
})

// Compile the template and hydrate it with data to generate HTML
const template = handlebars.compile(source)
const html = template(data)
console.log(html)
})
```

And the `handlebars-example.html` *template* file that uses `custom_title` helper has the following content that calls the helper and outputs some other properties:

```
<div class="header">
    <h1>{{custom_title title}}</h1>
</div>
<div class="body">
    <p>{{body}}</p>
</div>
<div class="footer">
    <div><a href="http://twitter.com/{{author.twitter}}">
    {{autor.name}}</a>
    </div>
    <ul>
      {{#each tags}}
        <li>{{this}}</li>
      {{/each}}
    </ul>
</div>
```

To produce this HTML when we run $ `node handlebars-example.js 'email body'`, use the following:

```
<div class="header">
    <h1>Practical Node.js</h1>
</div>
<div class="body">
    <p>email body</p>
</div>
<div class="footer">
    <div><a href="http://twitter.com/"></a>
    </div>
    <ul>
        <li>express</li>
        <li>node</li>
        <li>javascript</li>
    </ul>
</div>
```

To use Handlebars in the browser, download the library in a straightforward manner from the official web site (`http://handlebarsjs.com`) and include it in your pages. Alternatively, it's possible to use just the runtime version from the same web site (which is lighter in size) with precompiled templates. Templates can be precompiled with the Handlebars command-line tool.

Pug and Handlebars Usage in Express.js

By default, Express.js uses either a template extension provided to the response.render (or res.render) method or the default extension set by the `view engine` setting, to invoke the `require` and `_express` methods on the template library. In other words, for Express.js to utilize a template engine library out of the box, that library needs to have the `_express` method.

When the template engine library doesn't provide the `_express` method, or a similar one with `(path, options, callback)` parameters, it's recommended that you use Consolidate.js (`https://github.com/visionmedia/consolidate.js/`).

Let's look at a quick example of an abstraction library for templates called Consolidate.js. In this example, I use the template engine Swig. I picked this template engine because most likely you never heard of it and this makes it a good illustration for an abstraction library like Consolidate. So Swig comes from the `consolidate` module. I connected it to express with the `app.engine('html', cons.swig)` statement. See the full server implementation that renders Swig templates:

```
const express = require('express')
const cons = require('consolidate')
const path = require('path')

let app = express()

app.engine('html', cons.swig)

app.set('view engine', 'html')
app.set('views', path.join(__dirname, 'templates'))

var platforms = [
  { name: 'node' },
  { name: 'ruby' },
  { name: 'python' }
]

app.get('/', (req, res) => {
  res.render('index', {
    title: 'Consolidate This'
  })
})

app.get('/platforms', (req, res) => {
  res.render('platforms', {
    title: 'Platforms',
    platforms: platforms
  })
})

app.listen(3000, () => {
  console.log('Express server listening on port 3000')
})
```

As usual, the source code is in the GitHub repository, and the snippet is in the `code/ch4/consolidate` folder.

For more information on how to configure Express.js settings and use Consolidate.js, refer to the still- up-to-date book on Express.js version 4—*Pro Express.js* (Apress, 2014), which is available on all major book stores, and of course at `https://amzn.to/2t1SwNw`.

Pug and Express.js

Pug is compatible with Express.js out of the box (in fact, it's the default choice), so to use Pug with Express.js, you just need to install a template engine module (`pug`) (`https://www.npmjs.org/package/pug`) and provide an extension to Express.js via the `view engine` setting.

For example, in the main Express server file we set the `view engine` setting as `pug` to let Express know which library to use for templates:

```
app.set('view engine', 'pug')
```

Of course, developers need to install the `pug` npm module into their project so the pug package is stored locally in `node_modules`. Express will use the name `pug` provided to `view engine` to import the `pug` package and *also* use the `pug` as a template files extension in the `views` folder (`views` is the default name).

Note   If you use the `$ express <app_name>` command-line tool, you can add the option for engine support, i.e., the `-e` option for EJS and –H for Hogan. This will add EJS or Hogan automatically to your new project. Without either of these options, the `express-generator` (versions 4.0.0–4.2.0) will use Pug.

In the route file, we can call the template—for example, `views/page.pug` (the `views` folder name is another Express.js default, which can be overwritten with the `view` setting):

```
app.get('/page', (req, res, next) => {
  //get the data dynamically
  res.render('page', data)
})
```

If we don't specify the `view engine` setting, then the extension must be passed explicitly to `res.render()` as a first argument, such as:

```
res.render('page.pug', data)
```

Next, let's cover the Express usage for Handlebars.

Handlebars and Express.js

Contrary to Pug, the Handlebars library from `http://handlebarsjs.com` doesn't come with the `express` method, but there are a few options to make Handlebars work with Express.js:).

- `consolidate` (`https://github.com/tj/consolidate.js`): A Swiss-army knife of Express.js template engine libraries (shown in one of the previous sections)

- `hbs` (`https://github.com/pillarjs/hbs`): Wrapper library for Handlebars

- `express-handlebarss` (`https://github.com/ericf/express-handlebars`): A module to use Handlebars with Express

Here's how we can use the `hbs` approach (extension `hbs`). Somewhere in the configuration section of the main Express file (file that we launch with the `$ node` command), write the following statements:

```
// Imports
app.set('view engine', 'hbs')
// Middleware
```

Or, if another extension is preferable, such as `html`, we see the following:

```
app.set('view engine', 'html')
pp.engine('html', require('hbs').__express)
```

The `express-handlebars` approach usage is as follows:

```
const exphbs = require('express-handlebars')
app.engine('handlebars', exphbs({defaultLayout: 'main'}))
app.set('view engine', 'handlebars')
```

Good. Now we can put our knowledge to practice.

Project: Adding Pug Templates to Blog

Lastly, we can continue with Blog. In this section we add main pages using Pug, plus we add a layout and some partials:

- `layout.pug`: Global app-wide template
- `index.pug`: Home page with the list of posts
- `article.pug`: Individual article page
- `login.pug`: Page with a login form
- `post.pug`: Page for adding a new article
- `admin.pug`: Page to administer articles after logging in

Because the templates in this mini-project require data, we'll skip the demo until Chapter 5, where we'll plug in the MongoDB database. So the source code for the Pug templates is exactly the same as in the `code/ch5` folder of the GitHub repository `azat-co/practicalnode`: `https://github.com/azat-co/practicalnode`. Feel free to copy it from there or follow the instructions to implement listed below in this section.

layout.pug

Let's open the project where we left off in the previous chapter and add `layout.pug` with the document type statement:

```
doctype html
```

Now we can add the main tags of the page:

```
html
  head
```

The title of the each page is provided from the `appTitle` variable (a.k.a., local):

```
    title= appTitle
```

Then, in the `head` tag, we list all the front-end assets that we need app-wide (on each page):

```
script(type="text/javascript", src="js/jquery-2.0.3.min.js")
link(rel="stylesheet", href="/css/bootstrap-3.0.2/css/bootstrap.
min.css")
link(rel="stylesheet", href="/css/bootstrap-3.0.2/css/bootstrap-
theme.min.css")
link(rel="stylesheet", href="/css/style.css")
script(type="text/javascript", src="/css/bootstrap-3.0.2/js/
bootstrap.min.js")
script(type="text/javascript", src="/js/blog.js")
meta(name="viewport", content="width=device-width, initial-
scale=1.0")
```

The main content lives in `body`, which has the same level indentation as `head`:

```
body
```

Inside the body, we write an id and some classes for the styles that we'll add later:

```
#wrap
  .container
```

The `appTitle` value is printed dynamically, but the `p.lead` element only has text:

```
h1.page-header= appTitle
p.lead Welcome to example from Express.js Experience by
  a(href="http://twitter.com/azat_co") @azatmardan
  |. Please enjoy.
```

The `block` sections can be overwritten by the children templates (templates that extend this file):

```
block page
block header
  div
```

Menu is a partial (i.e., an include) that is stored in the `views/includes` folder. Note the absence of quotation marks:

```
include includes/menu
```

In this block named `alert`, we can display messages for users, so let's use special alerty classes on a `div` (the indentation is preserved to show hierarchy):

```
block alert
    div.alert.alert-warning.hidden
```

Main content goes in this block. It is empty now because other template will define it:

```
.content
    block content
```

Lastly, the footer block with `div` with the `container` class and with `p` with text and a link (link is wrapped in text) looks as follows:

```
block footer
    footer
        .container
            p
                | Copyright &copy; 2018 | Issues? Submit to
                a(href="https://github.com/azat-co/blog-express/
                issues") GitHub
                | .
```

To give you a full picture as well as preserve proper indentation (which is *PARAMOUNT* in Pug), the full code of `layout.pug` is as follows:

```
doctype html
html
  head
    title= appTitle
    script(type="text/javascript", src="js/jquery-2.0.3.min.js")
    link(rel="stylesheet", href="/css/bootstrap-3.0.2/css/bootstrap.
    min.css")
    link(rel="stylesheet", href="/css/bootstrap-3.0.2/css/
    bootstrap-theme.min.css")
```

```
link(rel="stylesheet", href="/css/style.css")
script(type="text/javascript", src="/css/bootstrap-3.0.2/js/
bootstrap.min.js")
script(type="text/javascript", src="/js/blog.js")
meta(name="viewport", content="width=device-width, initial-
scale=1.0")
body
  #wrap
    .container
      h1.page-header= appTitle
      p.lead Welcome to example from Express.js Experience by
        a(href="http://twitter.com/azat_co") @azatmardan
        |. Please enjoy.
      block page
      block header
        div
          include includes/menu
      block alert
        div.alert.alert-warning.hidden
      .content
        block content
  block footer
    footer
      .container
        p
          | Copyright &copy; 2014 | Issues? Submit to
          a(href="https://github.com/azat-co/blog-express/issues")
          GitHub
          |.
```

Next is the home page.

index.pug

Now, we can look at the home page template index.pug that extends layout.pug. Remember the syntax? It's extends name:

```
extends layout
```

Because we can overwrite some blocks, we set the menu variable to index, so the menu include (i.e., menu.pug) can determine which tab to show as active:

```
block page
  - var menu = 'index'
```

Of course, we need to overwrite the content block. Ergo, the main content with the list of articles that comes from locals iterates over the blog posts (articles). Each article link has a title and, needless to say, a URL that is formed by the article.slug value. When there are no posts/articles, then we show a message that nothing has been published yet. The code is as follows:

```
block content
  if (articles.length === 0)
    | There's no published content yet.
    a(href="/login") Log in
    | to post and publish.
  else
    each article, index in articles
      div
        h2
          a(href="/articles/#{article.slug}")= article.title
```

For your reference and to show the ease of comprehension in Pug's style, the full code of index.pug is as follows. You can see extends and two block overwrites (of layout):

```
extends layout

block page
  - var menu = 'index'
block content
```

```
if (articles.length === 0)
  | There's no published content yet.
 a(href="/login") Log in
 | to post and publish.
else
  each article, index in articles
    div
      h2
        a(href="/articles/#{article.slug}")= article.title
```

Figure 4-4 shows how the home page looks after adding style sheets.

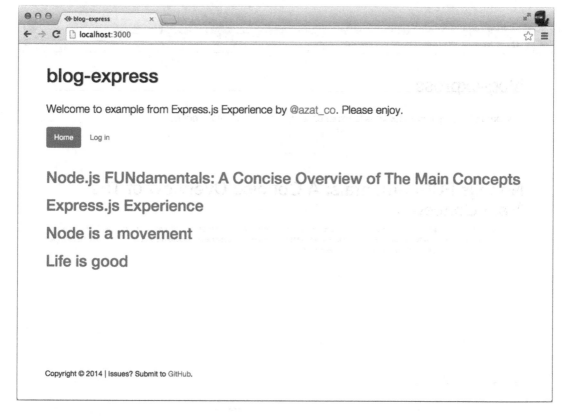

Figure 4-4. *The home page of Blog shows menu and the titles of the published articles*

Phew. Next is the page for the actual blog posts/articles.

article.pug

The individual article page (Figure 4-5) is relatively unsophisticated because most of the elements are abstracted into `layout.pug`. We only have `extends` and then overwrite the `content` block without the article title (`h1` heading) and article's text (`p` for paragraph).

```
extends layout

block content
  p
    h1= title
    p= text
```

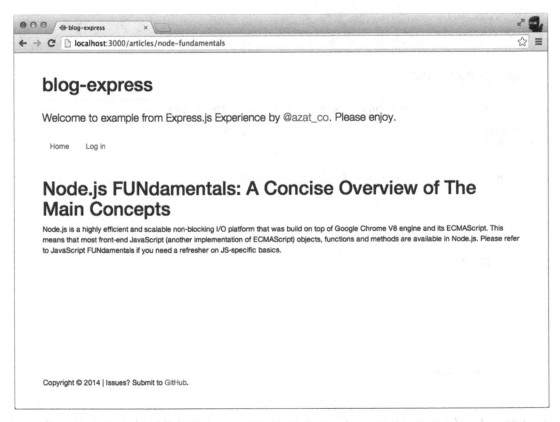

Figure 4-5. *The article page*

This is the awesomeness which we receive for free thanks to Twitter Bootstrap and h1 and p elements. You can clearly see that even despite defining only h1 and p, the webpage /articles/node-fundamentals has a page title menu and the footer. That's due to the inheritance, extends, and layout.pug.

Did you notice that "Log in" link? Let's implement the login page next.

login.pug

Similarly to article.pug, the login page uses login.pug, which contains... not much! *Only* a form and a button with some minimal Twitter Bootstrap classes/markup.

So as with article.pug, we extend layout and overwrite two blocks—one for the active menu value and the other for the content, which is the main part of the page. This main part has guess what? A LOGIN FORM! This is file login.pug:

```
extends layout

block page
  - var menu = 'login'

block content
  .col-md-4.col-md-offset-4
    h2 Log in
    div= error
    div
      form(action="/login", method="POST")
        p
          input.form-control(name="email", type="text",
          placeholder="hi@azat.co")
        p
          input.form-control(name="password", type="password",
          placeholder="***")
        p
          button.btn.btn-lg.btn-primary.btn-block(type="submit")
          Log in
```

Again, thanks to Twitter Bootstrap, our page looks stellar. It has a menu because of extends and layout.pug. Figure 4-6 shows how the login page looks.

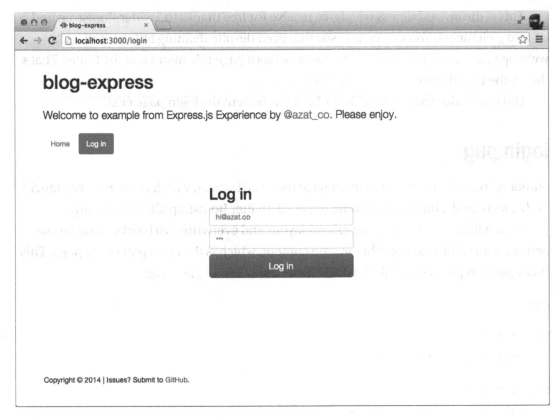

Figure 4-6. *The login page*

But how to create a new article? Easy! By posting its title and text.

post.pug

The post page (Figure 4-7) has another form and it also extends `layout.pug`. This time, the form contains a text area element that will become the main text of the article. In addition to the article text, there are `title`, and the URL segment (or path) to the article which is called `slug`.

```
extends layout
block page
  - var menu = 'post'
block content
    h2 Post an Article
    div= error
```

```
div.col-md-8
  form(action="/post", method="POST", role="form")
    div.form-group
      label(for="title") Title
      input#title.form-control(name="title", type="text",
      placeholder="JavaScript is good")
    div.form-group
      label(for="slug") Slug
      input#slug.form-control(name="slug", type="text",
      placeholder="js-good")
      span.help-block This string will be used in the URL.
    div.form-group
      label(for="text") Text
      textarea#text.form-control(rows="5", name="text",
      placeholder="Text")
    p
      button.btn.btn-primary(type="submit") Save
```

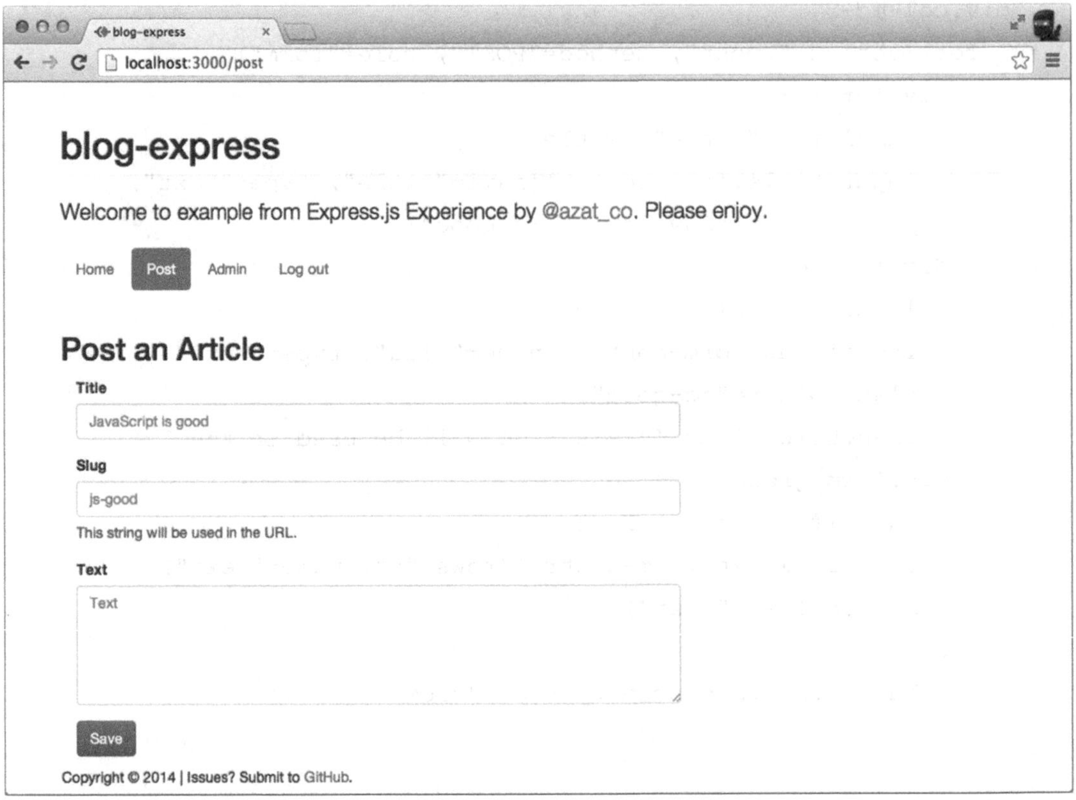

Figure 4-7. *The post page*

To give you some visual of the Pug of `post.pug`, take a look at the page for posting new articles. The action attribute of `<form>` will allow browsers to send the data to the backend and then Express will take care of it by processing, and our Node code will save it to the database.

If a valid administrator user is logged in, then we want to show an admin interface. See the Admin link in the menu? Let's implement the admin page to which this menu link leads to.

admin.pug

The admin page (Figure 4-8) has a loop of articles just like the home page, but in addition to just showing articles, we can include a front-end script (`js/admin.js`) specific to this page. This script will do some AJAX-y calls to publish and unpublish articles. These functions will be available only to admins. Of course we will need an server-side validation on the backend later. Don't trust only the front-end validation or authorization!

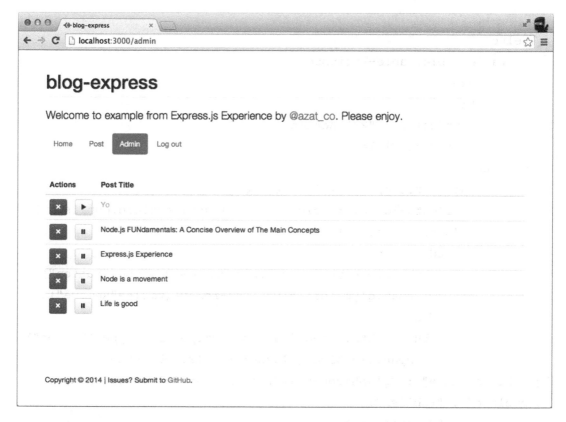

Figure 4-8. *The admin page shows the list of published and draft articles*

So the `admin.pug` file starts with the layout extension and has content overwrite, in which there's a table of articles. In each row of the table, we use `glyphicon` to show a fancy icon for pause or play ▶. The icons come from Twitter Bootstrap and are enabled via classes:

```
extends layout

block page
  - var menu = 'admin'

block content
  div.admin
    if (articles.length === 0 )
      p
        | Nothing to display. Add a new
        a(href="/post") article
```

```
        |.
   else
     table.table.table-stripped
       thead
         tr
           th(colspan="2") Actions
           th Post Title
       tbody
         each article, index in articles
           tr(data-id=`${article._id}`, class=(!article.published)?
           'unpublished':")
             td.action
               button.btn.btn-danger.btn-sm.remove(type="button")
                 span.glyphicon.glyphicon-remove(title="Remove")
             td.action
               button.btn.btn-default.btn-sm.publish(type="button")
                 span.glyphicon(class=(article.published) ?
"glyphicon-pause" : "glyphicon-play", title=(article.published) ?
"Unpublish" : "Publish")
             td= article.title
       script(type="text/javascript", src="js/admin.js")
```

Please notice that we use ES6 string template (or interpolation) to print article ids as attributes data- id (indentation was removed):

```
tr(data-id=`${article._id}`, class=(!article.published) ?
'unpublished':")
```

And a conditional (ternary) operator (https://github.com/donpark/hbs)
is used for classes and title attributes. Remember, it's JavaScript! (Indentation has was removed for better viewing.)

```
span.glyphicon(class=(article.published) ? "glyphicon-pause" :
"glyphicon-play", title=(article.published) ? "Unpublish" :
"Publish")
```

The result is a beautiful admin page (Okay, enough with sarcasm and saying Twitter Bootstrap is stellar, pretty or cute. It's not... but compared to standard HTML, which puts me to sleep, Twitter Bootstrap style is a HUGE improvement.) It has functionality to publish and unpublish articles.

Summary

In this chapter, you learned about the Pug and Handlebars templates (variables, iterations, condition, partials, unescaping, and so forth), and how to use them in a standalone Node.js script or within Express.js. In addition, the main pages for Blog were created using Pug.

In the next chapter, we'll learn how to extract the data from a database and save new data to it. You'll become familiar with MongoDB. Onwards.

CHAPTER 5

Persistence with MongoDB and Mongoskin

I really like using MongoDB with Node. Many other Node developers would agree with me because this database has JavaScript interface and uses JSON-like data structure. MongoDB belongs to a category of a NoSQL databases.

NoSQL databases (DBs), also called *non-relational databases*, are more horizontally scalable, and better suited for distributed systems than traditional SQL ones (a.k.a., RDMBS). NoSQL DBs built in a way that they allow data duplication and can be well tailored to specific queries. This process is called denormalization. In short, NoSQL comes to help when RDMBS can't scale. It's often the case that NoSQL databases deal routinely with larger data sizes than traditional ones.

The key distinction in implementation of apps with NoSQL DBs comes from the fact that NoSQL DBs are schema-less. There's no table, just a simple store indexed by IDs. A lot of data types are not stored in the database itself (no more `ALTER TABLE` queries); they are moved to the application or object- relational mapping (ORM) levels—in our case, to Node. js code. Another good reason to use NoSQL databases is because they are schema-less. For me, this is the best advantage of NoSQL. I can quickly prototype prototyping and iterate (more git pushes!). Once I am more or less done, or think I am done, I can implement schema and validation in Node. This workflow allows me to not waste time early in the project lifecycle while still having the security at a more mature stage.

MongoDB is a document store NoSQL database (as opposed to key value and wide-column store NoSQL databases, `http://nosql-database.org`). It's the most mature and dependable NoSQL database available thus far. I know that some people just hate MongoDB for its bugs but when I ask them if there's a better alternative they can't name anything. Interestingly, some traditional databases added NoSQL field type which allows them to rip the benefits of flexibility before available only to NoSQl databases.

© Azat Mardan 2018
A. Mardan, *Practical Node.js*, https://doi.org/10.1007/978-1-4842-3039-8_5

In addition to efficiency, scalability, and lightning speed, MongoDB has a JavaScript interface! This alone is magical, because now there's no need to switch context between the front end (browser JavaScript), back end (Node.js), and database (MongoDB). This is my favorite feature because in 90% of my projects I don't handle that my data or traffic, but I used the JavaScript interface all the time.

The company behind MongoDB is an industry leader, and provides education and certification through its online MongoDB University (`https://university.mongodb.com`). I once was invited by Mongo to interview for a Director of Software Engineering, but declined to continue after first few rounds. Well, that's a topic for a different book.

To get you started with MongoDB and Node.js, I'll show the following in this chapter:

- Easy and proper installation of MongoDB

- How to run the Mongo server

- Data manipulation from the Mongo console

- MongoDB shell in detail

- Minimalistic native MongoDB driver for Node.js example

- Main Mongoskin methods

- Project: Storing Blog data in MongoDB with Mongoskin

Easy and Proper Installation of MongoDB

Next, I'll show the MongoDB installation from the official package, as well as using HomeBrew for macOS users (recommended).

The following steps are better suited for macOS/Linux–based systems, but with some modifications they can be used for Windows systems as well, i.e., modify the `$PATH` variable, and the slashes. For more instructions for non-macOS/Linux users, go and check many other ways to install Mongo (`http://docs.mongodb.org/manual/installation`).

I'll continue with the installation for macOS users. The HomeBrew installation is recommended and is the easiest path (assuming macOS users have `brew` installed already, which was covered in Chapter 1):

```
$ brew install mongodb
```

If this doesn't work, try the manual installation. It's basically downloading an archive file for MongoDB at `http://www.mongodb.org/downloads` and then configuring it. For the latest Apple laptops, such as MacBook Air, select the OS X 64-bit version. The owners of older Macs should browse the link `http://dl.mongodb.org/dl/osx/i386`. The owners of other laptops and OSs, select the appropriate package for the download.

Tip   If you don't know the architecture type of your processor when choosing a MongoDB package, type `$ uname -p` in the command line to find this information.

After the download, unpack the package into your web development folder or any other as long as you remember it. For example, my development folder is `~/Documents/Code` (~ means home). If you want, you could install MongoDB into the `/usr/local/mongodb` folder.

Optional: If you would like to access MongoDB commands from anywhere on your system, you need to add your `mongodb` path to the `$PATH` variable. For macOS, you need the open-system `paths` file, which is located at `/etc/paths` with:

```
$ sudo vi /etc/paths
```

Or, if you prefer VS Code and have the `code` shell command installed, use this VS Code command:

```
$ code /etc/paths
```

Then, add the following line to the `/etc/paths` file:

```
/usr/local/mongodb/bin
```

Create a data folder; by default, MongoDB uses `/data/db`. Please note this might be different in newer versions of MongoDB. To create the data folder, type and execute the following commands:

```
$ sudo mkdir -p /data/db
$ sudo chown `id -u` /data/db
```

This data folder is where your local database instance will store all databases, documents, and so on- all data. The figure 5-1 below shows how I created my data folder in /data/db (root, then data then db), and changed ownership of the folder to my user instead of it being a root or whatever it was before. Science proved that not having folders owned by root, reduces the number of permission denied errors by 100%. Figure 5-1 shows how this looks onscreen.

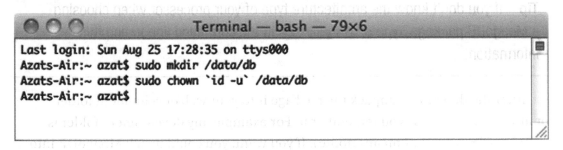

Figure 5-1. *Initial setup for MongoDB: create the data directory*

If you prefer to store data somewhere else rather than /data/db, then you can do it. Just specify your custom path using the --dbpath option to mongod (the main MongoDB service) when you launch your database instance (server).

If some of these steps weren't enough, then another interpretation of the installation instructions for MongoDB on various OSs is available at MongoDB.org, "Install MongoDB on OS X" (http://docs.mongodb.org/manual/tutorial/install-mongodb-on-os-x). Windows users can read a good walk-through article titled "Installing MongoDB" (http://www.tuanleaded.com/blog/2011/10/installing-mongodb).

How to Run the Mongo Server

To run the Mongo server (a.k.a. DB instance, service, or daemon), there's the mongod command. It's not mongodb or mongo. It's mongod. Remember the "d". It's stands for daemon.

If you installed in manually and didn't link the location to PATH, then go to the folder where you unpacked MongoDB. That location should have a bin folder in it. From that folder, type the following command:

```
$ ./bin/mongod
```

If you are like most normal developers, and prefer to type `mongod` anywhere on your computer, I assume you exposed the MongoDB `bin` folder in your `PATH` environment variable. So if you added `$PATH` for the MongoDB location, type the following *anywhere you like*:

```
$ mongod
```

Note   Oh, yeah. Don't forget to restart the terminal window after adding a new path to the `$PATH` variable (Figure 5-2). That's just how terminal apps work. They might not pick up your newest PATH value until you restart them.

```
●○○                      Terminal — mongod — 122×30
Last login: Sun Aug 25 17:29:16 on ttys000
Azats-Air:~ azat$ mongod
mongod --help for help and startup options
Sun Aug 25 17:31:00
Sun Aug 25 17:31:00 warning: 32-bit servers don't have journaling enabled by default. Please use --journal if you want dur
ability.
Sun Aug 25 17:31:00
Sun Aug 25 17:31:00 [initandlisten] MongoDB starting : pid=738 port=27017 dbpath=/data/db/ 32-bit host=Azats-Air.local
Sun Aug 25 17:31:00 [initandlisten]
Sun Aug 25 17:31:00 [initandlisten] ** NOTE: This is a development version (2.3.0) of MongoDB.
Sun Aug 25 17:31:00 [initandlisten] **       Not recommended for production.
Sun Aug 25 17:31:00 [initandlisten]
Sun Aug 25 17:31:00 [initandlisten] ** NOTE: This is a 32 bit MongoDB binary.
Sun Aug 25 17:31:00 [initandlisten] **       32 bit builds are limited to less than 2GB of data (or less with --journal).
Sun Aug 25 17:31:00 [initandlisten] **       Note that journaling defaults to off for 32 bit and is currently off.
Sun Aug 25 17:31:00 [initandlisten] **       See http://www.mongodb.org/display/DOCS/32+bit
Sun Aug 25 17:31:00 [initandlisten]
Sun Aug 25 17:31:00 [initandlisten] ** WARNING: soft rlimits too low. Number of files is 256, should be at least 1000
Sun Aug 25 17:31:00 [initandlisten]
Sun Aug 25 17:31:00 [initandlisten] db version v2.3.0, pdfile version 4.5
Sun Aug 25 17:31:00 [initandlisten] git version: 86d6c3b316da2fffc1001e665442ba679b51fd26
Sun Aug 25 17:31:00 [initandlisten] build info: Darwin bs-osx-106-i386-1.local 10.8.0 Darwin Kernel Version 10.8.0: Tue Ju
n  7 16:33:36 PDT 2011; root:xnu-1504.15.3~1/RELEASE_I386 i386 BOOST_LIB_VERSION=1_49
Sun Aug 25 17:31:00 [initandlisten] options: {}
Sun Aug 25 17:31:00 [initandlisten] Unable to check for journal files due to: boost::filesystem::directory_iterator::const
ruct: No such file or directory: "/data/db/journal"
Sun Aug 25 17:31:00 [websvr] admin web console waiting for connections on port 28017
Sun Aug 25 17:31:00 [initandlisten] waiting for connections on port 27017
```

Figure 5-2.   Successful starting of the MongoDB server outputs "waiting for connections on port 27017"

There's tons of info on the screen after `mongod`. If you can find something saying about "waiting" and "port 27017", then you are all set. Look for a message this:

```
waiting for connections on port 27017
```

That text means the MongoDB database server is running. Congrats!

By default, it's listening at http://localhost:27017. This is the host and port for the scripts and applications to access MongoDB. In our Node.js code, we use 27017 for for the database and port 3000 for the server.

If you see anything else, then you probably have one of the two:

- The `data` or `db` folders are not created or were created with root permissions. The solution is to create them with non-root.

- The MongoDB folder is not exposed, and `mongod` cannot be found. The solution is to use the correct location or expose the location in PATH.

Please fix the issue(s) if you have any. If you are all set with the "waiting" notice, the let's go and play with the database using Mongo Console.

Data Manipulation from the Mongo Console

Akin to the Node.js REPL, MongoDB has a console/shell that acts as a client to the database server instance. This means that we have to keep the terminal window with the server open and running while using the console in a different window/tab.

From the folder where you unpacked the archive, launch the `mongod` service with the command pointing to the `bin` folder:

```
$ ./bin/mongod
```

Or, if you installed MongoDB globally (recommended), launch the `mongod` service with just the command without path:

```
$ mongod
```

You should be able to see information in your terminal saying "waiting for connections on 27017". Now, we will launch a separate process or an application, if you will. It's called the MongoDB console or shell, and it allows developers to connect to the database instance and perform pretty much anything they want: create new documents, update them, and delete. In other words, Mongo console is a client. Its benefit is that it comes with MongoDB and does NOT require anything fancy or complex. It works in the terminal, which means you can use it on almost any OS (yes, even on Windows).

The name of the command is `mongo`. Execute this command in a *new* terminal window (*important!*). Again, if you didn't expose your MongoDB to `PATH`, then in the same folder in which you have MongoDB, type the `mongo` command with path to this `mongo` file, which is in the `bin` of the MongoDB installation. Open another terminal window in the same folder and execute:

```
$ ./bin/mongo
```

Or, if you have `mongo` "globally" by exposing the MongoDB's `bin` into `PATH`, simply type from any folder (you don't have to be in the MongoDB folder or specify bin since you already have that path in your PATH environment variable):

```
$ mongo
```

When you successfully connect to the database instance, then you should see something like this. Of course, the exact version will depend on your version of the MongoDB shell. My Mongo shell is 2.0.6:

```
MongoDB shell version: 2.0.6
connecting to: test
```

Did you notice the cursor change? It's now >, as shown in Figure 5-3. It mean you are in a different environment than bash or zsh (which I use). You cannot execute shell command anymore, so don't try to use `node server.js` or `mkdir my-awesome-pony-project`. It won't work. But what will work is JavaScript, Node.js, and some special MongoDB code. For example, type and execute the following two commands to save a document `{a: 1}` (super creative, I know, thanks) and then query the collection to see the newly created document there:

```
> db.test.save( { a: 1 } )
> db.test.find()
```

Figure 5-3 shows that I saved my record `{a:1}`. Everything went well. The commands `find()` and `save()` do exactly what you might think they do ;-), only you need to prefix them with `db.COLLECTION_NAME` where you substitute `COLLECTION_NAME` for your own name.

```
● ○ ○          Terminal — mongo — 79×14
Last login: Sun Aug 25 17:30:33 on ttys000
Azats-Air:~ azat$ mongo
MongoDB shell version: 2.3.0
connecting to: test
Welcome to the MongoDB shell.
For interactive help, type "help".
For more comprehensive documentation, see
        http://docs.mongodb.org/
Questions? Try the support group
        http://groups.google.com/group/mongodb-user
> db.test.save( { a: 1} )
> db.test.find()
{ "_id" : ObjectId("521a169d6421d0d4d6f3190f"), "a" : 1 }
>
```

Figure 5-3. *Running the MongoDB shell/console client and executing queries in the test collection*

Note   On macOS (and most Unix systems), to close the process, use control+C. If you use control+Z, it puts the process to sleep (or detaches the terminal window). In this case, you might end up with a lock on data files and then have to use the "kill" command (e.g., $ killall node) or Activity Monitor and delete the locked files in the data folder manually. For a vanilla macOS terminal, command+. is an alternative to control+C.

What are some other MongoDB console commands that seasoned Node developers like you and I can use? We will study the most important of them next.

MongoDB Console in Detail

MongoDB console syntax is JavaScript. That's wonderful. The last thing we want is to learn a new complex language like SQL. However, MongoDB console methods are not without their quirks. For example, db.test.find() has a class name db, then my collection name test, and then a method name find(). In other words, it's a mix of arbitrary (custom) and mandatory (fixed) names. That's unusual.

Let's take a look at the most useful MongoDB console (shell) commands, which I listed here:

- > `help`: prints a list of available commands

- > `show dbs`: prints the names of the databases on the database server to which the console is connected (by default, localhost:27017; but, if we pass params to `mongo`, we can connect to any remote instance)

- > `use db_name`: switches to `db_name`

- > `show collections`: prints a list of collections in the selected database

- > `db.collection_name.find(query);`: finds all items matching `query`

- > `db.collection_name.findOne(query);`: finds one item that matches `query`

- > `db.collection_name.insert(document)`: adds a document to the `collection_name` collection

- > `db.collection_name.save(document);`: saves a document in the `collection_name` collection—a shorthand of upsert (no `_id`) or insert (with `_id`)

- > `db.collection_name.update(query,{$set: data});`: updates items that match `query` in the `collection_name` collection with `data` object values

- > `db.collection_name.remove(query);` removes all items from `collection_name` that match `query` criteria

- > `printjson(document);`: prints the variable `document`

It's possible to use good old JavaScript. For example, storing a document in a variable is as easy as using an equal sign =. Then, `printjson()` is a utility method that outputs the value of a variable. The following code will read one document, add a field `text` to it, print and save the document:

```
> var a = db.messages.findOne()
> printjson(a)
> a.text = "hi"
```

```
> printjson(a)
> db.messages.save(a)
```

save() works two ways. If you have _id, which is a unique MongoDB ID, then the document will be updated with whatever new properties were passed to the save() method. That's the previous example in which I create a new property text and assigned a value of hi to it.

When there's no _id, then MongoDB console will insert a new document and create a new document ID (ObjectId) in _id. That's the very first example where we used db.test.save({a:1}). To sum up, save() works like an upsert (update or insert).

For the purpose of saving time, the API listed here is the bare minimum to get by with MongoDB in this book and its projects. The real interface is richer and has more features. For example, update accepts options such as multi: true, and it's not mentioned here. A full overview of the MongoDB interactive shell is available at http://bit.ly/2QWCyDI.

I'm sure you all enjoyed typing those brackets and parentheses in the terminal just to get a typo somewhere (#sarcasm). That's why I created MongoUI, which is a web-based database admin interface. It allows you to view, edit, search, remove MongoDB documents without typing commands. Check out MongoUI at https://github.com/azat-co/mongoui. You can install MongoUI with npm by executing npm i -g mongoui and then start it with mongoui. It'll open the app in your default browser and connect to your local DB instance (if there's one).

MongoUI is a web-based app which you can host on your own application. For an even better desktop tool than my own MongoUI, download Compass at TK. It's built in Node using Electron and React.

One more useful MongoDB command (script) is mongoimport. It allows developers to supply a JSON file that will be imported to a database. Let's say you are migrating a database or have some initial data that you want to use, but the database is empty right now. How do you create multiple records? You can copypasta to MongoDB console, but that's not fun. Use mongoimport. Here's an example of how to inject a data from a JSON file with an array of object:

```
$ mongoimport --db dbName --collection collectionName
--file fileName.json --jsonArray
```

You don't need to do anything extra to install `mongoimport`. It's already part of the MongoDB installation and lives in the same folder as `mongod` or `mongo`, i.e., `bin`. And JSON is not the only format that `mongoimport` takes. It can be CSV, or TSV as well. Isn't it neat?

Connecting and working with a database directly is a superpower. You can debug or seed the data without the need for writing any Node code. But sooner or later, you'll want to automate the work with the database. Node is great for that. To be able to work with MongoDB from Node, we need a driver.

Minimalistic Native MongoDB Driver for Node.js Example

To illustrate the advantages of Mongoskin, I will show how to use the Node.js native driver for MongoDB (`https://github.com/christkv/node-mongodb-native`) which is somewhat more work than to use Mongoskin. I create a basic script that accesses the database.

Firstly, create `package.json` with `npm init -y`. Then, install the MongoDB native driver for Node.js with `SE` to save the exact version as a dependency:

```
$ npm install mongodb@2.2.33 -SE
```

This is an example of a good `package.json` file with the driver dependency listed in there. It's from `code/ch5/mongodb-examples`. There are two more packages. You can ignore them for now. One of them is validating code formatting (`standard`) and another is an advanced MongoDB library (`mongoskin`):

```
{
  "name": "mongodb-examples",
  "version": "1.0.1",
  "description": "",
  "main": "mongo-native-insert.js",
  "scripts": {
    "test": "echo \"Error: no test specified\" && exit 1"
  },
```

```
"keywords": [],
"author": "Azat Mardan (http://azat.co/)",
"license": "MIT",
"dependencies": {
  "mongodb": "2.2.33",
  "mongoskin": "2.1.0"
},
"devDependencies": {
  "standard": "10.0.3"
}
}
```

It's a good learning approach to start from something small and then build skills gradually. For this reason let's study a small example that tests whether we can connect to a local MongoDB instance from a Node.js script and run a sequence of statements analogous to the previous section:

1. Declare dependencies

2. Define the database host and port

3. Establish a database connection

4. Create a database document

5. Output a newly created document/object

The file name for this short script is `code/ch5/mongo-native-insert.js`. We'll start this file with some imports. Then we will connect to the database using host and port. This is one of the ways to establish a connection to the MongoDB server in which the db variable holds a reference to the database at a specified host and port:

```
const mongo = require('mongodb')
const dbHost = '127.0.0.1'
const dbPort = 27017
const {Db, Server} = mongo
const db = new Db('local', new Server(dbHost, dbPort), {safe: true})
```

Once the connection is established with db.open, we can work with the database. So to open a connection, type the following:

```
db.open((error, dbConnection) => {
    // Do something with the database here
    // console.log(util.inspect(db))
    console.log(db._state)
    db.close()
})
```

For example, to create a document in MongoDB, we can use the insert() method. Unlike Mongo console, this insert() is *asynchronous* which means it won't execute immediately. The results will be coming later. That's why there's a callback. The callback has error as its first argument. It's called error-first pattern. The result that is the newly created document is the second argument of the callback. In the console, we don't really have multiple clients executing queries so in the console methods are synchronous. The situation is different in Node because we want to process multiple clients while we wait for the database to respond.

It's important to handle the error by checking for it and then exiting with an error code of 1:

```
dbConnection
  .collection('messages')
  .insert(item, (error, document) => {
    if (error) {
      console.error(error)
      return process.exit(1)
    }
    console.info('created/inserted: ', document)
    db.close()
    process.exit(0)
  })
```

Here is the entire code to accomplish these five steps. The most important thing to observe and remember is that *ENTIRE* working code of insert() is **inside** of the open() callback. This is because open() is asynchronous, which in turn is because dbConnection becomes available with a delay and we don't want to block the Node's

event loop waiting for the dbConnection. The full source code of this script is in the
mongo-native-insert.js file and included next for convenience in case you don't have
the GitHub open right now:

```js
const mongo = require('mongodb')
const dbHost = '127.0.0.1'
const dbPort = 27017

const {Db, Server} = mongo
const db = new Db('local',
  new Server(dbHost, dbPort),
  {safe: true}
)

db.open((error, dbConnection) => {
  if (error) {
    console.error(error)
    return process.exit(1)
  }
  console.log('db state: ', db._state)
  const item = {
    name: 'Azat'
  }
    dbConnection
      .collection('messages')
      .insert(item, (error, document) => {
      if (error) {
        console.error(error)
        return process.exit(1)
      }
      console.info('created/inserted: ', document)
      db.close()
      process.exit(0)
      }
    )
})
```

Now we can build a few more methods. For example, another `mongo-native.js` script looks up any object and modifies it:

1. Get one item from the `message` collection

2. Print it

3. Add a property text with the value `hi`

4. Save the item back to the `message` collection

After we install the library, we can include the MongoDB library in our `mongo-native.js` file as well as create host and port values:

```
const mongo = require('mongodb')
const dbHost = '127.0.0.1'
const dbPort = 27017
const {Db, Server} = mongo
const db = new Db('local', new Server(dbHost, dbPort), {safe: true})
```

Next open a connection. It's always a good practice to check for any errors and exit gracefully:

```
db.open((error, dbConnection) => {
  if (error) {
    console.error(error)
    process.exit(1)
  }
  console.log('db state: ', db._state)
```

Now, we can proceed to the first step mentioned earlier—getting one item from the `message` collection. The first argument to `findOne()` is a search or query criteria. It works as a logical AND, meaning the properties passed to `findOne()` will be matched against the documents in the database. The returned document will be in the callback's argument. This document is in the `item` variable.

The variable name doesn't matter that much. What matters is the order of an argument in the callback function. Ergo, **first argument is always an error object even when it's null. The second is the result of a method.** This is true for almost all MongoDB native driver methods but not for every Node library. Node developers need to read the documentation for a particular library to see what arguments are provided to a callback. But in the case of MongoDB native drive, error and result is the convention to remember and use.

```
dbConnection.collection('messages').findOne({},
(error, item) => {
  if (error) {
    console.error(error)
    process.exit(1)
  }
}
```

The second step, print the value, is as follows:

```
console.info('findOne: ', item)
```

As you can see, methods in the console and Node.js are not much different except that in Node, developers *must use callbacks.*

Next let's proceed to the remaining two steps: adding a new property and saving the document. `save()` works like an upsert: if a valid `_id` is provided, then the documents will be updated; if not, then the new documents will be created:

```
item.text = 'hi'
var id = item._id.toString() // we can store ID in a string
console.info('before saving: ', item)
dbConnection
  .collection('messages')
  .save(item, (error, document) => {
    if (error) {
      console.error(error)
      return process.exit(1)
    }
    console.info('save: ', document)
```

To convert a string into the `ObjectId` type, use `mongo.ObjectID()` method. To double-check the saved object, we use the document ID that we saved before in a string format (in a variable `id`) with the `find()` method. This method returns a cursor, so we apply `toArray()` to extract the standard JavaScript array:

```
dbConnection.collection('messages')
  .find({_id: new mongo.ObjectID(id)})
  .toArray((error, documents) => {
    if (error) {
      console.error(error)
      return process.exit(1)
    }
    console.info('find: ', documents)
    db.close()
    process.exit(0)
  }
)
})
})
})
```

The full source code of this script is available in the `mongo-native-insert.js` and `mongo-native.js` files. If we run them with `$ node mongo-native-insert` and, respectively, `$ node mongo-native`, while running the `mongod` service, the scripts should output something similar to the results in Figure 5-4. There are three documents. The first is without the property text; the second and third documents include it.

```
● ○ ○                    🗁 practicalnode — bash                      ↖↗
Azats-Air:practicalnode azat$ node mongo-native-insert
db state:  connected
created/inserted:  [ { name: 'Azat', _id: 5330adfd159337cd57825dcb } ]
Azats-Air:practicalnode azat$ node mongo-native.js
db state:  connected
findOne:  { name: 'Azat', _id: 5330adfd159337cd57825dcb }
before saving:  { name: 'Azat', _id: 5330adfd159337cd57825dcb, text: 'hi' }
save:  1
find:  [ { name: 'Azat', _id: 5330adfd159337cd57825dcb, text: 'hi' } ]
Azats-Air:practicalnode azat$ |
```

Figure 5-4. *Running a simple MongoDB script with a native driver*

From teaching dozens of MongoDB workshops, I can be sure that the majority of readers will be good with the methods studied here since these methods provide all the CRUD functionality (create, read, update, and delete). But for more advanced developers, the full documentation of this library is available at `http://bit.ly/2Lao9UW` and on the MongoDB website.

Main Mongoskin Methods

Meet Mongoskin (don't confuse with DC's Redskins). It provides a better API than the native MongoDB driver. To illustrate this, compare the following Mongoskin implementation with the example in prior section, which written using native MongoDB driver for Node.js.

As always, to install a module, run npm with install:

```
$ npm i mongoskin@2.1.0 -SE
```

The connection to the database is a bit easier with Mongoskin. We don't have to put all of our code into the `open()` callback. Yay! All we need is to invoke `db()`:

```
const mongoskin = require('mongoskin')
const { toObjectID } = mongoskin.helper
const dbHost = '127.0.0.1'
const dbPort = 27017
const db = mongoskin.db(`mongodb://${dbHost}:${dbPort}/local`)
```

As you can see, the Mongoskin method to connect to the database does *not* require you to put all the rest of the code in the callback. That's because Mongoskin buffers up the upcoming queries and execute them when the connection is ready. I like not having to put all of my Node code in one giant callback.

We can also create our own methods on collections. This might be useful when implementing an model-view-controller-like (MVC-like) architecture by incorporating app-specific logic into these custom methods. See how we can create a custom method `findOneAndAddText()` that takes some text (duh) and executes two MongoDB methods to first find that document and then update it in the database with the passed text. Custom methods are your own project-specific methods and they are great at reusing code.

Did you notice that there's no fat arrow function for the custom method `findOneAndAddText()`? That's because we need to let Mongoskin to pass the collection to use `this` inside of this method. If we use the fat arrow `()=>{}`, then we can's use `this.findOne()` inside of the custom method:

```
db.bind('messages').bind({
  findOneAndAddText: function (text, fn) {
  // no fat arrow fn because we need to let bind pass the collection
  to use this on the next line... this can be replaced with
  db.messages too
    this.findOne({}, (error, document) => {
      if (error) {
        console.error(error)
        return process.exit(1)
      }
```

```
    console.info('findOne: ', document)
    document.text = text
    var id = document._id.toString() // We can store ID in a string
    console.info('before saving: ', document)
    this.save(document, (error, count) => {
      if (error) {
        console.error(error)
        return process.exit(1)
      }
      console.info('save: ', count)
      return fn(count, id)
    })
  })
})
```

Last, we call the custom method like any other methods such as `find()` or `save()`. The more we use this custom in our code the more is the benefit of the code reuse and this pattern. It's important to use the `toArray()` method for the `find()` because the result of the query `documents` is more useful as an array.

```
db.messages.findOneAndAddText('hi', (count, id) => {
  db.messages.find({
    _id: toObjectID(id)
  }).toArray((error, documents) => {
    if (error) {
      console.error(error)
      return process.exit(1)
    }
    console.info('find: ', documents)
    db.close()
    process.exit(0)
  })
})
```

Mongoskin is a subset of the native Node.js MongoDB driver, so most of the methods, as you have observed from the latter are available in the former. For example, `find()`, `findOne()`, `update()`, `save()`, and `remove()`. They are from the native MongoDB driver and they are available in the Mongoskin straight up. But there are more methods. Here is the list of the main Mongoskin-only methods:

- `findItems(..., callback)`: Finds elements and returns an array instead of a cursor

- `findEach(..., callback)`: Iterates through each found element

- `findById(id, ..., callback)`: Finds by `_id` in a string format

- `updateById(_id, ..., callback)`: Updates an element with a matching `_id`

- `removeById(_id, ..., callback)`: Removes an element with a matching `_id`

Of course, there are alternatives to Mongoskin and the native MongoDB driver, including but not limited to:

- `mongoose`: An asynchronous JavaScript driver with optional support for modeling (recommended for large apps)

- `mongolia`: A lightweight MongoDB ORM/driver wrapper

- `monk`: A tiny layer that provides simple yet substantial usability improvements for MongoDB use within Node.js

Data validation is super important. Most of the MongoDB libraries will require developers to create their own validation, with Mongoose being an exception. Mongoose has a built-in data validation. Thus, for data validation at the Express level, these modules are often used:

- `node-validator`: validates data

- `express-validator`: validates data in Express.js 3/4

It is time to utilize our skills and build something interesting with MongoDB by enhancing our Blog project.

Project: Storing Blog Data in MongoDB with Mongoskin

Let's now return to our Blog project. I've split this feature of storing Blog data in MongoDB with Mongoskin into the following three tasks:

1. Adding MongoDB seed data

2. Writing Mocha tests

3. Adding persistence

The task numero uno is to populate the database with some test data. (Numero uno is number one in Chinese.)

Project: Adding MongoDB Seed Data

First of all, it's not much fun to enter data manually each time we test or run an app. So, in accordance with the Agile principles, we can automate this step by creating a shell seed data script db/seed.sh:

```
mongoimport --db blog --collection users --file
./db/users.json -jsonArray
mongoimport --db blog --collection articles --file
./db/articles.json --jsonArray
```

This script uses MongoDB's mongoimport feature, which inserts data conveniently into the database straight from JSON files.

The users.json file contains information about authorized users:

```
[{
  "email": "hi@azat.co",
  "admin": true,
  "password": "1"
}]
```

Here's some of the content of the `articles.json` file that has the seed content of the blog posts and testing (please use the file provided in GitHub instead of typing from the book):

```json
[
  {
    "title": "Node is a movement",
    "slug": "node-movement",
    "published": true,
    "text": "In one random deployment, it is often assumed that the
    number of scattered sensors are more than that required by the
    critical sensor density. Otherwise, complete area coverage may
    not be guaranteed in this deployment, and some coverage holes may
    exist. Besides using more sensors to improve coverage, mobile
    sensor nodes can be used to improve network coverage..."
  }, {
    "title": "Express.js Experience",
    "slug": "express-experience",
    "text": "Work in progress",
    "published": false
  }, {
    "title": "Node.js FUNdamentals: A Concise Overview of The Main
    Concepts",
    "slug": "node-fundamentals",
    "published": true,
    "text": "Node.js is a highly efficient and scalable nonblocking
    I/O platform that was built on top of a Google Chrome V8 engine
    and its ECMAScript. This means that most front-end JavaScript
    (another implementation of ECMAScript) objects, functions, and
    methods are available in Node.js. Please refer to JavaScript
    FUNdamentals if you need arefresher on
    JS-specific basics."
  }
]
```

To populate our seed data, simply run `$ ./db/seed.sh` from the project folder.

Project: Writing Mocha Tests

If you remember, Mocha uses `describe` for test suites and `it` for test cases. Thus, the test file `code/ch5/blog-express/tests/index.js` has this structure at a high level:

```
// Import/require statements

describe('server', () => {

  before(() => {
    boot()
  })

  describe('homepage', () => {

    it('should respond to GET', (done) => {
      // ...
    })

    it('should contain posts', (done) => {
      // ...
    })

  })

  describe('article page', () => {

    it('should display text or 401', (done) => {
      // ...
    })

  })

  after(() => {
    shutdown()
  })

})
```

Let's start the implementation with import/require statement (import not in a sense we are using ES6

`import` statement, but in a sense that `require()` method imports):

```
const boot = require('../app').boot
const shutdown = require('../app').shutdown
const port = require('../app').port
const superagent = require('superagent')
const expect = require('expect.js')
```

Next, we can import test data from seed files via `require` because it's a JSON format:

```
const seedArticles = require('../db/articles.json')
```

Let's add this test to the home page suite to check whether our app shows posts from seed data on the front page:

```
it('should contain posts', (done) => {
  superagent
    .get(`http://localhost:${port}`)
    .end((error, res) => {
      expect(error).to.be(null)
      expect(res.text).to.be.ok
      seedArticles.forEach((item, index, list) => {
        if (item.published) {
          expect(res.text).to.contain(`<h2>
          <a href="/articles/${item.slug}">${item.title}`)
        } else {
          expect(res.text).not.to.contain(`<h2>
          <a href="/articles/${item.slug}">${item.title}`)
        }
      })
      done()
    })
})
```

In a new-article page suite, let's test for presentation of the text with `contains`:

```
describe('article page', () => {
  it('should display text or 401', (done) => {
    let n = seedArticles.length
    seedArticles.forEach((item, index, list) => {
      superagent
        .get(`http://localhost:${port}/articles/${seed
        Articles[index].slug}`)
        .end((error, res) => {
          if (item.published) {
            expect(error).to.be(null)
            expect(res.text).to.contain(seedArticles[index].text)
          } else {
            expect(error).to.be.ok
            expect(res.status).to.be(401)
          }
          // console.log(item.title)
          if (index + 1 === n) {
            done()
          }
        })
    })
  })
})
```

To make sure that Mocha doesn't quit earlier than `superagent` calls the response callback, we implemented a countertrick. Instead of it, you can use async. The full source code is in the file `tests/index.js` under the `ch5` folder.

Running tests with either $ `make test` or $ `mocha test` should fail miserably, but that's expected because we need to implement persistence and then pass data to Pug templates, which we wrote in the previous chapter.

Project: Adding Persistence

This example builds on the previous chapter, with Chapter 3 having the latest code (Chapter 4 code is in `ch5`). Let's go back to our `ch3` folder, and add the tests, duplicate them, and then start adding statements to the `app.js` file.

The full source code of this example is available under `ch5` folder. First, we refactor dependencies importations to utilize Mongoskin:

```
const express = require('express')
const routes = require('./routes')
const http = require('http')
const path = require('path')
const mongoskin = require('mongoskin')
const dbUrl = process.env.MONGOHQ_URL || 'mongodb:
//@localhost:27017/blog'
const db = mongoskin.db(dbUrl)
const collections = {
  articles: db.collection('articles'),
  users: db.collection('users')
}
```

These statements are needed for the Express.js middleware modules to enable logging (`morgan`), error handling (`errorhandler`), parsing of the incoming HTTP request bodies (`body-parser`), and to support clients that do not have all HTTP methods (`method-override`):

```
const logger = require('morgan')
const errorHandler = require('errorhandler')
const bodyParser = require('body-parser')
const methodOverride = require('method-override')
```

Then we create an Express.js instance and assign the title to use this title in the templates:

```
const app = express()
app.locals.appTitle = 'blog-express'
```

Now we add a middleware that exposes Mongoskin/MongoDB collections in each Express.js route via the `req` object. It's called a *decorator* pattern. You can learn more about the decorator pattern as well as other Node patterns in my online course Node Patterns: From Callbacks to Observer. The idea is to have `req.collections` in all other subsequent middleware and routes. It's done with the following code. And don't forget to call `next()` in the middleware; otherwise, each request will stall:

```
app.use((req, res, next) => {
  if (!collections.articles || !collections.users)
    return next(new Error('No collections.'))
  req.collections = collections
  return next()
})
```

Next, we define the Express settings. We set up port number and template engine configurations to tell Express what folder to use for templates (`views`) and what template engine to use to render those templates (`pug`):

```
app.set('port', process.env.PORT || 3000)
app.set('views', path.join(__dirname, 'views'))
app.set('view engine', 'pug')
```

Now is the time for the usual suspects functionality of most of which should be already familiar to you: middleware for logging of requests, parsing of JSON input, using Stylus for CSS and serving of static content. Node developers use the `app.use()` statements to plug these middleware modules in the Express apps. I like to remain disciplined and use `path.join()` to construct cross-platform absolute paths out of relative folder names so that there's a guarantee the paths will work on Windows.

```
app.use(logger('dev'))
app.use(bodyParser.json())
app.use(bodyParser.urlencoded({extended: true}))
app.use(methodOverride())
app.use(require('stylus').middleware(path.join(__dirname, 'public')))
app.use(express.static(path.join(__dirname, 'public')))
```

For development, we use the standard Express.js error handler that we imported earlier with `require()`:

```
if (app.get('env') === 'development') {
  app.use(errorHandler('dev'))
}
```

The next section of the `app.js` file deals with the server routes. So, instead of a single catch-all * route in the `ch3` examples, we have the following GET and POST routes (that mostly render HTML from Pug templates):

```
app.get('/', routes.index)
app.get('/login', routes.user.login)
app.post('/login', routes.user.authenticate)
app.get('/logout', routes.user.logout)
app.get('/admin', routes.article.admin)
app.get('/post', routes.article.post)
app.post('/post', routes.article.postArticle)
app.get('/articles/:slug', routes.article.show)
```

REST API routes are used mostly for the admin page. That's where our fancy AJAX browser JavaScript will need them. They use GET, POST, PUT, and DELETE methods and don't render HTML from Pug templates, but instead output JSON:

```
app.get('/api/articles', routes.article.list)
app.post('/api/articles', routes.article.add)
app.put('/api/articles/:id', routes.article.edit)
app.delete('/api/articles/:id', routes.article.del)
```

In the end, we have a 404 catch-all route. It's a good practice to account for the cases when users type a wrong URL. If the request makes it to this part of the configuration (top to bottom order), we return the "404: Not found" status:

```
app.all('*', (req, res) => {
  res.status(404).send()
})
```

The way we start the server is the same as in Chapter 3, which means we determine whether this file is loaded by another file. In this case, we export the server object. If not, then we proceed to launch the server directly with `server.listen()`.

```
const server = http.createServer(app)
const boot = function () {
  server.listen(app.get('port'), function () {
    console.info(`Express server listening on port
    ${app.get('port')}`)
  })
}
const shutdown = function () {
  server.close(process.exit)
}
if (require.main === module) {
  boot()
} else {
  console.info('Running app as a module')
  exports.boot = boot
  exports.shutdown = shutdown
  exports.port = app.get('port')
}
```

Again, for your convenience, the full source code of `app.js` is under `ch5/blog-example` folder.

We must add `index.js`, `article.js`, and `user.js` files to the `routes` folder, because we need them in `app.js`. The `user.js` file is bare bones for now (we'll add authentications in Chapter 6).

The method for the GET `/users` route, which should return a list of existing users (which we'll implement later), is as follows:

```
exports.list = (req, res, next) => {
  res.send('respond with a resource')
}
```

The method for the GET /login page route that renders the login form (login.pug) is as follows:

```
exports.login = (req, res, next) => {
  res.render('login')
}
```

The method for the GET /logout route that eventually destroys the session and redirects users to the home page (to be implemented) is as follows:

```
exports.logout = (req, res, next) => {
  res.redirect('/')
}
```

The method for the POST /authenticate route that handles authentication and redirects to the admin page (to be implemented) is as follows:

```
exports.authenticate = (req, res, next) => {
  res.redirect('/admin')
}
```

The full code of user.js is in code/ch5/blog-example/routes. We will add more logic to user.js later. Now the most database action happens in the article.js routes.

Let's start with the GET article page where we call findOne with the slug from the req.params object:

```
exports.show = (req, res, next) => {
  if (!req.params.slug) return next(new Error('No article slug.'))
  req.collections.articles.findOne({slug: req.params.slug},
    (error, article) => {
      if (error) return next(error)
      if (!article.published) return res.status(401).send()
      res.render('article', article)
  })
}
```

The GET /api/articles API route (used in the admin page), where we fetch all articles with the find() method and convert the results to an array before sending them back to the requestee:

```
exports.list = (req, res, next) => {
  req.collections
    .articles
    .find({})
    .toArray((error, articles) => {
      if (error) return next(error)
      res.send({articles: articles})
  })
}
```

The POST /api/articles API routes (used in the admin page), where the insert method is used to add new articles to the articles collection and to send back the result (with _id of a newly created item):

```
exports.add = (req, res, next) => {
  if (!req.body.article) return next(new Error('No article payload.'))
  let article = req.body.article
  article.published = false
  req.collections.articles.insert(article,
    (error, articleResponse) => {
      if (error) return next(error)
      res.send(articleResponse)
  })
}
```

The PUT /api/articles/:id API route (used on the admin page for publishing), where the updateById shorthand method is used to set the article document to the payload of the request (req.body). (The same thing can be done with a combination of update and _id query.)

```
exports.edit = (req, res, next) => {
  if (!req.params.id) return next(new Error('No article ID.'))
  req.collections.articles.updateById(req.params.id,
```

```
    {$set: req.body.article},
    (error, count) => {
      if (error) return next(error)
      res.send({affectedCount: count})
  })
}
```

The DELETE `/api/articles/:id` API which is used on the admin page for removing articles in which, again, a combination of `remove` and `_id` can be used to achieve similar results:

```
exports.del = (req, res, next) => {
  if (!req.params.id) return next(new Error('No article ID.'))
  req.collections.articles.removeById(req.params.id, (error, count)
  => {
    if (error) return next(error)
    res.send({affectedCount: count})
  })
}
```

The GET `/post` create a new post page. This page is a blank form and thus requires NO data:

```
exports.post = (req, res, next) => {
  if (!req.body.title) { res.render('post') }
}
```

Next, there's the POST article route for the post page form (the route that actually handles the post addition). In this route we check for the non-empty inputs (`req.body`), construct the `article` object, and inject it into the database via the `req.collections.articles` object exposed to us by middleware. Lastly, we render HTML from the `post` template:

```
exports.postArticle = (req, res, next) => {
  if (!req.body.title || !req.body.slug || !req.body.text) {
    return res.render('post', {error: 'Fill title, slug and text.'})
  }
  const article = {
    title: req.body.title,
```

```
    slug: req.body.slug,
    text: req.body.text,
    published: false
  }
  req.collections.articles.insert(article, (error, articleResponse)
  => {
    if (error) return next(error)
    res.render('post',
      {error: 'Article was added. Publish it on Admin page.'})
  })
}
```

The GET `/admin` page route in which we fetch sorted articles (`{sort: {_id:-1}}`) and manipulate them:

```
exports.admin = (req, res, next) => {
  req.collections
    .articles.find({}, {sort: {_id: -1}})
    .toArray((error, articles) => {
      if (error) return next(error)
      res.render('admin', {articles: articles})
  })
}
```

Note   In real production apps that deal with thousands of records, programmers usually use pagination by fetching only a certain number of items at once (5, 10, 100, and so on). To do this, use the `limit` and `skip` options with the `find` method, e.g., HackHall example: `https://github.com/azat-co/hackhall/blob/master/routes/posts.js#L37`.

This time we won't duplicate the code since it's rather long. So for the full code of `article.js`, please refer to the `code/ch5/blog-example/routes`.

From the project section in Chapter 4, we have the `.pug` files under the `views` folder. Lastly, the `package.json` file looks as follows. Please compare your npm scripts and dependencies.

```
{
  "name": "blog-express",
  "version": "0.0.5",
  "private": true,
  "scripts": {
    "start": "node app.js",
    "seed": "sh ./seed.sh",
    "test": "make test",
    "st": "standard app.js && standard tests/index.js && standard
    routes/*"
  },
  "dependencies": {
    "body-parser": "1.18.2",
    "cookie-parser": "1.4.3",
    "errorhandler": "1.5.0",
    "express": "4.16.2",
    "express-session": "1.15.6",
    "method-override": "2.3.10",
    "mongodb": "2.2.33",
    "mongoskin": "2.1.0",
    "morgan": "1.9.0",
    "pug": "2.0.0-rc.4",
    "serve-favicon": "2.4.5",
    "stylus": "0.54.5"
  },
  "devDependencies": {
    "standard": "10.0.3",
    "mocha": "4.0.1",
    "superagent": "3.8.0",
    "expect.js": "0.3.1"
  }
}
```

For the admin page to function, we need to add some AJAX-iness in the form of the `js/admin.js` file under the `public` folder. (I don't know why I keep calling HTTP requests done with the XHR object the AJAX calls, since AJAX is *Asynchronous JavaScript And XML*, and no one is using XML anymore.#shrug)

In this file, we use `ajaxSetup` to configure all requests because these configs will be used in many requests. Most importantly, `withCredentials` will send the cookies which is needed for admin authentication.

```
$.ajaxSetup({
  xhrFields: {withCredentials: true},
  error: function (xhr, status, error) {
    $('.alert').removeClass('hidden')
    $('.alert').html('Status: ' + status + ', error: '
    + error)
  }
})
```

The function `findTr` is a helper that we can use in our event handlers:

```
var findTr = function (event) {
  var target = event.srcElement || event.target
  var $target = $(target)
  var $tr = $target.parents('tr')
  return $tr
}
```

Overall, we need three event handlers to remove, publish, and unpublish an article. This following code snippet is for removing, and it simply sends a request to our Node.js API route `/api/articles/:id`, which we wrote a page or two ago:

```
var remove = function (event) {
  var $tr = findTr(event)
  var id = $tr.data('id')
  $.ajax({
    url: '/api/articles/' + id,
    type: 'DELETE',
    success: function (data, status, xhr) {
```

```
        $('.alert').addClass('hidden')
        $tr.remove()
      }
    })
}
```

Publishing and unpublishing are coupled together, because they both send PUT to /api/articles/:id but with different payloads (`data`). Then type is of course PUT. The data is turned into a string because that is what this method $.ajax uses. If we were to use a different library like axios or fetch then the actual data format and the syntax of the call to make the request would be different. An interesting feature is coded in the callback. It allows to change the icons depending on the status of a particular article (`data.published`).

```
var update = function (event) {
  var $tr = findTr(event)
  $tr.find('button').attr('disabled', 'disabled')
  var data = {
    published: $tr.hasClass('unpublished')
  }
  var id = $tr.attr('data-id')
  $.ajax({
    url: '/api/articles/' + id,
    type: 'PUT',
    contentType: 'application/json',
    data: JSON.stringify({article: data}),
    success: function (dataResponse, status, xhr) {
      $tr.find('button').removeAttr('disabled')
      $('.alert').addClass('hidden')
      if (data.published) {
        $tr.removeClass('unpublished').find('.glyphicon-play').
        removeClass('glyphiconplay').addClass('glyphicon-pause')
      } else {
        $tr.addClass('unpublished').find('.glyphicon-pause').
        removeClass('glyphicon-pause').addClass('glyphicon-play')
```

```
      }
    }
  })
}
```

That's not all. Defining functions won't make them work when a user clicks a button. We need to attach event listeners. We attach event listeners in the `ready` callback to make sure that the `tbody` is in the DOM—otherwise, it might be not found:

```
$(document).ready(function () {
  var $element = $('.admin tbody')
  $element.on('click', 'button.remove', remove)
  $element.on('click', 'button', update)
})
```

The full source code of the front-end `admin.js` file is in `code/ch5/blog-example/public/js`. And now is the time to run the app!

Running the App

To run the app, simply execute $ `npm start`, which will execute $ `node app.js`, but if you want to seed and test it, execute $ `npm run seed`, which will execute $ `make db`. To run tests, use $ `npm test`, which executes $ `make test`, respectively (Figure 5-5). (There's no difference between running npm script commands or the commands directly.)

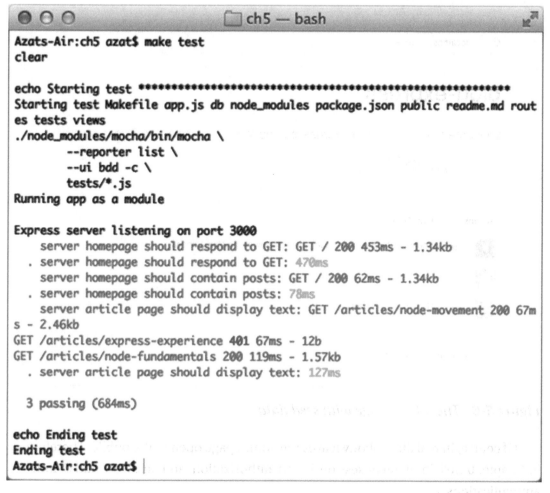

```
● ● ●                        ☐ ch5 — bash                              ⌐

Azats-Air:ch5 azat$ make test
clear

echo Starting test ●●●●●●●●●●●●●●●●●●●●●●●●●●●●●●●●●●●●●●●●●●●●●●●●●●●●●●●●●●●●●●●●●●
Starting test Makefile app.js db node_modules package.json public readme.md rout
es tests views
./node_modules/mocha/bin/mocha \
        --reporter list \
        --ui bdd -c \
        tests/*.js
Running app as a module

Express server listening on port 3000
    server homepage should respond to GET: GET / 200 453ms - 1.34kb
  . server homepage should respond to GET: 470ms
    server homepage should contain posts: GET / 200 62ms - 1.34kb
  . server homepage should contain posts: 78ms
    server article page should display text: GET /articles/node-movement 200 67m
s - 2.46kb
GET /articles/express-experience 401 67ms - 12b
GET /articles/node-fundamentals 200 119ms - 1.57kb
  . server article page should display text: 127ms

  3 passing (684ms)

echo Ending test
Ending test
Azats-Air:ch5 azat$ |
```

Figure 5-5. *The results of running Mocha tests*

Oh, yeah! Don't forget that $ mongod service must be running on the localhost
and port 27017. The expected result is that all tests now pass (hurray!), and if users visit
http://localhost:3000, they can see posts and even create new ones on the admin page
(http://localhost:3000/admin) as shown in Figure 5-6.

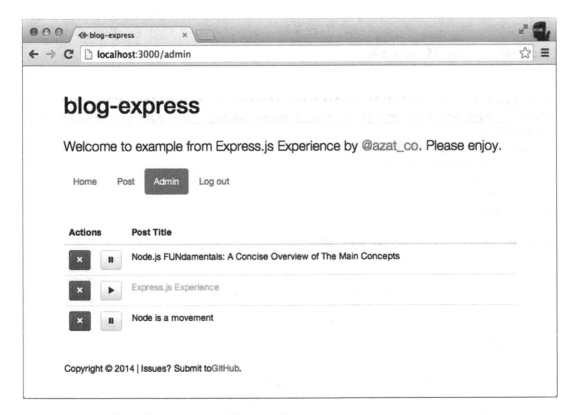

Figure 5-6. *The admin page with seed data*

Of course, in real life, nobody leaves the admin page open to the public. Therefore, in Chapter 6 we'll implement session-based authorization, and password and OAuth authentications.

Summary

In this chapter, I taught and you've learned how to install MongoDB, and use its console and native Node.js driver, for which we wrote a small script and refactored it to see Mongoskin in action. We also wrote tests, seeded scripts, implemented the persistence layer and the front-end admin page logic for Blog.

In the next chapter, we'll dive into misty and mysterious world of auth, and implement authorization and authentication for Blog.

CHAPTER 6

Security and Auth in Node.js

You know that security is an important aspect of any real-world web application. This is especially true nowadays, because our apps don't function in silos anymore. What if I tell you that you don't have to spend days studying for security certifications or read sketchy dark-web hacker forums to implement a secure Node app? I'll show you a few tricks.

We can makes our apps and communications secure by using various approaches, such as token-based authentication and/or OAuth (`http://oauth.net`). We can leverage numerous third-party services (e.g., Google, Twitter, GitHub) or become service providers ourselves (e.g., provide a public API).

In this practical book, I dedicate the whole chapter to matters of authorization, authentication, OAuth, and best practices. We'll look at the following topics:

- Authorization with Express.js middleware

- Token-based authentication

- Session-based authentication

- Project: Adding e-mail and password login to Blog

- Node.js OAuth

- Project: Adding Twitter OAuth 1.0 sign-in to Blog with Everyauth
  (`https://github.com/bnoguchi/everyauth`)

© Azat Mardan 2018
A. Mardan, *Practical Node.js*, https://doi.org/10.1007/978-1-4842-3039-8_6

Authorization with Express.js Middleware

Authorization in web apps usually means restricting certain functions to privileged clients. These functions can either be methods, pages, or REST API endpoints.

Express.js middleware allows us to apply certain rules seamlessly to all routes, groups of routes (namespacing), or individual routes.

- *All routes*: `app.get('*', auth)`

- *Groups of routes*: `app.get('/api/*', auth)`

- *Individual routes*: `app.get('/admin/users', auth)`

For example, if we want to protect all `/api/` endpoints, we utilize the following middleware with `*`:

```
app.all('/api/*', auth)
app.get('/api/users', users.list)
app.post('/api/users', users.create)
```

Interestingly enough, `app.all()` with a URL pattern and an `*` is functionally the same as utilizing `app.use()` with a URL in a sense that they both will be triggered only on those URLs that are matching the URL pattern:

```
app.use('/api', auth)
```

Another way of doing the same thing is to use `auth` middleware on each route which requires it:

```
app.get('/', home) // no Auth needed
app.get('/api/users', auth, users.list) // Auth needed
app.post('/api/users', auth, users.create) // Auth needed
```

In the previous examples, `auth()` is a function with three parameters: `req`, `res`, and `next`. For example in this middleware, you can call the OAuth service or query a database to get the user profile to *authorize* it (check for permissions) or to check for JWT (JSON Web Tokens) or web session to *authenticate* the user (check who it is). Or, most likely, do both!

```
const auth = (req, res, next) => {
  // ...
  // Assuming you get user profile and user.auth is true or false
  if (user.auth) return next()
  else next(new Error('Not authorized'))
  // or res.send(401)
}
```

The `next()` part is important, because this is how Express.js proceeds to execute subsequent request handlers and routes (if there's a match in a URL pattern). If `next()` is invoked without anything, then the normal execution of the server will proceed. That is Express will go to the next middleware and then to the routes that match the URL.

If `next()` is invoked with an error object such as `next(new Error('Not authorized'))`, then Express will jump straight to the first error handler, and none of the subsequent middleware or routes will be executed.

Token-Based Authentication

For applications to know which privileges a specific client has (e.g., admin), we must add an authentication step. In the previous example, this step went inside the `auth()` function.

The most common authentication is a cookie&session–based authentication, and the next section deals with this topic. However, in some cases, more REST-fulness is required, or cookies/sessions are not supported well (e.g., mobile). In this case, it's beneficial to authenticate each request with a token (probably using the OAuth2.0 (`http://tools.ietf.org/html/rfc6749`) scheme). The token can be passed in a query string or in HTTP request headers. Alternatively, we can send some other authentication combination of information, such as e- mail/username and password, or API key, or API password, instead of a token.

In our example of token-based authentication, each request can submit a token in a query string (accessed via `req.query.token`). And if we have the correct value stored somewhere in our app (database, or in this example just a constant `SECRET_TOKEN`), we can check the incoming token against it. If the token matches our records, we call `next()` to proceed with the request executions; if not, then we call `next(error)`, which triggers Express.js error handler execution (see the upcoming note):

```
const auth = (req, res, next) => {
  if (req.query.token && token === SECRET_TOKEN) {
    // client is fine, proceed to the next route
    return next()
  } else {
    return next(new Error('Not authorized'))
      // or res.send(401)
  }
}
```

In a more realistic example, we use API keys and secrets to generate HMAC-SHA1 (hash-based message authentication code—secure hash algorithm strings), and then compare them with the value in `req.query.token`.

Note   Calling `next()` with an error argument is analogous to throwing in the towel (i.e., giving up). The Express.js app enters the error mode and proceeds to the error handlers.

We just covered the token-based authentication, which is often used in REST APIs. But user-facing web apps (i.e., browser-enabled users & consumers) often use with cookies. We can use cookies to store and send session IDs with each request.

Cookies are similar to tokens, but require less work for us, the developers! This approach is the cornerstone of session-based authentication. The session-based method is the recommended way for basic web apps, because browsers already know what to do with session headers. In addition, in most platforms and frameworks, the session mechanism is built into the core. So, let's jump straight into session-based authentication with Node.js.

JSON Web Token (JWT) Authentication

Developers use JSON Web Tokens (JWT) to encrypted data, which is then stored on the client. JWTs have all the any information unlike regular tokens (API keys or OAuth access tokens), which are more like passwords. Thus, JWTs remove the need for a database to store user information.

In my opinion, JWT is less secure than web sessions. This is because web sessions store the data on the server (usually in a database) and only store a session ID on the client. Despite JWT using encryption, anyone can break any encryption given enough time and processing power.

Nevertheless, JWT is a very common technique that frontend web apps developers use. JWTs eliminate the need for the server-side database or a store. All info is in this token, which has three parts: header, payload and signature. Whereas the structure of JWT is the same, the encryption method can vary depending on what a developer's choice: HS256, RS512, ES384, and so on. I'm always paranoid about security, so the stronger the algorithm, the better. RS512 will be good for most of the cases circa 2020.

To implement a simple JWT login, let's use the `jsonwebtoken` library for signing tokens and `bcrypt` for hashing passwords. When a client wants to create an account, the system takes the password and hashes it asynchronously so as not to block the server from processing other requests The slower the hashing, the worse for attackers and the better for you. For example, this is how to get the password from the incoming request body and store the hash into the `users` array using 10 rounds of hashing, which is good enough:

```
app.post('/auth/register', (req, res) => {
    bcrypt.hash(req.body.password, 10, (error, hash)=>{
    if (error) return res.status(500).send()
    users.push({
        username: req.body.username,
        passwordHash: hash
    })
    res.status(201).send('registered')
  })
})
```

Once the user record is created (which has the hash), we can log in users to exchange the username and password for the JWT. They'll use this JWT for all other requests like a special key to authenticate and maybe unlock protected and restricted resources (that's *authorization* because not all users will have access to all the restricted resources).

The GET route is not a protected route, but POST is a protected one, because there's an extra `auth` middleware there that will check for the JWT:

```
app.get('/courses', (req, res) => {
    res.send(courses)
  })
app.post('/courses', auth, (req, res) => {
    courses.push({title: req.body.title})
    res.send(courses)
  })
```

The login route checks for the presence of this username in the `users` array but this can be a database call or a call to another API, not a simple `find()` method. Next, `bcrypt` has a `compare()` method that asynchronously compares the hash with the plain password. If they match (`matched == true`), then `jwt.sign()` will issue a signed (encrypted) token that has the username in it. (It can have many other fields, not just one field.)

```
app.post('/auth/login', (req, res) => {
    const foundUser = users.find((value, index, list) => {
      if (value.username === req.body.username) return true
      else return false
    })
    if (foundUser) {
      bcrypt.compare(req.body.password, foundUser.passwordHash,
      (error, matched) => {
        if (!error && matched) {
          res.status(201).json({token: jwt.sign({ username:
          foundUser.username}, SECRET)})
        } else res.status(401).send()
      })
    } else res.status(401).send()
})
```

JWT uses a special value SECRET to encrypt the data. Preferably when the app goes to production, an environment variable or a public key will populate the SECRET value. However now, SECRET is just a hard-coded const string.

When you get this JWT, you can make requests to POST /courses. The auth, which checks for JWT, uses the jwt module and the data from the headers. I use the auth header name. The name of the header doesn't matter as long as you use the same name on the server and on the client. For the server, I set the header name in the auth middleware.

Some developers like to use Authorization, but it's confusing to me since we're not authorizing, but authenticating. The authorization, which controls who can do what, is happening in the Node middleware. Here, we are performing authentication, which identifies who is this.

My auth header will look like this JWT TOKEN_VALUE. Ergo, to extract the token value out of the header, I use a string function split(' '):

```
const auth = (req, res, next) => {
  if (req.headers && req.headers.auth && req.headers.auth.split(' ')
  [0] === 'JWT') {
    jwt.verify(req.headers.auth.split(' ')[1], SECRET, (error,
    decoded) => {
      if (error) return res.status(401).send()
      req.user = decoded
      console.log('authenticated as ', decoded.username)
      next()
    })
  }
  else return res.status(401).send()
}
```

You can play with the full working and tested code in code/ch6/jwt-example. I like to use CURL, but most of my Node workshop attendees like Postman (a cross-platform GUI app), so in Figure 6-2 I show how to use Postman to extract the JWT (on login). And Figure 6-3 uses the token on POST /courses by having the token in the header auth after JWT with a space (JWT TOKEN_VALUE).

We finished the implementation. Now test the JWT example with these step-by-step instructions in CURL, Postman or any other HTTP client:

1. GET `/courses` will return a list of two courses that are hard-coded in `server.js`.

2. POST `/courses` with JSON data `{"title": "blah blah blah"}` will return 401 Not Authorized. Now we know that this is a protected route, and we need to create a new user to proceed.

3. POST `/auth/register` with username and password will create a new user, as shown in Figure 6-1. Next we can log in to the server to get the token.

4. POST `/auth/login` with username and password that match the existing records will return JWT, as shown in Figure 6-2.

5. POST `/courses` with title and JWT from step 4 in the `auth` header will create a new course (response status 201), as shown in Figures 6-3 and 6-4.

6. GET `/courses` will show your new title. Verify it. No need for JWT for this request, but it won't hurt either. Figure 6-5.

7. Celebrate and get a cup of tea with a (paleo) cookie.

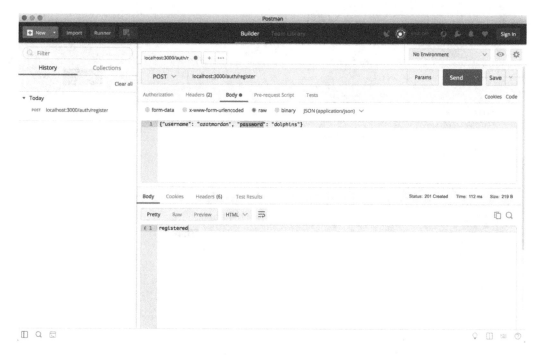

Figure 6-1. *Registering a new user by sending JSON payload*

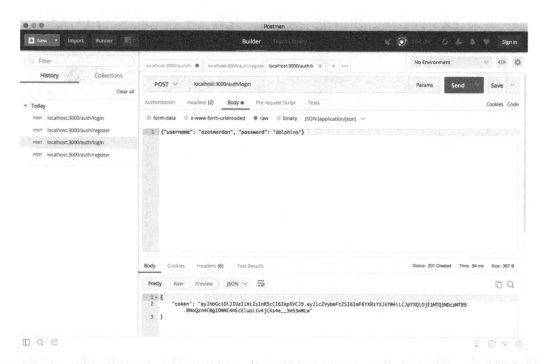

Figure 6-2. *Logging in to get JWT*

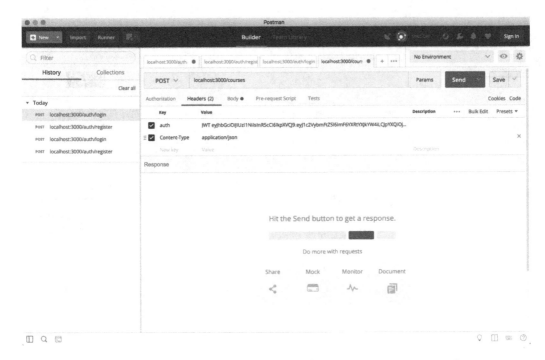

Figure 6-3. *Using JWT in the header auth*

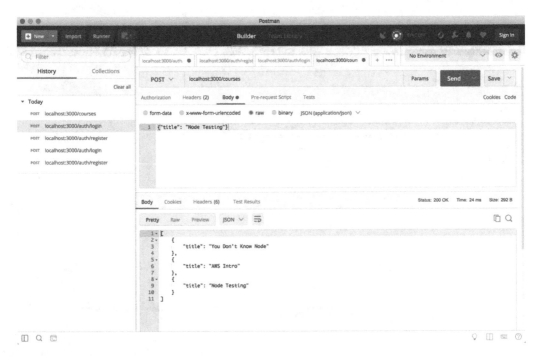

Figure 6-4. *200 status for the new course request with JWT in the header and the JSON payload*

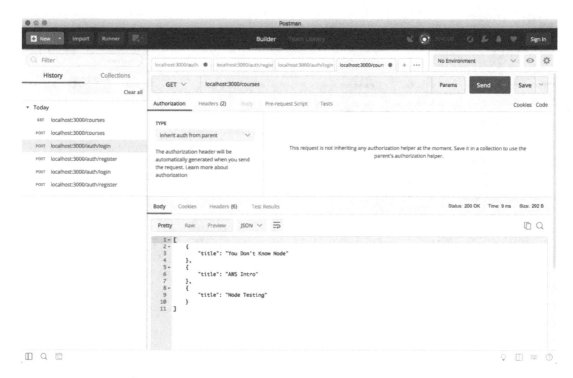

Figure 6-5. *Verifying new course*

Don't forget to select `raw` and `application/json` when registering (POST `/auth/register`) and when making other POST requests. And now that you saw my password, please don't hack my accounts (`https://github.com/danielmiessler/SecLists/pull/155`).

Finally, you can uncheck the `auth` header that has the JWT value and try to make another POST `/courses` request, as shown in Figure 6-6. The request will fail miserably (401), as it should because there's no JWT this time (see `auth` middleware in `server.js`).

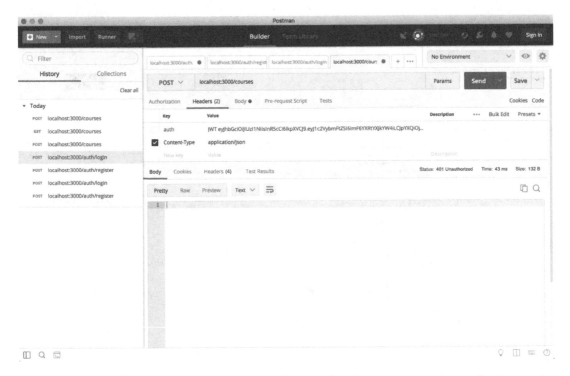

Figure 6-6. *Unchecking auth header with JWT leads to 401 as expected*

JWT is easy to implement. Developers don't need to create and maintain a shared database for the services. That's the main benefit. Clients get JWTs after the login request.

Once on the client, client code stores JWT in browser or mobile local storage or cookies (also in the browser). React, Vue, Elm, or Angular front-end apps send this token with each request. If you plan to use JWT, it's important to protect your secret and to pick a strong encryption algorithm to make it harder for attackers to hack your JWT data.

If you ask me, sessions are more secure because with sessions I store my data *on the server* instead of on the client. Let's talk about sessions.

Session-Based Authentication

Session-based authentication is done via the `session` object in the request object `req`. A web session in general is a secure way to store information about a client so that subsequent requests from that same client can be identified.

In the main Express.js file, we'll need to import (`require()`) two modules to enable sessions. We need to include and use `cookie-parser` and `express-session`:

1. `express.cookieParser()`: Allows for parsing of the client/ request cookies

2. `express.session()`: Exposes the `res.session` object in each request handler, and stores data in the app memory or some other persistent store like MongoDB or Redis

---

Note In `express-session` version 1.5.0 and higher, there's no need to add the `cookie-parser` middleware. In fact, it might lead to some bad behavior. So it's recommended to use `express-sesison` by itself because it will parse and read cookie by itself.

Needless to say, `cookie-parser` and `express-session` must be installed via npm into the project's `node_modules` folder. You can install them with:

```
$ npm i cookie-parser express-session -SE
```

In the main Express file such as `app.js` or `server.js`, import with `require()` and apply to the Express app with `app.use()`:

```
const cookieParser = require('cookie-parser')
const session = require('express-session')
...
app.use(cookieParser())
app.use(session())
```

The rest is straightforward. We can store any data in `req.session` and it appears automagically on each request from the same client (assuming their browser supports cookies). Hence, the authentication consists of a route that stores some flag (true/false) in the session and of an authorization function in which we check for that flag (if true, then proceed; otherwise, exit). For example to log in, we set the property `auth` on the `session` to `true`. The `req.session.auth` value will persist on future requests from the same client.

```
app.post('/login', (req, res, next) => {
  if (checkForCredentials(req)) {
  // checkForCredentials checks for credentials passed in the
    request's payload
    req.session.auth = true
    res.redirect('/dashboard') // Private resource
  } else {
    res.status(401).send() // Not authorized
  }
})
```

Warning   Avoid storing any sensitive information in cookies. The best practice is not to store any info in cookies manually—except session ID, which Express. js middleware stores for us automatically—because cookies are not secure. Also, cookies have a size limitation that is very easy to reach and which varies by browser with Internet Explore having the smallest limit.

By default, Express.js uses in-memory session storage. This means that every time an app is restarted or crashes, the sessions are wiped out. To make sessions persistent and available across multiple servers, we can use a database such as Redis or MongoDB as a session store that will save the data on restarts and crashes of the servers.

In fact, having Redis for the session store is one of the best practices that my team and I used at Storify and DocuSign. Redis provided one source of truth for the session data among multiple servers. Our Node apps were able to scale up well because they were stateless. We also used Redis for caching due to its efficiency.

Project: Adding E-mail and Password Login to Blog

To enable session-based authentication in Blog, we need to do the following:

1. Import and add the session middleware to the configuration part of app.js.

2. Implement the authorization middleware authorize with a session-based authorization so we can reuse the same code for many routes.

3. Add the middleware from step 2 to protected pages and routes
   in `app.js` routes, e.g., `app.get('/api/, authorize,`
   `api.index)`.

4. Implement an authentication route POST `/login`, and a logout
   route, GET `/logout`, in `user.js`.

We will start with the session middleware.

Session Middleware

Let's add the automatic cookie parsing and support for session middleware in these two
lines by putting them in the middle of configurations in `app.js`:

```
const cookieParser = require('cookie-parser')
const session = require('express-session')
// Other middleware
app.use(cookieParser('3CCC4ACD-6ED1-4844-9217-82131BDCB239'))
app.use(session({secret: '2C44774A-D649-4D44-9535-46E296EF984F'}))
// Routes
```

Warning   You should replace randomly generated values with your own ones.

`session()` must be preceded by `cookieParser()` because session depends on
cookies to work properly. For more information about these and other Express.js/
Connect middleware, refer to *Pro Express.js 4* (Apress, 2014).

Beware of another cookie middleware. Its name is `cookie-session` and it's not as
secure as `cookie-parser` with `express-session`. This is because `cookie-session`
stores all information in the cookie, not on the server. `cookie-session` can be used in
some cases but I do not recommend it. The usage is to import the module and to apply it
to the Express.js `app`:

```
const cookieSession = require('cookie-session')
app.use(cookieSession({secret: process.env.SESSION_SECRET}))
```

Again, the difference is that `express-session` uses secure in-memory or Redis storage—and cookies store only for the session ID, i.e., `sid`—whereas `cookie-session` uses browser cookies to store session information. In other words, the entire session is serialized into cookie-based storage, not just the session key. This approach should be avoided because of cookie size limitations and security concerns.

It's useful to pass request authentication information to the templates. We can do so by adding middleware that checks the `req.session.admin` value for truthyness and adds an appropriate property to `res.locals`:

```
app.use(function(req, res, next) {
  if (req.session && req.session.admin)
    res.locals.admin = true
  next()
})
```

Let's add authorization to the Blog project.

Authorization in Blog

Authorization is also done via middleware, but we won't set it up right away with `app.use()` like we did in the snippet for `res.locals`. Instead, we define a function that checks for `req.session.admin` to be true, and proceeds if it is. Otherwise, the 401 Not Authorized error is thrown, and the response is ended.

```
// Authorization
const authorize = (req, res, next) => {
  if (req.session && req.session.admin)
    return next()
  else
    return res.send(401)
}
```

Now we can add this middleware to certain protected endpoints (another name for routes). Specifically, we will protect the endpoints to see the admin page (GET `/admin`), to create a new article (POST `/post`), and to see the create new article page (GET `/post`):

```
app.get('/admin', authorize, routes.article.admin)
app.get('/post', authorize, routes.article.post)
app.post('/post', authorize, routes.article.postArticle)
```

We add the authorize middleware to API routes as well... to *all* of them, using `app.all()`:

```
app.all('/api', authorize)
app.get('/api/articles', routes.article.list)
app.post('/api/articles', routes.article.add)
app.put('/api/articles/:id', routes.article.edit)
app.delete('/api/articles/:id', routes.article.del)
```

The `app.all('/api', authorize)` statement is a more compact alternative to adding `authorize` to all `/api/...` routes manually. Less copy and paste and more code reuse, please.

I know a lot of readers like to see the entire source code. Thus, the full source code of the `app.js` file after adding session support and authorization middleware is as follows (under the `ch6/blog-password` folder):

```
const express = require('express')
const routes = require('./routes')
const http = require('http')
const path = require('path')
const mongoskin = require('mongoskin')
const dbUrl = process.env.MONGOHQ_URL || 'mongodb:
//@localhost:27017/blog'

const db = mongoskin.db(dbUrl)
const collections = {
  articles: db.collection('articles'),
  users: db.collection('users')
}
```

```
const cookieParser = require('cookie-parser')
const session = require('express-session')
const logger = require('morgan')
const errorHandler = require('errorhandler')
const bodyParser = require('body-parser')
const methodOverride = require('method-override')

const app = express()
app.locals.appTitle = 'blog-express'

// Expose collections to request handlers
app.use((req, res, next) => {
  if (!collections.articles || !collections.users)
  return next(new Error('No collections.'))
  req.collections = collections
  return next()
})

// Express.js configurations
app.set('port', process.env.PORT || 3000)
app.set('views', path.join(__dirname, 'views'))
app.set('view engine', 'pug')

// Express.js middleware configuration
app.use(logger('dev'))
app.use(bodyParser.json())
app.use(bodyParser.urlencoded({extended: true}))
app.use(methodOverride())
app.use(require('stylus').middleware(path.join(__dirname, 'public')))
app.use(express.static(path.join(__dirname, 'public')))
app.use(cookieParser('3CCC4ACD-6ED1-4844-9217-82131BDCB239'))
app.use(session({secret: '2C44774A-D649-4D44-9535-46E296EF984F',
  resave: true,
  saveUninitialized: true}))
```

```
// Authentication middleware
app.use((req, res, next) => {
  if (req.session && req.session.admin) {
    res.locals.admin = true
  }
  next()
})

// Authorization Middleware
const authorize = (req, res, next) => {
  if (req.session && req.session.admin)
    return next()
  else
    return res.status(401).send()
}

if (app.get('env') === 'development') {
  app.use(errorHandler())
}

// PAGES&ROUTES
app.get('/', routes.index)
app.get('/login', routes.user.login)
app.post('/login', routes.user.authenticate)
app.get('/logout', routes.user.logout)
app.get('/admin', authorize, routes.article.admin)
app.get('/post', authorize, routes.article.post)
app.post('/post', authorize, routes.article.postArticle)
app.get('/articles/:slug', routes.article.show)

// REST API ROUTES
app.all('/api', authorize)
app.get('/api/articles', routes.article.list)
app.post('/api/articles', routes.article.add)
app.put('/api/articles/:id', routes.article.edit)
app.delete('/api/articles/:id', routes.article.del)
```

```
app.all('*', function (req, res) {
  res.status(404).send()
})

// http.createServer(app).listen(app.get('port'), function(){
  // console.log('Express server listening on port ' + app.
  get('port'));
// });

const server = http.createServer(app)
const boot = function () {
  server.listen(app.get('port'), function () {
    console.info(`Express server listening on port ${app.get('port')}`)
  })
}
const shutdown = function () {
  server.close(process.exit)
}
if (require.main === module) {
  boot()
} else {
  console.info('Running app as a module')
  exports.boot = boot
  exports.shutdown = shutdown
  exports.port = app.get('port')
}
```

Now we can implement authentication (different from authorization).

Authentication in Blog

The last step in session-based authorization is to allow users and clients to turn the `req.session.admin` switch on and off. We do this by having a login form and processing the POST request from that form.

For authenticating users as admins, we set the appropriate flag (admin=true), in the `routes.user.authenticate` in the `user.js` file. This is done in the POST `/login` route, which we defined in the `app.js` —a line that has this statement:

```
app.post('/login', routes.user.authenticate)
```

In `user.js`, expose the method to the importer, i.e., the file that imports this `user.js` module:

```
exports.authenticate = (req, res, next) => {
```

The form on the login page submits data to this route. In general, a sanity check for the input values is always a good idea. If values are falsy (including empty values), we'll render the login page again with the message `error`.

The `return` keyword ensures the rest of the code in this method isn't executed. If the values are non-empty (or otherwise truthy), then the request handler will not terminate yet and will proceed to the next statements:

```
exports.authenticate = (req, res, next) => {
  if (!req.body.email || !req.body.password)
    return res.render('login', {
      error: 'Please enter your email and password.'
    })
```

Thanks to the database middleware in `app.js`, we can access database collections in `req.collections`. In our app's architecture, e-mail is a unique identifier (there are no two accounts with the same e-mail), so we use the `findOne()` function to find a match of the e-mail and password combination (logical AND):

```
req.collections.users.findOne({
  email: req.body.email,
  password: req.body.password
}, (error, user) => {
```

Warning   In virtually all cases, we don't want to store passwords as a plain text; we should store salts and password hashes instead. In this way, if the database gets compromised, passwords are not seen. For salting, use the core Node.js module crypto.

`findOne()` returns an error object and the `user` result object. However, we should still do error processing manually:

```
if (error) return next(error)
if (!user) return res.render('login', {error: 'Incorrect
email&password combination.'})
```

If the program has made it thus far (avoiding a lot of `return` statements prior), we can authenticate the user as administrator, thus enabling the authentication and the `auth` (authorization) method:

```
    req.session.user = user
    req.session.admin = user.admin
    res.redirect('/admin')
  })
}
```

The `logout` route is trivial. We clear the session by calling `destroy()` on `req.session`:

```
exports.logout = (req, res, next) => {
  req.session.destroy()
  res.redirect('/')
}
```

The full source code of `code/ch6/blog-password/routes/user.js` for your reference is as follows:

```
exports.list = function (req, res) {
  res.send('respond with a resource')
}

exports.login = function (req, res, next) {
  res.render('login')
}

exports.logout = function (req, res, next) {
  req.session.destroy()
  res.redirect('/')
}
```

```
exports.authenticate = function (req, res, next) {
  if (!req.body.email || !req.body.password) { return res.
  render('login', {error: 'Please enter your email and password.'}) }
  req.collections.users.findOne({
    email: req.body.email,
    password: req.body.password
  }, function (error, user) {
    if (error) return next(error)
    if (!user) return res.render('login', {error: 'Incorrect
    email&password combination.'})
    req.session.user = user
    req.session.admin = user.admin
    res.redirect('/admin')
  })
}
```

It's better to test the enhancements earlier. Everything should be ready for running the app.

Running the App

Now everything should be set up properly to run Blog. In contrast, to the example in Chapter 5, we see protected pages only when we're logged in. These protected pages enable us to create new posts, and to publish and unpublish them. But as soon as we click Logout in the menu, we no longer can access the administrator page.

The executable code is under the `code/ch6/blog-password` folder of the `practicalnode` repository: `https://github.com/azat-co/practicalnode`.

The oauth Module

The `oauth` module is the powerhouse of OAuth 1.0/2.0 schemes and flows for Node.js. It's a module that generates signatures, encryptions, and HTTP headers, and makes requests. You can find it on npm at `https://www.npmjs.org/package/oauth` and on GitHub at `https://github.com/ciaranj/node-oauth`.

We still need to initiate the OAuth flows (i.e., requests back and forth between consumer, provider, and our system), write the callback routes, and store information in sessions or databases. Refer to the service provider's (e.g., Facebook, Twitter, Google) documentation for endpoints, methods, and parameter names.

It is recommended that `node-auth` be used when complex integration is needed or when only certain pieces of OAuth are needed (e.g., header signatures are generated by node-auth, but the request is made by the `superagent` library).

To add OAuth version 0.9.15 (the latest as of this writing) to your project, simply say the following incantation:

```
$ npm install oauth@0.9.15
```

Once you install the oauth module, you can start implementing OAuth flows such as Twitter OAuth 2.0.

Twitter OAuth 2.0 Example with Node.js OAuth

OAuth 2.0 is less complicated and, some might argue, less secure than OAuth 1.0. You can find plenty of blog posts, flame wars and rants on OAuth 1 vs 2 online, if you wish. I'll give you my short version here.

In essence, OAuth 2.0 doesn't prescribe encryption and instead relies on SSL (https) for encryption. On the other hand, OAuth 1 dictates the encryption.

The way OAuth 2.0 works is similar to the token-based authorization we examined earlier, for which we have a single token, called a *bearer*, that we pass along with each request. Think about bearer as a special kind of a password that unlocks all the treasures. To get that token, all we need to do is exchange our app's token and secret for the bearer.

Usually, this bearer can be stored for a longer time than OAuth 1.x tokens (depending on the rules set by a specific service provider) and can be used as a single key/password to open protected resources. This bearer acts as our token in the token-based auth.

The following is an OAuth 2.0 request example, which I wrote for the `oauth` docs: `https://github.com/ciaranj/node-oauth#oauth20`. It'll illustrate how to make an OAuth 2 request to Twitter API.

First, we create an `oauth2` object that has a Twitter consumer key and secret (replace the values with yours):

```
const OAuth = require('oauth')
const OAuth2 = OAuth.OAuth2
const twitterConsumerKey = 'your key'
```

```
const twitterConsumerSecret = 'your secret'
const oauth2 = new OAuth2(twitterConsumerKey,
  twitterConsumerSecret,
  'https://api.twitter.com/',
  null,
  'oauth2/token',
  null
)
```

Then, we request access to the token/bearer from the service provider:

```
oauth2.getOAuthAccessToken(
  '',
  {'grant_type': 'client_credentials'},
  function (e, access_token, refresh_token, results) {
    console.log('bearer: ', access_token)
    // Store bearer
    // Make OAuth2 requests using this bearer to protected endpoints
  }
)
```

Now we can store the bearer for future use and make requests to protected endpoints with it.

Note Twitter uses OAuth 2.0 for endpoints (resources) which don't require users permissions. These endpoints use what's called *app-only authorization*, because they are accessible on behalf of apps, not on behalf of users of apps. Not all endpoints are available through app-only auth, and quotas/limitations are different. Conversely, Twitter uses OAuth 1.0 for authorization of requests made on behalf of the users of the apps. To learn what endpoints use OAuth 2 and what OAuth 1, please refer to the official documentation at `http://dev.twitter.com`.

Everyauth

The Everyauth module allows for multiple OAuth strategies to be implemented and added to any Express.js app in just a few lines of code. Everyauth comes with strategies for most of the service providers, so there's no need to search and implement service provider-specific endpoints, parameters names, and so forth. Also, Everyauth stores user objects in a session, and database storage can be enabled in a `findOrCreate` callback using a promise pattern.

Tip   Everyauth has an e-mail and password strategy that can be used instead of the custom-built auth. More information about it can be found in the Everyauth documentation at the GitHub repository (`https://github.com/bnoguchi/ everyauth#password-authentication`).

Each one of the third-party services may be different. You can implement them all yourself. But Everyauth has lots of submodules that implement exactly what OAuth flow each third-party service need. You simply provide credentials to submodules, configure them, and avoid any worries in regards to the details of OAuth flow(s). That's right, you just plug in your app secret and client ID and boom! You are rolling, all dandy like a candy.

Everyauth submodules are specific implementations of authorizations. And boy, open source contributors wrote tons of these submodules (strategies), so developers don't have to reinvent the wheel: password (simple email and password), Facebook, Twitter, Google, LinkedIn, Dropbox, Tumblr, Evernote, GitHub, Instagram, Foursquare, Yahoo!, Justin.tv, Vimeo, Basecamp, AngelList, Dwolla, OpenStreetMap, VKontakte (Russian social network famous for its pirated media), Mail.ru, SoundCloud, MailChimp, Stripe, Salesforce, Box.net, OpenId, LDAP and Windows Azure Access Control Service, and the list goes on and on at `http://bit.ly/2QV2dMM`.

Project: Adding Twitter OAuth 1.0 Sign-in to Blog with Everyauth

A typical OAuth 1.0 flow consists of these three steps (simplified):

1. Users go to a page/route to initiate the OAuth dance. There, our app requests a token via GET/POST requests using the signed app's consumer key and secret. For example, `/auth/twitter` is added automatically by Everyauth.

2. The app uses the token extracted in step 1 and redirects users to the service provider (Twitter) and waits for the callback.

3. The service provider redirects users back to the app, which catches the redirect in the callback route (e.g., `/auth/twitter/callback`). Then, the app extracts the access token, the access token secret, and the user information from the Twitter incoming request body/payload.

However, because we're using Everyauth, we don't need to implement requests for the initiation and the callback routes!

Let's add a Sign in with Twitter button to our project. We need the button itself (image or a link), app key, and secret (obtainable at dev.twitter.com), and then we must augment our authorization route to allow for specific Twitter handlers to be administrated on Blog.

Adding a Sign-in with a Twitter Link

By default, Everyauth uses the `/auth/:service_provider_name` pattern to initiate the three-legged OAuth 1.0 strategy. This, of course, can be customized, but to keep it short and simple (KISS), we can just add this link to `code/ch6/blog-everyauth/views/includes/menu.pug`:

```
li(class=(menu === 'login') ? 'active' : '')
  a(href='/auth/twitter') Sign in with Twitter
```

The whole menu.pug has if/else ternary expressions and looks like this:

```
.menu
  ul.nav.nav-pills
    li(class=(menu === 'index') ? 'active' : '')
      a(href='/') Home
    if (admin)
      li(class=(menu === 'post') ? 'active' : '')
        a(href="/post") Post
      li(class=(menu === 'admin') ? 'active' : '')
        a(href="/admin") Admin
      li
        a(href="/logout") Log out
    else
      li(class=(menu === 'login')? 'active' : '')
        a(href='/login') Log in
      li
        a(href='/auth/twitter') Sign in with Twitter
```

Configuring the Everyauth Twitter Strategy

To add the Everyauth module (everyauth) to Blog, type the following in the terminal:

```
$ npm i everyauth@0.4.9 -SE
```

The configuration of the Everyauth Twitter strategy is implemented in app.js, but in larger apps it's a good idea to abstract these types of strategies into separate files. The most important thing to remember is that Everyauth middleware needs to precede the app.route call.

To procure the Twitter app consumer key and secret, we harness environmental variables via process.env:

```
const TWITTER_CONSUMER_KEY = process.env.TWITTER_CONSUMER_KEY
const TWITTER_CONSUMER_SECRET = process.env.TWITTER_CONSUMER_SECRET
```

To pass these variables, we can use Makefile. In the Makefile, add these lines, substituting ABC and XYZ with your values:

```
start:
    TWITTER_CONSUMER_KEY=ABCABC \
    TWITTER_CONSUMER_SECRET=XYZXYZXYZ \
    node app.js
```

Also, add the `start` command to `.PHONY`:

```
.PHONY: test db start
```

As another option, we can create a bash file start.sh :

```
TWITTER_CONSUMER_KEY=ABCABC \
TWITTER_CONSUMER_SECRET=XYZXYZXYZ \
node app.js
```

Now we go back to the `app.js` file, in which we need to import the Everyauth module:

```
everyauth = require('everyauth')
```

It's a good practice to run the module in debug mode the first few times:

```
everyauth.debug = true
```

Each submodule is enabled using chained commands and promises. To define the previously mentioned key and secret, execute the following:

```
everyauth.twitter
  .consumerKey(TWITTER_CONSUMER_KEY)
  .consumerSecret(TWITTER_CONSUMER_SECRET)
```

Then, to tell the module what to do when Twitter sends back the authorized user object `twitterUserMetadata`, type this chained method with four arguments:

```
  .findOrCreateUser((session,
    accessToken,
    accessTokenSecret,
    twitterUserMetadata) => {
```

We can return the user object right away, but to emulate async writing to a database, let's create a promise

```
const promise = this.Promise()
```

and use the `process.nextTick` call, which is analogous to `setTimeout` `(callback, 0);`, and acts in an asynchronous manner. In a real-world app, you might want to find or save the data to the database:

```
process.nextTick(function(){
```

Change Azat's username to yours:

```
if (twitterUserMetadata.screen_name === 'azat_co') {
```

Store the `user` object in the in-memory session, just like we did in the `/login` route:

```
session.user = twitterUserMetadata
```

Most importantly, set admin flag to `true`:

```
session.admin = true
}
```

Everyauth expects us to fulfill the promise when it's ready:

```
promise.fulfill(twitterUserMetadata)
})
return promise
// return twitterUserMetadata
})
```

After all the steps are done, instruct Everyauth where to redirect the user:

```
.redirectPath('/admin')
```

Everyauth is so smart that it automatically adds a `/logout` route, which means our route (`app.get('/logout', routes.user.logout);`) won't be used. So we need to add some extra logic to the default Everyauth strategy. Otherwise, the session will always keep admin = true. In the `handleLogout` step, we clear our session by calling the exact same method from `user.js`:

```
everyauth.everymodule.handleLogout(routes.user.logout)
```

The next line tells Everyauth how to find a user object based on the `user` argument, but because we stored the whole user object in the session and we don't store user info in `findOrCreate`, we can just return back the same object:

```
everyauth.everymodule.findUserById( (user, callback) => {
  callback(user)
})
```

Last but not least, the line that follows enables Everyauth routes and it must go after cookie and session middleware, but must come before normal routes (e.g., app.get(), app.post()):

```
app.use(everyauth.middleware())
```

The full source code of the `code/ch6/blog-everyauth/app.js` file after adding the Everyauth Twitter OAuth1.0 strategy is rather lengthy, so I won't print it here, but you can find it on GitHub at the book's repository.

To run the app, execute $ `make start`, and **don't forget to replace** the Twitter username, consumer key, and secret with yours. Then when you click on the "Sign in with Twitter" button, you'll be redirected to Twitter to authorize this application. After that you'll be redirected back to the localhost app and should see the admin page menu. We have been authorized by a third-party service provider!

Also, the user information is available to your app so it can be stored in the database for future use. If you already gave permissions, the redirect to and from Twitter might happen very fast. I captured the terminal output in Figure 6-7. The logs show each step of Everyauth process such as getting tokens and sending responses. You can customize each step.

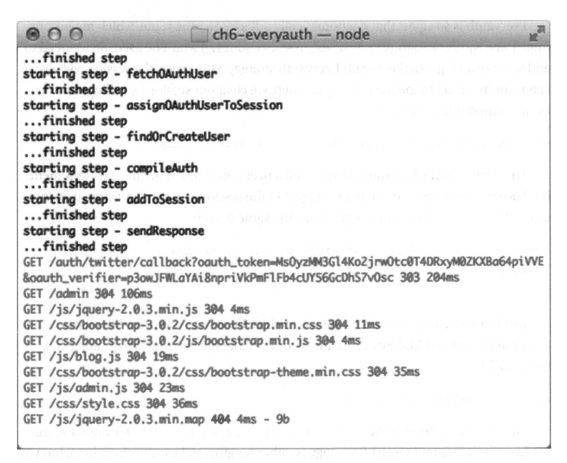

Figure 6-7. *Everyauth Twitter strategy with debug mode in action*

Auths are important. Good job.

Summary

In this chapter, we learned how to implement standard e-mail and password authentication, and used Express.js middleware to protect sensitive pages and endpoints in Blog. Then, we covered OAuth 1.0 and OAuth 2.0 with Everyauth and OAuth modules, respectively.

Now we have a few security options for Blog. In the next chapter, we'll explore Mongoose (`http://mongoosejs.com`), the object-relational mapping object-document mapping (ODM) Node.js library for MongoDB.

The Mongoose library is a good choice for complex systems with a lot of interdependent business logic between entities, because it completely abstracts the database and provides developers with tools to operate with data only via Mongoose objects. The chapter will touch on the main Mongoose classes and methods, explain some of the more advanced concepts, and refactor persistence in Blog.

## CHAPTER 7

Boosting Node.js and MongoDB with Mongoose

I first learned about Mongoose when I worked at Storify. Mongoose is a fully developed object document mapping (ODM) library for Node.js and MongoDB. We used it to simplify business logic in our Node API apps. We had a lot of connections between different database documents and Mongoose models allows us to save all the related logic. Mongoose worked fine except for one extra complex query which I wrote using native driver, not Mongoose.

The disadvantage of Mongoose is that it could make certain queries slower due to a lot of code that Mongoose has to go through. Contrary, the advantages of using ODM are many and go far beyond code organization or the ease of development. Typical ODM is a crucial piece of modern software engineering, especially enterprise engineering.

The main benefit of Mongoose is that it abstracts everything from the database, and the application code interacts only with objects and their methods. ODM also allows specifying relationships between different types of objects and putting business logic (related to those objects) in the classes.

In addition, Mongoose has built-in validation and type casting that can be extended and customized according to needs. When used together with Express.js, Mongoose makes the stack truly adherent to the MVC concept.

Also, Mongoose uses a similar interface to those of Mongo shell, native MongoDB driver, and Mongoskin. Mongoose provides its own methods while making available methods from the native driver. The main Mongoose functions such as `find`, `update`, `insert`, `save`, `remove`, and so on, do what you they say they do. It'll help us to get started with Mongoose faster.

© Azat Mardan 2018
A. Mardan, *Practical Node.js*, https://doi.org/10.1007/978-1-4842-3039-8_7

Buckle up because in this chapter we learn at the following:

- Mongoose installation

- Connection establishment in a standalone Mongoose script

- Mongoose schemas

- Hooks for keeping code organized

- Custom static and instance methods

- Mongoose models

- Relationships and joins with population

- Nested documents

- Virtual fields

- Schema type behavior amendment

- Express.js + Mongoose = true MVC

The source code for this chapter is in the `code/ch7/blog-express` directory of the practical node GitHub repository (`https://github.com/azat-co/practicalnode`).

Mongoose Installation

First, we should install Mongoose with npm. Among many variations, this is one of the ways we can install Mongoose 4.13.0 into an empty folder:

```
$ npm init -y
$ npm i mongoose@4.13.0 -SE
```

DB Connection in a Standalone Mongoose Script

Mongoose can be used as a standalone MongoDB library. To illustrate this, here's a banal script that establishes a connection, creates a Mongoose model definition, instantiates the `practicalNodeBook` object, and then saves it to the database.

Let's create a rather simple `mongoose-example` (that's in the folder in `code/ch7`). To have access to the library, we need to include the mongoose module in our program:

```
const mongoose = require('mongoose')
```

Unlike the Node.js native MongoDB driver, which requires us to write a few lines of code, Mongoose can connect to the database server in one line. Mongoose requests are buffered, so we don't have to wait for the established connection like we do with the native driver, which requires developers to put all the code in the callback of `open()`.

To connect to DB, just call `mongoose.connect()` with at least the `uri` argument (first) or with optional `options` and `callback` (second and third). The uniform resource identifier (URI), a.k.a. a connection string, is the only required parameter. It follows a standard format of:

```
mongodb://username:password@host:port/database_name
```

In our example we use the default values. The host is `localhost`, and the port is 27017. The database name is `test` while there's no password or username:

```
mongoose.connect('mongodb://localhost:27017/test', {useMongoClient:
true})
mongoose.Promise = global.Promise
```

The line with `Promise` makes Mongoose use native ES6 promise implementation. Developers can supply another promise implementation if they want (for example, flow bluebird).

For situations that are more advanced, options and callbacks can be passed to `connect`. The `options` object supports all properties of the native MongoDB driver (`http://bit.ly/2QPFkul`).

Note   It's a common practice in Node.js apps (and Mongoose) to open a database connection once, when the program starts, and then to keep it open until termination. This applies to web apps and servers as well. Ergo, there's no need to open and close connections.

This is easy so far, right? The next step is an important distinction that Mongoose introduces compared with Mongoskin and other lightweight MongoDB libraries. The step creates a model with the `model()` function by passing a string and a schema (more on schemas later). The model is usually stored in a capitalized literal:

```
const Book = mongoose.model('Book', { name: String })
```

Now the configuration phase is over, and we can create a document that represents a particular instance of the model `Book`:

```
const practicalNodeBook = new Book({ name: 'Practical Node.js' })
```

Mongoose documents come with very convenient built-in methods (http://bit.ly/2QVTb23) such as `validate`, `isNew`, `update`, and so on. Just keep in mind that these methods apply to this particular document, not the entire collection or model.

The difference between documents and models is that *a document is an instance of a model*; a model is something abstract. It's like your real MongoDB collection, but it is supported by a schema and is presented as a Node.js class with extra methods and attributes. Collections in Mongoose closely resemble collections in Mongoskin or the native driver. Strictly speaking, models, collections, and documents are different Mongoose classes.

Usually we don't use Mongoose collections directly, and we manipulate data via models only. Some of the main model methods look strikingly familiar to the ones from Mongoskin or native MongoDB driver, such as `find`, `insert()`, `save()`, and so forth.

To finish our small script and make it write a document to the database, let's use one of the document methods— `document.save()`. This method is a document methods that will save the document into the database. The method is asynchronous, which by now you know will require a callback (or a promise or an async/await function). The method's callback has an error-first signature:

```
practicalNodeBook.save((err, results) => {
  if (err) {
    console.error(err)
    process.exit(1)
  } else {
```

```
    console.log('Saved: ', results)
    process.exit(0)
  }
})
```

Here is the full source code for the `mongoose.js` file from the `code/ch7/`
`mongoose-example`, which creates a new document with the property name:

```
const mongoose = require('mongoose')
mongoose.connect('mongodb://localhost:27017/test', {useMongoClient:
true})
mongoose.Promise = global.Promise
const Book = mongoose.model('Book', { name: String })

const practicalNodeBook = new Book({ name: 'Practical Node.js' })
practicalNodeBook.save((err, results) => {
  if (err) {
    console.error(err)
    process.exit(1)
  } else {
    console.log('Saved: ', results)
    process.exit(0)
  }
})
```

To run this snippet, execute the `$ node mongoose.js` command (MongoDB server
must be running in parallel). The results of the script should output the newly created
object with its ObjectId, as seen in Figure 7-1.

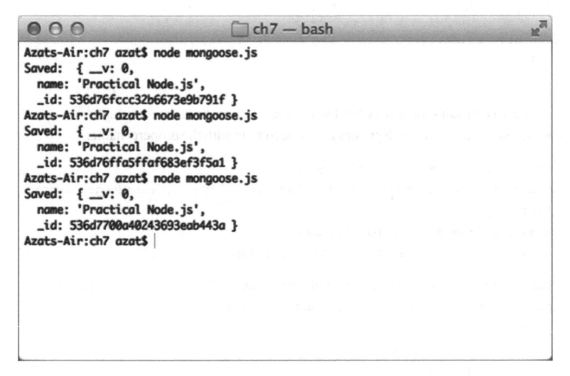

Figure 7-1. *Running a standalone Mongoose script that creates objects*

So far, our schema was very basic. It had only one field `name` with the type String. Next we'll study what other type of fields are supported.

Mongoose Schemas

Schema is a JSON-ish class that has information about properties/field types of a document. It also can store information about validation and default values, and whether a particular property is required. Schemas can contain business logic and other important information. In other words, schemas serve as blueprints for documents.

Schemas include validation and enables more robust adherence to the data structure. This is a major benefit. For example, upon saving a document, Mongoose will ignore fields that are not in the schema. Or as another example, Mongoose will not save a document when fields required in its schema are missing from the document.

To work with Mongoose, developers use documents (it's ODM after all), but Mongoose documents and models require schemas. That's why first developers create schemas to define models, which they in turn use to create documents.

Thus, before we can use models properly, we need to define their schemas, e.g., the book schema with the name property of string type can be defined right in the model as you saw before or by itself with the `Schema` method from `mongoose`. Simply invoke `Schema` with an object and save it in a variable:

```
const bookSchema = mongoose.Schema({
  name: String
})
```

Warning Mongoose ignores those properties that aren't defined in the model's schema but allows the documents to be created, updated, or saved. On the other hand, any violation of a type or omission of a required field will lead to an error and the document NOT being saved, updated, or created.

Mongoose `Schema` supports various types of data. Some of these types are similar to JavaScript and thus Node types, but some are new. These are the Mongoose data types:

- `String`: A standard JavaScript/Node.js string (a sequence of characters) type

- `Number`: A standard JavaScript/Node number type up to 253 (64-bit); larger numbers with mongoose-long `https://www.npmjs.org/package/mongoose-long` and `https://github.com/aheckmann/mongoose-long`

- `Boolean`: A standard JavaScript/Node Boolean type—true or false

- `Buffer`: A Node.js binary type (images, PDFs, archives, and so on)

- `Date`: An ISODate-formatted date type, such as 2014–12–31T12:56:26.009Z

- `Array`: A standard JavaScript/Node array type

- `Schema.Types.ObjectId` A typical, MongoDB 24-character hex string of a 12-byte binary number (e.g., 52dafa354bd71b30fa12c441)

- `Schema.Types.Mixed`: Any type of data (i.e., flexible free type)

Warning   Mongoose does not listen to mixed-type object changes, so call `markModified()` before saving the object to make sure changes in the mixed-type field are persistent.

`ObjectId` is added automatically as a primary `_id` key if omitted in the `insert()` or `save()` methods; `_id` key can be used to sort documents chronologically (`http://bit.ly/2LfpcTu`). They are available through `Schema.Types` or `mongoose.Schema.Types`, e.g., `Schema.Types.Mixed`.

We have a great deal of flexibility in defining our document schemas—for example, here's a schema with strings, dates, buffers, objects (mixed type), and ObjectIds. Moreover, you can set the default values right there in the schema. Default values simplify development because they allow to omit values. How? Default values will be used when no values are provided.

But that's not all. We can define a function as a default value too. This is a dynamic way to set the value. Finally, using `[]` means the fields, value will be an array with each individual item of that array having the type specified in the square braces `[]`. For example, `contributors` is an array of ObjectIds (referring to the collection of contributors).

```
const ObjectId = mongoose.Schema.Types.ObjectId
const Mixed = mongoose.Schema.Types.Mixed

const bookSchema = mongoose.Schema({
  name: String,
  created_at: Date,
  updated_at: {
    type: Date,
    default: Date.now // Current timestamp
  },
  published: Boolean,
  authorId: {
    type: ObjectId,
    required: true // Require field
  },
```

```
description: {
  type: String,
  default: null
},
active: {
  type: Boolean,
  default: false
},
keywords: { // Array of strings
  type: [String],
  default: []
},
description: {
  body: String,
  image: Buffer // Binary or string data
},
version: {
  type: Number,
  default: () => { // Dynamic value
    return 1
  }
},
notes: Mixed,
contributors: [ObjectId]
})
```

It's possible to create and use custom types that already have the rules for the ubiquitous email and URL types, e.g., there's a module mongoose-types (`https://github.com/bnoguchi/mongoose-types`).

Mongoose schemas are *pluggable*, which means, by creating a plugin, certain functionality can be extended across all schemas of the application.

For better code organization and code reuse, in the schema, we can set up static and instance methods, apply plugins, and define hooks.

> **Tip** For validation in Node.js in addition to Mongoose and before it, consider using the `validator.js` and `express-validator` modules.

Hooks for Keeping Code Organized

In a complex application with a lot of interrelated objects, we might want to execute certain logic before saving an object. Hooks are a good place to store such logic. For example, we might want to upload a PDF to the web site before saving a book document:

```
bookSchema.pre('save', (next) => {
  // Prepare for saving
  // Upload PDF
  return next()
})
```

On the other hand, before removing, we need to make sure there are no pending purchase orders for this book:

```
bookSchema.pre('remove', (next) => {
  // Prepare for removing
  return next(e) // e is an instance of Error or null
})
```

Developers can set up pre and post hooks on save, remove, and validate as well as on custom methods.

Custom Static and Instance Methods

In addition to dozens of built-in Mongoose model methods, we can add custom ones. For example, to initiate a purchase, we can call the `buy` method on the document `practicalNodeBook` after we implement the custom instance method `buy()`:

```
bookSchema.method({ // Instance methods
  buy: function (quantity, customer, callback) {
    const bookToPurchase = this // Exact book with id, title, etc.
```

```
    // Create a purchase order and invoice customer
    // Any document/instance method like save, valid, etc.
    will work on "this"
    return callback(results)
  },
  refund: function (customer, callback) {
    // Process the refund
    return callback(results)
  }
})
```

The custom instance methods are better to use instead of re-implementing the same logic over and over again.

On the other hand, there are static methods. Static methods are useful when we either don't have a particular document object or we don't need it. For example, we don't need a particular book ID to run a report to get how much books have 0 inventory in the warehouse or to get how many books of a particular kind we have in the store:

```
bookSchema.static({ // Static methods for generic, not instance/
document specific logic
  getZeroInventoryReport: function(callback) {
    // Run a query on all books and get the ones with zero inventory
    // Document/instance methods would not work on "this"
    return callback(books)
  },
  getCountOfBooksById: function(bookId, callback){
    // Run a query and get the number of books left for a given book
    // Document/instance methods would not work on "this"
    return callback(count)
  }
})
```

Note   Hooks and methods must be added to the schemas before compiling them to models—in other words, before calling the `mongoose.model()` method.

Mongoose Models

As in many other ORMs/ODMs, in Mongoose, the cornerstone object is a model. To compile a schema into a model, use `mongoose.model(name, schema)`. For example, to create a book model from `bookSchema`, use `mongoose.model`:

```
const Book = mongoose.model('Book', bookSchema)
```

The first parameter is just a string, which we can use later to pull an instance of this model. Usually, this string is the same as the object literal for the model. It's usually capitalized, e.g., `Book`. By default, Mongoose will use the model name to tie it to a collection name by pluralizing it. For example, the `Book` model will use `books` collection.

Models are used to create documents (actual data). To do so, call `new ModelName(data)`—for example, this is how to create two documents for two different books using one `Book` model:

```
const practicalNodeBook = new Book({ name: 'Practical Node.js' })
const javascriptTheGoodPartsBook = new Book({ name: "JavaScript The
Good Parts"})
```

It's better to assign the initial value through the constructor `new Book()` versus using the `document.set()` method later, because Mongoose has to process fewer function calls and our code remains more compact and better organized. Of course, this is possible only if we know the values when we create the instances. ;-)

Don't confuse static with instance model methods. If we call a method on `practicalNodeBook`, it's an instance method; if we call it on the `Book` object, it's a static class method.

Models have static built-in methods that are very similar to Mongoskin and native MongoDB methods, such as `find()`, `create()`, and `update()`.

A list of the static Mongoose model methods (invoked on a capitalized object, e.g., `Book`) along with their meaning, follows:

- `Model.create(data, [callback (error, doc)])`: Creates a new Mongoose document and saves it to the database

- `Model.remove(query, [callback(error)])`: Removes documents from the collection that match the query; when finished, calls `callback` with `error`

- `Model.find(query, [fields], [options], [callback(error, docs)])`: Finds documents that match the query (as a JSON object); possible to select fields (`http://mongoosejs.com/docs/api.html#query_Query-select`) and use options (`http://bit.ly/2QUNBNx`)

- `Model.update(query, update, [options], [callback(error, affectedCount, raw)])`: Updates documents, similar to native `update`

- `Model.populate(docs, options, [callback(error, doc)])`: Populates documents using references to other collections; an alternative to another approach described in the next section

- `Model.findOne(query, [fields], [options], [callback(error, doc)])`: Finds the first document that matches the query

- `Model.findById(id, [fields], [options], [callback(error, doc)])`: Finds the first element for which `_id` equals the `id` argument (cast based on the schema)

- `Model.findOneAndUpdate([query], [update], [options], [callback(error, doc)])`: Finds the first document that matches the query (if present) and updates it, returning the document; uses `findAndModify` (`http://bit.ly/2QW1zP1`)

- `Model.findOneAndRemove(query, [options], [callback(error, doc)])`: Finds the first document that matches the query and removes it when returning the document

- `Model.findByIdAndUpdate(id, [update], [options], [callback(error, doc)])`: Similar to `findOneAndUpdate` using only the ID

- `Model.findByIdAndRemove(id, [options], [callback(error, doc)])`: Similar to `findOneAndRemove` using only the ID

Warning   Not all the Mongoose model methods trigger hooks. Some of them are executed directly. For example, calling `Model.remove()` does not trigger the `remove` hook, because no Mongoose documents are involved (instances of `Model` that use lowercase literals, e.g., `practicalNodeBook`).

The complete list of the methods is extensive; therefore, refer to the official Mongoose API documentation (`http://mongoosejs.com/docs/api.html#model-js`). The most used instance (document) methods are as follows:

- `doc.model(name)`: Returns another Mongoose model

- `doc.remove([callback(error, doc)])`: Removes this document

- `doc.save([callback(error, doc, affectedCount)])`: Saves this document

- `doc.update(doc, [options], [callback(error, affectedCount, raw)])`: Updates the document with `doc` properties, and `options` parameters, and then upon completion fires a callback with `error`, number of `affectedCount`, and the database output

- `doc.toJSON([option])`: Converts a Mongoose document to JSON (options are listed later)

- `doc.toObject([option])`: Converts a Mongoose document to a plain JavaScript object (options are listed later)

- `isModified([path])`: True/false, respectively, if some parts (or the specific path) of the document are or are not modified

- `markModified(path)`: Marks a path manually as modified, which is useful for mixed (`Schema.Types.Mixed`) data types because they don't trigger the modified flag automatically

- `doc.isNew`: True/false, respectively, whether the document is new or not new

- `doc.id`: Returns the document ID

- `doc.set(path, value, [type], [options])`: Sets `value` at a path

- `doc.validate(callback(error))`: Checks validation manually (triggered automatically before `save()`)

Most often, you'll need to get data from your document, e.g., to send back to a client using `res.send()`. But the document object will have some additional Mongoose properties and methods. The two methods listed above will help you to get just the data. They are `toObject()` and `toJSON()`. They take options, listed for `toObject()` and `toJSON()` are as follows:

- `getters`: True/false, calls all `getters` including path and virtual types

- `virtuals`: True/false, includes virtual `getters` and can override the `getters` option

- `minimize`: True/false, removes empty properties/objects (defaults to true)

- `transform`: Transforms the function called right before returning the object

That's it for Mongoose methods for the most part. Of course, Mongoose has other methods for more edge case scenarios and advanced uses. You can learn about them by opening this Mongoose document API link: `http://mongoosejs.com/docs/api.html#document-js`.

Relationships and Joins with Population

Although, Node developers cannot query MongoDB on complex relationships (like they can in MySQL), they can do so in the application layer with the help of Mongoose. This becomes really convenient in larger applications because they tend to have complex relationships between documents.

To give you an example, in an e-commerce store, an order refers to its products by IDs. To get more than just product ID, developers need to write two queries: one to fetch order and another to fetch its products. Instead of making two queries developers can one Mongoose query. They can use Mongoose to fetch order with products fields.

Mongoose makes connecting two entities by their relationship easier. Mongoose provides a feature called *population*. No. This population is not about people living in a certain area but it somehow related. Mongoose population is about adding more data to your query using relationships. It allows us to fill certain parts of the document from a different collection.

Let's say we have `posts` and `users` documents. Users can write posts. There are two approaches to implement this. We can use one collection. The `users` collection can have the `posts` array field. This will require a single query, but this structure is limited in many ways because posts cannot be indexed or accessed separately from users.

Or we can use two collections (and models). In this case, the structure is more flexible but requires at least two queries if we want to fetch a user and his posts.

Don't fret. Mongoose is here to help. We can reference posts in the user schema and then populate the posts. In order to use `populate()`, we must define `ref` and the name of the model such as in the posts field of `userSchema`:

```
const mongoose = require('mongoose')
const Schema = mongoose.Schema

const userSchema = Schema({
  _id: Number,
  name: String,
  posts: [{
    type: Schema.Types.ObjectId,
    ref: 'Post'
  }]
})
```

The actual `postSchema` does not have any mentions about the user model. It just has some string fields:

```
const postSchema = Schema({
  _creator: { type: Number, ref: 'User' },
  title: String,
  text: String
})
```

The next few lines are where we create models, and then bang! We can pull posts data with a single query, not two as we would have done without referencing and without `populate()`. Here's how to construct the query and then call `exec()` to run it:

```
const Post = mongoose.model('Post', postSchema)
const User = mongoose.model('User', userSchema)

User.findOne({ name: /azat/i })
  .populate('posts')
  .exec((err, user) => {
    if (err) return handleError(err) // Defined elsewhere
    console.log('The user has % post(s)', user.posts.length)
  })
```

Note   `ObjectId`, `Number`, `String`, and `Buffer` are valid data types to use as references, meaning they will work as *foreign keys* in the relational DB terminology.

In the previous query, we used a regular expression (RegExp) `/azat/i`, which means "Find me all the names matching the string `azat` case-insensitively". This feature is not exclusive to Mongoose. In fact, the native driver and its other wrappers, along with the `mongo` console, all support RegExps. The syntax is the same as in normal JavaScript/Node.js RegExp patterns. Therefore, in a way, we perform a join query on our `Post` and `User` models.

Okay. It's possible to return only a portion of populated results. For example, we can limit the number of posts to the first ten (10) only:

```
.populate({
  path: 'posts',
  options: { limit: 10, sort: 'title' }
})
```

Sometimes it's more practical to return only certain fields instead of the full document. This can be done with `select`:

```
.populate({
    path: 'posts',
    select: 'title',
```

```
    options: {
      limit: 10,
      sort: 'title'
    }
  })
```

In addition, Mongoose can filter the populated results by a query! For example, we can apply RegExp for "node.js" to the text (a `match` query property):

```
.populate({
  path: 'posts',
  select: '_id title text',
  match: {text: /node\.js/i},
  options: {
    limit: 10,
    sort: '_id'
  }
})
```

The query selects properties using `select` by the field names of `_id`, `title`, `text`. You see, queries can be as customized as you want them to be! The best practice is to query and populate only the required fields because this avoids potential leakage of sensitive information and reduces overhead on the system.

The `populate` method also works on multiple document queries. For example, we can use `find` instead of findOne:

```
User.find({}, {
    limit: 10,
    sort: { _id: -1}})
  .populate('posts')
  .exec((err, user) => {
    if (err) return handleError(err)
    console.log('The user has % post(s)', user.posts.length)
  })
```

> **Tip**   For custom sorting, we can add properties using `name: -1` or `name: 1` patterns and can pass the resulting object to the `sort` option. Again, this is a standard MongoDB interface and is not exclusive to Mongoose.

Nested Documents

In the previous section, we saw how to populate a query on one collection with the data from another collection. That's a more traditional approach to designing your database in the sense that it mimics relational database design with its normal forms and strict atomization of data.

The document storage model in NoSQL databases is well suited to use nested documents. This is better when you know what queries are run most frequently. You can optimize your database to make it be biased to a certain query. For example, if we know that the most typical use case is to read user profiles, then instead of having two collections— `posts` and `users` —we can have a single collection (`users`), with each item of that collection having `posts`.

The decision whether to use separate collections or nested documents is more of an architectural question, and its answer depends on usage. For example, if posts are used only in the context of users (their authors)—say, on the users' profile pages—then it's best to use nested documents. However, if the blog features multiple users' posts that need to be queried independently of their (posts) user context, then separate collections fit better.

To implement nested documents, we can use the type `Schema.Types.Mixed` in Mongoose schemas (`Schema`, e.g., `bookSchema` or `postSchema`) or we can create a new schema for the nested document. An example of the former approach is as follows:

```
const userSchema = new mongoose.Schema({
  name: String,
  posts: [mongoose.Schema.Types.Mixed]
})
// Attach methods, hooks, etc.
const User = mongoose.model('User', userSchema)
```

However, the latter approach of using a distinct new subschema is more flexible and powerful. Take a look at the next example in which we define two schemas and then one is used in an array field of another schema. This approach is better for code reuse because it lets you to use the nested schema elsewhere, maybe in several more schemas.

Here I nested `postSchema` in an array field of `userSchema`, because users can have posts, and querying by users is the most typical use case for this app:

```
const postSchema = new mongoose.Schema({
  title: String,
  text: String
})
// Attach methods, hooks, etc., to post schema
const userSchema = new mongoose.Schema({
  name: String,
  posts: [postSchema]
})
// Attach methods, hooks, etc., to user schema
const User = mongoose.model('User', userSchema)
```

To create a new user document or to save a post to an existing user when working with a nested posts document, treat the `posts` property as an array and just use the `push` method from the JavaScript/Node.js API, or use the MongoDB `$push` operand (`http://bit.ly/2QVBTCf`).

For example, we can use MongoDB's `$push` in the `update()` query to add a post (`newPost`) to a user object, which is found by a matching ID (`_id` is `userId`):

```
User.update(
  {_id: userId},
  {$push: {posts: newPost}},
  function (error, results) {
    // Handle error and check results
})
```

Fields can be like ghosts. Sometimes you see 'em, other times you don't. Let's study yet another Mongoose feature—virtual fields.

Virtual Fields

Virtual fields (or virtuals) are fields that don't exist in the database, but act just like regular fields in a Mongoose document when accessed in a document. To oversimplify, virtual fields are mock or fake fields that pretend to act like and be normal ones.

Virtual fields are awesome for dynamic data or creating aggregate fields. For example, if our system requires to have first name, last name, and the full name (which is just a concatenation of the first two names)—there's no need to store the full name values in addition to the first and last name values! All we need to do is concatenate the first and last name in a full-name virtual field.

Another use case is to make the database backward compatible. That's how I avoided writing and running database migrations at Storify. Every time there was a new DB schema, I just added a virtual to support old documents.

For example, we might have thousands of user items in a MongoDB collection, and we want to start collecting their locations. We have two options: run a migration script to add the default location ("none") to the thousands of old user documents or use a virtual field and apply defaults at runtime!

To define a virtual we need to do two things:

1. Call the `virtual(name)` method to create a virtual type (Mongoose API) (`http://mongoosejs.com/docs/api.html#document-js`).

2. Apply a getter function with `get(fn)` (Mongoose API) (`http://bit.ly/2QV1I5q`).

As an example, let's build a Gravatar link generator to pull images from Gravatar. (`http://en.gravatar.com` is a service that hosts profile images, a.k.a., avatars, to be used universally by various websites.)

A Gravatar URL is always an md5 hash of the user's email: (`http://en.gravatar.com/site/implement/hash`). This allows us to construct a Gravatar link for any user by his/her email. Therefore, we can get the virtual value (`gravatarUrl`) on the fly by hashing instead of storing the value (less overhead!).

In this example, I intentionally made the input email mixed cased and with a trailing space, and then applied core Node module `crypto` for the md5 hashing:

```
const crypto = require('crypto')

Identity.virtual('gravatarUrl')
  .get(function() { // Not fatty catty ()=>{}
    if (!this.email) return null // "this" is an instance/document
    let email = this.email // For example: email = "HI@azat.co "
    email = email.trim().toLowerCase()
    const hash = crypto
      .createHash('md5')
      .update(email)
      .digest('hex')
    const gravatarBaseUrl = 'https://secure.gravatar.com/avatar/'
    return gravatarBaseUrl + hash
})
```

Or the case mentioned earlier, getting a full name out of first and last, is implemented by concatenating the names into one string, as follows:

```
userSchema.virtual('fullName')
  .get(function() {
    // "this" is an instance/document
    return `${this.firstName} ${this.lastName}`
})
```

Another example is when only a subset of the full document *must* be exposed and not the full details, as in the user model, which has tokens and passwords. Thus we omit fields that we want to hide by whitelisting only the fields we want to expose, such as username and avatar, but not token, password, or salt:

```
userSchema.virtual('info')
  .get(function() {
    return {
      service: this.service,
      username: this.username,
```

```
    name: this.name,
    date: this.date,
    url: this.url,
    avatar: this.avatar
  }
})
```

We used `get` for the virtual. Let's dig deeper into the getter, as well as it's close kin setter.

Schema Type Behavior Amendment

Schemas are not just static boring type definitions. Developers can add functions to bring the dynamism to the fields in the schema. Mongoose allows us to define/write getters (`get`), setters (`set`), and defaults (`default`) right in the Schema! Same goes for validate and some other useful methods.

`get` is invoked when a field is read, while `set` when the field is assigned a value. Developers can modify the actual value being read or assigned from/to the actual database document. For example, the URL field can have a `set()` method that enforces all strings into lowercase. Validate is triggered for the field validation and is typically used for some custom types such as emails.

Mongoose offers four methods: `set()`, `get()`, `default()` and `validate()`. They do what you think they do. Here are examples of defining methods and their purpose

- `set()`: To transform a string to a lower case when the value is assigned

- `get()`: To add a "thousands" comma to a number when the number is extracted/accessed

- `default()`: To generate a new ObjectId,

- `validate()`: To check for email patterns; is triggered upon `save()`

We can define the aforementioned four methods all right there, in the fields of the JSON-like Mongoose `Schema` on the same level as `type`:

```
postSchema = new mongoose.Schema({
  slug: {
    type: String,
    set: function(slug) {
      return slug.toLowerCase()
    }
  },
  numberOfLikes: {
    type: Number,
    get: function(value) {
      return value.toString().replace(/\B(?=(\d{3})+
      (?!\d))/g, ",")
    }
  },
  posted_at: {
    type: String,
    get: function(value) {
      if (!value) return null;
      return value.toUTCString()
    }
  },
  authorId: {
    type: ObjectId,
    default: function() {
      return new mongoose.Types.ObjectId()
    }
  },
  email: {
    type: String,
    unique: true,
    validate: [
      function(email) {
        return (email.match(/[a-z0-9!#$%&'*+\/=?^_`{|}~-]+(?:\.
        [a-z0-9!#$%&'*+\/=?^_`{|}~-]+)*@(?:[a-z0-9](?:[a-z0-9-]*
        [a-z0-9])?\.)+[a-z0-9](?:[a-z0-9-]*[a-z0-9])?/i) != null)},
      'Invalid email'
```

```
        ]
    }
})
```

If defining custom methods in the `Schema` definition is not an option for some reason (maybe our system requires us to do it dynamically), Mongoose offers another approach to amending `Schema` behavior—chained methods, which require two steps:

1. Use `Schema.path(name)` to get `SchemaType` (official docs) (`http://bit.ly/2R0ZBNE`).

2. Use `SchemaType.get(fn)` to set the getter method (official docs) (`http://bit.ly/2QVDyaX`).

For example, we can create a getter method for the `numberOfPosts` field not in the Schema definition, but after `userSchema` is created:

```
userSchema
  .path('numberOfPosts')
  .get(function() {
    return this.posts.length
  })
```

In Mongoose, *path* is just a fancy name for the nested field name and its parent objects. For example, if we have ZIP code (`zip`) as a child of `contact.address`, such as `user.contact.address.zip`, then the `contact.address.zip` is a path.

Express.js + Mongoose = True MVC

To avoid rebuilding all other components unrelated to ODM, such as templates, routes, and so forth, we can factor the existing Blog from the previous chapter by making it use Mongoose instead of Mongoskin. This requires minimal effort but produces an abstraction layer between MongoDB and the request handlers. As always, the fully functional code is available on GitHub, in the `ch7` folder. (`https://github.com/azat-co/practicalnode/tree/master/ch7`).

The process of refactoring starts with the creation of a new branch: `mongoose`. You can use the final solution in the GitHub repository. (`https://github.com/azat-co/blog-express/tree/mongoose`). First, we need to remove Mongoskin and install Mongoose:

```
$ npm uninstall mongoskin -save
$ npm install mongoose@4.13.0 --save
```

`package.json` is amended to include `mongoose` and looks similar to this:

```
{
  "name": "blog-mongoose",
  "version": "1.0.1",
  "private": true,
  "scripts": {
    "start": "make start",
    "seed": "sh ./seed.sh",
    "test": "make test",
    "st": "standard app.js && standard tests/index.js && standard
    routes/*"
  },
  "author": "Azat Mardan (http://azat.co/)",
  "license": "MIT",
  "dependencies": {
    "body-parser": "1.18.2",
    "cookie-parser": "1.4.3",
    "errorhandler": "1.5.0",
    "everyauth": "0.4.9",
    "express": "4.16.2",
    "express-session": "1.15.6",
    "method-override": "2.3.10",
    "mongoose": "4.13.0",
    "morgan": "1.9.0",
    "pug": "2.0.0-rc.4",
    "serve-favicon": "2.4.5",
    "stylus": "0.54.5"
  },
```

```
"devDependencies": {
  "expect.js": "0.3.1",
  "mocha": "4.0.1",
  "standard": "10.0.3",
  "superagent": "3.8.0"
 }
}
```

Now, in the `app.js` file, we can remove the Mongoskin inclusion (`mongoskin = require('mongoskin'),`) and add a new import statement for Mongoose:

```
const mongoose = require('mongoose')
```

Mongoose uses models, but Mongoskin does not. So let's create a folder `models` in our project folder (use bash: `$ mkdir models`) and include the folder with (it really includes `index.js`, which we have yet to create):

```
const models = require('./models')
```

Substitute the Mongoskin `db`, and `articles` and `users` `db.collection()` statements shown next:

```
const db = mongoskin.db(dbUrl, {safe: true})
const collections = {
  articles: db.collection('articles'),
  users: db.collection('users')
}
```

with just the Mongoose connection statement, **leaving out** the `collections` object entirely because in Mongoose we'll be working with models not collections directly:

```
const db = mongoose.connect(dbUrl, {useMongoClient: true})
```

In the collection middleware, we remove if/else and `req.collections` lines inside the `app.use()`:

```
app.use((req, res, next) => {
  if (!collections.articles || ! collections.users)
  // <--- REMOVE
```

```
  return next(new Error('No collections.'))
    // <--- UPDATE
  req.collections = collections // <--- REMOVE
})
```

Then, add the if/else validation for `Article` and `User` models (coming from `models/article.js` and models/user.js), and the models in the request with the req. models = models statement:

```
app.use((req, res, next) => {
  if (!models.Article || !models.User) { // <--- ADD
    return next(new Error('No models.')) // <--- UPDATE
  }
  req.models = models // <--- ADD
  return next()
})
```

That's it! The upgrade from Mongoskin to Mongoose is complete. For your reference, the full code of the resulting app.js is in the `code/ch7/blog-mongoose/app.js.`

Next, let's implement the schemas. In the `Article` schema, `title` is required and it's limited to 120 characters with `validate`. The `published` defaults to `false` if not specified upon object creation. The slug should never have spaces due to the `set` method.

To illustrate code reuse, we abstract the `find` method from the routes (`routes/article.js`) into the model (`models/article.js`). This can be done with all database methods:

```
articleSchema.static({
  list: function (callback) {
    this.find({}, null, {sort: {_id: -1}}, callback)
  }
})
```

Then, we compile the schema and methods into a model:

```
module.exports = mongoose.model('Article', articleSchema)
```

The full source code of `article.js` with schema and a static method is as follows:

```
const mongoose = require('mongoose')

const articleSchema = new mongoose.Schema({
  title: {
    type: String,
    required: true,
    validate: [function (value) {
      return value.length <= 120
    }, 'Title is too long (120 max)'],
    default: 'New Post'
  },
  text: String,
  published: {
    type: Boolean,
    default: false
  },
  slug: {
    type: String,
    set: function (value) {
      return value.toLowerCase().replace(' ', '-')
    }
  }
})

articleSchema.static({
  list: function (callback) {
    this.find({}, null, {sort: {_id: -1}}, callback)
  }
})

module.exports = mongoose.model('Article', articleSchema)
```

The `models/user.js` file also begins with an inclusion and a schema:

```
const mongoose = require('mongoose')

const userSchema = new mongoose.Schema({
  email: {
    type: String,
    required: true,
    set: function (value) {
      return value.trim().toLowerCase()
    },
    validate: [
      function (email) {
        return (email.match(/[a-z0-9!#$%&'*+\/=?^_`{|}~-]+(?:\.
        [a-z0-9!#$%&'*+\/=?^_`{|}~-]+)*@(?:[a-z0-9](?:[a-z0-9-]*[a-
        z0-9])?\.)+[a-z0-9](?:[a-z0-9-]*[a-z0-9])?/i) != null)
      },
      'Invalid email'
    ]
  },
  password: String,
  admin: {
    type: Boolean,
    default: false
  }
})

module.exports = mongoose.model('User', userSchema)
```

The `email` field is validated with RegExp, and is then is trimmed and forced to lowercase when it's set.

To connect `app.js` and models, there must be a `models/index.js` file that simply acts as a layer of abstraction by importing and exporting all the models:

```
exports.Article = require('./article')
exports.User = require('./user')
```

We have `models/index.js` so that we don't need to import all schemas individually in our `app.js` and other files (potentially).

Now we modify the routes files. The `routes/article.js` file now needs to switch to Mongoose models instead of Mongoskin collections. So, in the `show` method, this Mongoskin line goes away:

```
req.collections.articles.findOne({slug: req.params.slug},
  (error, article) => {
```

Then this Mongoose line comes in to use the `Article` model from `req.models`:

```
req.models.Article.findOne({slug: req.params.slug},
  (error, article) => {
```

The resulting `show` uses the Mongoose method `findOne()` from `Article` model and has `slug` presence validation before that:

```
exports.show = (req, res, next) => {
  if (!req.params.slug) return next(new Error('No article slug.'))
  req.models.Article.findOne({slug: req.params.slug}, (error,
  article) => {
    if (error) return next(error)
    if (!article.published && !req.session.admin) return res.
    status(401).send()
    res.render('article', article)
  })
}
```

In the `list` method, remove the Mongoskin code show next, since we are not working with collections directly anymore:

```
req.collections.articles.find({}).toArray((error, articles) => {
```

and replace it with Mongoose model code of `Article.list()`:

```
req.models.Article.list((error, articles) => {
```

to get the request handler that resembles this:

```
exports.list = (req, res, next) => {
  req.models.Article.list((error, articles) => {
```

```
    if (error) return next(error)
    res.send({articles: articles})
  })
}
```

Next, in the `exports.add` method, find this line of Mongoskin code:

```
req.collections.articles.insert(
  article,
  (error, articleResponse) => {
```

is replaced with this Mongoose code that uses the `Article` model instead of a collection:

```
req.models.Article.create(article, (error, articleResponse) => {
```

The `exports.edit` method is trickier, and there are a few possible solutions:

1. Find a Mongoose document (e.g., `findById()`) and use document methods (e.g., `update()`).

2. Use the static model method `findByIdAndUpdate()`.

In both cases, this Mongoskin piece of code goes away:

```
req.collections.articles.updateById(
  req.params.id,
  {$set: req.body.article},
  (error, count) => {
```

Although there's `update()` in Mongoose as well, we'll use another, better approach with `save()`, because `save()` executes all the schema logic such as pre and post hooks, and proper schema validation. It's smarter than the direct `update()`. `save()` is the special sauce that Mongoose brings to the table, and it's a pity not to harness its power. So the preceding Mongoskin snippet with `updateById()` is replaced by this code with Mongoose's `set()` and `save()`:

```
exports.edit = (req, res, next) => {
  if (!req.params.id) return next(new Error('No article ID.'))
  if (!req.body.article) return next(new Error('No article
  payload.'))
  req.models.Article.findById(req.params.id, (error, article) => {
```

```
    if (error) return next(error)
    article.set(req.body.article)
    article.save((error, savedDoc) => {
      if (error) return next(error)
      res.send(savedDoc)
    })
  })
}
```

Just to show you a more elegant one-step approach that uses one method
`findByIdAndUpdate()` (the latter from the new exports.edit implementation shown
earlier):

```
req.models.Article.findByIdAndUpdate(
  req.params.id,
  {$set: req.body.article},
  (error, doc) => {
    if (error) return next(error)
    res.send(doc)
  }
)
```

Lastly, in the `exports.del` request handler, we will find the document by its ID and
then invoke `remove()`:

```
exports.del = (req, res, next) => {
  if (!req.params.id) return next(new Error('No article ID.'))
  req.models.Article.findById(req.params.id, (error, article) => {
    if (error) return next(error)
    if (!article) return next(new Error('Article not found'))
    article.remove((error, doc) => {
      if (error) return next(error)
      res.send(doc)
    })
  })
```

The `exports.postArticle` and `exports.admin` functions look like these (the functions' bodies are the same as when we used Mongoskin):

```
req.models.Article.create(article, (error, articleResponse) => {
  // ...
})
req.models.Article.list((error, articles) => {
  // ...
})
```

Again, that's all we have to do to switch to Mongoose for this route. However, to make sure there's nothing missing, here's the full code of the `routes/article.js` file:

```
exports.show = (req, res, next) => {
  if (!req.params.slug) return next(new Error('No article slug.'))
  req.models.Article.findOne({slug: req.params.slug}, (error,
  article) => {
  if (error) return next(error)
  if (!article.published && !req.session.admin) return res.
  status(401).send()
  res.render('article', article)
  })
}

exports.list = (req, res, next) => {
  req.models.Article.list((error, articles) => {
    if (error) return next(error)
    res.send({articles: articles})
  })
}

exports.add = (req, res, next) => {
  if (!req.body.article) return next(new Error('No article
  payload.'))
  var article = req.body.article
  article.published = false
  req.models.Article.create(article, (error, articleResponse) => {
```

```
    if (error) return next(error)
    res.send(articleResponse)
  })
}

exports.edit = (req, res, next) => {
  if (!req.params.id) return next(new Error('No article ID.'))
  if (!req.body.article) return next(new Error('No article
  payload.'))
  req.models.Article.findById(req.params.id, (error, article) => {
    if (error) return next(error)
    article.set(req.body.article)
    article.save((error, savedDoc) => {
      if (error) return next(error)
      res.send(savedDoc)
    })
  })
}

exports.del = (req, res, next) => {
  if (!req.params.id) return next(new Error('No article ID.'))
  req.models.Article.findById(req.params.id, (error, article) => {
    if (error) return next(error)
    if (!article) return next(new Error('Article not found.'))
    article.remove((error, doc) => {
      if (error) return next(error)
      res.send(doc)
    })
  })
}

exports.post = (req, res, next) => {
  if (!req.body.title) { res.render('post') }
}
```

```
exports.postArticle = (req, res, next) => {
  if (!req.body.title || !req.body.slug || !req.body.text) {
    return res.render('post', {error: 'Fill title, slug and text.'})
  }
  var article = {
    title: req.body.title,
    slug: req.body.slug,
    text: req.body.text,
    published: false
  }
  req.models.Article.create(article, (error, articleResponse) => {
    if (error) return next(error)
    res.render('post', {error: 'Article was added. Publish it on
    Admin page.'})
  })
}

exports.admin = (req, res, next) => {
  req.models.Article.list((error, articles) => {
    if (error) return next(error)
    res.render('admin', {articles: articles})
  })
}
```

The `routes/index.js` file, which serves the home page, is as follows:

```
exports.article = require('./article')
exports.user = require('./user')

exports.index = (req, res, next) => {
  req.models.Article.find(
    {published: true},
    null,
    {sort: {_id: -1}},
    (error, articles) => {
      if (error) return next(error)
```

```
      res.render('index', {articles: articles})
    }
  )
}
```

Finally, `routes/user.js` has a single line (JUST ONE LINE) to change in `authenticate`. Do this! Invoke `findOne()` from the `req.models.User` model to fetch the user with username and password (plain). This will check the user validity:

```
exports.authenticate = (req, res, next) => {
  if (!req.body.email || !req.body.password) {
    return res.render('login', {error: 'Please enter your email and
    password.'})
  }
  req.models.User.findOne({
    email: req.body.email,
    password: req.body.password
  }, function (error, user) {
    if (error) return next(error)
    if (!user) return res.render('login', {error: 'Incorrect
    email&password combination.'})
    req.session.user = user
    req.session.admin = user.admin
    res.redirect('/admin')
  })
}
```

Of course, in real life you would not store plain passwords but use encrypted hash and salt. In other words, store salt and hash but never the plain password to prevent attackers stealing the plain passwords, which they can and will use on other websites. Most people can't remember more than 2–3 passwords, so they keep using the same ones everywhere. Gosh, they should download a password manager like Keepass, Padlock, enpass or something similar, to store unique 50-character passwords and randomly generated answers to silly questions like "What was the name of your first pet?".

To check if everything went well, simply run Blog as usual with $ `node app` and navigate the pages on http://localhost:3000/. In addition, we can run Mocha tests with $ `npm test` (which triggers a `make` command, which in turn triggers the `mocha` command).

Summary

In this chapter, we learned what Mongoose is, how to install it, how to establish a connection to the database, and how to create Mongoose schemas while keeping the code organized with hooks and methods. We also compiled schemas into models and populated references automatically, and used virtual fields and custom schema type properties. And we refactored Blog to use Mongoose and made our app gain a true MVC architecture.

Next, we'll cover how to build REST APIs with the two Node.js frameworks: Express. js and Hapi. This is an important topic, because more and more web development is shifting toward heavy front-end logic and thin backend. Some systems even go as far as building/using free-JSON APIs or back-as-a- service services. This tendency allows teams to focus on what is the most important for end users— user interface and features—as well as what is vital for businesses: reduced iteration cycles, and lower costs of maintenance and development.

Another essential piece in this puzzle is test-driven practice. To explore it, we'll cover Mocha, a widely used Node.js testing framework. Onward to REST APIs and TDD.

CHAPTER 8

Building Node.js REST API Servers with Express.js and Hapi

Modern-day web developers use an architecture consisting of a *thick* client and a a *thin* back-end layer. They use frameworks such as Backbone.js (`http://backbonejs.org`), AngularJS (`https://angularjs.org`), Ember.js (`http://emberjs.com`), and the like to build the thick client. On the other hand, they use REST APIs for the *thin* back-end layer. (typically represented by a representational state transfer (REST) web application programing interface (API) service). This architecture, dubbed thick client or single-page application (SPA), has become more and more popular. No surprise here. There are many advantages to this thick-client approach:

- SPA (single-page applications) are faster because they render elements of the webpage in the browser without the need to always fetch the HTML from the server.

- The bandwidth is smaller since most of the page layout stays the same once it's loaded, thus the browser only needs the data in JSON format for the changing elements of the webpage.

- The same back-end REST API can serve multiple client apps/ consumers, with web applications being just one of them (mobile and public third-party apps are examples of others).

- There is a separation of concerns, i.e., the clients can be replaced without compromising the integrity of the core business logic, and vice versa.

© Azat Mardan 2018
A. Mardan, *Practical Node.js*, https://doi.org/10.1007/978-1-4842-3039-8_8

- User interface / user experience (UI/UX) are inherently hard to test, especially with event-driven, single-page apps, and then there's an added complexity of cross-browser testing; but, with separation of business logic into the back-end REST API, that logic becomes easy to test in both unit and functional testing.

Therefore, the majority of new projects take the REST API and clients approach. Development teams may take this approach even if they have just one client for the time being, which is typically a web app, because they realize that otherwise, when they eventually add more apps, they'll have to redo their work.

That's why we've seen a rise of the back-end-as-a-service niche in which a back-end RESTful API can be rented on a monthly or hourly basis which offloads the need for developing and maintenance away from developers. Examples are AWS Lambda, MongoLab, Firebase, and now discontinued Parse.com. Of course, we can't always rent a service. Sometimes we need the control or customization, and other times we need more security. That's why developers still implement their own services. With Node, to create a RESTful API services is as easy as stealing a vegan burrito from a San Francisco hipster (not that vegan burritos are any good).

To get started with Node.js REST servers, in this chapter we cover the following:

- RESTful API basics

- Project dependencies

- Test coverage with Mocha (`http://visionmedia.github.io/mocha`) and superagent (`http://visionmedia.github.io/superagent`)

- REST API server implementation with Express and Mongoskin (`https://github.com/kissjs/node-mongoskin`)

- Refactoring: Hapi.js (`http://hapijs.com`) REST API Server

The REST API server is able to process the creation of objects, and retrieval of objects and collections, and make changes to objects and remove objects. For your convenience, all the source code is in the `ch8` folder in github.com/azat-co/practicalnode (`https://github.com/azat-co/practicalnode`).

RESTful API Basics

RESTful API (`http://bit.ly/2zqJqlJ`)[1] became popular because of the demand in distributed systems in which each transaction needs to include enough information about the state of the client. This standard is stateless, because no information about the clients' states is stored on the server, making it possible for each request to be served by a different system. This make scaling systems up or down a breeze.

In a sense, the stateless servers are like loosely coupled classes in programming. Lots of infrastructure techniques use the best programming practices; in addition to loose coupling, versioning, automation, and continuous integration can all be applied to infrastructure to a great benefit.

Distinct characteristics of RESTful API (i.e., if API is RESTful, it usually follows these principles) are as follows:

- RESTful API has better scalability support because different components can be deployed independently to different servers.

- It replaced the Simple Object Access Protocol (SOAP) (`http://bit.ly/2zqJrpN`)[2] because of the simpler verb and noun structure.

- It uses HTTP methods such as GET, POST, DELETE, PUT, OPTIONS, and so forth.

- JSON is not the only option (although it is the most popular). Unlike SOAP, which is a protocol, the REST methodology is flexible in choosing formats. For example alternative formats might be Extensible Markup Language (XML) or comma-separated values formats (CSV).

Table 8-1 shows an example of a simple create, read, update, and delete (CRUD[3]) (`http://bit.ly/2zrmG53`) REST API for message collection.

---

[1]https://en.wikipedia.org/wiki/Representational_state_transfer#Applied_to_Web_services
[2]http://en.wikipedia.org/wiki/SOAP
[3]http://en.wikipedia.org/wiki/Create,_read,_update_and_delete

Table 8-1. *Example of the CRUD REST API structure*

Method	URL	Meaning
GET	`/messages.json`	Return list of messages in JSON format
PUT	`/messages.json`	Update/replace all messages and return status/error in JSON
POST	`/messages.json`	Create new message and return its ID in JSON format
GET	`/messages/{id}.json`	Return message with ID `{id}` in JSON format
PUT	`/messages/{id}.json`	Update/replace message with id `{id}`; if `{id}` message doesn't exist, create it
DELETE	`/messages/{id}.json`	Delete message with ID `{id}`, return status/error in JSON format

REST is not a protocol; it's an architecture in the sense that it's more flexible than SOAP, which we know is a protocol. Therefore, REST API URLs could look like `/messages/list.html` or `/messages/list.xml`, in case we want to support these formats.

PUT and DELETE are idempotent methods. (Idempotent is another fancy word that computer scientists invented to charge high tuition fees for college degrees.) An idempotent method basically means that if the server receives two or more similar requests, the end result is the same. Ergo idempotent are safe to replicate.

And GET is nullipotent (safe), while POST is not idempotent (not safe). POST might affect the state and cause side effects.

More information on REST API can be found at Wikipedia (`http://en.wikipedia.org/wiki/Representational_state_transfer`) and in the article "A Brief Introduction to REST (`http://www.infoq.com/articles/rest-introduction`)."

In our REST API server, we perform CRUD operations and harness the Express.js middleware (`http://expressjs.com/api.html#middleware`) concept with the `app.param()` and `app.use()` methods. So, our app should be able to process the following commands using the JSON format (`collectionName` is the name of the collection, typically pluralized nouns, e.g., messages, comments, users):

- *POST* `/collections/{collectionName}`: request to create an object; responds with the of newly created object ID

- *GET* `/collections/{collectionName}/{id}`: request with ID to retrieve an object

- *GET* `/collections/{collectionName}/`: request to retrieve any items from the collection (`items`); in our example, we'll have this query options: up to 10 items and sorted by ID

- *PUT* `/collections/{collectionName}/{id}`: request with ID to update an object

- *DELETE* `/collections/{collectionName}/{id}`: request with ID to remove an object

Let's start our project by declaring dependencies.

Project Dependencies

To get started with our project, we need to install packages. In this chapter, we use Mongoskin (`https://github.com/kissjs/node-mongoskin`), a MongoDB library, which is a better alternative to the plain, good-ol' native MongoDB driver for Node.js (`https://github.com/mongodb/node-mongodb-native`). In addition, Mongoskin is more lightweight than Mongoose and it is schemaless (which I personally like, but I know some devs might prefer to have the safety and consistency of a schema).

The second choice is the framework. We are going to use the most popular, the most used, the framework with the most plugins—Express.js (`http://expressjs.com`). Express.js extends the core Node.js `http` module (`http://nodejs.org/api/http.html`) to provide more methods and features. Needless to say, I'm a huge fan of Express. Partially because I wrote a book on it (*Pro Express.js* (Apress, 2014)), which is still the most comprehensive book on the framework, and partially, because my team and I used Express at Storify, DocuSign, and Capital One to build multiple heavily trafficked apps.

The Express.js framework has boatloads of plugin modules called *middleware*. These middleware modules allow devs to pick and choose whatever functionality they need without having to buy in into some large, bulky, cookie-cutter, opinionated framework. In a way, Express serves as a foundation for a custom-built framework that is exactly what a project needs, not more and not less. Some people compare the Express.js framework with Ruby's Sinatra because it's non-opinionated and configurable.

First, we need to create a `ch8/rest-express` folder (or download the source code):

```
$ mkdir rest-express
$ cd rest-express
$ npm init -y
```

As mentioned in the previous chapter, Node.js/npm provides multiple ways to install dependencies, including the following:

- Manually, one by one

- As a part of `package.json`

- By downloading and copying modules

To keep things simple, let's just use the `package.json` approach. You can create the `package.json` file, or copy the dependencies section or the whole file:

```
{
  "name": "rest-express",
  "version": "0.2.1",
  "description": "REST API application with Express, Mongoskin,
  MongoDB, Mocha and Superagent",
  "main": "index.js",
  "directories": {
    "test": "test"
  },
  "scripts": {
    "start": "node index.js",
    "test": "PORT=3007 ./node_modules/.bin/mocha test -R spec"
  },
  "author": "Azat Mardan (http://azat.co/)",
  "license": "MIT",
```

```
"dependencies": {
  "body-parser": "1.18.2",
  "express": "4.16.2",
  "mongodb": "2.2.33",
  "mongoskin": "2.1.0",
  "morgan": "1.9.0"
},
"devDependencies": {
  "expect.js": "0.3.1",
  "mocha": "4.0.1",
  "standard": "10.0.3",
  "superagent": "3.8.0"
  }
}
```

Then, simply run this command to install modules for the application:

```
$ npm install
```

As a result, the node_modules folder should be created with the superagent, express, mongoskin, and expect libraries. If you change the versions specified in package.json to the later ones, please make sure to update the code according to the packages' change logs.

Test Coverage with Mocha and Superagent

Before the app implementation, let's write functional tests that make HTTP requests to our soon-to-be- created REST API server. In a test-driven development (TDD) manner, let's use these tests to build a Node.js free JSON REST API server using the Express.js framework and Mongoskin library for MongoDB.

In this section, we'll walk through the writing of functional tests using the Mocha (http://visionmedia.github.io/mocha) and superagent (http://visionmedia.github.io/superagent) libraries. The tests need to perform basic CRUD by posting HTTP requests to our server.

If you know how to use Mocha or just want to jump straight to the Express.js app implementation, feel free to do so. You can use CURL terminal commands for testing, too.

Assuming we already have Node.js, npm, and MongoDB installed, let's create a *new* folder (or, if you wrote the tests, use that folder). Let's use Mocha as a command-line tool, and Expect.js and superagent as local libraries. To install the Mocha CLI (if it's not available via $ `mocha -V`), run this command from the terminal:

```
$ npm install -g mocha@4.0.1
```

Expect.js and superagent should be available already as part of the installation done in the previous section.

Tip   Installing Mocha locally gives us the ability to use different versions at the same time. To run tests, simply point to `./node_modules/.bin/mocha`. Use `npm i mocha@4.0.1-DE` to install Mocha locally.

To launch tests, use the `npm test` alias to `mocha test` (global) or `./node_modules/.bin/mocha test` (local). A better alternative is to use Makefile, as described in Chapter 6.

Now let's create a `test/index.js` file in the same folder (`ch8/rest-express`), which will have six suites:

1. Create a new object

2. Retrieve an object by its ID

3. Retrieve the whole collection

4. Update an object by its ID

5. Check an updated object by its ID

6. Remove an object by its ID

HTTP requests are a breeze with Superagent's chained functions, which we can put inside each test suite.

So, we start with dependencies and then have three Mocha statements:

```
const boot = require('../index.js').boot
const shutdown = require('../index.js').shutdown
const port = require('../index.js').port
```

```
const superagent = require('superagent')
const expect = require('expect.js')

before(() => {
  boot()
})

describe('express rest api server', () => {
  // ...
})

after(() => {
  shutdown()
})
```

Then, we write our first test case wrapped in the test case (`describe` and its callback). The main thing happens in the request (made by `superagent`) callback. There, we put multiple assertions that are the bread and butter (or meat and veggies for paleo readers) of TDD. To be strictly correct, this test suite uses BDD language, but this difference is not essential for our project.

The idea is simple. We make a POST HTTP request to a local instance of the server which we required and booted right from the test file. When we send the request, we pass some data. This creates the new object. We can expect that there are no errors, that the body of a certain composition, etc. We save the newly created object ID into `id` to use it for requests in the next test cases.

```
describe('express rest api server', () => {
  let id

  it('post object', (done) => {
    superagent.post(`http://localhost:${port}
    /collections/test`)
      .send({
        name: 'John',
        email: 'john@rpjs.co'
      })
      .end((e, res) => {
        expect(e).to.eql(null)
        expect(res.body.length).to.eql(1)
```

```
        expect(res.body[0]._id.length).to.eql(24)
        id = res.body[0]._id
        done()
      })
  })
  // ...
})
```

As you may have noticed, we're checking for the following:

- The error object should be null (`eql(null)`).

- The response body array should have one item (`to.eql(1)`).

- The first response body item should have the `_id` property, which is 24 characters long, i.e., a hex string representation of the standard MongoDB ObjectId type.

To finish, we save the newly created object's ID in the `id` global variable so we can use it later for retrievals, updates, and deletions. Speaking of object retrievals, we test them in the next test case. Notice that the `superagent` method has changed to `get()`, and the URL path contains the object ID. You can "uncomment" `console.log` to inspect the full HTTP response body:

```
it('retrieves an object', (done) => {
  superagent.get(`http://localhost:${port}
  /collections/test/${id}`)
    .end((e, res) => {
      expect(e).to.eql(null)
      expect(typeof res.body).to.eql('object')
      expect(res.body._id.length).to.eql(24)
      expect(res.body._id).to.eql(id)
      done()
    })
})
```

The `done()` callback allows us to test async code. Without it, the Mocha test case ends abruptly, long before the slow server has time to respond.

The next test case's assertion is a bit more interesting because we use the `map()` function on the response results to return an array of IDs. In this array, we find our ID (saved in the `id` variable) with the `contain` method. The `contain` method is a more elegant alternative to native `indexOf()`. It works because the results, which are limited to 10 records, come sorted by IDs, and our object was created just moments ago.

```
it('retrieves a collection', (done) => {
  superagent.get(`http://localhost:${port}
  /collections/test`)
    .end((e, res) => {
      expect(e).to.eql(null)
      expect(res.body.length).to.be.above(0)
      expect(res.body.map(function (item) { return item._id })).
      to.contain(id)
      done()
    })
})
```

When the time comes to update our object, we actually need to send some data. We do this by passing an object to superagent's function. Then, we assert that the operation was completed with `(msg=success)`:

```
it('updates an object', (done) => {
  superagent.put(`http://localhost:${port}
  /collections/test/${id}`)
    .send({
      name: 'Peter',
      email: 'peter@yahoo.com'
    })
    .end((e, res) => {
      expect(e).to.eql(null)
      expect(typeof res.body).to.eql('object')
      expect(res.body.msg).to.eql('success')
      done()
    })
})
```

The last two test cases, which assert retrieval of the updated object and its deletion, use methods similar to those used before:

```
it('checks an updated object', (done) => {
  superagent.get(`http://localhost:${port}
  /collections/test/${id}`)
    .end((e, res) => {
      expect(e).to.eql(null)
      expect(typeof res.body).to.eql('object')
      expect(res.body._id.length).to.eql(24)
      expect(res.body._id).to.eql(id)
      expect(res.body.name).to.eql('Peter')
      done()
    })
})
it('removes an object', (done) => {
  superagent.del(`http://localhost:${port}
  /collections/test/${id}`)
    .end((e, res) => {
      expect(e).to.eql(null)
      expect(typeof res.body).to.eql('object')
      expect(res.body.msg).to.eql('success')
      done()
    })
})
})
```

It's important to finish the work of the server when we are done with testing:

```
after(() => {
  shutdown()
})
```

The full source code for testing is in the ch8/rest-express/test/index.js file.

To run the tests, we can use the $ mocha test command, $ mocha test/index.js, or $ npm test. For now, the tests should fail because we have yet to implement the server!

For those of you who require multiple versions of Mocha, another alternative, which is better, is to run your tests using local Mocha binaries: `$ ./node_modules/mocha/bin/mocha ./test`. This, of course, assumes that we have installed Mocha locally into `node_modules`.

Note By default, Mocha doesn't use any reporters, and the result output is lackluster. To receive more explanatory logs, supply the `-R <name>` option (e.g., `$ mocha test -R spec` or `$ mocha test -R list`).

REST API Server Implementation with Express and Mongoskin

Create and open `code/ch8/rest-express/index.js`, which will be the main application file. First things first. Let's import our dependencies into the application, that's in `index.js`:

```
const express = require('express')
const mongoskin = require('mongoskin')
const bodyParser = require('body-parser')
const logger = require('morgan')
const http = require('http')
```

Express.js instantiation of an app instance follows:

```
const app = express()
```

Express middleware is a powerful and convenient feature of Express.js to organize and reuse code. Why write our own code if we can use a few middleware modules? To extract parameters and data from the requests, let's use the `bodyParser.json()` middleware from `body-parser`. `logger()`, which is `morgan` npm module, is optional middleware that allows us to print requests. We apply them with `app.use()`. In addition, we can use port configuration and server logging middleware.

```
app.use(bodyParser.json())
app.use(logger())
app.set('port', process.env.PORT || 3000)
```

Mongoskin makes it possible to connect to the MongoDB database in one effortless line of code:

```
const db = mongoskin.db('mongodb://@localhost:27017/test')
```

Note   If you wish to connect to a remote database (e.g., Compose (`https://www.compose.com`) or mLab), substitute the string with your username, password, host, and port values. Here is the format of the uniform resource identifier (URI) string (no spaces): `mongodb://[username:password@] host1[:port1][,host2[:port2],...[,hostN[:portN]]] [/[database][?options]]`.

The next statement is a helper function that converts hex strings into MongoDB ObjectID data types:

```
const id = mongoskin.helper.toObjectID
```

The `app.param()` method is another form of Express.js middleware. It basically allows to *do something every time there is this value in the URL pattern of the request handler.* In our case, we select a particular collection when a request pattern contains a string `collectionName` prefixed with a colon (we'll see this when we examine routes):

```
app.param('collectionName', (req, res, next, collectionName) => {
  req.collection = db.collection(collectionName)
  return next()
})
```

I had many students at my workshop exclaim, "It's not working", when they were staring at the root `localhost:3000` instead of using a path like `localhost:3000/collections/messages`. To avoid such confusion, let's include a root route with a message that asks users to specify a collection name in their URLs:

```
app.get('/', (req, res, next) => {
  res.send('Select a collection, e.g., /collections/messages')
})
```

Now the real work begins. The GET `/collections/:collectionName` is your typical REST read operation, that is, we need to retrieve a list of items. We can sort it by `_id` and use a limit of 10 to make it a bit more interesting. Here is how we can harness `find()` using the `req.collection`, which was created in the `app.param` middleware.

```
app.get('/collections/:collectionName', (req, res, next) => {
  req.collection.find({}, {limit: 10, sort: [['_id', -1]]})
    .toArray((e, results) => {
      if (e) return next(e)
      res.send(results)
    }
  )
})
```

So have you noticed a `:collectionName` string in the URL pattern parameter? This and the previous `app.param()` middleware are what give us the `req.collection` object, which points to a specified collection in our database. `toArray` create either an error `e` or array of items `results`.

Next is the object-creating endpoint POST `/collections/:collectionName`. It is slightly easier to grasp because we just pass the whole payload to the MongoDB. Again we use `req.collection`. The second argument to `insert()` is optional. Yeah. I know it's not super secure to pass unfiltered and not-validated payloads to the database, but what can go wrong? (Sarcasm font.)

```
app.post('/collections/:collectionName', (req, res, next) => {
  // TODO: Validate req.body
  req.collection.insert(req.body, {}, (e, results) => {
    if (e) return next(e)
    res.send(results.ops)
  })
})
```

This approach when we create a RESTful API without schema or restrictions on the data structure is often called *free JSON REST API*, because clients can throw data structured in any way, and the server handles it perfectly. I found this architecture very advantageous for early prototyping due to the ability to use this API for any data just by changing the collection name or the payload that I'm sending from my client, i.e., a front-end app.

Next is GET /collections/:collectionName/:id, e.g., /collections/messages/123. For that we'll be using a single-object retrieval function findOne(), which is more convenient than find(). This is because findOne() returns an object directly instead of a cursor, as find(). That's good. We can drop awkward toArray(). The function signature for findOne() is different because now it has to take the callback.

We're also extracting the ID from the :id part of the URL path with req.params.id Express.js magic because we need the ID of this particular document and because we can have multiple URL parameters defined in the URL path of the Express route.

```
app.get('/collections/:collectionName/:id', (req, res, next) => {
  req.collection.findOne({_id: id(req.params.id)},
  (e, result) => {
    if (e) return next(e)
    res.send(result)
  })
})
```

Of course, the same functionality can be achieved with find, using {_id: ObjectId(req.params.id)} as the query and with toArray(), but you know that already.

The PUT request handler gets more interesting because update() doesn't return the augmented object. Instead, it returns a count of affected objects. Also, {$set:req.body} is a special MongoDB operator that sets values. MongoDB operators tend to start with a dollar sign $, like $set or $push.

The second parameter {safe:true, multi:false} is an object with options that tell MongoDB to wait for the execution before running the callback function and to process only one (the first) item. The callback to update() is processing error e, and if it's null and the number of update documents is 1 (it could be 0 if the ID is not matching—no error e in this case), it sends back the success to the client.

```
app.put('/collections/:collectionName/:id', (req, res, next) => {
  req.collection.update({_id: id(req.params.id)},
    {$set: req.body},
    {safe: true, multi: false}, (e, result) => {
      if (e) return next(e)
      res.send((result.result.n === 1) ? {msg: 'success'} :
      {msg: 'error'})
    })
})
```

Lastly, we define the DELETE `/collections/:collectionName/:id` route to remove one document. The ID is coming from the `req.params.id` like in the other individual-document routes. The callback will have two arguments, with the second having the `result` property. Thus we use `result.result`.

In the callback of `remove()`, we create an if/else to output a custom JSON message with `msg`, which equals either a `success` string for one (1) removed document, or the `error` message for a value different from one (1). The error `e` is a MongoDB error like "cannot connect".

```
app.delete('/collections/:collectionName/:id', (req, res, next) => {
  req.collection.remove({_id: id(req.params.id)}, (e, result) => {
    if (e) return next(e)
    res.send((result.result.n === 1) ? {msg: 'success'} :
    {msg: 'error'})
  })
})
```

The last few lines of the `index.js` file (`code/ch8/rest-express/index.js`) make our file compatible with either starting the server or exporting it to be used/started elsewhere, i.e., in the tests:

```
const server = http.createServer(app)
const boot = () => {
  server.listen(app.get('port'), () => {
    console.info(`Express server listening
      on port ${app.get('port')}`)
  })
}
```

```
const shutdown = () => {
  server.close(process.exit)
}

if (require.main === module) {
  boot()
} else {
  console.info('Running app as a module')
  exports.boot = boot
  exports.shutdown = shutdown
  exports.port = app.get('port')
}
```

Just in case something is not working well, the full code of the Express.js REST API server is in the `code/ch8/rest-express/index.js` file.

Now exit your editor and run `index.js` file with the `node` command. If it's Linux or macOS, you can use this command in your terminal:

```
$ node .
```

The command above with the dot (`.`) is the equivalent of `$ node index.js`. Sadly, if you are on Windows, then `node .` will not work, so you have to use the full file name.

Test your server manually or automatically. Just do it, then do it again. To test automatically, execute the tests with Mocha. Tests will start a new server, so you may want to close/terminate/kill your own server to avoid the annoying "error address in use" error.

```
$ mocha test
```

If you are bored of a standard Mocha result report, then a slightly cuter reporter is nyan (Figure 8-1).

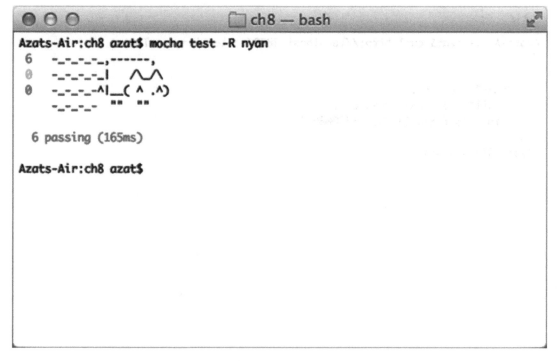

Figure 8-1. *Who wouldn't like a library with Nyan Cat?*

You can use it with -R nyan as follows:

```
$ mocha test -R nyan
```

If you really don't like Mocha, BDD or TDD, manual testing with CURL is always there for you. :-) At least on POSIX (Linux, Unix, macOS), CURL is built-in and comes with those OSs. On Windows, you can download the CURL tool manually.

For GET CURLing, simply provide the URL, and you will get the server response which is the JSON of the object, as shown in Figure 8-2:

```
$ curl http://localhost:3000/collections/curl-test
```

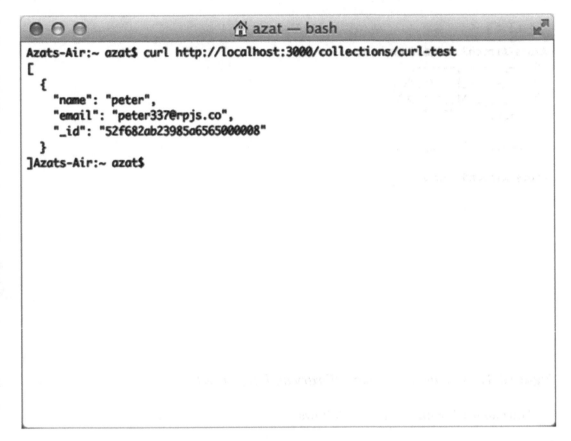

Figure 8-2. A GET request made with CURL

Note   GET requests also work in the browser because every time you open a URL in a browser, you make a GET request. For example, open (`http://localhost:3000/test`) while your server is running.

CURLing data to make a POST request is easy (Figure 8-3). Provide `-d` for data. Use the urlencoded format with `key=value&key1=value1`, etc. or use a JSON file with the at (`@`) symbol: `-d@testplace.json`. Most likely you need to provide the header too: `--header "Content-Type: application/json"`.

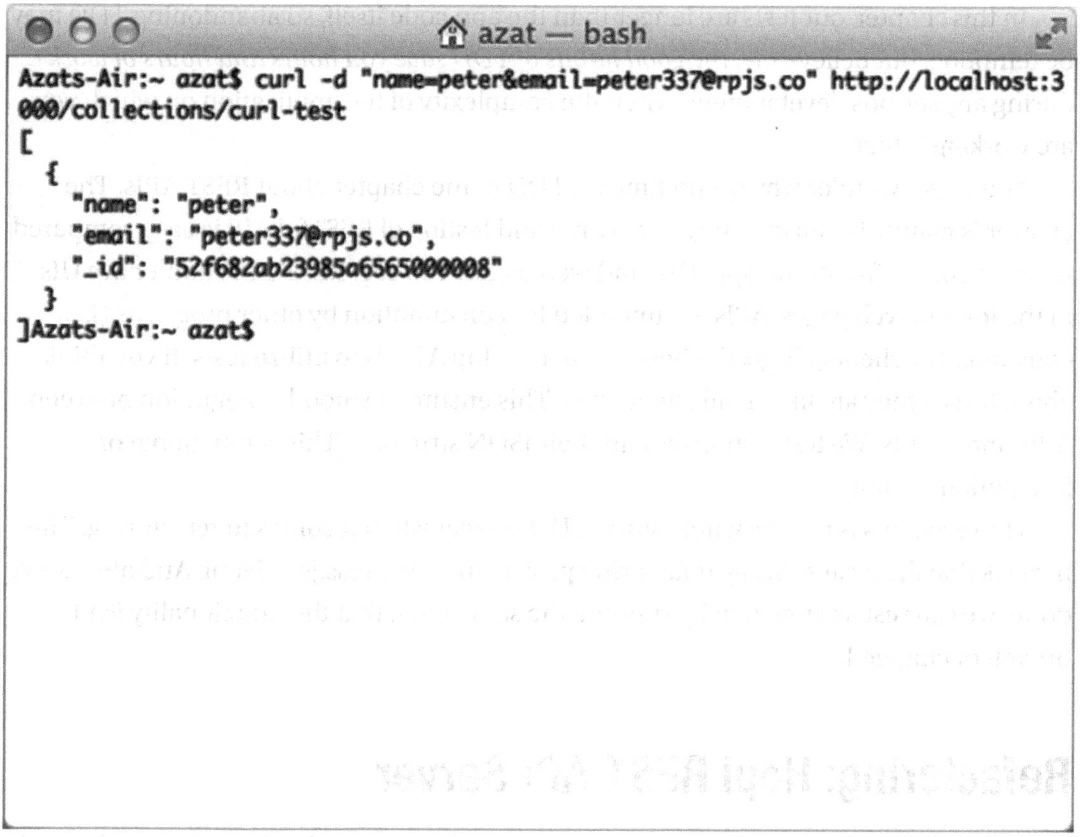

```
Azats-Air:~ azat$ curl -d "name=peter&email=peter337@rpjs.co" http://localhost:3
000/collections/curl-test
[
  {
    "name": "peter",
    "email": "peter337@rpjs.co",
    "_id": "52f682ab23985a6565000008"
  }
]Azats-Air:~ azat$
```

Figure 8-3. *The result of sending a POST request via CURL*

Here's an example of sending name and email values with POST:

```
$ curl -d "name=peter&email=peter337@rpjs.co" --header "Content-Type:
application/json" http://localhost:3000/collections/curl-test
```

DELETE or PUT can be made with the option --request NAME. Remember to add the ID in the URL, such as:

```
$ curl --request DELETE http://localhost:3000/collections/
curl-test/52f6828a23985a6565000008
```

For a short, nice tutorial on the main CURL commands and options, take a look at *CURL Tutorial with Examples of Usage* at http://bit.ly/2zslIWr.

In this chapter, our tests are longer than the app code itself, so abandoning TDD may be tempting, but believe me, *the good habits of TDD save you hours and hours of work* during any serious development, when the complexity of the application on which you are working is high.

You might wonder why spend time on TDD in the chapter about REST APIs. The answer is mainly because testing saves time and testing of RESTful API is easy compared to testing of the frond-end app, UIs, and web pages. You see, REST APIs don't have UIs in the form of web pages. APIs are intended for consumption by other programs (i.e., consumers or clients). Ergo, the best way to develop APIs is to utilize tests. If you think about tests—they are like small client apps. This ensures a smooth integration between APIs and clients. We test responses and their JSON structure. This is functional or integration testing.

However, this is not the whole story. TDD is great when it comes to refactoring. The next section illustrates this by refactoring project from Express.js to Hapi. And after we're done, we can rest assured that by running the same tests, that the functionality isn't broken or changed.

Refactoring: Hapi REST API Server

Hapi (`https://hapijs.com`) is an enterprise-grade framework. It's more complex and feature rich than Express.js, and it's easier to develop in large teams. Hapi was started by (and used at) Walmart Labs that support Walmart's heavily trafficked e-commerce website. So Hapi has been battle-tested at a YUGE scale (think releasing Node on Black Friday sales).

The goal of this section is to show you alternative patterns in implementing the REST API server in Node.js. Now, because we have Mocha tests, we can refactor our code with peace of mind. Here's the `package.json` for this project:

```
{
  "name": "rest-hapi",
  "version": "0.0.1",
  "description": "REST API application with Express, Mongoskin,
  MongoDB, Mocha and Superagent",
  "main": "index.js",
```

```
"directories": {
  "test": "test"
},
"scripts": {
  "start": "node index.js",
  "test": "mocha test -R spec"
},
"author": "Azat Mardan (http://azat.co/)",
"license": "MIT",
"dependencies": {
  "good": "7.3.0",
  "hapi": "16.6.2",
  "mongodb": "2.2.33",
  "mongoskin": "2.1.0"
},
"devDependencies": {
  "mocha": "4.0.1",
  "superagent": "3.8.0",
  "expect.js": "0.3.1"
}
}
```

You can either use `package.json` with $ `npm install` or, for Hapi installation only, simply run $ `npm install hapi@16.6.2 good@7.3.0--save` from the `ch8/rest-hapi` folder. `hapi` is the framework's module and `good` is its logger. The `npm install` command downloads the modules and unpacks them in the `node_modules` folder. Next, we need to create a `hapi-app.js` file and open it in the editor.

As usual, at the beginning of a Node.js program (`code/ch8/rest-hapi/index.js`), we import dependencies. Then, we define domain (localhost) and port (3000). Next we create the Hapi server object using `new Hapi.server()`:

```
const port = process.env.PORT || 3000
const Hapi = require('hapi')
server.connection({ port: port, host: 'localhost' })
const server = new Hapi.Server()
```

And we create the database connection db, just like in the Express.js example:

```
const mongoskin = require('mongoskin')
const db = mongoskin.db('mongodb://@localhost:27017/test', {})
const id = mongoskin.helper.toObjectID
```

Instead of middleware like we used in Express, in Hapi we will create a function that will load the database collection asynchronously based on the provided name argument, which is a URL param. The loadCollection() function gives us the database collection that is corresponding to the name value (use an enum in a real project):

```
const loadCollection = (name, callback) => {
  callback(db.collection(name))
}
```

The next part is the most distinct compared with Express.js. Developers use properties for methods and paths, and instead of res (or response) we use reply inside of the handler property. Every route is an item in the array passed to server.route(). The first such route is for the home page (/):

```
server.route([
  {
    method: 'GET',
    path: '/',
    handler: (req, reply) => {
      reply('Select a collection, e.g., /collections/messages')
    }
  },
  // ...
])
```

The next item in this array passed to server.route() (that is the argument to the route method), is the route that returns a list of items as a response to a GET /collection/:collectionName request. The main logic happens in the handler function again, where we call the loadCollection() function, find any objects (find({})), and output sorted results limited to 10 items:

```
{
  method: 'GET',
  path: '/collections/{collectionName}',
  handler: (req, reply) => {
    loadCollection(req.params.collectionName, (collection) => {
      collection.find({}, {limit: 10, sort: [['_id', -1]]})
        .toArray((e, results) => {
          if (e) return reply(e)
          reply(results)
        })
    })
  }
},
```

The third route handles the creation of new objects (POST /collections/collectionName). Again, we use loadCollection() and then call the insert method with a request body (req.payload):

```
{
  method: 'POST',
  path: '/collections/{collectionName}',
  handler: (req, reply) => {
    loadCollection(req.params.collectionName, (collection) => {
      collection.insert(req.payload, {}, (e, results) => {
        if (e) return reply(e)
        reply(results.ops)
      })
    })
  }
},
```

Please note that each URL parameter is enclosed in { }, unlike the :name convention that Express.js uses. This is in part because colon (:) is a valid URL symbol, and by using it as a parameter identifier we cannot use colon (:) in our URL addresses. (Although I don't know why you would colon when you can use slash /.)

The next route is responsible for getting a single record by its ID (`/collection/collectionName/id`). The main logic of using the `findOne()` method is the same as in the Express.js server example:

```
{
  method: 'GET',
  path: '/collections/{collectionName}/{id}',
  handler: (req, reply) => {
    loadCollection(req.params.collectionName, (collection) => {
      collection.findOne({_id: id(req.params.id)}, (e, result) => {
        if (e) return reply(e)
        reply(result)
      })
    })
  }
},
```

This route updates documents in the database and, again, most of the logic in the handler remains the same, as in the Express.js example, except that we call `loadCollection()` to get the right collection based on the URL parameter `collectionName`:

```
{
  method: 'PUT',
  path: '/collections/{collectionName}/{id}',
  handler: (req, reply) => {
    loadCollection(req.params.collectionName, (collection) => {
      collection.update({_id: id(req.params.id)},
        {$set: req.payload},
        {safe: true, multi: false}, (e, result) => {
          if (e) return reply(e)
          reply((result.result.n === 1) ? {msg: 'success'} :
          {msg: 'error'})
        })
    })
  }
},
```

The last route handles deletions. First, it gets the right collection via the URL parameter (`collectionName`). Then, it removes the object by its ID and sends back the message (`success` or `error`):

```
  {
    method: 'DELETE',
    path: '/collections/{collectionName}/{id}',
    handler: (req, reply) => {
      loadCollection(req.params.collectionName, (collection) => {
        collection.remove({_id: id(req.params.id)}, (e, result) => {
          if (e) return reply(e)
          reply((result.result.n === 1) ? {msg: 'success'} :
          {msg: 'error'})
        })
      })
    }
  }
]) // for "server.route(["
```

The next configuration is optional. It configures server logging with `good`:

```
const options = {
  subscribers: {
    'console': ['ops', 'request', 'log', 'error']
  }
}

server.register(require('good', options, (err) => {
  if (!err) {
    // Plugin loaded successfully, you can put console.log here
  }
}))
```

The next statement of `ch8/rest-hapi/index.js` creates a function that starts the server with the `server.start()` method:

```
const boot = () => {
  server.start((err) => {
    if (err) {
      console.error(err)
      return process.exit(1)
    }
    console.log(`Server running at: ${server.info.uri}`)
  })
}
```

The next statement creates a function to close the process:

```
const shutdown = () => {
  server.stop({}, () => {
    process.exit(0)
  })
}
```

Lastly, we put an if/else to boot up the server straightaway when this file is run directly or export `boot`, `shutdown`, and `port` when this file is loaded as a module (with `require()`):

```
if (require.main === module) {
  console.info('Running app as a standalone')
  boot()
} else {
  console.info('Running app as a module')
  exports.boot = boot
  exports.shutdown = shutdown
  exports.port = port
}
```

The following summarizes what we did differently while switching from Express.js to Hapi:

- Defined routes in an array

- Used method, path, and handler properties of the route object

- Used the `loadCollection` method instead of middleware

- Used `{name}` instead of `:name` for defining URL parameters

As alway, the full source code is in the GitHub repository. The file and its path is `ch8/rest-hapi/index.js`.

If we run the newly written Hapi server with `$ node index.js` (or `$ npm start`) and then run tests in a separate tab/window, the tests pass! If they don't for some reason, then download and run the source code from the GitHub repository github.com/azat-co/practicalnode (`http://github.com/azat-co/practicalnode`).

Summary

The loosely coupled architecture of REST API servers and clients (mobile, web app, or front end) allows for better maintenance and works perfectly with TDD/BDD. In addition, NoSQL databases such as MongoDB are good at handling free REST APIs. We don't have to define schemas, and we can throw any data at it and the data is saved!

The Express.js and Mongoskin libraries are great when you need to build a simple REST API server using a few lines of code. Later, if you need to expand the libraries, they also provide a way to configure and organize your code. If you want to learn more about Express.js, take a look at *Pro Express.js* (Apress, 2014). Also, it's good to know that for more complex systems, the Hapi server framework is there for you.

In this chapter, in addition to Express.js, we used MongoDB via Mongoskin. We also used Mocha and Superagent to write functional tests that, potentially, save us hours in testing and debugging when we refactor code in the future.

Then we easily flipped Express.js for Hapi and, thanks to the tests, we are confident that our code works as expected. The differences between the Express and Hapi frameworks as we observed are in the way we defined routes and URL parameters and output the response.

CHAPTER 9

Real-Time Apps with WebSocket, Socket.IO, and DerbyJS

Real-time apps are becoming more and more widespread in financial trading, gaming, social media, various DevOps tools, cloud services, and of course, news. The main factor contributing to this trend is that technologies have become much better. They allow for a greater bandwidth to transmit data and for more calculations to process and retrieve the data.

HTML5 pioneered the new standard of real-time connections called *WebSocket*. The way it works: in browser JavaScript you get a global object called `WebSocket`. This object is a class and it has all kinds of methods for developers to implement the WebSocket protocol client.

The WebSocket protocol (or `ws://` in the URL format) is very different from HTTP or HTTPS. Hence, developers need a special ws server. Just having an HTTP server won't cut it. And as you know, Node.js is a highly efficient, non-blocking input/output platform.

Implementing WebSocket servers with Node is pure joy because Node is fast and because Node is also JavaScript, just like the WebSocket clients (i.e., browser JavaScript). Thus, Node is very well suited for the task of being a back-end pair to the browser with its WebSocket API.

© Azat Mardan 2018
A. Mardan, *Practical Node.js*, https://doi.org/10.1007/978-1-4842-3039-8_9

To get you started with WebSocket and Node.js, we'll keep things simple stupid (KISS) (`http://azat.co/blog/kiss`) and cover the following:

- What is WebSocket?

- Native WebSocket and Node.js with the ws module example

- Socket.IO and Express.js example

- Collaborative online editor example with DerbyJS, Express.js, and MongoDB

What Is WebSocket?

WebSocket is a special communication "channel" between browsers (clients) and servers. It's an HTML5 protocol. WebSocket's connection is constant, in contrast to traditional HTTP requests, which are always initiated by the client, which means there's no way for a server to notify the client if there are updates (except for Server-side Events).

By maintaining a duplex open connection between the client and the server, updates can be pushed in a timely fashion without clients needing to poll at certain intervals. This main factor makes WebSocket ideal for real-time apps for which data needs to be available on the client immediately. For more information on WebSocket, take a look at the extensive resource About HTML5 WebSocket (`http://www.websocket.org/aboutwebsocket.html`).

There's no need to use any special libraries to use WebSocket in modern browsers. The following StackOverflow has a list of such browsers: What browsers support HTML5 WebSockets API? (`http://bit.ly/2zrwH2f`). For older browser support, the workaround includes falling back on polling.

As a side note, *polling* (both short and long), can also be used to emulate the real-time responsiveness of web apps. In fact, some advanced libraries (Socket.IO) fall back to polling when WebSocket becomes unavailable as a result of connection issues or users not having the latest versions of browsers. Polling is relatively easy, and I don't cover it here. It can be implemented with just a `setInterval()` callback and an endpoint on the server. However, there's no true real-time communication with polling; each request is separate.

Native WebSocket and Node.js with the ws Module Example

Sometimes it's easier to start from the simplest thing and build things on top of it. With this in mind, our mini project includes building a native WebSocket implementation that talks with the Node.js server with the help of the ws module:

- Browser WebSocket implementation

- Node.js server with ws module implementation

Let's examine this with a quick example.

Browser WebSocket Implementation

This is our front-end code (file ch9/basic/index.html) for Chrome version 32.0.1700.77. We start with typical HTML tags:

```
<html>
  <head>
  </head>
  <body>
```

The main code lives in the script tag, where we instantiate an object from global WebSocket. When we do so, we provide the server URL. Notice the ws:// instead of a familiar http://. The letters ws:// stand for the WebSocket protocol:

```
<script type="text/javascript">
  var ws = new WebSocket('ws://localhost:3000');
```

As soon as the connection is established, we send a message to the server:

```
ws.onopen = function(event) {
  ws.send('front-end message: ABC');
};
```

Usually, messages are sent in response to user actions, such as mouse clicks. When we get any message from the WebSocket location, the following handler is executed:

```
ws.onmessage = function(event) {
  console.log('server message: ', event.data);
};
```

A good practice is to have an `onerror` event handler. We log the error message:

```
ws.onerror = function(event) {
  console.log('server error message: ', event.data);
};
```

We then close the tags and save the file:

```
    </script>
  </body>
</html>
```

To make sure you don't miss anything, here's the full source code of `ch9/basic/` `index.html`, which is very straightforward and rather small:

```
<html>
  <head>
  </head>
  <body>
    <script type="text/javascript">
      var ws = new WebSocket('ws://localhost:3000');
      ws.onopen = function(event) {
        ws.send('front-end message: ABC');
      };
      ws.onerror = function(event) {
        console.log('server error message: ', event.data);
      };
      ws.onmessage = function(event) {
        console.log('server message: ', event.data);
      };
    </script>
  </body>
</html>
```

Node.js Server with ws Module Implementation

WebSocket.org provides an echo service for testing the browser WebSocket, but we can build our own small Node.js server with the help of the ws library (`http://npmjs.org/ws`). You can create `package.json` and install `ws`:

```
$ npm init -y
$ npm install ws@3.3.0 -SE
```

In the `code/ch9/basic/server.js` file, we import `ws` and initialize the server into the `wss` variable:

```
const WebSocketServer = require('ws').Server
const wss = new WebSocketServer({port: 3000})
```

Akin to the front-end code, we use an event pattern to wait for a connection. When the connection is ready, in the callback we send the string `XYZ` and attach an event listener `on('message')` to listen to incoming messages from the page:

```
wss.on('connection', (ws) => {
  ws.send('XYZ')
  ws.on('message', (message) => {
    console.log('received: %s', message)
  })
})
```

Moreover, let's add some continuous logic that will provide current time to the browser using `ws.send()` and `new Date`:

```
wss.on('connection', (ws) => {
  ws.send('XYZ')
  setInterval(()=>{
    ws.send((new Date).toLocaleTimeString())
  }, 1000)
  ws.on('message', (message) => {
    console.log('received: %s', message)
  })
})
```

The full code of the server code is in `code/ch9/basic/server.js`.

Start the Node.js server with `$ node server`. Then, open `index.html` in the browser and you should see this message in the JavaScript console (option + command + j on Macs): `server message: XYZ` (Figure 9-1).

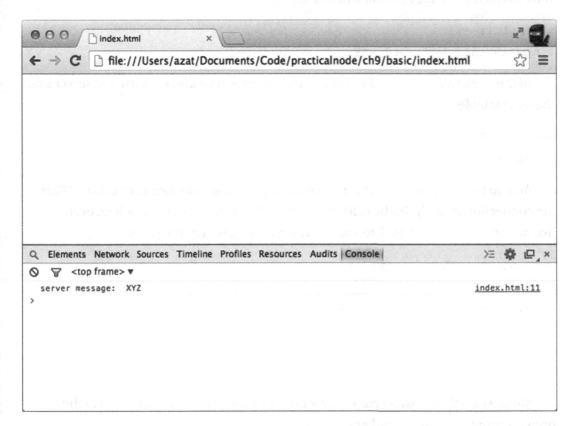

Figure 9-1. *Browser outputs a message received via WebSocket*

While in the terminal, the Node.js server output is `received: front-end message: ABC`, as is illustrated in Figure 9-2.

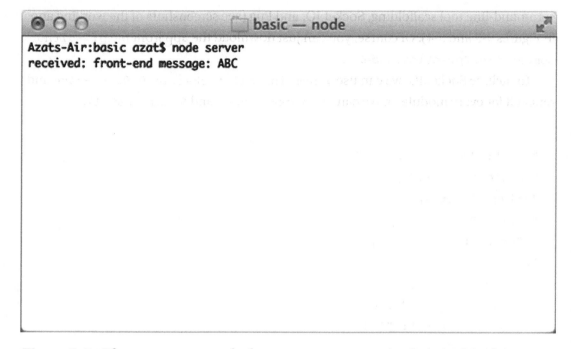

Figure 9-2. *The server outputs the browser message received via WebSocket*

Native HTML5 WebSocket is an amazing technology. However, WebSocket is a protocol and an evolving standard. This means that each browser implementation might vary. And, of course, if support for older browsers is needed, you should do your research and test.

In addition, often the connection may be lost and may need to be re-established. To handle cross- browser and backward compatibility, as well as re-opening, a lot of developers depend on the Socket.IO library, which we will explore in the next section.

Socket.IO and Express.js Example

Full coverage of the Socket.IO (`http://socket.io`) library absolutely deserves its own book. Nevertheless, because it's such a popular library, and getting started with it is very easy with Express.js, I include in this chapter an example that covers the basics. This mini project illustrates duplex-channel communication between browser and server.

As in most real-time web apps, the communication between a server and a client happens in response either to some user actions or as a result of updates from the server. So, in our example, the web page renders a form field in which each character echoes (browser to server and back) in reverse in real time. The example harnesses Express.js command-line tool scaffolding, Socket.IO, and Pug (see screenshots of the working app in Figures 9-3 and 9-4). Of course, you can just download the app from `http://github.com/azat-co/practicalnode`.

To include Socket.IO, we can use `$ npm install socket.io@0.9.16--save` and repeat it for every module, or we can use `package.json` and `$ npm install`:

```json
{
  "name": "socket-express",
  "version": "0.1.0",
  "private": true,
  "scripts": {
    "start": "node app.js"
  },
  "dependencies": {
    "body-parser": "1.18.2",
    "cookie-parser": "1.4.3",
    "debug": "3.1.0",
    "express": "4.16.2",
    "morgan": "1.9.0",
    "pug": "2.0.0-rc.4",
    "socket.io": "2.0.4"
  }
}
```

Socket.IO, in some way, might be considered another server, because it handles socket connections and not our standard HTTP requests. This is how we refactor autogenerated Express.js code:

```js
const http = require('http')
const express = require('express')
const path = require('path')
const logger = require('morgan')
const bodyParser = require('body-parser')
```

The standard Express.js configuration is as follows:

```
const routes = require('./routes/index')
const app = express()

// view engine setup
app.set('views', path.join(__dirname, 'views'))
app.set('view engine', 'pug')

app.use(logger('dev'))
app.use(bodyParser.json())
app.use(bodyParser.urlencoded({extended: true}))
app.use(express.static(path.join(__dirname, 'public')))

app.use('/', routes)
```

Then, the Socket.IO piece is as follows:

```
const server = http.createServer(app)
const io = require('socket.io').listen(server)
```

When the Socket server connection is established, we attach a `messageChange` event listener that implements logic that is reversing an incoming string:

```
io.sockets.on('connection', (socket) => {
  socket.on('messageChange', (data) => {
    console.log(data)
    socket.emit('receive', data.message.split('').reverse().join(''))
  })
})
```

We finish by starting the server with `listen()` as we always do:

```
app.set('port', process.env.PORT || 3000)
server.listen(app.get('port'), () => {
  console.log(`Express server listening on port
  ${app.get('port')}`)
})
```

Just in case if these snippets are confusing, the full content of the Express app with SocketIO is in `code/ch9/socket-express/app.js`.

A quick remark about port numbers: by default, WebSocket connections can use the standard ports: 80 for HTTP and 443 for HTTPS.

Last, our app needs some front-end love in `index.pug`. Nothing fancy—just a form field and some front-end JavaScript in the Pug template:

```
extends layout

block content
  h1= title
  p Welcome to
    span.received-message #{title}
  input(type='text', class='message', placeholder='what is on your
  mind?', onkeyup='send(this)')
  script(src="/socket.io/socket.io.js")
  script.
    var socket = io.connect('http://localhost:3000');
    socket.on('receive', function (message) {
      console.log('received %s', message);
      document.querySelector('.received-message').innerText =
      message;
    });
    var send = function(input) {
      console.log(input.value)
      var value = input.value;
      console.log('sending %s to server', value);
      socket.emit('messageChange', {message: value});
    }
```

Again, start the server and open the browser to see real-time communication. Typing text in the browser field logs data on the server without messing up HTTP requests and waiting. The approximate browser results are shown in Figure 9-3; the server logs are shown in Figure 9-4.

Figure 9-3. *The input of* `!stekcoS` *yields* `Sockets!`

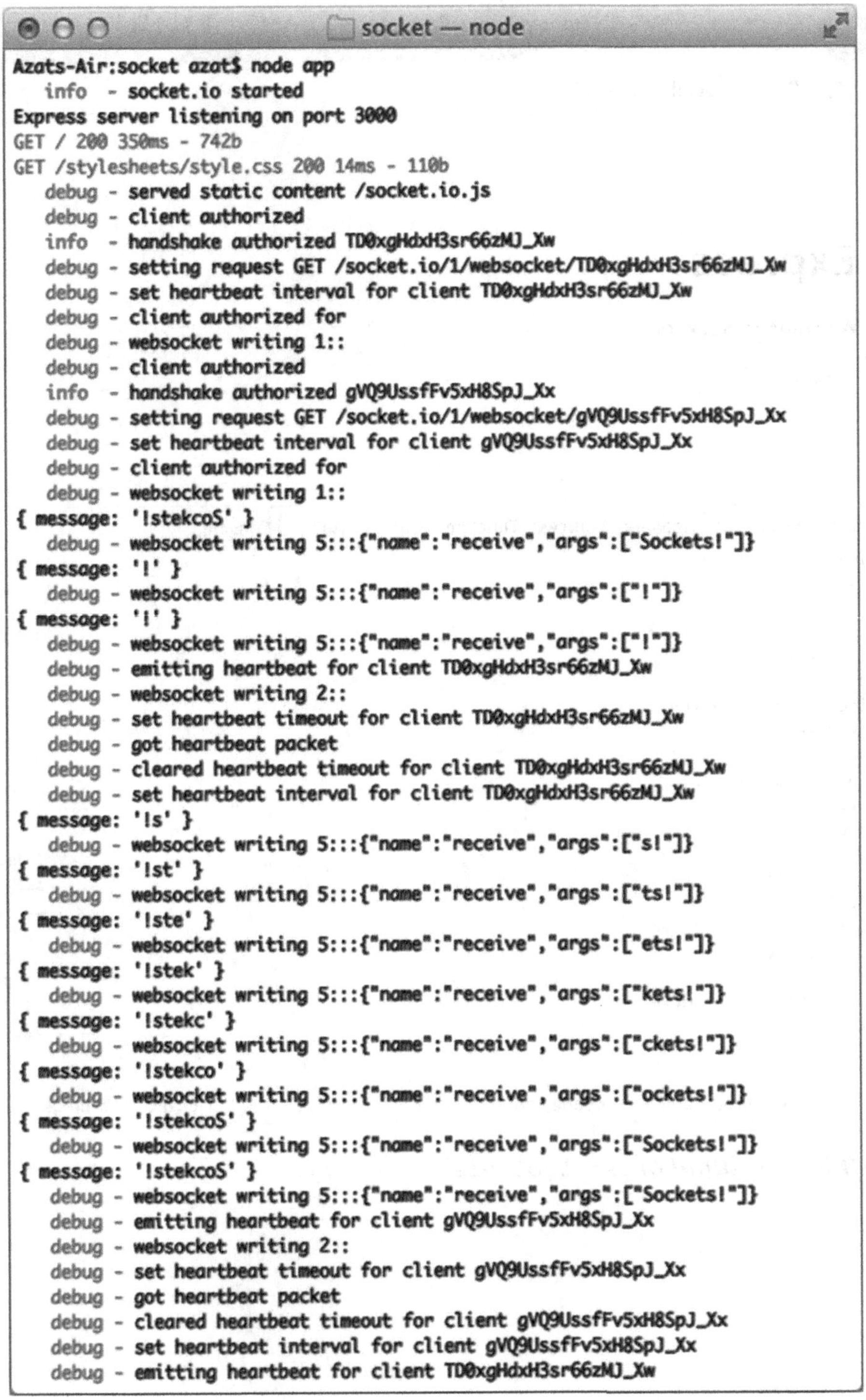

Figure 9-4. Express.js server catching and processing input in real time

For more Socket.IO examples, go to socket.io/#how-to-use (`http://socket.io/#how-to-use`).

Collaborative Online Code Editor Example with DerbyJS, Express.js, and MongoDB

Derby (`http://derbyjs.com`) is an interesting and sophisticated MVC framework designed to be used with Express (`http://expressjs.com`) as its middleware, whereas Express.js is a popular node framework that uses the middleware concept to enhance the functionality of applications. Derby also comes with the support of Racer (`https://github.com/codeparty/racer`), a data synchronization engine, and a Handlebars-like template engine (`http://handlebarsjs.com`), among many other features.

Meteor (`http://meteor.com`) and Sails.js (`http://sailsjs.org`) are other reactive (real-time) full-stack MVC Node.js frameworks comparable with DerbyJS. However, Meteor is more opinionated and often relies on proprietary solutions and packages.

The following example illustrates how easy it is to build a real-time application using Express.js, DerbyJS, MongoDB, and Redis.

The structure for this DerbyJS mini project is as follows:

- Project dependencies and `package.json`

- Server-side code

- DerbyJS app

- DerbyJS view

- Editor tryout

Project Dependencies and package.json

If you haven't installed Node.js, npm, MongoDB, or Redis, you can do it now by following instructions in these resources:

- Installing Node.js via package manager (`https://nodejs.org/en/download/package-manager/`)

- Installing npm (`https://www.npmjs.com/get-npm`)

- Install MongoDB (`http://bit.ly/2zrogUx`)

- Redis Quick Start (`http://redis.io/topics/quickstart`)

Create a project folder, `editor`, and a file `package.json` with the following content:

```json
{
  "name": "editor",
  "version": "0.0.1",
  "description": "Online collaborative code editor",
  "main": "index.js",
  "scripts": {
    "test": "mocha test"
  },
  "git repository": "http://github.com/azat-co/editor",
  "keywords": "editor node derby real-time",
  "author": "Azat Mardan",
  "license": "BSD",
  "dependencies": {
    "derby": "~0.5.12",
    "express": "~3.4.8",
    "livedb-mongo": "~0.3.0",
    "racer-browserchannel": "~0.1.1",
    "redis": "~0.10.0"
  }
}
```

This gets us the `derby` (DerbyJS), `express` (Express.js), `livedb-mongo`, `racer-browserchannel`, and `redis` (Redis client) modules. DerbyJS and Express.js are for routing and they use corresponding frameworks (versions 0.5.12 and 3.4.8). Redis, `racer-browserchannel`, and `livedb-mongo` allow DerbyJS to use Redis and MongoDB databases.

Server-side Code

As an entry point for our application, create `editor/server.js` with a single line of code that starts a Derby server we have yet to write:

```
require('derby').run(__dirname + '/server.js');
```

Create and start adding the following lines to `editor/server.js`. First, import the dependencies:

```
var path = require('path'),
  express = require('express'),
  derby = require('derby'),
  racerBrowserChannel = require('racer-browserchannel'),
  liveDbMongo = require('livedb-mongo'),
```

Then, define the Derby app file:

```
app = require(path.join(__dirname, 'app.js')),
```

Instantiate the Express.js app:

```
expressApp = module.exports = express(),
```

And the Redis client:

```
redis = require('redis').createClient(),
```

And the local MongoDB connection URI:

```
mongoUrl = 'mongodb://localhost:27017/editor';
```

Now we create a `liveDbMongo` object with the connection URI and `redis` client object:

```
var store = derby.createStore({
  db: liveDbMongo(mongoUrl + '?auto_reconnect', {
    safe: true
  }),
  redis: redis
});
```

Define a public folder with static content:

```
var publicDir = path.join(__dirname, 'public');
```

Then, declare Express.js middleware in chained calls:

```
expressApp
  .use(express.favicon())
  .use(express.compress())
```

It's important to include DerbyJS-specific middleware that exposes Derby routes and model objects:

```
  .use(app.scripts(store))
  .use(racerBrowserChannel(store))
  .use(store.modelMiddleware())
  .use(app.router())
```

Regular Express.js router middleware follows:

```
  .use(expressApp.router);
```

It's possible to mix Express.js and DerbyJS routes in one server—the 404 catchall route:

```
expressApp.all('*', function(req, res, next) {
  return next('404: ' + req.url);
});
```

The full source code of `server.js` is as follows:

```
var path = require('path'),
  express = require('express'),
  derby = require('derby'),
  racerBrowserChannel = require('racer-browserchannel'),
  liveDbMongo = require('livedb-mongo'),
  app = require(path.join(__dirname, 'app.js')),
  expressApp = module.exports = express(),
  redis = require('redis').createClient(),
  mongoUrl = 'mongodb://localhost:27017/editor';
```

```
var store = derby.createStore({
  db: liveDbMongo(mongoUrl + '?auto_reconnect', {
    safe: true
  }),
  redis: redis
});

var publicDir = path.join(__dirname, 'public');

expressApp
  .use(express.favicon())
  .use(express.compress())
  .use(app.scripts(store))
  .use(racerBrowserChannel(store))
  .use(store.modelMiddleware())
  .use(app.router())
  .use(expressApp.router);

  expressApp.all('*', function(req, res, next) {
  return next('404: ' + req.url);
});
```

DerbyJS App

The DerbyJS app (`app.js`) shares code smartly between the browser and the server, so you can write functions and methods in one place (a Node.js file). However, parts of `app.js` code become browser JavaScript code (not just Node.js) depending on the DerbyJS rules. This behavior allows for better code reuse and organization, because you don't have to duplicate routes, the helper function, and utility methods. One of the places where the code from the DerbyJS app file becomes browser code only is inside `app.ready()`, which we will see later.

Declare the variable and create an app (`editor/app.js`):

```
var app;
app = require('derby').createApp(module);
```

Declare the root route so that when a user visits it, the new snippet is created and the user is redirected to the `/:snippetId` route:

```
app.get('/', function(page, model, _arg, next) {
  snippetId = model.add('snippets', {
    snippetName: _arg.snippetName,
    code: 'var'
  });
  return page.redirect('/' + snippetId);
});
```

DerbyJS uses a route pattern similar to Express.js, but instead of response (`res`), we use `page`, and we get data from the `model` argument.

The `/:snippetId` route is where the editor is displayed. To support real-time updates to the Document Object Model (DOM), all we need to do is to call `subscribe`:

```
app.get('/:snippetId', function(page, model, param, next) {
  var snippet = model.at('snippets.'+param.snippetId);
  snippet.subscribe(function(err){
    if (err) return next(err);
    console.log (snippet.get());
    model.ref('_page.snippet', snippet);
    page.render();
  });
});
```

The `model.at` method with a parameter in a `collection_name.ID` pattern is akin to calling `findById()`—in other words, we get the object from the store/database.

`model.ref()` allows us to bind an object to the view representation. Usually in the view we would write `{{_page.snippet}}` and it would update itself reactively. However, to make the editor look beautiful, we use the Ace editor from Cloud9 (`http://ace.c9.io`). Ace is attached to the `editor` object (global browser variable).

Front-end JavaScript code in DerbyJS is written in the `app.ready` callback. We need to set Ace content from the Derby model on app start:

```
app.ready(function(model) {
  editor.setValue(model.get('_page.snippet.code'));
```

Then, it listens to model changes (coming from other users) and updates the Ace editor with new text (front-end code):

```
model.on('change', '_page.snippet.code', function(){
  if (editor.getValue() !== model.get('_page.snippet.code')) {
    process.nextTick(function(){
      editor.setValue(model.get('_page.snippet.code'), 1);
    })
  }
});
```

`process.nextTick` is a function that schedules the callback (passed as a parameter to it) in the next event loop iteration. This trick allows us to avoid an infinite loop when the updated model from one user triggers a change event on the Ace editor, and that triggers an unnecessary update on the remote model.

The code that listens to Ace changes (e.g., new character) and updates the DerbyJS model:

```
editor.getSession().on('change', function(e) {
  if (editor.getValue() !== model.get('_page.snippet.code')) {
    process.nextTick(function(){
      model.set('_page.snippet.code', editor.getValue());
    });
  }
});
});
```

`_page` is a special DerbyJS name used for rendering/binding in the views.

For reference, the full source code of `editor/app.js` is as follows:

```
var app;

app = require('derby').createApp(module);

app.get('/', function(page, model, _arg, next) {
  snippetId = model.add('snippets', {
    snippetName: _arg.snippetName,
    code: 'var'
  });
```

```
  return page.redirect('/' + snippetId);
});

app.get('/:snippetId', function(page, model, param, next) {
  var snippet = model.at('snippets.'+param.snippetId);
  snippet.subscribe(function(err){
    if (err) return next(err);
    console.log (snippet.get());
    model.ref('_page.snippet', snippet);
    page.render();
  });
});

app.ready(function(model) {
  editor.setValue(model.get('_page.snippet.code'));
  model.on('change', '_page.snippet.code', function(){
    if (editor.getValue() !== model.get('_page.snippet.code')) {
      process.nextTick(function(){
        editor.setValue(model.get('_page.snippet.code'), 1);
      });
    }
  });
  editor.getSession().on('change', function(e) {
    if (editor.getValue() !== model.get('_page.snippet.code')) {
      process.nextTick(function(){
        model.set('_page.snippet.code', editor.getValue());
      });
    }
  });
});
```

DerbyJS View

The DerbyJS view (`views/app.html`) is quite straightforward. It contains built-in tags such as `<Title:>`, but most of the things are generated dynamically by the Ace editor after the page is loaded.

Let's start by defining the title and head:

```
<Title:>
  Online Collaborative Code Editor
<Head:>
  <meta charset="UTF-8">
  <meta http-equiv="X-UA-Compatible" content="IE=edge,chrome=1">
  <title>Editor</title>
  <style type="text/css" media="screen">
    body {
        overflow: hidden;
    }

    #editor {
        margin: 0;
        position: absolute;
        top: 0px;
        bottom: 0;
        left: 0;
        right: 0;
    }
  </style>
```

Then, load jQuery and Ace from content delivery networks (CDNs):

```
<script src="//cdnjs.cloudflare.com/ajax/libs/ace/1.1.01/ace.js">
</script>
<script src="//code.jquery.com/jquery-2.1.0.min.js"></script>
```

Apply a hidden `input` tag and editor element inside the body tag:

```
<Body:>
  <input type="hidden" value="{_page.snippet.code}" class="code"/>
  <pre id="editor" value="{_page.snippet.code}"></pre>
```

Initialize the Ace editor object as global (the `editor` variable), then set the theme and language (of course, JavaScript!) with `setTheme()` and `setMode()`, respectively:

```
<script>
    var editor = ace.edit("editor");
    editor.setTheme("ace/theme/twilight");
    editor.getSession().setMode("ace/mode/javascript");
</script>
```

The full source code of `views/app.html` is as follows:

```
<Title:>
  Online Collaborative Code Editor
<Head:>
  <meta charset="UTF-8">
  <meta http-equiv="X-UA-Compatible" content="IE=edge,chrome=1">
  <title>Editor</title>
  <style type="text/css" media="screen">
    body {
        overflow: hidden;
    }

    #editor {
        margin: 0;
        position: absolute;
        top: 0px;
        bottom: 0;
        left: 0;
        right: 0;
    }
  </style>
  <script src="//cdnjs.cloudflare.com/ajax/libs/ace/1.1.01/ace.js">
  </script>
  <script src="//code.jquery.com/jquery-2.1.0.min.js"></script>
<Body:>
  <input type="hidden" value="{_page.snippet.code}" class="code"/>
  <pre id="editor" value="{_page.snippet.code}"></pre>
```

```
<script>
    var editor = ace.edit("editor");
    editor.setTheme("ace/theme/twilight");
    editor.getSession().setMode("ace/mode/javascript");
</script>
```

Note   It's vital to preserve the same view name (i.e., `app.html`) as the DerbyJS app file (`app.js`), because this is how the framework knows what to use.

Editor Tryout

If you followed all the previous steps, there should be `app.js`, `index.js`, `server.js`, `views/app.html`, and `package.json` files.

Let's install the modules with `$ npm install`. Start the databases with `$ mongod` and `$ redis- server`, and leave them running. Then, launch the app with `$ node .` or `$ node index`.

Open the first browser window at `http://localhost:3000/` and it should redirect you to a new snippet (with ID in the URL). Open a second browser window at the same location and start typing (Figure 9-5). You should see the code updating in the first window! Congratulations! In just a few minutes, we built an app that might have taken programmers a few months to build back in the 2000s, when front-end JavaScript and AJAX-y web sites were first gaining popularity.

Figure 9-5. *Collaborative online code editor*

The working project is available on GitHub at `https://github.com/azat-co/` `editor`.

Summary

In this chapter, we saw that there's native support for WebSocket in modern HTML5 browsers, and we learned how to get started with Socket.IO and Express.js to harness the power of WebSocket in Node.js. In addition, we explored the mighty full-stack framework of DerbyJS in the editor example.

In the next chapter we'll move to the essential part of any real-world project, which is getting Node.js apps to a production-level readiness by adding extra configuration, monitoring, logging, and other things.

CHAPTER 10

Getting Node.js Apps Production Ready

Getting Node.js apps to a production-ready state is probably the most unexplored and skipped topic in the Node.js literature. The reason could be the lack of expertise in production deployments or the vast number of options and edge cases. However, getting apps to the production level is one of the most important topics in this entire book in my humble opinion.

Yes, the apps differ in structures, the frameworks they use, and the goals they try to achieve; however, there are a few commonalities worth knowing about—for example, environmental variables, multithreading, logging, and error handling. So, in this chapter, we cover the following topics:

- Environment variables

- Express.js in production

- Socket.IO in production

- Error handling

- Node.js domains for error handling

- Multithreading with Cluster

- Multithreading with Cluster2

- Event logging and monitoring

- Building tasks with Grunt

- Locking dependencies

- Git for version control and deployments

- Running tests in Cloud with TravisCI

331

© Azat Mardan 2018
A. Mardan, *Practical Node.js*, https://doi.org/10.1007/978-1-4842-3039-8_10

Environment Variables

Before deployment to the production environment, it's good to prepare our app's code. Let's start with information that needs to be private and can't be shared in a version control system. Sensitive information such as API keys, passwords, and database URIs are best stored in environment variables, not in the source code itself. Node.js makes it fairly easy to access these variables:

```
console.log(process.env.NODE_ENV,
  process.env.API_KEY,
  process.env.DB_PASSWORD)
```

Then, before the application is started, set these variables:

```
$ NODE_ENV=test API_KEY=XYZ DB_PASSWORD=ABC node envvar.js
```

Note   There's no space between `NAME` and value (`NAME=VALUE`).

Typically, the environment variable setting is a part of the deployment or operations setup. In the next chapter, we deal with putting these variables on the server.

Express.js in Production

In Express.js, use if/else statements to check for `NODE_ENV` values to use different levels of server logs. For development, we want more information, but in production, stack and exceptions might reveal a vulnerability, so we hide them:

```
const errorHandler = require('errorhandler')
if (process.env.NODE_ENV === 'development') {
  app.use(errorHandler({
    dumpExceptions: true,
    showStack: true
  }))
} else if (process.env.NODE_ENV === 'production') {
  app.use(errorHandler())
}
```

You might be wondering, where this mystical and mysterious `process.env.NODE_ENV` comes from. Very easy. It is an environment variable, and as with all other environment variables, developers can set them outside, in the shell (bash or zsh or other) environment. The environment variables are set with `KEY=VALUE` syntax or prefixed with `export KEY=VALUE` when set for the duration of the entire shell session. For example, to run the server in a production mode, just set an environment variable to production:

```
$ NODE_ENV=production node app.js
```

Notice that the env var `NODE_ENV` and the command `node` were on the same command and line (unless you continue the command on a new line with \). You must have them in one command. If you want to set the environment variable once for multiple commands, then `export` is your friend:

```
$ export NODE_ENV=production
$ node app.js
```

Note   By default, Express.js falls back to development mode as we see in the source code (`http://bit.ly/1l7UEi6`). Thus, set the `NODE_ENV` environment variable to `production` when in the production environment.

Let's talk about sessions now. When using in-memory session store (the default choice), the data can't be shared across different processes/servers (which we want in production mode). Conveniently, Express.js and Connect notify us about this as we see in this source code (`http://bit.ly/1nnvvhf`) with this message:

```
Warning: connect.session() MemoryStore is not
designed for a production environment, as it will leak
memory, and will not scale past a single process.
```

What we need here is a single source of truth—one location where all the session data is stored and can be accessed by multiple Node servers. This problem is solved easily by using a shared Redis instance as a session store. For example, for Express.js, execute the following:

```
const session = require('express-session')
const RedisStore = require('connect-redis')(session)

app.use(session({
  store: new RedisStore(options),
  secret: '33D203B7-443B'
}))
```

The secret is just some random string to make hacking of the session harder. Ideally, you would take it from an environment variable to make it not be in the source code:

```
app.use(session({
  store: new RedisStore(options),
  secret: process.env.SESSION_SECRET
}))
```

Let me give you a more advanced example with session options that includes a special key and cookie domain:

```
const SessionStore = require('connect-redis')
const session = require('express-session')

app.use(session({
  key: process.env.SESSION_KEY',
  secret: process.env.SESSION_SECRET,
  store: new SessionStore({
    cookie: {domain: '.webapplog.com'},
    db: 1, // Redis DB
    host: 'webapplog.com'
}))
```

Options for `connect-redis` are `client`, `host`, `port`, `ttl`, `db`, `pass`, `prefix`, and `url`. For more information, please refer to the official `connect-redis` documentation (`https://github.com/visionmedia/connect-redis`).

Error Handling

As a rule of thumb, when readying your code for production, make sure to listen to *all* error events from `http.Server` and `https.Server`, i.e., always have `error` event listeners doing something like this:

```
server.on('error', (err) => {
  console.error(err)
  // ...
})
```

Then have a catchall event listener (`uncaughtException`) for unforeseen cases. This event is the *last* step before the app will crash, terminate the process, and burn your computer to ashes. Do not try to resume a normal operation when you have this event. Log, save work (if you have anything left), and exit like this:

```
process.on('uncaughtException', (err) => {
  console.error('uncaughtException: ', err.message)
  console.error(err.stack)
  process.exit(1) // 1 is for errors, 0 is okay
})
```

Alternatively, you can use the `addListener` method:

```
process.addListener('uncaughtException', (err) => {
  console.error('uncaughtException: ', err.message)
  console.error(err.stack);
  process.exit(1)
})
```

Just to give you another example, the following snippet is devised to catch uncaught exceptions, log them, notify development and operations (DevOps) via email/text messages (`server.notify`), and then exit:

```
process.addListener('uncaughtException', (err) => {
  server.statsd.increment('errors.uncaughtexception')
  log.sub('uncaughtException').error(err.stack || err.message)
```

```
if (server.notify && server.set('env') === 'production') {
    server.notify.error(err)
  }
  process.exit(1)
})
```

You might wonder what to do in the event of these uncaught exceptions (the `server.notify.error()` method). It depends. Typically, at a minimum, we want them to be recorded, most likely in the logs. For this purpose, later we'll cover a more advanced alternative to `console.log`—the Winston library (`https://github.com/winstonjs`).

At a maximum, you can implement text message alerts effortlessly using the Twilio API (`http://www.twilio.com`). The following is an example in which helpers can send Slack or HipChat messages via their REST API and send an email containing an error stack:

```
const sendHipChatMessage = (message, callback) => {
  const fromhost = server
    .set('hostname')
    .replace('-','')
    .substr(0, 15); //truncate the string
  try {
    message = JSON.stringify(message)
  } catch(e) {}
  const data = {
    'format': 'json',
    auth_token: server.config.keys.hipchat.servers,
    room_id: server.config.keys.hipchat.serversRoomId,
    from: fromhost,
    message: `v ${server.set('version')} message: ${message}`
  }
  request({
    url:'http://api.hipchat.com/v1/rooms/message',
    method:'POST',
```

```
      qs: data}, function (e, r, body) {
        if (e) console.error(e)
        if (callback) return callback();
    })
}
server.notify = {}
server.notify.error = (e) => {
  const message = e.stack || e.message || e.name || e
  sendHipChatMessage(message)
  console.error(message)
  server.sendgrid.email({
    to: 'error@webapplog.com',
    from: server.set('hostname') + '@webapplog.com',
    subject: `Webapp ${server.set('version')} error: "${e.name}"`,
    category: 'webapp-error',
    text: e.stack || e.message
  }, exit)
  return
}
```

Multithreading with Cluster

There are a lot of opinions out there against Node.js that are rooted in the myth that Node.js-based systems *have* to be single-threaded. Although a single Node.js process *is* single-threaded, nothing could be further from the truth about the systems. And with the core `cluster` module (`http://nodejs.org/api/cluster.html`), we can spawn many Node.js processes effortlessly to handle the system's load. These individual processes use the same source code, and they can listen to the same port. Typically, each process uses one machine's CPU. There's a master process that spawns all other processes and, in a way, controls them (it can kill, restart, and so on).

Here is a working example of an Express.js (version 4.x or 3.x) app that runs on four processes. At the beginning of the file, we import dependencies:

```
const cluster = require('cluster')
const http = require('http')
const numCPUs = require('os').cpus().length
const express = require('express')
```

The `cluster` module has a property that tells us whether the process is master or child (master controls children). We use it to spawn four workers (the default workers use the same file, but devs can overwrite that with `setupMaster` (http://bit. ly/2zs9Bsn)). In addition, we can attach event listeners and receive messages from workers (e.g., `kill`).

```
if (cluster.isMaster) {
  console.log (' Fork %s worker(s) from master', numCPUs)
  for (let i = 0; i < numCPUs; i++) {
    cluster.fork()
  }
  cluster.on('online', (worker) => {
    console.log ('worker is running on %s pid', worker.process.pid)
  })
  cluster.on('exit', (worker, code, signal) => {
    console.log('worker with %s is closed', worker.process.pid)
  })
}
```

The worker code is just an Express.js app with a twist. We would like to see that a request was handled by a different process. Each process has a unique ID. Let's get the process ID:

```
} else if (cluster.isWorker) {
  const port = 3000
  console.log(`worker (${cluster.worker.process.pid}) is now
  listening to http://localhost:${port}`)
  const app = express()
  app.get('*', (req, res) => {
    res.send(200, `cluser ${cluster.worker.process.pid} responded \n`)
  })
  app.listen(port)
}
```

The full source code of `cluster.js` can be found in `practicalnode/code/ch10/examples/cluster.js`.

As usual, to start an app, run $ `node cluster`. There should be four (or two, depending on your machine's architecture) processes, as shown in Figure 10-1.

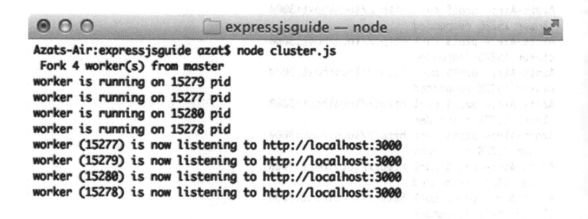

```
Azats-Air:expressjsguide azat$ node cluster.js
 Fork 4 worker(s) from master
worker is running on 15279 pid
worker is running on 15277 pid
worker is running on 15280 pid
worker is running on 15278 pid
worker (15277) is now listening to http://localhost:3000
worker (15279) is now listening to http://localhost:3000
worker (15280) is now listening to http://localhost:3000
worker (15278) is now listening to http://localhost:3000
```

Figure 10-1. *Starting four processes with Cluster*

When we CURL with $ `curl http://localhost:3000`, there are different processes that listen to the *same* port and respond to us (Figure 10-2).

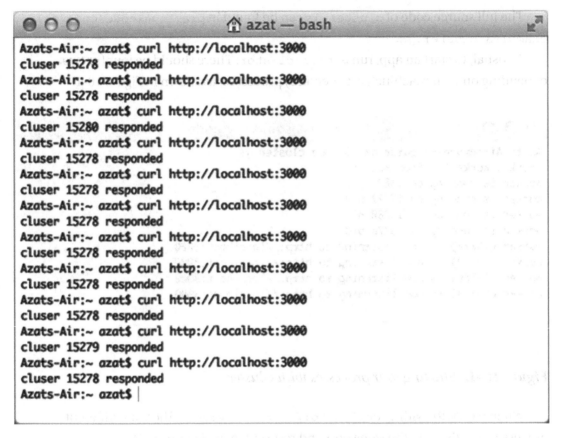

Figure 10-2. *Server response is rendered by different processes.*

Multithreading with pm2

Achieving multithreading with pm2 is even simpler than with cluster because there's no need to modify the source code. pm2 will pick up your `server.js` file and fork it into multiple processes. Each process will be listening on the same port, so your system will have load balanced between the processes. pm2 goes into the background because it works as a service. You can name each set of processes, view, restart, or stop them.

To get started with pm2, first you need to install it. You can do it globally on your production VM:

```
$ npm i -g pm2
```

Once you have `pm2`, use `start` command with the option `-i 0`, which means automatically determine the number of CPUs and launch that many processes. Here's an example of launching a multithreaded server from `app.js`:

```
$ pm2 start -i 0 app.js
```

Once the processes are running, get the list of them by using

```
$ pm2 ls
```

You can terminate all processes with

```
$ pm2 stop all
```

Alternatively, you can name your application which you want to scale up with `--name`:

```
$ pm2 start ./hello-world.js -i 0 --name "node-app"
```

and then restart or stop only that app by its name.

What's good about `pm2` is that you can use it for development too, because when you install pm2 with npm, you get the `$ pm2-dev` command. The way it works is very similar to `$ nodemon` or `$ node-dev`. It will monitor for any file changes in the project folder and restart the Node code when needed.

For Docker containers, use `$ pm2-docker`. It has some special features that make running Node inside of a container better. To get the `$ pm2-docker` command, simply install `pm2` with npm globally, as was shown before.

Event Logging and Monitoring

When things go south (e.g., memory leaks, overloads, crashes), there are two things software engineers can do:

1. Monitor via dashboard and health statuses (monitoring and REPL)

2. Analyze postmortems after the events have happened (Winston and Papertrail)

Monitoring

When going to production, software and development operations engineers need a way to get current status quickly. Having a dashboard or just an endpoint that spits out JSON-formatted properties is a good idea, including properties such as the following:

- `memoryUsage`: Memory usage information
- `uptime`: Number of seconds the Node.js process is running
- `pid`: Process ID
- `connections`: Number of connections
- `loadavg`: Load average
- `sha`: Secure Hash Algorithm (SHA) of the Git commit deploy and/or version tag of the deploy

Here's an example of the Express.js route `/status`:

```
app.get('/status', (req, res) => {
  res.send({`
    pid: process.pid,`
    memory: process.memoryUsage(),`
    uptime: process.uptime()
  })
})
```

A more informative example with connections and other information is as follows:

```
const os = require('os')
const exec = require('child_process').exec
const async = require('async')
const started_at = new Date()

module.exports = (req, res, next) => {
  const server = req.app
  if(req.param('info')) {
    let connections = {}
    let swap
```

```
async.parallel([
  (done) => {
    exec('netstat -an | grep :80 | wc -l', (e, res) => {
      connections['80'] = parseInt(res,10)
      done()
    })
  },
  (done) => {
    exec(
      'netstat -an | grep :'
        + server.set('port')
        + ' | wc -l',
      (e, res) => {
        connections[server.set('port')] = parseInt(res,10)
        done()
      }
    )
  },
  (done) => {
    exec('vmstat -SM -s | grep "used swap" | sed -E "s/
    [^0-9]*([0-9]{1,8}).*/\1/"', (e, res) => {
      swap = res
      done()
    })
  }], (e) => {
    res.send({
      status: 'up',
      version: server.get('version'),
      sha: server.et('git sha'),
      started_at: started_at,
      node: {
        version: process.version,
        memoryUsage: Math.round(process.memoryUsage().rss / 1024
        / 1024)+"M",
        uptime: process.uptime()
      },
```

```
        system: {
          loadavg: os.loadavg(),
          freeMemory: Math.round(os.freemem()/1024/1024)+"M"
        },
          env: process.env.NODE_ENV,
          hostname: os.hostname(),
          connections: connections,
          swap: swap
        })
      })
    }
    else {
      res.send({status: 'up'})
    }
  }
```

REPL in Production

What can be better than poking around a live process and its context using the REPL
tool? We can do this easily with production apps if we set up REPL as a server:

```
const net = require('net')
const options = {name: 'azat'}

net.createServer(function(socket) {
  repl.start(options.name + "> ", socket).context.app = app
}).listen("/tmp/repl-app-" + options.name)
```

Then, connect to the remote machine by using Secure Shell (SSH). Once on the
remote machine, run:

```
$ telnet /tmp/repl-app-azat
```

You should be prompted with a more sign (>), which means you're in the REPL.
Or, if you want to connect to the remote server right away, i.e., bypassing the SSH
step, you can modify the code to this:

```
const repl = require('repl')
const net = require('net')
```

```
const options = { name: 'azat' }
const app = {a: 1}
net.createServer(function(socket) {
  repl.start(options.name + "> ", socket).context.app = app
}).listen(3000)
```

Please use `iptable` to restrict the Internet protocol addresses (IPs) when using this approach. Then, straight from your local machine (where the hostname is the IP of the remote box), execute:

```
$ telnet hostname 3000
```

Winston

Winston provides a way to have one interface for logging events while defining multiple transports, e.g., email, database, file, console, Software as a Service (SaaS), and so on. In other words, Winston is an abstraction layer for the server logs.

The list of transports supported by Winston includes lots of good services: Loggly (`https://www.loggly.com`), Riak, MongoDB, SimpleDB, Mail, Amazon SNS, Graylog2, Papertrail, Cassandra, and you can write to console and file too! (We used Papertrail at Storify.com to debug and it went so well that later we got acquired by a bigger company, and now Storify is a part of Adobe.)

It's easy to get started with Winston. Install it into your project:

```
$ npm i -SE winston
```

In the code, implement the import and then you can log:

```
var winston = require('winston')
winston.log('info', 'Hello distributed log files!')
winston.info('Hello again distributed logs')
```

The power of Winston comes when you add transporters. To add and remove transporters, use the `winston.add()` and `winston.remove()` functions.

To add a file transporter, provide a file name:

```
winston.add(winston.transports.File, {filename: 'webapp.log'})
```

To remove a transporter, use:

```
winston.remove(winston.transports.Console)
```

For more information, go to the official documentation (`http://bit.ly/2zs4xEm`).

Papertrail App for Logging

Papertrail (`https://papertrailapp.com`) is a SaaS that provides centralized storage and a web GUI to search and analyze logs. To use Papertrail with the Node.js app, do the following:

1. Write logs to a file and `remote_sync` (`https://github.com/papertrail/remote_syslog2`) them to Papertrail

2. Send logs with `winston` (`http://bit.ly/2zs4xEm`), which is described earlier, and winston-papertrail (`https://github.com/kenperkins/winston-papertrail`), directly to the service

Building Tasks with Grunt

Grunt is a Node.js-based task runner. It performs compilations, minifications, linting, unit testing, and other important tasks for automation.

Install Grunt globally with npm:

```
$ npm install -g grunt-cli
```

Grunt uses `Gruntfile.js` to store its tasks. For example:

```
module.exports = function(grunt) {
  // Project configuration

  grunt.initConfig({
    pkg: grunt.file.readJSON('package.json'),
    uglify: {
      options: {
        banner: '/*! <%= pkg.name %> <%= grunt.template.today
        ("dd-mm-yyyy") %> */\n'
      },
```

```
    build: {
      src: 'src/<%= pkg.name %>.js',
      dest: 'build/<%= pkg.name %>.min.js'
    }
  }
})

// Load the plugin that provides the "uglify" task
grunt.loadNpmTasks('grunt-contrib-uglify')

// Default task
grunt.registerTask('default', ['uglify'])
}
```

package.json should have plugins required by the grunt.loadNpmTasks()
method. For example:

```
{
  "name": "grunt-example",
  "version": "0.0.1",
  "devDependencies": {
    "grunt": "~0.4.2",
    "grunt-contrib-jshint": "~0.6.3",
    "grunt-contrib-uglify": "~0.2.2",
    "grunt-contrib-coffee": "~0.10.1",
    "grunt-contrib-concat": "~0.3.0"
  }
}
```

Let's move to the more complex example in which we use jshint, uglify, coffee,
and concat plugins in the default task in Gruntfile.js.

Start by defining package.json:

```
module.exports = function(grunt) {

  grunt.initConfig({
    pkg: grunt.file.readJSON('package.json'),
```

And then the `coffee` task:

```
coffee: {
  compile: {
    files: {
```

The first parameter is the destination, and the second is `source`:

```
      'source/<%= pkg.name %>.js': ['source/**/*.coffee']
      // Compile and concatenate into single file
    }
  }
},
```

`concat` merges multiple files into one to reduce the number of HTTP requests:

```
concat: {
  options: {
    separator: ';'
  },
```

This time, our target is in the `build` folder:

```
  dist: {
    src: ['source/**/*.js'],
    dest: 'build/<%= pkg.name %>.js'
  }
},
```

The `uglify` method minifies our `*.js` file:

```
uglify: {
  options: {
    banner: '/*! <%= pkg.name %> <%= grunt.template.today
    ("dd-mm-yyyy") %> */\n'
  },
  dist: {
    files: {
```

Again, the first value is the destination; the second dynamic name is from the concat task:

```
            'build/<%= pkg.name %>.min.js': ['<%= concat.dist.dest %>']
        }
      }
    },
```

jshint is a linter and shows errors if the code is not compliant:

```
  jshint: {
    files: ['Gruntfile.js', 'source/**/*.js'],
    options: {
      // options here to override JSHint defaults
      globals: {
        jQuery: true,
        console: true,
        module: true,
        document: true
      }
    }
  }
})
```

Load the modules to make them accessible for Grunt:

```
grunt.loadNpmTasks('grunt-contrib-uglify')
grunt.loadNpmTasks('grunt-contrib-jshint')
grunt.loadNpmTasks('grunt-contrib-concat')
grunt.loadNpmTasks('grunt-contrib-coffee')
```

Lastly, define the default task as a sequence of subtasks:

```
  grunt.registerTask('default', [ 'jshint', 'coffee','concat',
  'uglify'])
}
```

To run the task, simply execute $ `grunt` or $ `grunt` `default`.
`Gruntfile.js` is in `code/ch10/grunt-example`.
The results of running $ `grunt` are shown in Figure 10-3.

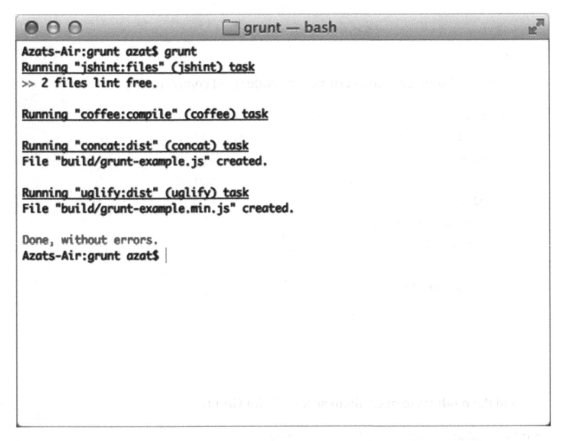

Figure 10-3. *The results of the Grunt default task*

A Brief on Webpack

Someone might argue that a better alternative to Grunt might be Webpack. Maybe. Let's see how to get started with Webpack. You need to have the `webpack.config.js` file in your project root. Luckily, this file is not of some weird format such as YML or JSON but of a good old Node module. So we start the `webpack.config.js` implementation with `module.exports`.

At a bare minimum, you would have a starting point from which Webpack will unfold all the source code and its dependencies. This is `entry`. And you would have `output` that is the bundled and compiled file. Everything else is just extra and adds extra transpilers, source maps, and other features.

```
module.exports = {
  entry: "./jsx/app.jsx",
  output: {
    path: __dirname + '/js',
    filename: "bundle.js"
  },
  // ... More configurations
}
```

For example, here's a Webpack configuration file from my new book on React.js called React Quickly (Manning, 2017) (`http://bit.ly/1RbD616`). In this config file, I point to the source file `app.jsx`, which is in the `jsx` folder. I write the resulting bundle file into the folder `js`. This bundle file is named `bundle.js`. It comes with source maps `bundle.map.js` because I included the `devtool` setting. `module` ensures that my JSX (a special language designed just for React) is converted into regular JavaScript. I use Babel for that via the library called `babel-loader`. Take a look at the entire config file:

```
module.exports = {
  entry: "./jsx/app.jsx",
  output: {
    path: __dirname + '/js',
    filename: "bundle.js"
  },
  devtool: '#sourcemap',
  stats: {
    colors: true,
    reasons: true
  },
```

```
module: {
  loaders: [
    {
      test: /\.jsx?$/,
      exclude: /(node_modules)/,
      loader: 'babel-loader'
    }
  ]
}
}
```

The command to install Webpack locally is `npm i webpack -ES` (or without `S` if you are using npm v5+). Then execute the bundling/compilation with `node_modules/.bin/webpack`. As with other tools, I do not recommend installing Webpack globally because that might lead to conflicts between versions.

So Webpack by default will look for the `webpack.config.js` file. Of course, you can name your file something other than `webpack.config.js`, but in this case you would have to tell Webpack what file to use. You can do so with the option `--config`, such as in `node_modules/.bin/webpack --config my-weird-config-filename-example.config.js`.

There's also a `watch` option that will rebuild the bundle file on any file change in the source. Just add `--watch` to the `webpack` command.

The way webpack works is by using loaders and plugins. What's the difference? Plugins are more powerful, while loaders are more simplistic. For example, `babel-loader` is a loader that converts JSX into regular JavaScript. Contrary, the Hot Module Replacement (HMR) plugin is a plugin that enables partial updates on the Webpack server by sending chunks of data on WebSockets.

Speaking of HMR. It's very cool and awesome. It can save you a lot of time. The idea is that you can modify your front-end app partially without losing app state. For example, after logging in, performing a search, and clicking a few times, you are deep down in your front-end application looking at a detailed view of some item. Without HMR, you have to perform this entire process each time you want to see a change in your code appear. Log in, enter search, find item, click, click, click. You get the idea. With HMR, you just edit code, save the file, and boom! Your app has the change (or not) at the exact same view. In other words, your app retains state. Hot Module Replacement is a wonderful feature.

You want to use webpack dev server for HMR. This dev server is built on Express, by the way. For an HMR guide, see this documentation because Webpack HMR changes fast and by the time you read this my example may be out-of-date.

Loaders are awesome too. Example of loaders include libraries to work with CSS, images, and of course JavaScript. For example, `css-loader` will allow to use `import` and `require` in the Node code to import CSS code, while `style-loader` will inject a CSS style into the DOM with a `<script>` tag. Crazy, huh?

The bottom line is that Webpack is powerful. Use it.

Locking Dependencies

Consider this scenario: we use Express.js that depends on, say, Pug of the latest version (*). Everything works until, unknown to us, Pug is updated with breaking changes. Express.js now uses Pug that breaks our code. No bueno.

Not-locking versions is a common convention for npm modules (as discussed in Chapter 12), i.e., they don't lock the versions of *their* dependencies. So, as you might guess, this may lead to a trouble because when a dependency (or a dependency of a dependency) gets a breaking change, our apps won't work.

Using ^ or * or leaving the version field in `package.json` blank will lead to higher versions of dependencies down the road when, after some time, you or someone else (or automated CI/CD server) executes `npm install`.

One solution is to commit `node_modules`. Why do this? Because, even if we lock dependency A in our `package.json`, most likely this module A has a wild card * or version range in its `package.json`. Therefore, our app might be exposed to unpleasant surprises when an update to the A module dependency breaks our system.

And don't send me hate mail (I delete it anyway). We committed `node_modules` to Git at DocuSign and it worked fine. We slept well at night knowing that if npm goes down, which happened frequently, we can re-deploy at any moment. (And look how good and beautiful the new DocuSign web app is now: `http://bit.ly/2j2rWEF`.)

Committing modules to your version control system (Git, SVN) is still a good choice because 5, 10, or 15 years down the road, when your production application is still in use, npm may not be around. It's just a startup and is still not profitable. Or npm registry may become corrupted—it's just CouchDB after all. Or the library maintainers can decide to remove the library that you rely on from their repository. (`left-pad` unpublish broke half the web: `http://bit.ly/2zqQuyN`). Or the version you use might be removed.

Or someone may put some malicious code into a dependency you're using, or the Internet in your area might be down. Or npm version 16 will be incompatible with your code (very likely, since last few npm releases made drastic changes and broke a lot of good projects, such as Create React Native App which is still incompatible with npm v5 many months after the npm 5 release). Or the aliens might cut the wire, and your npm i won't reach npmjs.org. Having your own repository and not depending on npm is a better choice. Consider private repositories with Nexus or Artifactory as well.

There's a significant drawback in committing modules: binaries often need to be rebuilt on different targets (e.g., macOS vs. Linux). So, by skipping $ npm install and not checking binaries, development operations engineers have to use $ npm rebuild on targets. Of course, the size of the module can blow up your Git repo drastically.

The same problem might be (somewhat better) mitigated by using $ npm shrinkwrap (http://bit.ly/2zroWti). This command creates npm-shrinkwrap. json, which has *every* subdependency listed/locked at the current version. Now, magically, $ npm install skips package.json and uses npm-shrinkwrap.json instead!

When running Shrinkwrap, be careful to have all the project dependencies installed and to have only them installed (run $ npm install and $ npm prune to be sure). For more information about Shrinkwrap and locking versions with node_modules, see the article by core Node.js contributors: "Managing Node.js Dependencies with Shrinkwrap" at http://bit.ly/2zrHyJK.

In version of npm 5, a new file is created automatically. It's called package-lock.json. It has all the dependencies with their exact versions saved. No chance for a screwup. The package-lock.json file could look like this:

```
{
  "name": "blog-mongoose",
  "version": "1.0.1",
  "lockfileVersion": 1,
  "requires": true,
  "dependencies": {
    "accepts": {
      "version": "1.3.4",
      "resolved": "https://registry.npmjs.org/accepts/-/accepts-
      1.3.4.tgz",
      "integrity": "sha1-hiRnWMfdbSGmR0/whKR0DsBesh8=",
```

```
    "requires": {
      "mime-types": "2.1.17",
      "negotiator": "0.6.1"
    }
  },
  "acorn": {
    "version": "3.3.0",
    "resolved": "https://registry.npmjs.org/acorn/-/acorn-
    3.3.0.tgz",
    "integrity": "sha1-ReN/s56No/JbruP/U2niu18iAXo="
  },
  "acorn-globals": {
    "version": "3.1.0",
    "resolved": "https://registry.npmjs.org/acorn-globals/-/acorn-
    globals-3.1.0.tgz",
    "integrity": "sha1-/YJw9x+7SZawBPqIDuXUZXOnMb8=",
    "requires": {
      "acorn": "4.0.13"
    },
```

When there's `package-lock.json`, npm will use that file to reproduce
`node_modules`. `npm-shrinkwrap.json` is backwards-compatible with npm v2–4 and
it takes precedence over `package-lock.json`, which developers actually shouldn't
publish to npm if they are publishing an npm module (see Chapter 12 on publishing
npm modules). Another difference is that `package-lock.json` is opt-out, since it's the
default in version 5, while `npm-shrinkwrap.json` is opt-in, since you have to execute
an extra command to generate it (`$ npm shrinkwrap`). For an attempt at explanation,
see the official docs at `https://docs.npmjs.com/files/package-locks`.

Are you confused when to use lock and when shrinkwrap? Here's my rule of thumb:
for your own apps, use `package-lock.json` because it's automatic (only in npm v5)
or `npm-shrinkwrap.json` to be on a safer side. Commit them to Git or just commit the
entire `node_modules`. For the npm modules that you publish, don't lock the versions
at all.

If npm is slow or not locking your dependencies enough (as was the case with version 4, but version 5 is fast enough), then take a look at two other package managers: yarn and pnpm.

- yarn: Uses npm registry but often faster and more predictable due to lock files

- pnpm: Fully command-compatible-with-npm tool which uses symlinks and thus is blazingly fast and space efficient.

Git for Version Control and Deployments

Git has become not only a standard version control system, but also—because of its distributed nature —Git has become the default transport mechanism of deployment because it enables you to send source code.

Platform as a service (PaaS) solutions often leverage Git for deploys, because it's already a part of many development flows. Instead of "pushing" your code to GitHub or BitBucket, the destination becomes a PaaS-like Heroku, Azure, or Nodejitsu. Git is also used for continuous deployment and continuous integration (e.g., TravisCI, CircleCI).

Even when Infrastructure-as-a-Service (IaaS) solutions are used, developers can leverage automated systems like Chef (`http://docs.opscode.com`).

Installing Git

To install Git for your OS, download a package from the official website (`http://git-scm.com/downloads`). Then, follow these steps:

1. In your terminal, type these commands, *substituting* `"John Doe"` and johndoe@example.com with your name and email address:

   ```
   $ git config --global user.name "John Doe"
   $ git config --global user.email johndoe@example.com
   ```

2. To check the installation, run:

   ```
   $ git version
   ```

3. You should see something like the following in your terminal
    window, as shown in Figure 10-4 (your version might vary—in our
    case, it's 1.8.3.2):

```
git version 1.8.3.2
```

```
● ● ○              Terminal — bash — 78×8
Last login: Sun Aug 25 16:42:13 on ttys000
Azats-Air:~ azat$ git config --global user.name "John Doe"
Azats-Air:~ azat$ git config --global user.email johndoe@example.com
Azats-Air:~ azat$ git version
git version 1.8.3.2
Azats-Air:~ azat$
```

Figure 10-4. *Configuring and testing the Git installation*

Generating SSH Keys

SSH keys provide a secure connection without the need to enter a username and
password every time. For GitHub repositories, the latter approach is used with HTTPS
URLs (e.g., `https://github.com/azat-co/rpjs.git`,) and the former with SSH URLs
(e.g., `git@github.com:azat-co/rpjs.git`).

To generate SSH keys for GitHub on macOS/Unix machines, do the following:

1. Check for existing SSH keys:

```
$ cd ~/.ssh
$ ls -lah
```

2. If you see some files like `id_rsa` (please refer to Figure 10-5 for an
    example), you can delete them or back them up into a separate
    folder by using the following commands:

```
$ mkdir key_backup
$ cp id_rsa* key_backup
$ rm id_rsa*
```

```
Azats-Air:~ azat$ ssh-keygen -t rsa -C "johny@example.com"
Generating public/private rsa key pair.
Enter file in which to save the key (/Users/azat/.ssh/id_rsa):
Created directory '/Users/azat/.ssh'.
Enter passphrase (empty for no passphrase):
Enter same passphrase again:
Your identification has been saved in /Users/azat/.ssh/id_rsa.
Your public key has been saved in /Users/azat/.ssh/id_rsa.pub.
The key fingerprint is:
df:08:f9:a0:0c:87:ed:e8:38:33:92:11:54:c3:bb:0f johny@example.com
The key's randomart image is:
+--[ RSA 2048]----+
|  oo             |
| . ..            |
|.  .             |
|.  . o  .        |
| .  + o S        |
|.  E *  . = o    |
| o ++    +  .    |
|o +o .           |
| ..+.            |
+-----------------+
Azats-Air:~ azat$ open id_rsa.pub
The file /Users/azat/id_rsa.pub does not exist.
Azats-Air:~ azat$ open ~/.ssh/id_rsa.pub
No application knows how to open /Users/azat/.ssh/id_rsa.pub.
Azats-Air:~ azat$ pbcopy < ~/.ssh/id_rsa.pub
Azats-Air:~ azat$
```

Figure 10-5. *Generating an RSA key pair for SSH and copying the public RSA key to a clipboard*

3. Now we can generate a new SSH key pair using the `ssh-keygen` command, assuming we are in the `~/.ssh` folder:

```
$ ssh-keygen -t rsa -C "your_email@youremail.com"
```

4. Next, answer the questions. It's better to keep the default name `id_rsa`. Then, copy the content of the `id_rsa.pub` file to your clipboard:

```
$ pbcopy < ~/.ssh/id_rsa.pub
```

Alternatively, you can open the `id_rsa.pub` file in the default editor:

```
$ open id_rsa.pub
```

or in TextMate:

```
$ mate id_rsa.pub
```

> **Tip**   SSH connections are also used to connect to IaaS remote machines.

After you have copied the public key, go to github.com (`http://github.com`), log in, go to your account settings, select "SSH key," and add the new SSH key. Assign a name (e.g., the name of your computer) and paste the value of your *public* key.

To check whether you have an SSH connection to GitHub, type and execute the following command in your terminal:

```
$ ssh -T git@github.com
```

If you see something such as,

```
Hi your-GitHub-username! You've successfully authenticated,
but GitHub does not provide shell access.
```

then everything is set up.

While connecting to GitHub for the first time, you may receive the warning "authenticity of host … can't be established." Please don't be confused with this message; just proceed by answering yes, as shown in Figure 10-6.

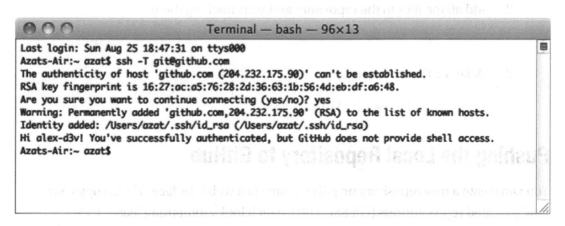

Figure 10-6. *Testing the SSH connection to GitHub for the very first time*

If, for some reason, you have a different message, please repeat steps 3 and 4 from the previous section on SSH Keys and/or reupload the content of your `*.pub` file to GitHub.

Warning   Keep your `id_rsa` file private. Don't share it with anybody!

More instructions are available at GitHub: Generating SSH Keys (`https://help.github.com/articles/generating-ssh-keys`). Windows users might find useful the SSH key generator feature in PuTTY (`http://www.putty.org`).

In case you've never used Git and/or GitHub, or you've forgotten how to commit code, the next section provides a short tutorial.

Creating a Local Git Repository

To create a GitHub repository, go to github.com (`http://github.com`), log in, and create a new repository. There will be an SSH address; copy it. In your terminal window, navigate to the project folder to which you would like to push GitHub. Then, do the following:

1. Create a local `Git` and `.git` folder in the root of the project folder:

   ```
   $ git init
   ```

2. Add all the files to the repository and start tracking them:

   ```
   $ git add .
   ```

3. Make the first commit:

   ```
   $ git commit -m "initial commit"
   ```

Pushing the Local Repository to GitHub

You can create a new repository on github.com via a web interface. Then, copy your newly created repo's address (Git SSH URI), which looks something like `git@github.com:username/reponame`. Follow the steps to add the address to your local Git:

1. Add the GitHub remote destination:

   ```
   $ git remote add your-github-repo-ssh-url
   ```

It might look something like this:

```
$ git remote add origin git@github.com:azat-co/simple-
message-board.git
```

2. Now everything should be set to push your local Git repository to the remote destination on GitHub with the following command:

```
$ git push origin master
```

3. You should be able to see your files at github.com (http://github.com) under your account and repository.

Later, when you make changes to the file, there is no need to repeat all these steps. Just execute:

```
$ git add .
$ git commit -am "some message"
$ git push origin master
```

If there are no new untracked files that you want to start tracking, type the following:

```
$ git commit -am "some message"
$ git push origin master
```

To include changes from individual files, run the following:

```
$ git commit filename -m "some message"
$ git push origin master
```

To remove a file from the Git repository, execute:

```
$ git rm filename
```

For more Git commands, go to:

```
$ git --help
```

> **Note** I advise against committing the `node_modules` folder to the repository for a project intended to be used in other applications, i.e., for a module. On the other hand, it's a good practice to commit that folder along with all the dependencies for a standalone application, because future updates might break something unintentionally.

Running Tests in Cloud with TravisCI

TravisCI is an SaaS continuous integration system that allows you to automate testing on each GitHub push (e.g., `$ git push origin master`). Alternative services include Codeship (`https://www.codeship.io`), CircleCI (`https://circleci.com`), and many others (`http://bit.ly/1ipdxxt`).

TravisCI is more common among open-source projects and has a similar configuration to other systems, i.e., a YAML file. In case of Node.js programs, it can look like this:

```
language: node_js
node_js:
  - "0.11"
  - "0.10"
```

In this configuration, 0.11 and 0.10 are versions of Node.js to use for testing. These multiple Node.js versions are tested on a separate set of virtual machines (VMs). The following configuration file can be copied and used (it's recommended by TravisCI):

```
language: node_js
node_js:
  - "0.11"
  - "0.10"
  - "0.8"
  - "0.6"
```

npm's `package.json` has a property `scripts.test` that is a string to execute scripts, so we can put the `mocha` command in it:

```
echo '{"scripts": {"test": "mocha test-expect.js"}}' > package.json
```

The previous line yields the following `package.json` file:

```
{"scripts": {"test": "mocha test-expect.js"}}
```

Then, we can run $ `npm test` successfully.

On the other hand, we can use any other command that invokes the execution of the test, such as the Makefile command $ `make test`:

```
echo '{"scripts": {"test": "make test"}}' > package.json
```

TravisCI uses this npm instruction to run the tests.

After all the preparation is done in the form of the `YAML` file and the `package.json` property, the next step is to sign up for TravisCI (free for open-source project/public repositories on GitHub) and select the repository from the web interface on `https://travis-ci.org`.

For more information on the TravisCI configuration, follow the project in this chapter or see *Building a Node.js* project (`http://bit.ly/2zrw7l7`).

TravisCI Configuration

There's no database in our application yet, but it's good to prepare the TravisCI configuration right now. To add a database to the TravisCI testing instance, use:

```
services:
  - mongodb
```

By default, TravisCI starts the MongoDB instance for us on the local host, port 27017:

```
language: node_js
node_js:
  - "0.11"
  - "0.10"
  - "0.8"
  - "0.6"
services:
  - mongodb
```

That's it! The test build will be synced on each push to GitHub.

If your tests fail even locally right now, don't despair, because that's the whole point of TDD. In the next chapter, we'll hook up the database and write more tests for fun.

Because of the GitHub hooks to TravisCI, the test build should start automatically. On their completion, contributors can get email/Internet Relay Chat (IRC) notifications.

Summary

In this chapter, we briefly touched on environment variables, went through the basics of Git, and generated SSH keys. We used Grunt for predeploy tasks such as concatenation, minification, and compilation; implemented clusters, monitoring, error handling, and logging; and configured TravisCI to run tests.

In the next chapter, we'll proceed to cover the deployment of the app to PaaS (Heroku) and IaaS (Amazon Web Services). We'll also show basic examples of Nginx, Varnish Cache and Upstart configurations.

CHAPTER 11

Deploying Node.js Apps

As we approach the end of the book, there's a vital step we have to explore: the deployment itself. To help you navigate between PaaS and IaaS options, and have some scripts you can use on your servers, we'll learn the following topics:

- Deploying to Heroku (PaaS)

- Deploying to Amazon Web Services (AWS)

- Keeping Node.js apps alive with forever, Upstart, and init.d

- Serving static resources properly with Nginx

- Caching with Varnish

Deploying to Heroku

Heroku (`http://www.heroku.com`) is a polyglot Agile application deployment Platform as a Service (PaaS). The benefits of using PaaS over other cloud solutions include the following:

1. It's easy to deploy, i.e., just one Git command to deploy: `$ git push heroku master`.

2. It's easy to scale, e.g., log in to Heroku.com and click a few options.

3. It's easy to secure and maintain, e.g., no need to set up startup scripts manually.

Heroku works similarly to AWS Beanstalk, Windows Azure (`http://azure.microsoft.com/en-us`), and many others in the sense that you can use Git to deploy applications. In other words, Heroku uses ubiquitous Git as its deployment mechanism. This means that after becoming familiar with Heroku and comfortable with Git, and after

© Azat Mardan 2018
A. Mardan, *Practical Node.js*, https://doi.org/10.1007/978-1-4842-3039-8_11

creating accounts with cloud PaaS providers, it's fairly easy to deploy Node.js apps to them as well.

To get started with the process, we need to follow these steps:

1. Install Heroku Toolbelt (`https://toolbelt.heroku.com`)—a bundle that includes Git and others tools.

2. Log in to Heroku, which should upload a public SSH key file (e.g., `id_rsa.pub`) to the cloud (i.e., heroku.com).

To set up Heroku, follow these steps:

1. Sign up at `http://heroku.com`. Currently, they have a free account. To use it, select all options as minimum (0) and the database as shared.

2. Download Heroku Toolbelt at `https://toolbelt.heroku.com`. Toolbelt is a package of tools, i.e., libraries, that consists of Heroku, Git, and Foreman (`https://github.com/ddollar/foreman`). For users of older Macs, get this client (`http://assets.heroku.com/heroku-client/heroku-client.tgz`) directly. If you use another OS, browse Heroku Client GitHub (`https://github.com/heroku/heroku`).

3. After the installation is done, you should have access to the `heroku` command. To check it and log in to Heroku, type:

```
$ heroku login
```

The system asks you for Heroku credentials (username and password), and if you've already created the SSH key, it uploads it automatically to the Heroku web site, as shown in Figure 11-1.

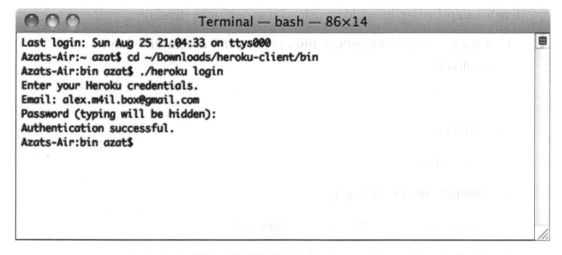

Figure 11-1. *The response to a successful command* `$ heroku login command`

4. If everything went well, to create a Heroku application inside your specific project folder, you should be able to run:

    ```
    $ heroku create
    ```

Official instructions are available at Heroku: Quickstart (`https://devcenter.heroku.com/articles/quickstart`) and Heroku: Node.js (`https://devcenter.heroku.com/articles/getting-started-with-nodejs`).

Then, for each app we need to deploy, perform the following setup steps:

1. Create the local Git repository.

2. Initialize the Heroku app with `$ heroku create` (adds a Git remote destination to Heroku cloud).

Last, initial deployment as well as each change is deployed by (1) staging the commit with `$ git add`, (2) committing the changes to the local repository with `$ git commit`, and (3) pushing the changes to the Heroku remote `$ git push heroku master`.

On deployment, Heroku determines which stack to use (Node.js, in our case). For this reason, we need to provide the mandatory files `package.json`, which tells Heroku what dependencies to install; `Procfile`, which tells Heroku what process to start; and Node.js app files (e.g., `server.js`). The content of `Procfile` can be as minimalistic as `web: node server.js`.

Here is a step-by-step breakdown using Git to deploy to Heroku:

1. Create a local Git repository and `.git` folder if you haven't done so already:

   ```
   $ git init
   ```

2. Add files:

   ```
   $ git add .
   ```

3. Commit files and changes:

   ```
   $ git commit -m "my first commit"
   ```

4. Create the Heroku Cedar stack application (Cedar stack is a special technology that Heroku uses to create and run its apps) and add the Git remote destination with this command:

   ```
   $ heroku create
   ```

   If everything went well, the system should tell you that the remote has been added and the app has been created, and it should give you the app name.

5. To look up the remote type and execute (*optional*), do the following:

   ```
   $ git remote show
   ```

6. Deploy the code to Heroku with:

   ```
   $ git push heroku master
   ```

   Terminal logs should tell you whether the deployment went smoothly (i.e., succeeded). If you have a different branch you'd like to use, you can use `$ git push heroku branch_name`, just like you would do with any other Git destination (e.g., GitHub).

7. To open the app in your default browser, type:

   ```
   $ heroku open
   ```

or just go to the URL of your app and type something like:
`http://yourappname-NNNN.herokuapp.com`.

8. To look at the Heroku logs for this app, type:

```
$ heroku logs
```

To update the app with the new code, type the following *only*:

```
$ git add -A
$ git commit -m "commit for deploy to heroku"
$ git push heroku master
```

Note   You'll be assigned a new application URL each time you create a new Heroku app with the command `$ heroku create`.

To propagate environment variables to the Heroku cloud, use the `heroku config` set of commands:

- `$ heroku config`: List of environment variables

- `$ heroku config:get NAME`: Value of NAME environment variable

- `$ heroku config:set NAME=VALUE`: Setting the value of NAME to VALUE

- `$ heroku config:unset NAME`: Removal of the environment variable

Note   Configuration variable data is limited to 16KB for each app.

To use the same environment variables locally, you can store them in the `.env` file in the root of your project. The format is NAME=VALUE. For example:

```
DB_PASSWORD=F2C9C45
API_KEY=7C311DA3126F
```

Warning   There shouldn't be any spaces between the name, equal sign, and the value. After the data are in `.env`, just use Foreman (part of Heroku Toolbelt):

```
$ foreman start
```

Tip   Don't forget to add your `.env` to `.gitignore` to avoid sharing it in the version control system.

As an alternative to Foreman and the `.env` file, it's possible just to set environment variables before starting an app:

```
$ DB_PASSWORD=F2C9C45 API_KEY=7C311DA3126F node server
```

or in your profile file (e.g., `~/.bashrc`):

```
export DB_PASSWORD=F2C9C45
export API_KEY=7C311DA3126F
```

Needless to say, if you have more than one app and/or API key, then you can use names such as `APPNAME_API_KEY`.

To sync your local `.env` seamlessly with cloud variables, use the heroku-config plugin (`http://bit.ly/2zqKarh`). To install it, run:

```
$ heroku plugins:install heroku-config
```

To get variables from the cloud to the local file, type:

```
$ heroku config:pull
```

To overwrite cloud data with local variables, type:

```
$ heroku config:push
```

For official information on setting up environment variables in Heroku, see Configuration and Config Vars (`https://devcenter.heroku.com/articles/config-vars`). The article might require Heroku login.

There are a multitude of add-ons for Heroku (`https://addons.heroku.com`). Each add-on is like a mini service associated with a particular Heroku app. For example, MongoHQ (`https://addons.heroku.com/mongohq`) provides the MongoDB database, and the Postgres add-on (`https://addons.heroku.com/heroku-postgresql`) does the same for the PostgreSQL database. SendGrid (`https://addons.heroku.com/sendgrid`) allows sending transactional emails. In Figure 11-2, you can see the beginning of the long list of Heroku add-ons.

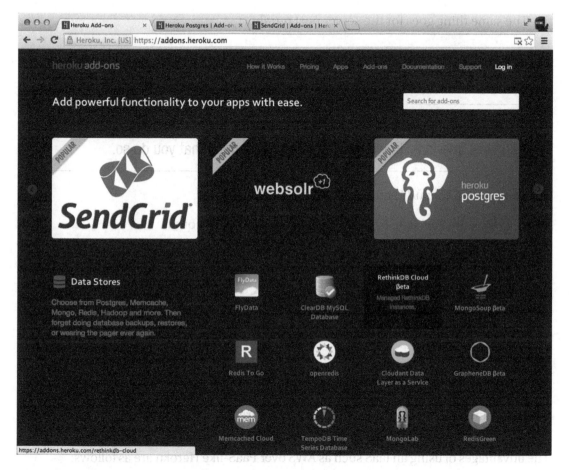

Figure 11-2. *Heroku supports a multitude of add-ons*

Most of the add-ons pass information to the Node.js app (and others, such as Rails) via environment variables. For example, the MongoHQ URI is provided in

```
process.env.MONGOHQ_URL
```

To make our Node.js apps work locally and remotely, all we need to do is to specify the local URI to fall back to when the environment variable is not set:

```
const databaseUrl = process.env.MONGOHQ_URL ||
"mongodb://@127.0.0.1:27017/practicalnode"
```

The same thing goes for the server port number:

```
const port = process.env.PORT || 5000
app.listen(port)
```

Note   It's possible to copy a database connection string (and other data) from the Heroku web interface. However, it's not recommended that you do so.

Some useful Git and Heroku commands are as follows:

- `$ git remote -v`: List defined remote destinations
- `$ git remote add NAME URL`: Add a new remote destination with `NAME` and `URL` (usually SSH or HTTPS protocols)
- `$ heroku start`: Start the app in the cloud
- `$ heroku info`: Pull the app's info

Deploying to Amazon Web Services

Cloud is eating the world of computing. There are private and public clouds. AWS, probably the most popular choice among the public cloud offerings, falls under the IaaS category. The advantages of using an IaaS such as AWS over PaaS-like Heroku are as follows:

1. It's more configurable (any services, packages, or operation systems).
2. It's more controllable. There are no restrictions or limitations.
3. It's cheaper to maintain. PaaS can quickly cost a fortune for high-performance resources.

In this tutorial, we use 64-bit Amazon Linux AMI (`http://aws.amazon.com/amazon-linux-ami`) with CentOS. It might be easier to use the Extra Packages for Enterprise Linux (EPEL) package manager to install Node.js and npm. If you don't have EPEL, skip to the manual C++ build instructions.

Assuming you have your Elastic Compute Cloud (EC2) instance up and running, make an SSH connection into it and see if you have `yum` with EPEL (`https://fedoraproject.org/wiki/EPEL`). To do so, just see if this command says `epel`:

```
$ yum repolist
```

If there's no mentions of `epel`, run:

```
$ rpm -Uvh http://download-i2.fedoraproject.org/pub/epel/6/i386/
epel-release-6-8.noarch.
rpm
```

Then, to install both Node.js and npm, simply run this command:

```
$ sudo yum install nodejs npm --enablerepo=epel
```

This might take a while. Answer with `y` as the process goes on. In the end, you should see something like this (your results may vary):

```
Installed:
  nodejs.i686 0:0.10.26-1.el6          npm.noarch 0:1.3.6-4.el6
Dependency Installed:
...
Dependency Updated:
...
Complete!
```

You probably know this, but just in case, to check installations, type the following:

```
$ node -V
$ npm -v
```

For more information on using `yum`, see Managing Software with yum (`https://www.centos.org/docs/5/html/yum`) and Tips on securing your EC2 instance (`http://aws.amazon.com/articles/1233`).

So, if the previous EPEL option didn't work for you, follow these build steps. On your EC2 instance, install all system updates with `yum`:

```
$ sudo yum update
```

Then, install the C++ compiler (again with `yum`):

```
$ sudo yum install gcc-c++ make
```

Do the same with `openssl`:

```
$ sudo yum install openssl-devel
```

Then install Git, which is needed for delivering source files to the remote machine. When Git is unavailable, `rsync` (`http://ss64.com/bash/rsync.html`) can be used:

```
$ sudo yum install git
```

Lastly, clone the Node repository straight from GitHub:

```
$ git clone git://github.com/joyent/node.git
```

and build Node.js:

```
$ cd node
$ git checkout v0.10.12
$ ./configure
$ make
$ sudo make install
```

Note   For a different version of Node.js, you can list them all with `$ git tag -l` and check out the one you need.

To install npm, run:

```
$ git clone https://github.com/isaacs/npm.git
$ cd npm
$ sudo make install
```

Relax and enjoy the build. The next step is to configure AWS ports/firewall settings. Here's a short example of `server.js`, which outputs "Hello readers" and looks like this:

```
const http = require('http')
http.createServer((req, res) => {
  res.writeHead(200, {'Content-Type': 'text/plain'})
  console.log ('responding')
```

```
res.end(`Hello readers!
  If you see this, then your Node.js server
  is running on AWS EC2!`)
}).listen(80, () => {
  console.log ('server is up')
})
```

On the EC2 instance, either configure the firewall to redirect connections (e.g., port to Node.js 3000, but this is too advanced for our example) or disable the firewall (okay for our quick demonstration and development purposes):

```
$ service iptables save
$ service iptables stop
$ chkconfig iptables off
```

In the AWS console, find your EC2 instance and apply a proper rule to allow for inbound traffic, as shown in Figure 11-3. For example:

```
Type: HTTP
```

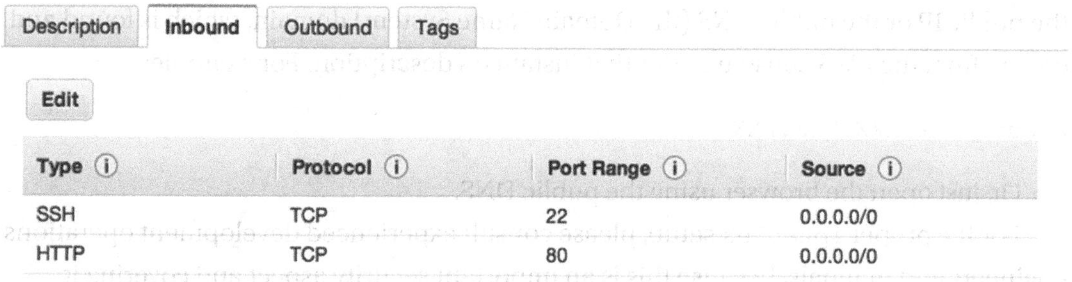

Description	Inbound	Outbound	Tags		

Edit

Type ⓘ	Protocol ⓘ	Port Range ⓘ	Source ⓘ
SSH	TCP	22	0.0.0.0/0
HTTP	TCP	80	0.0.0.0/0

Figure 11-3. *Allowing inbound HTTP traffic on port 80*

The other fields fill automatically:

```
Protocol: TCP
Port Range: 80
Source: 0.0.0.0/0
```

Or we can just allow all traffic (again, for development purposes only), as shown in Figure 11-4.

Description	Inbound	Outbound	Tags

Edit

Type ⓘ	Protocol ⓘ	Port Range ⓘ	Source ⓘ
SSH	TCP	22	0.0.0.0/0
All traffic	All	All	0.0.0.0/0

Figure 11-4. *Allowing all traffic for development mode only*

Now, while the Node.js app is running, executing `$ netstat -apn | grep 80`, the remote machine should show the process. For example,

```
tcp       0      0 0.0.0.0:80              0.0.0.0:*
LISTEN    1064/node
```

And from your local machine, i.e., your development computer, you can either use the public IP or the public DNS (the Domain Name System) domain, which is found and copied from the AWS console under that instance's description. For example:

```
$ curl XXX.XXX.XXX.XXX -v
```

Or, just open the browser using the public DNS.

For the proper `iptables` setup, please consult experienced development operations engineers and manuals, because this is an important security aspect and covering it properly is out of the scope of this book. However, here are some commands to redirect traffic to, say, port 3001:

```
$ sudo iptables -A PREROUTING -t nat -i eth0 -p tcp --dport 80 -j
REDIRECT --to-port 8080
$ sudo iptables -t nat -A INPUT -p tcp --dport 80 -j REDIRECT --to-
ports 3001
$ sudo iptables -t nat -A OUTPUT -p tcp --dport 80 -j REDIRECT --to-
ports 3001
```

You can also use commands such as the following:

```
$ service iptables save
$ service iptables start
$ service iptables restart
$ chkconfig iptables on
```

It's worth mentioning that AWS supports many other operating systems via its AWS Marketplace (`https://aws.amazon.com/marketplace`). Although AWS EC2 is a very popular and affordable choice, some companies opt for special Node.js tools available in the SmartOS (`http://smartos.org`), e.g., DTrace (`http://dtrace.org/blogs`), built on top of Solaris by Joyent (`http://www.joyent.com`), the company that maintains Node.js.

Keeping Node.js Apps Alive with forever, Upstart, and init.d

This section relates only to IaaS deployment—another advantage to PaaS deployments. The reason why we need this step is to bring the application back to life in case it crashes. Even if we have a master–child system, something needs to keep an eye on the master itself. You also need a way to stop and start processes for maintenance, upgrades, and so forth.

Luckily, there's no shortage of solutions to monitor and restart our Node.js apps:

- *forever* (`https://github.com/foreverjs/forever`): Probably the easiest method because the `forever` module is installed via npm and works on almost any Unix OS. Unfortunately, if the server itself fails (not our Node.js server, but the big Unix server), then nothing resumes forever.

- *Upstart* (`http://upstart.ubuntu.com`): The most recommended option. It solves the problem of starting daemons on startups, but it requires writing an Upstart script and having the latest Unix OS version support for it. I'll show you an Upstart script example for CentOS.

- *init.d* (`http://bit.ly/2zrCq8m`): An outdated analog of Upstart. init.d contains the last startup script options for systems that don't have Upstart capabilities.

forever

`forever` is a module that allows us to start Node.js apps/servers as daemons and keeps them running *forever*. Yes, that's right. If the node process dies for some reason, it brings it right back up!

`forever` is a very neat utility because it's an npm module (very easy to install almost anywhere) and it's very easy to use without any extra language. A simple use case is as follows:

```
$ sudo npm install forever -g
$ forever server.js
```

If you're starting from another location, prefix the file name with the absolute path, e.g., `$ forever /var/`. A more complex forever example looks like this:

```
$ forever start -l forever.log -o output.log -e error.log server.js
```

To stop the process, run:

```
$ forever stop server.js
```

To look up all the programs run by forever, run:

```
$ forever list
```

To list all available forever commands, run:

```
$ forever --help
```

Warning   The app won't start on server reboots without extra setup/utilities.

Upstart Scripts

"Upstart is an event-based replacement for the `/sbin/init` daemon that handles starting of tasks and services during boot..."—the Upstart website (`http://upstart. ubuntu.com`). The latest CentOS (6.2+), as well as Ubuntu and Debian OSes, comes with Upstart. If Upstart is missing, try typing `$ sudo yum install upstart` to install it on CentOS, and try `$ sudo apt-get install upstart` for Ubuntu.

First, we need to create the upstart script. A very basic Upstart script—to illustrate its structure—starts with metadata:

```
author        "Azat"
description   "practicalnode"
setuid        "nodeuser"
```

We then start the application on startup after the file system and network:

```
start on (local-filesystems and net-device-up IFACE=eth0)
```

We stop the app on server shutdown:

```
stop on shutdown
```

We instruct Upstart to restart the program when it crashes:

```
respawn
```

We log events to `/var/log/upstart/webapp.log`:

```
console log
```

We include environment variables:

```
env NODE_ENV=production
```

We write the command `exec` and the file to execute:

```
exec /usr/bin/node /var/practicalnode/webapp.js
```

Where to place the upstart script? We can save it in a file such as `webapp.conf` in a folder `/etc/init`:

```
$ cd /etc/init
$ sudo vi webapp.conf
```

Let me know you another Upstart script example that sets multiple env vars:

```
#!upstart
description "webapp.js"
author      "Azat"
env PROGRAM_NAME="node"
env FULL_PATH="/home/httpd/buto-middleman/public"
```

```
env FILE_NAME="forever.js"
env NODE_PATH="/usr/local/bin/node"
env USERNAME="springloops"

start on runlevel [2345]
stop on shutdown
respawn
```

This part of the script is responsible for launching the application webapp.js (similar to our local $ `node webapp.js` command, only with absolute paths). The output is recorded into the `webapp.log` file:

```
script
    export HOME="/root"

    echo $$ > /var/run/webapp.pid
    exec /usr/local/bin/node /root/webapp.js >> /var/log/webapp.log
    2>&1

end script
```

The following piece is not as important, but it provides us with the date in the log file:

```
pre-start script
    # Date format same as (new Date()).toISOString() for consistency
    echo "[`date -u +%Y-%m-%dT%T.%3NZ`] (sys) Starting" >> /var/log/
    webapp.log
end script
```

The following tells what to do when we're stopping the process:

```
pre-stop script
    rm /var/run/webapp.pid
    echo "[`date -u +%Y-%m-%dT%T.%3NZ`] (sys) Stopping" >> /var/log/
    webapp.log
end script
```

To start/stop the app, use:

```
$ /sbin/start myapp
$ /sbin/stop myapp
```

To determine the app's status, type and run:

```
$ /sbin/status myapp
```

Tip   With Upstart, the Node.js app restarts on an app crash and on server reboots.

The previous example was inspired by Deploy Nodejs app in Centos 6.2 (`http://bit.ly/1qwIeTJ`). For more information on Upstart, see How to Write CentOS Initialization Scripts with Upstart (`http://bit.ly/1pNFlxT`) and Upstart Cookbook (`http://bit.ly/206gMyI`).

init.d

If Upstart is unavailable, you can create an `init.d` script. init.d is a technology available on most Linux OSes. Usually, development operations engineers resort to init.d when Upstart is not available and when they need something more robust than forever. Without going into too much detail, Upstart is a newer alternative to `init.d` scripts. We put `init.d` scripts into the `/etc/` folder.

For example, the following `init.d` script for CentOS starts, stops, and restarts the node process from the `home/nodejs/sample/app.js` file:

```
#!/bin/sh

#
# chkconfig: 35 99 99
# description: Node.js /home/nodejs/sample/app.js
#

. /etc/rc.d/init.d/functions

USER="nodejs"

DAEMON="/home/nodejs/.nvm/v0.4.10/bin/node"
ROOT_DIR="/home/nodejs/sample"

SERVER="$ROOT_DIR/app.js"
LOG_FILE="$ROOT_DIR/app.js.log"

LOCK_FILE="/var/lock/subsys/node-server"
```

```
do_start()
{
        if [ ! -f "$LOCK_FILE" ] ; then
                echo -n $"Starting $SERVER: "
                runuser -l "$USER" -c "$DAEMON $SERVER >> $LOG_FILE
                &" && echo_success || echo_failure
                RETVAL=$?
                echo
                [ $RETVAL -eq 0 ] && touch $LOCK_FILE
        else
                echo "$SERVER is locked."
                RETVAL=1
        fi
}
do_stop()
{
        echo -n $"Stopping $SERVER: "
        pid=` ps -aefw | grep "$DAEMON $SERVER" | grep -v " grep " |
        awk '{print $2}'`
        kill -9 $pid > /dev/null 2>&1 && echo_success || echo_failure
        RETVAL=$?
        echo
        [ $RETVAL -eq 0 ] && rm -f $LOCK_FILE
}

case "$1" in
        start)
                do_start
                ;;
        stop)
                do_stop
                ;;
        restart)
```

```
                do_stop
                do_start
                ;;
        *)
                echo "Usage: $0 {start|stop|restart}"
                RETVAL=1

esac

exit $RETVAL
```

For more info on `init.d`, see this detailed tutorial (`http://bit.ly/1lDkRGi`).

Serving Static Resources Properly with Nginx

Adding static web servers is optional but recommended. Although, it's fairly easy to serve static files from Node.js applications, and we can use `sendFile` or Express.js static middleware, it's a big no-no for systems that require high performance. Let Node.js apps handle interactive and networking tasks only.

For serving static content, the best option is to use Nginx (`http://nginx.org`), Amazon S3 (`http://aws.amazon.com/s3`) or CDNs, e.g., Akamai (`http://www.akamai.com`) or CloudFlare (`https://www.cloudflare.com`). This is because these technologies were specifically designed for the task. They will allow to decrease the load on Node.js processes and improves the efficiency of your system.

Nginx is a popular choice among development operations engineers. It's an HTTP and reverse-proxy server. To install Nginx on a CentOS system (v6.4+), type and run the following shell command:

```
$ sudo yum install nginx
```

As a side note, for Ubuntu, you can use the `apt` packaging tool: `$ sudo apt-get install nginx`. For more information about `apt`, refer to the docs (`http://bit.ly/20aBltC`).

But, let's continue with our CentOS example. We need to open the `/etc/nginx/conf.d/virtual.conf` file for editing, e.g., using a VIM (Vi Improved) editor:

```
$ sudo vim /etc/nginx/conf.d/virtual.conf
```

Then, we must add this configuration:

```
server {
    location / {
        proxy_pass http://localhost:3000;
    }
    location /static/ {
        root /var/www/webapplog/public;
    }
}
```

The first `location` block acts as a proxy server and redirects all requests that are not `/static/*` to the Node.js app, which listens on port 3000. Static files are served from the `/var/www/webapplog/public` folder.

If your project uses Express.js or a framework that's built on top of it, don't forget to set the trust proxy to true by adding the following line to your server configuration:

```
app.set('trust proxy', true);
```

This little configuration enables Express.js to display true client IPs provided by proxy instead of proxy IPs. The IP address is taken from the `X-Forwarded-For` HTTP header of requests (see the next code snippet).

A more complex example with HTTP headers in the proxy-server directive, and file extensions for static resources, follows:

```
server {
    listen 0.0.0.0:80;
    server_name webapplog.com;
    access_log /var/log/nginx/webapp.log;

    location ~* ^.+\.(jpg|jpeg|gif|png|ico|css|zip|tgz|gz|rar|bz2|
    pdf|txt|tar|wav|bmp|rtf|js|flv|swf|html|htm)$ {
        root /var/www/webapplog/public;
    }
```

```
location / {
    proxy_set_header X-Real-IP $remote_addr;
    proxy_set_header HOST $http_host;
    proxy_set_header X-NginX-Proxy true;

    proxy_pass http://127.0.0.1:3000;
    proxy_redirect off;
}
```

Note   Replace `3000` with the Node.js app's port number, `webapplog.com` with our domain name, and `webapp.log` with your log's file name.

Alternatively, we can use upstream try_files (`http://wiki.nginx.org/ HttpCoreModule#try_files`). Then, start Nginx as a service:

```
$ sudo service nginx start
```

After Nginx is up and running, launch your Node app with forever or Upstart on the port number you specified in the proxy-server configurations.

To stop and restart Nginx, use:

```
$ sudo service nginx stop
$ sudo service nginx start
```

So far, we've used Nginx to serve static content while redirecting non-static requests to Node.js apps. We can take it a step further and let Nginx serve error pages and use multiple Node.js processes. For example, if we want to serve the 404 page from the `404.html` file, which is located in the `/var/www/webapplog/public` folder, we can add the following line inside the server directive:

```
error_page 404 /404.html;
location /404.html {
    internal;
    root /var/www/webapplog/public;
}
```

If there is a need to run multiple Node.js processes behind Nginx, we can set up location rules inside the server in exactly the same way we used `location` for dividing static and nonstatic content. However, in this case, both destinations are handled by Node.js apps. For example, we have a Node.js web app that is running on 3000, serving some HTML pages, and its URL path is /, whereas the Node.js API app is running on 3001, serving JSON responses, and its URL path is `/api`:

```
server {
  listen 8080;
  server_name webapplog.com;
  location / {
    proxy_pass http://localhost:3000;
    proxy_set_header Host $host;
  }
  location /api {
    proxy_pass http://localhost:3001;
    rewrite ^/api(.*) /$1 break;
    proxy_set_header Host $host;
  }
}
```

In this way, we have the following trafficking:

- The / requests go to `http://localhost:3000`.
- The `/api` requests go to `http://localhost:3001`.

Caching with Varnish

The last piece of the production deployment puzzle is setting up caching using Varnish Cache (`https://www.varnish-cache.org`). This step is optional for Node.js deploys, but, like an Nginx setup, it's also recommended, especially for systems that expect to handle large loads with the minimum resources consumed.

The idea is that Varnish allows us to cache requests and serve them later from the cache without hitting Nginx and/or Node.js servers. This avoids the overhead of processing the same requests over and over again. In other words, the more identical requests the server has coming, the better Varnish's optimization.

Let's use yum again, this time to install Varnish dependencies on CentOS:

```
$ yum install -y gcc make automake autoconf libtool ncurses-devel
libxslt groff pcre-devel pckgconfig libedit libedit-devel
```

Download the latest stable release (as of May 2014):

```
$ wget http://repo.varnish-cache.org/source/varnish-3.0.5.tar.gz
```

and build Varnish Cache with the following:

```
$ tar -xvpzf varnish-3.0.5.tar.gz
$ cd varnish-3.0.5
$ ./autogen.sh
$ ./configure
$ make
$ make check
$ make install
```

For this example, let's make only minimal configuration adjustments. In the file /etc/sysconfig/varnish, type:

```
VARNISH_LISTEN_PORT=80
VARNISH_ADMIN_LISTEN_ADDRESS=127.0.0.1
```

Then, in /etc/varnish/default.vcl, type:

```
backend default {
  .host = "127.0.0.1";
  .port = "8080";
}
```

Restart the services with:

```
$ /etc/init.d/varnish restart
$ /etc/init.d/nginx restart
```

Everything should be working by now. To test it, CURL from your local (or another remote) machine:

```
$ curl -I www.varnish-cache.org
```

If you see "Server: Varnish", this means that requests go through Varnish Cache first, just as we intended.

Summary

In this chapter, we covered deployment using the Git and Heroku command-line interfaces to deploy to PaaS. Then, we worked through examples of installing and building a Node.js environment on AWS EC2, running Node.js apps on AWS with CentOS. After that, we explored examples of forever, Upstart, and init.d to keep our apps running. Next, we installed and configured Nginx to serve static content, including error pages, and split traffic between multiple Node.js processes. Lastly, we added Varnish Cache to lighten the Node.js apps' loads even more.

## CHAPTER 12

Modularizing Your Code and Publishing Node.js Modules to npm

Two of the key factors that attributed to the rapid growth of the Node.js module ecosystem are its open-source nature and robust packaging systems (with registry). As of mid 2014, JavaScript and Node.js had surpassed any other language/platform in number of packages contributed per year (source):

- *Node.js*: 6742 *packages per year* (26,966 packages in 4 years)

- *Python*: 1351 packages per year (29,720 packages in 22 years)

- *Ruby*: 3022 packages per year (54,385 packages in 18 years)

Recent numbers are even higher with npm having over 620,000 packages. That's more than half a million! As you can see from the chart taken from `http://modulecounts.com` (Figure 12-1), Node's npm surpassed other platforms' package repositories in absolute numbers. Maven Central (Java) and Packagist (PHP) try to catch up but fail miserably. npm and Node are the top dogs.

© Azat Mardan 2018
A. Mardan, *Practical Node.js*, https://doi.org/10.1007/978-1-4842-3039-8_12

Module Counts

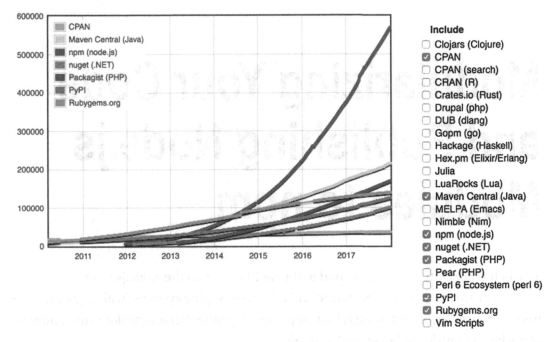

Figure 12-1. *Node's npm is dominating by the number of modules since mid 2014.*

Other factors that contribute to the Node.js's popularity include:

- Ability to share code between front-end/browser and server-side (with projects such as browserify and ender.js)

- Philosophy of small (in terms of lines of code and functionality) functional modules vs. large, standard/core packages (i.e., granularity)

- Evolving ECMAScript standard and expressive nature, and ease of adoption of the JavaScript language

With this in mind, many Node.js enthusiasts find it rewarding to contribute to the ever-growing open- source community. When doing so, there are a few conventions to follow as well as concepts to understand:

- Recommended folder structure

- Required patterns

- `package.json`

- Publishing to npm

- Locking versions

Recommended Folder Structure

Here is an example of a good, structured npm module in which you have documentation, project manifest, starting file, and a folder for dependencies:

```
webapp
  /lib
  webapp.js
  index.js
  package.json
  README.md
```

The `index.js` file does the initialization, whereas `lib/webapp.js` has all the principal logic.

If you're building a command-line tool, add the `bin` folder:

```
webapp
  /bin
  webapp-cli.js
  /lib
  webapp.js
  index.js
  package.json
  README.md
```

Also, for the CLI module, add the following to `package.json`:

```
...
"bin": {
    "webapp": "./bin/webapp-cli.js"
},
...
```

The `webapp-cli.js` file starts with the line `#!/usr/bin/env node`, but then has normal Node.js code.

It's a good idea to add unit tests to your external module, because it increases confidence and the likelihood of other people using it. Some programmers go as far as not using a module that doesn't have any tests! The added benefit is that tests serve as a poor man's examples and documentation.

TravisCI, which we covered in previous chapters, allows free testing for open-source projects. Its badges, which turn from red to green, depending on the status of tests (failing or passing), became the de facto standard of quality and are often seen on the README pages of the most popular Node.js projects.

Modularizing Patterns

Modularizing is the best practice because you can keep your application flexible and update different parts independently of each other. It's totally fine to have bunch of modules with only a single function in each one of them. In fact, a lot of module on npm are just that—a single function.

There are a few common patterns for writing external modules (meant for use by other users, not just within your app):

- `module.exports` as a function pattern (recommended)

- `module.exports` as a class pattern (not recommended)

- `module.exports` as an object pattern

- `exports.NAME` pattern, which could be an object or a function

Here is an example of the `module.exports` as a function pattern:

```
let _privateAttribute = 'A'
let _privateMethod = () => {...}
module.exports = function (options) {
  // Arrow function can also be used depending on
  // what needs to be the value of "this"
  // Initialize module/object
  object.method = () => {...}
  return object
}
```

And here is an example of an equivalent with a function declaration, but this time we used named function that we exported via the global `module.exports`:

```
module.exports = webapp
function webapp (options) {
  // Initialize module/object
  object.method = () => {...}
  return object
}
```

Tip   For info about named function expressions vs. function declarations, refer to Chapter 1.

The file in which we include the module looks like this:

```
const webapp = require('./lib/webapp.js')
const wa = webapp({...}) // Initialization parameters
```

More succinctly, it looks like this:

```
const webapp = require('./lib/webapp.js')({...})
```

The real-life example of this pattern is the Express.js module (source code).

The `module.exports` as a class pattern uses the so-called *pseudoclassical instantiating/inheritance pattern*, which can be recognized by the use of the `this` and `prototype` keywords:

```
module.exports = function(options) {
  this._attribute = 'A'
  // ...
}
module.exports.prototype._method = function() {
  // ...
}
```

Notice the capitalized name and the new operator in the including file:

```
const Webapp = require('./lib/webapp.js')
const wa = new Webapp()
// ...
```

The example of this module.exports as a class pattern is the OAuth module (source code).

The module.exports as an object pattern is similar to the first pattern (functional), only without the constructor. It may be useful for defining constants, locales, and other settings:

```
module.exports = {
  sockets: 10,
  limit: 200,
  whitelist: [
  'azat.co',
  'webapplog.com',
  'apress.com'
  ]
}
```

The including file treats the object as a normal JavaScript object. For example, we can set maxSockets with these calls:

```
const webapp = require('./lib/webapp.js')
const http = require('http')
http.globalAgent.maxSockets = webapp.sockets
```

Note   The require method can read JSON files directly. The main difference is that the JSON standard has the mandatory double quotes (") for wrapping property names.

The `exports.NAME` pattern is just a shortcut for `module.exports.NAME` when there's no need for one constructor method. For example, we can have multiple routes defined this way:

```
exports.home = function(req, res, next) {
  res.render('index')
}
exports.profile = function(req, res, next) {
  res.render('profile', req.userInfo)
}
// ...
```

And we can use it in the including file the following way:

```
const routes = require('./lib/routes.js')
// ...
app.get('/', routes.home)
app.get('/profile', routes.profile)
// ...
```

Composing package.json

Another mandatory part of an npm module is its `package.json` file. The easiest way to create a new `package.json` file, if you don't have one already (most likely you do), is to use `$ npm init`. The following is an example produced by this command:

```
{
  "name": "webapp",
  "version": "0.0.1",
  "description": "An example Node.js app",
  "main": "index.js",
  "devDependencies": {},
  "scripts": {
    "test": "test"
  },
```

```
  "repository": "",
  "keywords": [
    "math",
    "mathematics",
    "simple"
  ],
  "author": "Azat <hi@azat.co>",
  "license": "BSD"
}
```

The most important fields are `name` and `version`. The others are optional and self-explanatory, by name. The full list of supported keys is located at the npm web site: `http://bit.ly/2xIqmNK`.

Warning   `package.json` must have double quotes around values and property names, unlike native JavaScript object literals.

---

npm scripts is an important feature that benefits all projects and more so large one. See that `scripts` property in the `package.json` file? Inside of it developers can define any commands, which act as aliases. The left part is the alias, and the right part (after the : colon) is the actual command:

```
"scripts": {
  "test": "mocha test",
  "build": "node_modules/.bin/webpack --config webpack-dev.config.js",
  "deploy": "aws deploy push --application-name WordPress_App --s3-
  location s3://CodeDeployDemoBucket/WordPressApp.zip --source /tmp/
  MyLocalDeploymentFolder/",
  "start": "node app.js",
  "dev": "node_modules/.bin/nodemon app.js"
}
```

To run the command, you use $ `npm run NAME`, e.g., $ `npm run build` or $ `npm run deploy`. The two names are special. The don't need `run`. They are `test` and `start`. That is to execute `test` or `start`, simply use `npm test` and `npm start`.

It's possible to call other npm scripts from the right side (the values):

```
"scripts": {
  "test": "mocha test",
  "build": "node_modules/.bin/webpack --config webpack-dev.config.js",
  "prepare": "npm run build && npm test"
}
```

Lastly, there are `post` and `pre` hooks for each npm script. They are defined as pre and post prefixes to the names. For example, if I always want to build after the installation, I can set up `postinstall`:

```
"scripts": {
  "postinstall": "npm run build",
  "build": "node_modules/.bin/webpack --config webpack-dev.config.js"
}
```

npm scripts are very powerful. Some Node developers are even abandoning their build tools, such as Grunt or Gulp or Webpack, and implementing their build pipelines with npm scripts and some low-level Node code. I sort of agree with them. Having to learn and depend on myriads of Grunt, Gulp, or Webpack plugins is no fun. For more use cases of npm scripts, start at this page: `https://docs.npmjs.com/misc/scripts`.

It's worth noting that `package.json` and npm do not limit their use. In other words, you are encouraged to add custom fields and devise new conventions for their cases.

Publishing to npm

To publish to npm, you must have an account there. So first, you need to proceed to the website npmjs.org and register there. Once you do that, you will have an account, and you will have a username and password. The next step is to sign in on the command line. Do this by executing the following:

```
$ npm adduser
```

You just need to sign in with the npm CLI once. After you do it, you are read to publish as many times as you wish. To publish a new module or an update to an already published module, simply execute the following command from the module/package project folder:

```
$ npm publish
```

Some useful npm commands are as follows:

- `$ npm tag NAME@VERSION TAG`: Tag a version

- `$ npm version SEMVERSION`: Increment a version to the value of SEMVERSION (semver) and update `package.json`

- `$ npm version patch`: Increment the last number in a version (e.g., 0.0.1 to 0.0.2) and update `package.json`

- `$ npm version minor`: Increment a middle version number (e.g., 0.0.1 to 0.1.0 or 0.0.1 to 1.0.0) and update `package.json`

- `$ npm unpublish PACKAGE_NAME`: Unpublish package from npm (take optional version with `@`)

- `$ npm owner ls PACKAGE_NAME`: List owners of this package

- `$ npm owner add USER PACKAGE_NAME`: Add an owner

- `$ npm owner rm USER PACKAGE_NAME`: Remove an owner

Not-Locking Versions

The rule of thumb is that when we publish external modules, we don't lock dependencies' versions. However, when we deploy apps, we lock versions in `package.json`. You can read more on why and how lock versions in projects that are applications (i.e., not npm modules) in Chapter 10.

Then why not lock versions in the modules? The answer is that open source is often a part-time gig and an afterthought for most people. It's not like you'll make millions and can spend 40 hours per week on your FOSS npm module.

Let's say there's a security vulnerability or something is outdated in a dependency of your npm module. Most likely, you'll be patching your app that is your main full-time daily job, and not patching this poor little npm module. That's why it's a good idea to

NOT lock the version but let it use a caret symbol ^, which means the patches will be updated in dependencies.

Yes. If someone depends on your npm module, they may get a bug when it pulls a newer dependency, but the tradeoff is worth it. Your module will have the latest dependencies automatically, without requiring your attention (the next time someone installs your module).

That's the main reason why almost all popular npm modules such as Express, Webpack, and React do have ^ in package.json (`http://bit.ly/2xNJVo7`, `http://bit.ly/2xLUF6f` and `http://bit.ly/2xMFSbw`).

Summary

Open source factors have contributed to the success and widespread use of the Node. js platform. It's relatively easy to publish a module and make a name for yourself (unlike other mature platforms with solid cores). We looked at the recommended patterns and structures, and explored a few commands to get started with publishing modules to npm.

## CHAPTER 13

Node HTTP/2 Servers

It's almost 2020, and HTTP/2 is already here. It has been here for a few years now. If you are not using HTTP/2, then you are losing out on big improvements. Major browsers already support HTTP/2. A lot of services and websites switched to HTTP/2 as early as 2016 and more continue this trend.

HTTP/2 has some very big differences from HTTP/1 when it comes to delivering traffic. For example, HTTP/2 offers multiplexing and the server push of assets. If you are not optimizing your code for HTTP/2, then you probably have a slower app than you would have with HTTP/2. Lots of web- optimization practices of HTTP/1 are unnecessary and may even hurt with HTTP/2.

In this chapter, if you know the major features of HTTP/2, then jump straight to the sections on implementing an HTTP/2 server in Node and server push. If you don't know its major features, you should read the following brief overview and then follow it up with some more reading online.

Brief Overview of HTTP/2

The modern Internet with its TCP/IP protocol started around 1975, which is an astonishing 40+ years ago. For the most part of its existence, we used HTTP and its successor HTTP/1.1 (version 1.1) to communicate between clients and servers. Those served the web well, but the way developers build websites has dramatically changed. There are myriads of external resources, images, CSS files, and JavaScript assets. The number of resources is only increasing.

HTTP/2 (or just H2) is the first major upgrade to the good old HTTP protocol in over 15 years (first HTTP is circa 1991)! It is optimized for modern websites. The performance is better without complicated hacks like domain sharding (having multiple domains) or file concatenation (having one large file instead of many small ones).

© Azat Mardan 2018
A. Mardan, *Practical Node.js*, https://doi.org/10.1007/978-1-4842-3039-8_13

H2 is the new standard for the web, which started as Google's SPDY protocol. It's already being used by many popular websites and is supported by most major browsers. For example, I went to Yahoo's Flickr, and it was using h2 protocol (HTTP2) already (back in July of 2016, as shown in Figure 13-1).

Figure 13-1. *Yahoo!'s Flickr has been using the HTTP/2 protocol for many years now*

Semantically, HTTP/2 is no different from HTTP/1.1, meaning you have the same XML-like language in the body and also the same header fields, status codes, cookies, methods, URLs, etc. The stuff familiar to developers is still there in H2. But H2 offers a lot of the benefits, including:

- *Multiplexing*: Allows browsers to include multiple requests in a single TCP connection that enables browsers to request all the assets in parallel.

- *Server push*: Servers can push web assets (CSS, JS, images) before a browser knows it needs them, which speeds up page load times by reducing the number of requests.

- *Stream priority*: Allows browsers to specify priority of assets. For example, a browser can request HTML first to render it before any styles or JavaScript.

- *Header compression*: All HTTP/1.1 requests have to have headers which are typically duplicate the same info, while H2 forces all HTTP headers to be sent in a compressed format.

- *De facto mandatory encryption*: Although the encryption is not required, most major browsers implement H2 only over TLS (HTTPS).

While there's some criticism of H2, it's clearly a way forward for now (until we get something even better). What do you need to know about it as a web developer? Well, most of the optimization tricks you know have become unnecessary, and some of them will even hurt a website's performance. In particular, the file concatenation. Stop doing that (image sprites, bundled CSS and JS), because H2 can make parallel requests and because each small change in your big file will invalidate cache. It's better to have many small files with H2. I hope the need for build tools like Grunt, Gulp, and Webpack will drop because of that. They introduce additional complexity, steep learning curve, and dependencies to web projects.

Another thing that good developers did in the HTTP/1.1 world but that will hurt you in H2 is domain sharding (a trick to go over the browser limit on the number of active TCP connections). Okay, it might not hurt in all cases, but there's not benefit in it in H2 because H2 supports multiplexing. It might hurt because each domain incurs additional overhead. Don't do domain sharding in HTTP2. If you have to, then resolve domains to the same IP and make sure your SSL certificates has a wildcard which makes it valid for the subdomainsm or have a multidomain cert.

Please educate yourself on all the HTTP/2 details and how to optimize your applications and content for it. The official website is a good place to start.

SSL Key and Certificate

Before we can submerge into the HTTP/2 module code, we must do some preparation. You see, the HTTP/2 protocol must use an SSL connection. It's when you see `https` in your browser URL address bar, the browser shows you a lock symbol, and you can inspect the secure connection certificate, which hopefully was issued by a trusted source.

SSL, HTTPS and HTTP/2 are more secure than HTTP/1 (http in an URL) because they are encrypting your traffic between the client (browser) and the server. If an attacker tries to hijack it, they'll get only some gibberish.

For development purposes, you can create a self-signed certificate and the key instead of paying money to a trusted authority to issue a certificate for you. You will see a warning message in Chrome (Figure 13-2) when you use a self-signed certificate, but that's okay for the development purposes.

Figure 13-2. *Click on ADVANCED*

Create an empty folder and a self-signed SSL certificate in it. To create a folder named `http2` run the `mkdir`:

```
$ mkdir http2
$ cd http2
```

Once inside of the folder, use the `openssl` command to generate an RSA private key `server.pass.key`, as shown next. Never share a private key except with your sysadmin whom you know personally. If you don't have `openssl`, then download it from `https://www.openssl.org/` source.

```
$ openssl genrsa -des3 -passout pass:x -out server.pass.key 2048
```

The good message would look like this:

```
Generating RSA private key, 2048 bit long modulus
.....................................................................+++
..........+++
e is 65537 (0x10001)
```

Next, trade in your `server.pass.key` for the `server.key`, which will be your RSA key:

```
$ openssl rsa -passin pass:x -in server.pass.key -out server.key
```

You should see "writing RSA key" if everything went fine. If you don't see this message, most likely you are in a wrong folder, specified a wrong path, or made a type (irony intended). Please repeat by copying the commands correctly.

We don't need the `server.pass.key` anymore, so let's keep things clean and organized. Let's remove this file:

```
$ rm server.pass.key
```

We got the key `server.key`. That's not all. What we also need is the certificate. We want to generate an certificate (`csr`) file first using the `server.key`:

```
$ openssl req -new -key server.key -out server.csr
```

You will need to answer some trivial questions about your location. Just put anything. It doesn't matter, since this is for development only. For example, put US and California as country and state:

```
Country Name (2 letter code) [AU]:US
State or Province Name (full name) [Some-State]:California
```

Come up with some answers to other questions about organization, unit, email, and password when asked. You don't have to provide an accurate info since this is a development certificate.

Finally, sign (with key `server.key`) the certificate (`server.csr`) to generate the `server.crt`, which is the file to be used in Node:

```
$ openssl x509 -req -sha256 -days 365 -in server.csr -signkey server.
key -out server.crt
```

The successful message will have a subject with your answers—for example, mine had US, CA ,and SF among them:

```
Signature ok
subject=/C=US/ST=CA/L=SF/O=NO\x08A/OU=NA
Getting Private key
```

You should have at least two files:

```
server.crt
server.key
```

Keep them secret, especially the key and especially when it's a real production key. You can get rid of the `csr` file.

Here's a somewhat simpler command that generates `crt` and `key` files. The command will bypass the `csr` file and answer questions automatically (the `subj` option):

```
openssl req -x509 -newkey rsa:2048 -nodes -sha256 -subj
'/C=US/ST=CA/L=SF/O=NO\x08A/OU =NA' \
  -keyout server.key -out server.crt
```

HTTP/2 Node Server

Now we'll learn how to create an HTTP/2 server with Node.js. It's actually very straightforward because the `http2` interface is for the most part is *compatible* with `http` or `https` interfaces.

See for yourself. We import and define variables. Then we instantiate `server` with a special method `createSecureServer()`. This special method takes two arguments. The first argument is for the SSL encryption. We feed the contents of the two files, i.e., the key and signed certificate. In the second argument, we define the request handler, just as we would define a request handler with the `http` module.

```
const http2 = require('http2')
const fs = require('fs')

const server = http2.createSecureServer({
  key: fs.readFileSync('server.key'),
  cert: fs.readFileSync('server.crt')
}, (req, res) => {
```

```
  res.end('hello')
})
server.on('error', (err) => console.error(err))
server.listen(3000)
```

Alternatively, we can re-write our example to use stream. We would assign an event listener with the `on()` method to catch `stream` events. We can use `respond()` and `end()` on the `stream` object to set headers (text/html), status (200), and send back `<h1>`:

```
const http2 = require('http2')
const fs = require('fs')

const server = http2.createSecureServer({
  key: fs.readFileSync('server.key'),
  cert: fs.readFileSync('server.crt')
})

server.on('error', (err) => console.error(err))
server.on('socketError', (err) => console.error(err))

server.on('stream', (stream, headers) => {
  // stream is a Duplex
  stream.respond({
    'content-type': 'text/html',
    ':status': 200
  })
  stream.end('<h1>Hello World</h1>')
})

server.listen(3000)
```

To launch the HTTP/2 server, run your Node code as usual with node or nodemon or node-dev:

```
$ node server.js
```

If you see a message "(node:10536) ExperimentalWarning: The http2 module is an experimental API." that's totally fine. Just ignore it because it basically says that the methods in the http2 class might change in the future. I'm using Node version 8.9.3, which is the latest LTS version as of this writing. If you use a higher LTS version, this warning should not be there anymore.

On the contrary, if you are seeing "Error: Cannot find module 'http2'", that is a BAD sign. Warnings are okay to ignore (in most cases), albeit with some limitations, but errors won't allow the execution at all.

You might be wondering why the http2 cannot be found? You probably have an older version of Node that doesn't have the core http2 module. Your best bet is to use nvm to install a newer version, at least as high as my version 8.9.3. If nvm is too much of a hassle for you, then simply go to the Node website and use their installer. The downside of using the installer is that you won't be able to switch back and forth. You will always have to install. With nvm, you can switch back and forth between various versions once you install them. There's no need to repeat myself anymore on installations here because I covered a lot of different Node installations in Chapter 1.

Assuming you didn't get an error message, open your browser (preferably Chrome) at `https://localhost:3000`. Don't forget to use https and the correct port number 3000. Important! Also don't forget to allow your browser to use the self-signed certificate. When you're visiting your server, make sure to select "ADVANCED" (Figure 13-2) and click "Proceed to localhost (unsafe)" (Figure 13-3). You can also add localhost as an exception. The reason being is that browsers don't trust self-signed certificates by default.

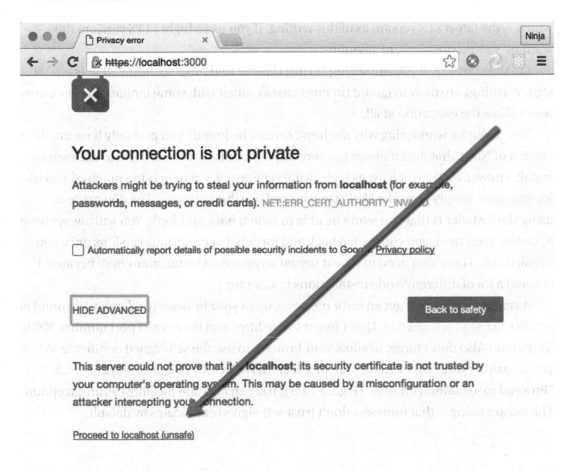

Figure 13-3. *Self-signed certificate will require to click on "Proceed to localhost (unsafe)"*

As a result, you will see a glorious Hello World from the future (HTTP/2). You can inspect the certificate by clicking on the "Not Secure" to the left of the URL address `https://localhost:3000`. See Figure 13-4 for my example, which has NA as the organization name and location as US and CA.

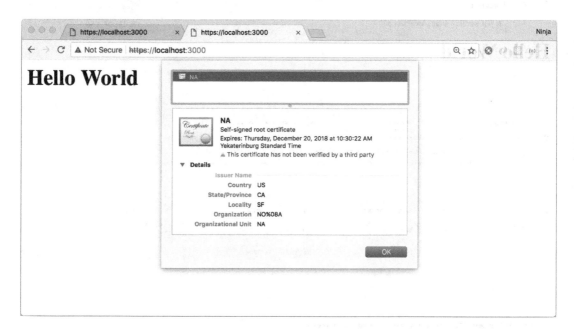

Figure 13-4. *Inspecting "Not Secure" but totally working development self-signed certificate*

And of course, we can check that the request itself was done using the HTTP/2 protocol and not the old, slow, and ugly HTTP/1 with SSL. You can easily check for the protocol in the Network tab of your Chrome browser, as I did in Figure 13-5.

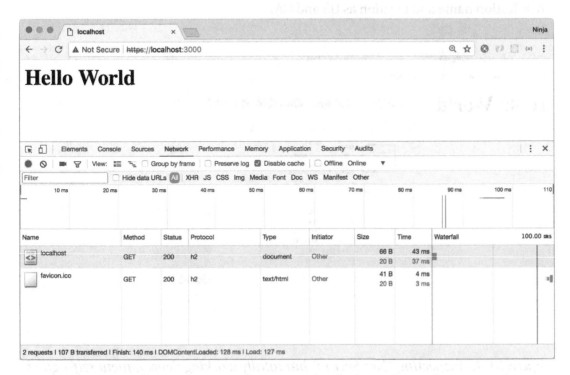

Figure 13-5.   *Localhost request in the Network tab shows h2 as the protocol.*

Another way to check that we've got H2 is to use CURL. To see the server response, you can make CURL requests with the following command (make sure you've got the latest version 7.46 with nghttp2):

```
$ curl https://localhost:3000/ -vik
```

Here are the explains of the `vik` options: `v` is for more information, `i` is for showing headers, and `k` is to make CURL to be okay with the self-signed certificate.

The successful CURL output should contain lines like these ones:

```
  Trying 127.0.0.1...
* Connected to localhost (127.0.0.1) port 3000 (#0)
* ALPN, offering h2
* ALPN, offering http/1.1
* Cipher selection:
```

Then there's stuff you don't need to bother with, followed by:

```
* SSL connection using TLSv1.2 / ECDHE-RSA-AES128-GCM-SHA256
* ALPN, server accepted to use h2
* Server certificate:
*  subject: C=US; ST=CA; L=SF; O=NOx08A; OU=NA
* Using HTTP2, server supports multi-use
* Connection state changed (HTTP/2 confirmed)
```

So it's HTTP/2. Like we didn't know, right? And see that US and CA? That's what I used with my `openssl` command, and that's what's in my certificate. Yours might be different.

Node HTTP/2 Server Push

Multiplexing is good but it's not as cool or awesome as sending assets (stylesheets, images, JavaScript, and other goodies) even before the browser requests or knows about them. Great feature.

The way server push works is by bundling multiple assets and resources into a single HTTP/2 call. Under the hood, the server will issue a PUSH_PROMISE. Clients (browsers included) can use it or not depending on whether the main HTML file needs it. If yes, it needs it, then client will match received push promises to make them look like a regular HTTP/2 GET calls. Obviously, if there's a match, then no new calls will be made, but the assets already at the client will be used.

Server push is not a guarantee to improve loading time. Educate yourself and experiment to see the improvement in your particular case. I give you three good articles for more info on server push benefits:

- What's the benefit of Server Push?

- Announcing Support for HTTP/2 Server Push

- Innovating with HTTP 2.0 Server Push

Now let's see the implementation. First go the imports with `require()`, and then the key and certificate that we must provide to the `createSecureServer()`.

```
const http2 = require('http2')
const fs = require('fs')
```

```
const server = http2.createSecureServer({
  key: fs.readFileSync('server.key'),
  cert: fs.readFileSync('server.crt')
})

server.on('error', (err) => console.error(err))
server.on('socketError', (err) => console.error(err))
```

Next, we copy the same stream event listener and response as we had in the previous example, except now we add `stream.pushStream()` and include `<script>` in the HTML. You might be wondering what is happening. Let me explain. The HTML is sent right away, but with it also goes `myfakefile.js` with an alert box code. The script file won't be loaded or executed until the browser sees `<script>` in the HTML. Then the browser will be like "OMG. I have this file already from the push. LOL. Let me just use it. TTYL."

```
server.on('stream', (stream, headers) => {
  stream.respond({
    'content-type': 'text/html',
    ':status': 200
  })
  stream.pushStream({ ':path': '/myfakefile.js' }, (pushStream) => {
    pushStream.respond({
      'content-type': 'text/javascript',
      ':status': 200
    })
    pushStream.end(`alert('you win')`)
  })
  stream.end('<script src="/myfakefile.js"></script>
  <h1>Hello World</h1>')
})

server.listen(3000)
```

The full source code is in the `ch13/http2-push/server.js` file. When you run this server and open `https://localhost:3000`, then the browser will show you the alert (Figure 13-6). And you can see in the Network tab in the Chrome DevTools the type of the protocol as h2 and the initiator as Push (Figure 13-7). The Network tab confirms that there was just *one* request, not *two* as you would normally have in HTTP/1.

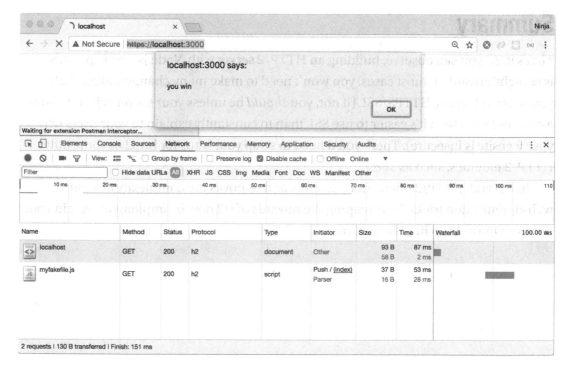

Figure 13-6. *Localhost request in the Network tab shows h2 as the protocol*

Figure 13-7. *Localhost request in the Network tab shows h2 as the protocol*

Remember that our server was never configured to respond to a different URL, i.e., it wasn't configured to send HTML for / and to send JavaScript for /myfakefile.js. In fact, any URL path will have the same HTML response. This proves that the alert code was pushed together with HTML not independently in a new request, as we would have without the HTTP/2 server push. The only way the browser can get its hands on the JavaScript is in the same response with HTML. That's the magic of the server push. Use it knowingly.

Summary

That's it. As you can observe, building an HTTP/2 server with Node.js and Express.js is straightforward. In most cases, you won't need to make many changes. Most likely, you're already using HTTPS/SSL (if not, you *should* be unless your server is just for static assets and even then it's easier to use SSL than to constantly explain to your users why your website is insecure). Then, you'd need to swap your https for http2 or some other HTTP/2 modules, such as `spdy`.

In the end, HTTP/2 offers more benefits and removes the complexity of some web-optimization tricks. Start reaping the rewards of H2 now by implementing it in your servers. Onward to a brighter future!

## CHAPTER 14

Asynchronous Code in Node

Asynchronous code is at the heart of Node because it allows developers to build non-blocking I/O systems that are more performant than traditional blocking system for the reason that non-blocking I/O systems use the waiting time and delegate by creating parallel executions.

Historically, Node developers were able to use only callbacks and event emitters (observer pattern in Node). However, in recent years, front-end developers and ECMAScript have pushed onto Node developers (for better or worse) a few asynchronous styles that allow for a different async syntax. In this chapter, we'll cover:

- `async` module
- Promises
- Async/await functions

My favorite is async/await functions, so if you want to just jump straight to that section in this chapter, do so. But I will still cover the others albeit briefly to show that async functions are better. :)

Here's a teaser for you. This code will continue to work even after the JSON error. In other words, try/catch will prevent the app from crashing:

```
try {
  JSON.parse('not valid json for sure')
} catch (e) {
  console.error(e)
}
```

© Azat Mardan 2018
A. Mardan, *Practical Node.js*, https://doi.org/10.1007/978-1-4842-3039-8_14

Now what about this async code with `setTimeout()`, which mimicks an IO operation?

```
try {
  setTimeout(()=>JSON.parse('not valid json for sure'), 0)
} catch (e) {
  console.error('nice message you will never see')
}
```

Can you guess? The `try/catch` is useless in async code! That's because mighty event loop separates the callback code in an I/O method. When that callback fires, it has lost all the memory of a try/catch. Argh.

The solution is to use the `error` argument and process it by having an if/else. That's for pure callbacks. There are other approaches as well.

async Module

A common scenarios is to run multiple tasks at once. Let's say you are migrating a database and you need to insert bunch of records into a database from a JSON file. Each record is independent of one another, so why not send many of them at once so they run in parallel? It might be a good idea to do so.

Node allows us to write parallel tasks. Here's a simple code that connects to a database and then uses a counter to finish up the loading:

```
const mongodb= require('mongodb')
const url = 'mongodb://localhost:27017'
const customers = require('./customer_data.json')

const finalCallback = (results)=>{
  console.log(results)
  process.exit(0)
}

let tasksCompleted = 0
const limit = 1000

mongodb.MongoClient.connect(url, (error, dbServer) => {
  if (error) return console.log(error)
  const db = dbServer.db('cryptoexchange')
```

```
  for (let i=0; i<limit; i++) {
    db.collection('customers')
      .insert(customers[i], (error, results) => {
        // Just a single insertion, not 1000 of them
      })
  }
})
// Putting finalCallback() here would NOT help
```

But how do we know when everything is done? Often you need to continue to execute some other code dependent upon the completion of ALL the tasks, such as these 1,000 MongoDB insertions. Where to put `finalCallback()`? You can have a counter. It's a crude approach but it works (file `code/ch14/async/parallel.js`):

```
const mongodb= require('mongodb')
const url = 'mongodb://localhost:27017'
const customers = require('./customer_data.json')

const finalCallback = (results)=>{
  console.log(results)
  process.exit(0)
}

let tasksCompleted = 0
const limit = customers.length

mongodb.MongoClient.connect(url, (error, dbServer) => {
  if (error) return console.log(error)
  const db = dbServer.db('cryptoexchange')
  for (let i=0; i<limit; i++) {
    db.collection('customers')
      .insert(customers[i], (error, results) => {
        tasksCompleted++
        if (tasksCompleted === limit) return finalCallback(`Finished
        ${tasksCompleted}insertions for DB migration`)
      })
  }
})
```

It's not very elegant to have this counter and also, how do you know whether one or two out of the 1,000s of the tasks have failed? That's why there's the async library. It solves the problem of running and error handling of parallel tasks, but not just them. It also has methods for sequential, and many other types of asynchronous execution. Another benefit of the async module's parallel method is that developers can pass the results of every individual task to the main final callback. Try that with the counter!

Here's the same database migration script but re-written with the async module (file code/ch14/async-example/parallel-async.js):

```javascript
const mongodb= require('mongodb')
const url = 'mongodb://localhost:27017'
const customers = require('./customer_data.json')
const async = require('async')

const finalCallback = (results)=>{
  console.log(results)
  process.exit(0)
}

let tasks = []
const limit = customers.length

mongodb.MongoClient.connect(url, (error, dbServer) => {
  if (error) return console.log(error)
  const db = dbServer.db('cryptoexchange')
  for (let i=0; i<limit; i++) {
    tasks.push((done) => {
      db.collection('customers').insert(customers[i], (error,
      results) => {
        done(error, results)
      })
    })
  }
  async.parallel(tasks, (errors, results) => {
    if (errors) console.error(errors)
    finalCallback(results)
  })
})
```

There are more methods in `async` than just `parallel()`. There are methods to execute tasks sequentially, with racing, with queue, with limits, with retries, and in tons of other ways. Almost all of them support multiple `error` and `result` objects in the final callback, which is a huge plus. For an up-to-date `async` API, see the docs at `https://caolan.github.io/async`.

Promises

Promises use `then`. They use `catch` sometimes too. That's how you can recognize them. That's how you can use them. As a Node developer, you will be using other people's promises a lot. They'll be coming from libraries such as `axios` or `mocha`.

In a rare case when you cannot find a promise-based library on npm, you will have to write your own promise. There's a global `Promise`, which is available in all and every Node v8+ program. This global `Promise` will help you to create your own promise.

Therefore, let's first cover how to use promises and then how to create them with `Promise`. We'll start with usage since most of you will never need to write your own promises (especially when you finish this chapter and learn better syntax such as async functions).

To use a promise, simply define `then` and put some code into it:

```
const axios = require('axios')
axios.get('http://azat.co')
  .then((response)=>response.data)
  .then(html => console.log(html))
```

You can chain and pass around data as much as you want. Try to avoid using nested callbacks inside of `then`. Instead, return a value and create a new `then`. When you get tired of writing `then`, consider writing one or more `catch` statements. For example, using `https://azat.co` will lead to an error because I don't have an SSL certificate on that domain:

```
Error: Hostname/IP doesn't match certificate's altnames: "Host: azat.
co. is not in thecert's altnames: DNS:*.github.com, DNS:github.com,
DNS:*.github.io, DNS:github.io"
```

That error came from this code:

```
axios.get('https://azat.co')
  .then((response)=>response.data)
  .then(html => console.log(html))
  .catch(e=>console.error(e))
```

The next topic is the creation of promises. Just call `new Promise` and use either the `resolve` or `reject` callbacks (yes, callbacks in promises). For example, the `fs.readFile()` is a callback-based function. It's good and familiar. Let's make an ugly promise out of that. Also, let's parse JSON with try/catch, because why not? In a promise it's okay to use try/catch.

```
const fs = require('fs')
function readJSON(filename, enc='utf8'){
  return new Promise(function (resolve, reject){
    fs.readFile(filename, enc, function (err, res){
      if (err) reject(err)
      else {
        try {
          resolve(JSON.parse(res))
        } catch (ex) {
          reject(ex)
        }
      }
    })
  })
}

readJSON('./package.json').then(console.log)
```

There are more features in `Promise`, such as `all`, `race`, and error handling. I will skip all of that because you can read about them in the docs, because async functions are better, and because I don't like promises.

Now that you know how to use a promise from a library (such as `axios`) and create a promise from the ES6 standard promise, I want to show you how a basic promise implementation works under the hood. You will smile and be pleasantly surprised that a promise is nothing more that some tiny-bitty JavaScript code around callback. Promises are not replacement for callbacks, because you still need callbacks for promises.

All know the `setTimeout()` method. It works similarly to any other async method, such as `fs.readFile()` or `superagent.get()`. You have normal argument(s) such as string, number, object, and other boring static data, and you have callbacks, which are not normal arguments, but functions (dynamic and lively, thus more interesting). You would create a new async function `myAsyncTimeoutFn` with your own callback. So when you call this new function, it calls timeout with the callback, and after 1000ms, the callback is executed (file `code/ch14/promise/basic-promise-1.js`):

```
function myAsyncTimeoutFn(data, callback) {
  setTimeout(() => {
    callback()
  }, 1000)
}

myAsyncTimeoutFn('just a silly string argument', () => {
  console.log('Final callback is here')
})
```

What we can do is to re-write the custom timeout function `myAsyncTimeoutFn` to return an object that will have a special method (file `code/ch14/promise/basic-promise-2.js`). This special method will set the callback. This process is called externalization of the callback argument. In other words, our callback won't be passed as an argument to the `myAsyncTimeoutFn` but to a method. Let's call this method `then` because why not.

```
function myAsyncTimeoutFn(data) {

  let _callback = null
  setTimeout( () => {
    if ( _callback ) callback()
  }, 1000)
```

```
    return {
      then(cb){
        _callback = cb
      }
    }
}

myAsyncTimeoutFn('just a silly string argument').then(() => {
  console.log('Final callback is here')
})
```

The code above functions well because our normal `setTimeout` does not actually need `_callback` right now. It needs the callback only long, long, long one thousand milliseconds in the future. By that time, we've executed `then`, which sets the value of the `_callback`.

Some engineers knowledgeable about OOP might call the `_callback` value a private method, and they would be correct. And yes, you actually don't need to prefix the `_callback` with the underscore (`_`), but that's a good convention in Node that tells other Node developers (at least the good ones, like yourself, who read my books) that this method is private. See Chapter 1 for more syntax conventions like that.

What about errors? Error handling is important in Node, right? We cannot just ignore errors or throw them under the rug (never throw an error). That's easy too, because we can add another argument to `then`. Here's an example with the core `fs` module and error handling (file `code/ch14/promise/basic-promise-2.js`):

```
const fs = require('fs')
function readFilePromise( filename ) {
  let _callback = () => {}
  let _errorCallback = () => {}

  fs.readFile(filename, (error, buffer) => {
    if (error) _errorCallback(error)
    else _callback(buffer)
  })
```

```
  return {
    then( cb, errCb ){
      _callback = cb
      _errorCallback = errCb
    }
  }
}

readFilePromise('package.json').then( buffer => {
  console.log( buffer.toString() )
  process.exit(0)
}, err => {
  console.error( err )
  process.exit(1)
})
```

The result of the code above (file `code/ch14/promise/basic-promise-3.js`) will be the content of the package.json file if you run it in my code folder `code/ch14/promise`. But you probably can't wait to see the error handling in action. Let's introduce a typo into the file name that will lead to the `errCb`, which is `_errorCallback`. This is the code that breaks the script:

```
readFilePromise('package.jsan').then( buffer => {
  console.log( buffer.toString() )
  process.exit(0)
}, err => {
  console.error( err )
  process.exit(1)
})
```

The output is just what we wanted:

```
{ Error: ENOENT: no such file or directory, open 'package.jsan'
  errno: -2,
  code: 'ENOENT',
  syscall: 'open',
  path: 'package.jsan' }
```

To summarize our basic promise implementation, we are not using the callback argument on the main function to pass the value, but we are using the callback argument on the `then` method. The callback argument value is a function that is executed later, just like with the regular callback pattern.

Of course standard (ES6 or ES2015) promises have more features. This was just a basic (naive) implementation to show you that promises are simple and mostly about syntax. This list has good resources on learning about promises in depth.

I hope this example has demystified promises and made them less scary… if not, then just use the async/await functions and you'll be good. The next section is about them.

Async Functions

In a nutshell, an `async/await` function is just a wrapper for a promise. They are very compatible. The advantage of the `async/await` function is that the syntax is smaller and that the `async/await` concept *already exists* in other languages such as C#.

Let's re-write the code from the previous section with an async function. The way to do it is to use the word `async` in front of the word `function` or before the fat arrow function `()=>`. Then you can use word `await` after that *inside* of the function. This `await` won't block the entire system, but it will "pause" the current function to get the asynchronous results from a promise or async function.

```
const axios = require('axios')
const getAzatsWebsite = async () => {
  const response = await axios.get('http://azat.co')
  return response.data
}
getAzatsWebsite().then(console.log)
```

So async functions and promises are compatible. Developers can resolve async functions with `then`. The difference is that inside of the `async` function developers don't need to create a mess of `then` statements or nested callbacks. Take a look at this neat Mocha example from my course Node Testing:

```
const axios = require('axios')
const {expect} = require('chai')
const app = require('../server.js')
const port = 3004
```

```
before(async function() {
  await app.listen(port, ()=>{console.log('server is running')})
  console.log('code after the server is running')
})

describe('express rest api server', async () => {
  let id

  it('posts an object', async () => {
    const {data: body} = await axios.post(`http://localhost:${port}
    /collections/test`,{ name: 'John', email: 'john@rpjs.co'})
    expect(body.length).to.eql(1)
    expect(body[0]._id.length).to.eql(24)
    id = body[0]._id
  })

  it('retrieves an object', async () => {
    const {data: body} = await axios.get(`http://localhost:${port}
    /collections/test/${id}`)
    // console.log(body)
    expect(typeof body).to.eql('object')
    expect(body._id.length).to.eql(24)
    expect(body._id).to.eql(id)
    expect(body.name).to.eql('John')
  })
  // ...
})
```

I hope you appreciate the succinctness of the `async` in the `before` and `it` statements. The full source code of this Mocha test with promise and callback versions are on GitHub.

The gist is that async functions are more awesome when you don't resolve them yourself but use them in a framework or a library. Let's see how to use Koa, which is a web framework similar to Express but which uses async functions.

Here's a basic example that has a single route (called middleware, remember?) `app.use()`. It take an async function and there's no `next()` callback. You simply set the body on the `ctx` (context) argument:

```
const Koa = require('koa')
const app = new Koa()

app.use(async ctx => {
  ctx.body = 'Hello World'
})

app.listen(3000)
```

What's especially nice with this approach in Koa is that you can call other asynchronous methods. For example, here's how you can make a non-blocking request to fetch my website azat.co and then send to the client its HTML as the response:

```
const Koa = require('koa')
const app = new Koa()

app.use(async ctx => {
  const response = await axios.get('http://azat.co')
  ctx.body = response.data
})

app.listen(3000)
```

Now let's go back full circle to `try/catch`. Remember, we couldn't use `try/catch` to handle asynchronous errors, right? Guess what. It'll work in the async/await function. See this:

```
const axios = require('axios')
const getAzatsWebsite = async () => {
  try {
    const response = await axios.get('https://azat.co')
    return response.data
  } catch(e) {
    console.log('oooops')
  }
}
getAzatsWebsite().then(console.log)
```

The code above will produce oooops because my website azat.co is hosted on http, not hosted on https.

And you know what else is cool when you use the async/await functions? You can throw errors. Take a look at this example:

```
const makeRequest = async () => {
  const data = await fetchData()
  const data2 = await processData(data)
  const data3 = await processData(data2)
  const data4 = await processData(data3)
  const data5 = await processData(data4)
  throw new Error("oops")
}

makeRequest()
  .catch(err => {
    console.log(err) // outputs Error: oops at makeRequest
  })
```

Technically, you can throw in the promise too, since the async/await functions use promises inside. However, the same error in promises will have a less useful message:

```
Error: oops at callAPromise.then.then.then.then.then (index.js:8:13)
```

For more on async/await vs promise, see this post: http://bit.ly/2xPHIs3.

Summary

Writing and understanding asynchronous code is hard. It's not your fault if this topic is tough on your mind because most of the Computer Science material teaches synchronous code. Also, human brains just aren't wired evolutionarily to deal with parallel and concurrent .

It doesn't matter if you are new to Node or are a seasoned Node developer like I am, you must know how to work and read new asynchronous code with async library promises and the async/await function. Now you can start writing your code using some of that new syntax which you learned in this chapter. And if you ask me, I really like the async/await function syntax for its eloquence and compatibility with the widely-supported promises.

## CHAPTER 15

Node Microservices with Docker and AWS ECS

Node and microservices go together like nuts and honey, like SPF 50 and Cancun, like hipsters and IPA. You get the idea. Some of you might not even know exactly what the heck microservices are. Let me give you my brief definition.

Microservices are small services. A microservice will have just one functionality, but it will have everything that functionality needs.

Let's say you have a service that is giving you an interface to a cookie machine. You can bake a cookie, save a template of a new cookie recipe (gluten-free!), get stats on cookie production, and do all the other boring but necessary stuff a service can do, such called CRUD, from create, read, update and delete.

To continue with this example, now your task is to break this monolithic service into microservices. One microservice will be baking cookies. Another microservice will be saving new cookie recipes for baking by the first microservice, or whatever. In other words, instead of a single application with one staging, one CI/CD, and one production, now you have several applications each with their own staging environment, CI/CD, production environment, and other hassles.

Why bother? Because microservices will allow you to scale different parts of your system up or down *independently*. Let's say there's very little need for new recipes, but there's a huge demand for the orders coming from chat bots (yet another microservice). Good. With microservices, you can scale just the chat bot cookie-ordering microservice (app) and not waste your precious pennies on scaling any other services. On the other hand, with a monolithic app, you have to scale everything at once, which of course takes up more RAM, CPU, and coffee consumed.

There's a fancy term in computer science that will make you look smart (if you work in enterprise) or snobbish (if you work in a startup). Nevertheless, the term describes the microservices philosophy nicely. It's *loose coupling*, and according to many CS books

© Azat Mardan 2018
A. Mardan, *Practical Node.js*, https://doi.org/10.1007/978-1-4842-3039-8_15

and classes, if you use it you'll get flexibility, ease of maintenance, and enough health to enjoy your retirement.

As with many tech concepts, microservices technology has gone through a cycle of overhype. It has advantages and disadvantages. Uber for example has over 2,500 microservices, and its engineers starting to see problems because of complexity and other issues of managing so many separate apps. Hate them or love, the best thing is to know and use microservices when you see a fit. Again, Node is brilliant for microservices because it's light weight, fast and because more and more developers prefer not to have switch of context and use JavaScript for their server-side language.

The project of creating a microservice in a container and deploying it to the cloud is divided into four parts:

1.   Creating a local Node project, a microservice RESTful API that connects to MongoDB

2.   Dockerizing Node project, i.e., turning a local project into a Docker image

3.   Setting up Docker networks for multi-container setup

4.   Deploying the Docker microservice image to the cloud, namely Amazon Web Services (AWS) Elastic Container Service (EC2)

Installing Installations

Before doing the exercise in this chapter, make sure you have the following:

1.   Docker engine

2.   Amazon Web Services (AWS) account

3.   AWS CLI (`aws-cli`)

Installing Docker Engine

Next, you would need to get the Docker engine (daemon). If you are a macOS user like I am, then the easiest way to install the daemon is to just go to and download it from the official Docker website: `https://docs.docker.com/docker-for-mac`.

And if you are not a macOS user, then you can select one of the options from this Docker website page: `https://docs.docker.com/engine/installation`.

To verify installation, run:

```
$ docker version
```

It's good if you see something like this:

```
Client:
  Version:        17.03.1-ce
  API version:    1.27
  Go version:     go1.7.5
  Git commit:     c6d412e
  Built:          Tue Mar 28 00:40:02 2017
  OS/Arch:        darwin/amd64

Server:
  Version:        17.03.1-ce
  API version:    1.27 (minimum version 1.12)
  Go version:     go1.7.5
  Git commit:     c6d412e
  Built:          Fri Mar 24 00:00:50 2017
  OS/Arch:        linux/amd64
  Experimental:   true
```

The next step is to verify that Docker can pull from Hub. Run this hello world image:

```
$ docker run hello-world
```

If you see a message like this, most likely you didn't start Docker:

```
Cannot connect to the Docker daemon. Is the docker daemon running on
this host?
```

Start Docker. If you used the macOS installer linked earlier, then you can utilize the GUI app from the menu bar. Figure 15-1 shows how running the Docker daemon looks on my macOS menu bar.

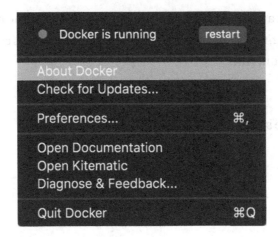

Figure 15-1. *Docker macOS client in the menu bar needs to show "running"*

On the contrary, if you see a message like the one below, then daemon is running and you are ready to work with Docker!

```
Unable to find image 'hello-world:latest' locally
latest: Pulling from library/hello-world

c04b14da8d14: Pull complete
Digest: sha256:0256e8a36e2070f7bf2d0b0763dbabdd67798512411de4cdcf943
1a1feb60fd9
Status: Downloaded newer image for hello-world:latest

Hello from Docker!
This message shows that your installation appears to be working
correctly.

To generate this message, Docker took the following steps:
 ...
```

Getting an AWS Account

You can easily get a free (trial) AWS account. You'll need a valid email and a credit card. Read about the free tier at https://aws.amazon.com/free, and when you are ready, sign up by clicking on "CREATE A FREE ACCOUNT".

Once you are in, make sure you can access EC2 dashboard. Sometimes AWS requires a phone call or a waiting period, but most people can get an account within 10 minutes. It's not always easy to navigate your way around the AWS web console, especially if you are a first-time user. EC2 is just one of many, many, many AWS services. EC2 belongs to the Compute family or category, while there are Database, Security, Tools, Networking and various other categories.

Take a look at Figure 15-2 where I point to the location of the EC2 services in "Recently visited services". If this is your first time using AWS console, you won't have EC2 in the list of recent services. Right below "Recently visited services" is the Compute category that gives you the access to the EC2 dashboard.

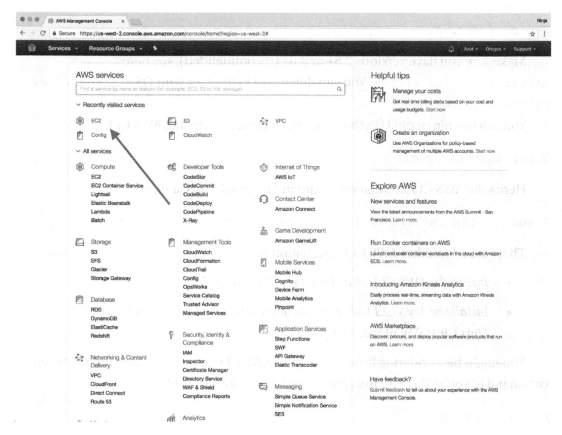

Figure 15-2. *AWS web console has Compute and EC2, which we need for microservices and containers, in the top left column*

Using the web console is easy, but it is limited when it comes to deployment of Docker containers and their images to the AWS container registry. We can later deploy those images from this cloud registry. AWS web console is also limited in the fact that it's hard or even impossible to automate the web interface, whereas it's very easy to automate the command-line interface by writing a few shell scripts. AWS CLI will allow us to upload Docker images to the cloud. Thus, let us proceed to install the AWS CLI.

Installing AWS CLI

Check for Python and pip with these commands:

```
$ phyton --version
$ pip --version
```

Make sure you have versions 2.6+ or 3.6+ (recommended), see here: https://amzn.to/2xPYZBu. You can download Python for your OS at https://www.python.org/downloads.

You can use pip or pip3 (Python package manager) to install AWS CLI:

```
$ pip install awscli
```

Here's the AWS CLI installation command for macOS El Capitan:

```
$ sudo -H pip install awscli --upgrade --ignore-installed six
```

There are a few other AWS CLI Installation options:

- *Install the AWS CLI with Homebrew*: For macOS

- *Install the AWS CLI Using the Bundled Installer (Linux, macOS, or Unix)*: Just download, unzip, and execute

You might be wondering how to verify the AWS CLI installation. Run the following command to verify AWS CLI installation and its version (1+ is ok):

```
$ aws --version
```

Dockerizing Node Microservice

Before deploying anything in the cloud, let's build Node app Docker images locally. Then we will run the image as a container *locally* in both the development and production modes. When you finish this project, you will know how to dockerize a Node project and get yummy.

Creating/Copying the Node Project

Firstly, you need to have the application code itself before you can containerize anything. Of course, you can copy the existing code from `code/banking-api`, but it's better for learning to create the project from scratch.

That's what we will do now. Create a new project folder somewhere on your local computer:

```
$ mkdir banking-api
$ cd banking-api
$ mkdir api
$ cd api
```

Create vanilla/default `package.json` and install required packages as regular dependencies with exact versions:

```
$ npm init -y
$ npm i express@4.15.2 errorhandler@1.5.0 express@4.15.2
globalog@1.0.0 monk@4.0.0 pm2@2.4.6 -SE
```

Add the following npm scripts: the first to test and the second to run the server using local pm2:

```
  "scripts": {
    "test": "sh ./test.sh",
    "start": "if [[ ${NODE_ENV} = production ]]; then
    ./node_modules/.bin/pm2-docker start -i 0 server.js; else
    ./node_modules/.bin/pm2-dev server.js; fi"
},
```

There are two CLI commands for pm2: `pm2-docker` for the container and `pm2-dev` for local development.

The full relative path `./node_modules/.bin` is recommended to make your command more robust. Local installation can be replaced with a global one with `$ npm i -g pm2`. However, global installation is an extra step outside of `package.json`, and the `npm i` command and doesn't allow developers to use different versions of `pm2` on one machine.

The source code for the Node+Express API (`code/ch15/banking-api/api/server.js`) is as follows:

```
require('globalog')
const http = require('http')
const express = require('express')
const errorhandler = require('errorhandler')
const app = express()
const monk = require('monk')

const db = monk(process.env.DB_URI, (err)=>{
  if (err) {
    error(err)
    process.exit(1)
  }
})

const accounts = db.get('accounts')

app.use(express.static('public'))
app.use(errorhandler())

app.get('/accounts', (req, res, next)=>{
  accounts.find({ }, (err, docs) =>{
    if (err) return next(err)
    return res.send(docs)
  })
})

app.get('/accounts/:accountId/transactions', (req, res)=>{
  accounts.findOne({_id: req.params.accountId}, (err, doc) =>{
    if (err) return next(err)
```

```
    return res.send(doc.transactions)
  })
})

http.createServer(app).listen(process.env.PORT, ()=>{
  log(`Listening on port ${process.env.PORT}`)
})
```

The key here is that we are using two environment variables: `PORT` and `DB_URI`. We would need to provide them in Dockerfile or in the command so the app has them set during running.

Let's verify that your application works without Docker by starting MondoGB and the app itself:

```
mongod
```

In a new terminal, launch the server with env vars:

```
DB_URI=mongodb://localhost:27017/db-dev PORT=3000 npm start
```

Yet, in another terminal make a request to your server:

```
curl http://localhost:3000/accounts
```

The result will be `[]%` because it's an empty database and accounts collection. If you use MongoUI or `mongo` shell to insert a document to db-dev database and accounts collections, then you'll see that document in the response. To learn about main `mongo` shell command, you can skim through Chapter 7 of my open-source book *Full Stack JavaScript, 2nd Edition*: `http://bit.ly/2KUjsui`.

The app is working, and now is the time to containerize it.

Creating a Node.js Dockerfile

Go back to the `banking-api` folder and create an empty `Dockerfile`, which must be exactly `Dockerfile`, with no extension and starting with the capital letter D:

```
$ cd ..
$ touch Dockerfile
```

Then, write in `banking-api/Dockerfile` the base image name `FROM node:8-alpine` that is Node v8 based on Alpine. Add `CMD` as shown below. Each `Dockerfile` needs statements like these two:

```
FROM node:8-alpine

CMD ["npm", "start"]
```

Alpine is a lightweight stripped-down Ubuntu which is Linux. It means Alpine is Linux-based. At Capital One, we used Alpine for Node microservices. It worked well. The Docker image size is a few megabytes vs. ~200Mb for a full Ubuntu.

The `Dockerfile` is not yet doing everything we need it do do. So next copy the rest of the `Dockerfile` file between `FROM` and `CMD` as shown below. We will learn shortly what these statements mandate Docker to do. You can copy or ignore the comments marked by the hash sign (#).

```
FROM node:8-alpine

# Some image metadata
LABEL version="1.0"
LABEL description="This is an example of a Node API server with
connection to MongoDB.\More details at https://github.com/azat-co/
node-in-production and https://node.university"
#ARG mongodb_container_name
#ARG app_env

# Environment variables
# Add/change/overwrite with docker run --env key=value
# ENV NODE_ENV=$app_env
ENV PORT=3000
# ENV DB_URI="mongodb://${mongodb_container_name}:27017/db-${app_
env}"
# agr->env->npm start->pm2-dev or pm2-docker
# User
#USER app
# Mount Volume in docker run command

# RUN npm i -g pm2@2.4.6
```

```
# Create api directory
RUN mkdir -p /usr/src/api
# From now one we are working in /usr/src/api
WORKDIR /usr/src/api

# Install api dependencies
COPY ./api/package.json.
# Run build if necessary with devDependencies then clean them up
RUN npm i --production

# Copy keys from a secret URL, e.g., S3 bucket or GitHub Gist
# Example adds an image from a remote URL
ADD "https://process.filestackapi.com/ADNupMnWyR7k
CWRvm76Laz/resize=height:60/https://www.filepicker.io/api/file/
WYqKiG0xQQ65DBnss8nD" ./public/node-university-logo.png

# Copy API source code
COPY ./api/.

EXPOSE 3000

# The following command will use NODE_ENV to run pm2-docker or
pm2-dev
CMD ["npm", "start"]
```

Firstly, we need to create an app directory in the Docker container. RUN will run any shell command. These next "commands" RUN and WORKDIR in your Dockerfile will tell Docker to create a folder and then to set up a default folder for subsequent commands:

```
# Create api directory
RUN mkdir -p /usr/src/api
# From now one we are working in /usr/src/api
WORKDIR /usr/src/api
```

COPY will get the project manifest file package.json into the container. This allows us to install app dependencies by executing npm i. Of course, let's skip the development dependencies (devDependencies in package.json) by using --production. devDependencies should include tools like Webpack, Babel, JSLint and so on, unless you want to test and build your project in a container.

```
# Install api dependencies
COPY ./api/package.json.
# Run build if necessary with devDependencies then clean them up
RUN npm i --production
```

Next, bundle app source by using COPY that takes files from the current folder on the host (using the dot .) and puts them into api folder in the container. Remember, the container folder is first, and the host is second:

```
# Copy API source code
COPY ./api/.
```

You want to open a port cause otherwise no incoming connections will ever get to the container (all outgoing connections are open by default).

```
EXPOSE 3000
```

Finally, you start the server with CMD which runs $ npm start. The list [] can contain more options or use a different command name.

```
CMD ["npm", "start"]
```

By now the Dockerfile, which is a blueprint for your Node microservice, is ready. The code for the microservice is ready too. It's REST API with Express.

Next, we are going to build, run and verify the container by running it *locally*.

Build the image from the banking-api folder where you should have Dockerfile and the api folder:

```
$ docker build .
```

Ah. Don't forget to start the Docker Engine (daemon) before building. Ideally, you'll see 13 steps such as shown next. These steps are statements in Dockerfile. They're called layers. Docker brilliantly reuses layers for images when there are no changes to them.

```
$ docker build .
Sending build context to Docker daemon 23.82 MB
Step 1/13: FROM node:6-alpine
6-alpine: Pulling from library/node
```

```
79650cf9cc01: Pull complete
db515f170158: Pull complete
e4c29f5994c9: Pull complete
Digest: sha256:f57cdd2969122bcb9631e02e632123235008245df8ea26fe6dde0
2f11609ec57
Status: Downloaded newer image for node:6-alpine
 ---> db1550a2d1e5
Step 2/13: LABEL version "1.0"
 ---> Running in 769ba6574e60
 ---> 63d5f68d2d01
Removing intermediate container 769ba6574e60
Step 3/13: LABEL description "This is an example of a Node API server
with connection to MongoDB. More details at https://github.com/azat-
co/node-in-production and https://node.university"
 ---> Running in f7dcb5dd35b6
 ---> 08f1211cbfe1

 ...

Step 13/13: CMD npm start
 ---> Running in defd2b5776f0
 ---> 330df9053088
Removing intermediate container defd2b5776f0
Successfully built 330df9053088
```

Each step has a hash. Copy the last hash of the image, e.g., 330df9053088 in my case.

As an interim step, we can verify our image by using a host database. In other words, our app will be connecting to the host database from a container. This is good for development. In production, you'll be using a managed database such as AWS RDS, Compose, mLabs, or a database in a separate (second) container.

To connect to your local MongoDB instance (which must be running), let's grab your host IP:

```
$ ifconfig | grep inet
```

Look for the value that says `inet`. For example, `inet 10.0.1.7 netmask 0xffffff00 broadcast 10.0.1.255` means my IP is 10.0.1.7.

Put the IP in the environment variable in the `docker run` command for the Docker build of the app image by substituting in the `{host-ip}` and `{app-image-id}` with *your* values:

```
$ docker run --rm -t --name banking-api -e NODE_ENV=development -e
DB_URI="mongodb://{host-ip}:27017/db-prod" -v $(pwd)/api:/usr/src/api
-p 80:3000 {app-image-id}
```

The command must be all on one line or two or more by lines joined by the backslash (\). As an example, the next command has my IP and my image ID in the command instead of the `{ }` values.

```
$ docker run --rm -t --name banking-api -e NODE_ENV=development -e
DB_URI="mongodb://10.0.1.7:27017/db-prod" -v $(pwd)/api:/usr/src/api
-p 80:3000 330df9053088
```

This is just an example. Don't copy my command as-is. Use your IP and image ID. Let me explain what each option is doing:

- `-e` passes environment variables

- `-p` maps host 80 to container 3000 (set in `Dockerfile`)

- `-v` mounts the local volume so you can change the files on the host and container app will pick up the changes automatically

Now after container is running, go ahead and verify by using `curl localhost/accounts`. You should see the response coming from the container app.

You can test the volume. Modify your `server.js` without re-building or stopping the container. You can add some text, a route, or mock data to the `/accounts`:

```
app.get('/accounts', (req, res, next)=>{
  accounts.find({}, (err, docs) =>{
    if (err) return next(err)
    docs.push({a:1})
    return res.send(docs)
  })
})
```

Hit save in your editor on your host, `curl` again and boom! You'll see the change in the response from the app container. The change is the `a:1` response instead of the empty response `[]` as before. This means that the code *in the container* is changing because of the volume and the changes *in the host*. See what I have here as the CURL request and microservice's response:

```
$ curl localhost/accounts
[{"a":1}]%
```

To stop the container, simply run the `dockea stop` command with the container name that you specified when you executed the `docker run` command. Here's the `stop` command for the `banking-api` name:

```
$ docker stop banking-api
```

Or get the container ID first with `$ docker ps` and then run `$ docker stop {container-id}`.

The bottom line is that our `Dockerfile` is production-ready, but we can run the container in dev mode (`NODE_ENV=development`) with volumes and a host database that allows us to avoid any modifications between images and/or Dockerfiles when we go from dev to prod.

Use Docker Networks for Multi-container Setup

Microservices are never used alone. They need to communicate with other micro and normal services.

As mentioned, `Dockerfile` you created is ready to be deployed to the cloud without modifications. However, if you want to run MongoDB or any other service in a container (instead of a host or managed solution like mLab or Compose), then you can do it with Docker networks. The idea is to create a network and launch two (or more) containers inside of this network. Every container in a network can "talk" to each other just by name.

Creating a Docker Network

Assuming you want to name your network `banking-api-network`, run this command:

```
$ docker network create --driver=bridge banking-api-network
```

Verify by getting `banking-api-network` details or a list of all networks:

```
$ docker network inspect banking-api-network
$ docker network ls
```

You should see a table with network ID, driver (bridge or host), name, and so on, like this:

```
$ docker network ls
NETWORK ID       NAME                  DRIVER    SCOPE
e9f653fffa25     banking-api-network   bridge    local
cd768d87acb1     bridge                bridge    local
0cd7db8df819     host                  host      local
8f4db39bd202     none                  null      local
```

Next, launch a vanilla `mongo` image in `banking-api-network` (or whatever name you used for your network). The name of the container `mongod-banking-api-prod-container` will become the host name to access it from our app:

```
$ docker run --rm -it --net=banking-api-network --name mongod-
banking-api-prod-container
mongo
```

Note   If you didn't have `mongo` image saved locally, Docker will download it for you. It'll take some time to download it but it'll happen just once, the first time.

Leave this MongoDB container running. Open a new terminal.

Launch App into a Network

This is my command to launch my Node app in a production mode and connect to my MongoDB container which is in the same network (`banking-api-network`):

```
$ docker run --rm -t --net=banking-api-network --name banking-api
-e NODE_ENV=production-e DB_URI="mongodb://mongod-banking-api-prod-
container:27017/db-prod" -p 80:3000 330df9053088
```

The `330df9053088` must be replaced with your app image ID from the previous section when you executed the `docker build .` command. If you forgot the app image ID, then run `docker images` and look up the ID.

This time, you'll see `pm2` in a production clustered mode. I have two (2) CPUs in my Docker engine settings, hence `pm2-docker` spawned two Node processes which both listen for incoming connections at 3000 (container, 80 on the host):

```
$ docker run --rm -t --net=banking-api-network --name banking-api
-e NODE_ENV=production-e DB_URI="mongodb://mongod-banking-api-prod-
container:27017/db-prod" -p 80:3000 330d
f9053088
npm info it worked if it ends with ok
npm info using npm@3.10.10
npm info using node@v6.10.3
npm info lifecycle banking-api@1.0.0~prestart: banking-api@1.0.0
npm info lifecycle banking-api@1.0.0~start: banking-api@1.0.0

> banking-api@1.0.0 start /usr/src/api
> if [[ ${NODE_ENV} = production ]]; then ./node_modules/.bin/
pm2-docker start -i 0 server.js; else ./node_modules/.bin/pm2-dev
server.js; fi

[STREAMING] Now streaming realtime logs for [all] processes
0|server    | Listening on port 3000
1|server    | Listening on port 3000
```

The command is different than in the previous section but the image is the same. The command does NOT have a volume and has different environment variables. There's no need to use a volume since we want to bake the code into an image for portability.

Again, open a new terminal (or use an existing tab) and run CURL:

```
$ curl http://localhost/accounts
```

If you see `[]%`, then all is good.

Inspecting your network with $ `docker network inspect banking-api-network` will show that you have two (2) running containers there:

```
...
    "Containers": {
        "02ff9bb083484a0fe2abb63ec79e0a78f9cac0d31440374
        f9bb2ee8995930414": {
            "Name": "mongod-banking-api-prod-container",
            "EndpointID": "0fa2612ebc14ed7af097f7287e0138
            02e844005fe66a979dfe6cfb1c08336080",
            "MacAddress": "02:42:ac:12:00:02",
            "IPv4Address": "172.18.0.2/16",
            "IPv6Address": ""
        },
        "3836f4042c5d3b16a565b1f68eb5690e062e5472a09caf56
        3bc9f11efd9ab167": {
          "Name": "banking-api",
          "EndpointID": "d6ae871a94553dab1fcd6660185be4
          029a28c80c893ef1450df8cad20add583e",
          "MacAddress": "02:42:ac:12:00:03",
          "IPv4Address": "172.18.0.3/16",
          "IPv6Address": ""
      }
    },
...
```

Using a similar approach, you can launch other apps and services into the same network and they'll be able to talk with each other.

Note   The older `--link` flag/option is deprecated. Don't use it. See `https://dockr.ly/2xW5jHZ`.

Let me share some of the common issues and their solutions for easy and effortless troubleshooting. Here's the top list:

- *No response:* Check that the port is mapped in the $ `docker run` command with `-p`. It's not enough to just have `EXPOSE` in `Dockerfile`. Developers need to have both.

- *The server hasn't updated after my code change:* Make sure you mount a volume with `-v`. You don't want to do it for production though.

- *I cannot get my IP because your command is not working on my Windows, ChromeOS, Apple Watch, etc.:* See `http://www.howtofindmyipaddress.com`.

- *I can't understand networks:* For more info on networks, see `http://bit.ly/2xNJbiL`.

Node Containers in AWS with EC2 ECS

For the next topics, we will learn how to deploy Node microservices into cloud. The goal is to deploy two containers (API and DB) using ECR and EC2 ECS. We will achieve this goal with the following steps:

1. Creating an AWS Elastic Cloud Registry (ECR) to store images in the cloud

2. Uploading the app image to the cloud (using ECR)

3. Creating a new ECS task definition with two (2) containers to connect them together

4. Creating a container cluster (using ECS)

5. Creating a container service and running it in the cloud (using ECS)

When you are done, you will know how to deploy scalable production-level Node microservices

Creating a Registry (ECR)

Each image needs to be uploaded to a registry before we can use it to run a container. There is registry from Docker: `https://hub.docker.com`. AWS provides its own registry service called EC2, which stands for Elastic Container Registry (ECR). Let's use it.

Log in to your AWS web console at `https://aws.amazon.com`. Navigate to `us-west-2` (or some other region, but we are using `us-west-2` in this lab) and click on CE2 Container Service under Compute, as shown in Figure 15-3.

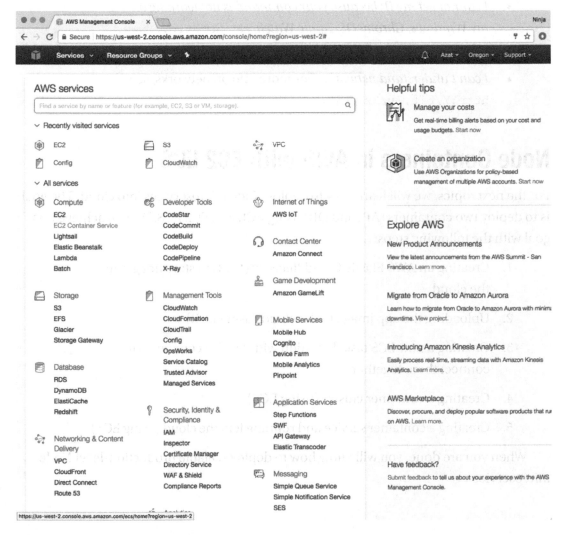

Figure 15-3. *Selecting EC2 Container Service under Compute from the AWS web console*

Then click on *Repositories* from a left menu and then on a blue button named *Create repository*. Then the new repository wizard will open. It might look similar to the one on my screenshot on Figure 15-4.

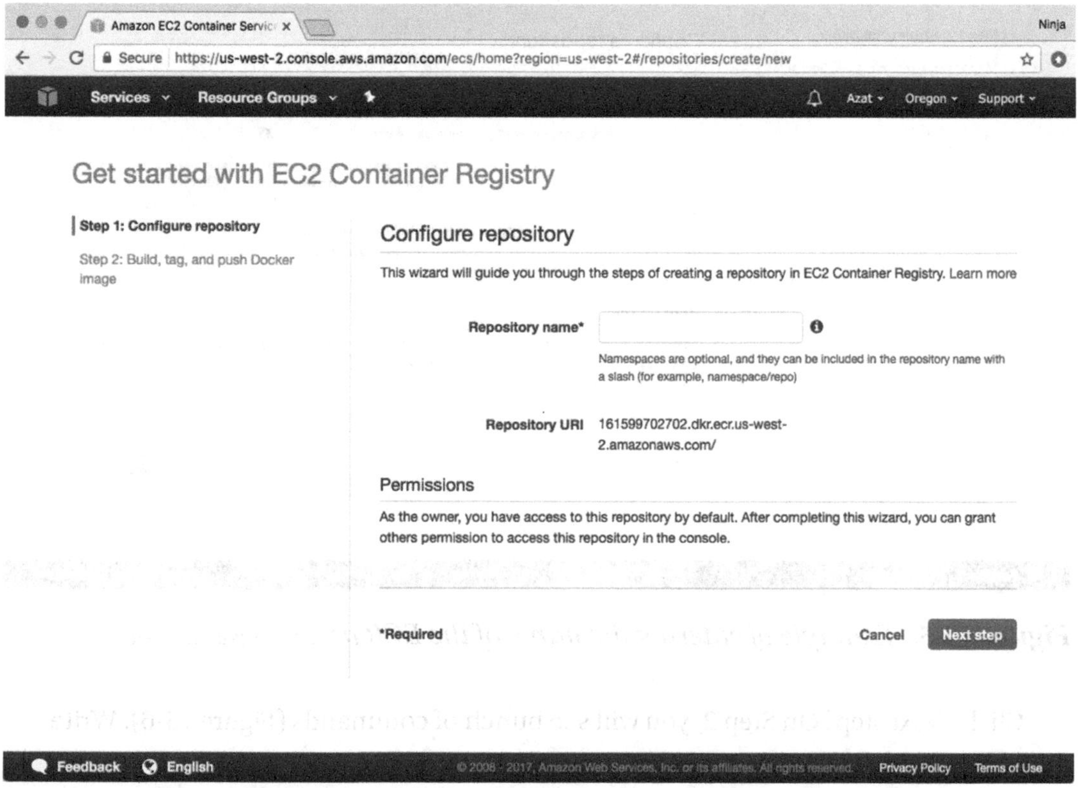

Figure 15-4. *Configure repository is step 1 of creating ECR that prompts for the container repository name*

Enter the name of your repository for container images. I picked `azat-main-repo` because my name is Azat and I have great imagination. Do the same. Not in the sense of picking the same name, but in the sense of naming your repository with some name which you can easily remember later. You can see my screen in Figure 15-5. It shows the future repository URI right away.

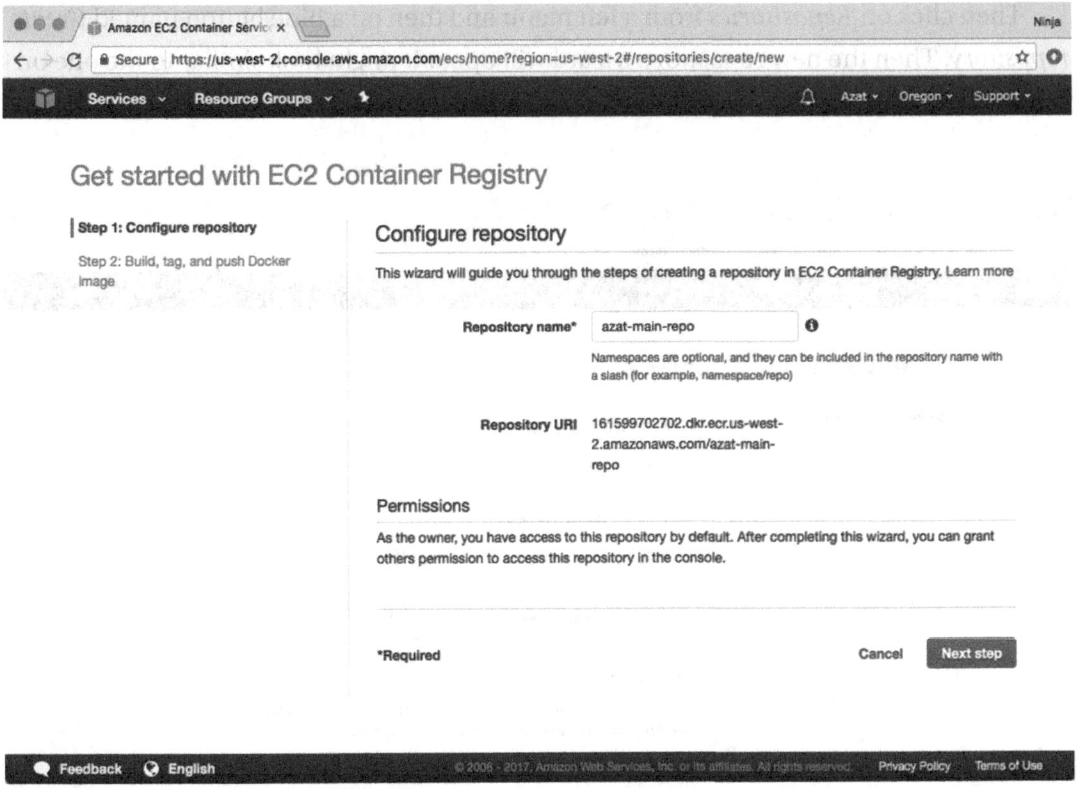

Figure 15-5. *Example of entering the name of the ECR as* `azat-main-repo`

Click "Next step". On Step 2, you will see bunch of commands (Figure 15-6). Write them down and put somewhere safe... away from a dog that can eat it.

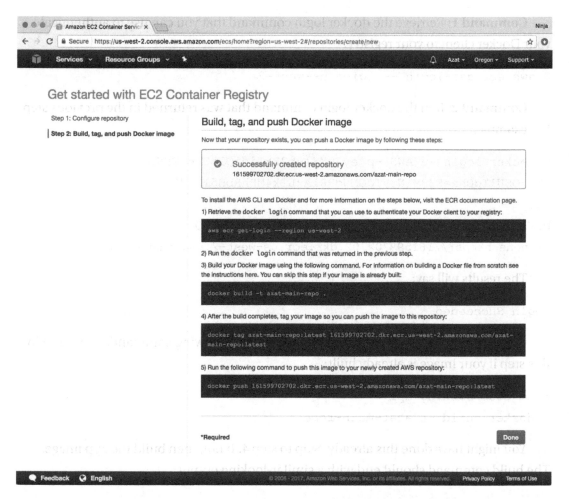

Figure 15-6. *Building and pushing instructions (step 2 of creating ECR) which explains how to upload Docker images*

I have successfully created the repository, and my URI is:

```
161599702702.dkr.ecr.us-west-2.amazonaws.com/azat-main-repo
```

What is your URI? Send me a postcard.

Next, follow instructions shown to you to upload an image. You must build it before uploading/pushing. You'll need AWS CLI. If you still don't have it, then install the AWS CLI and Docker now. I list the commands to build and upload the image next.

Command 1: Retrieve the docker login command that you can use to authenticate your Docker client to your registry:

```
$ aws ecr get-login --region us-west-2
```

Command 2: Run the docker login command that was returned in the previous step. For example,

```
$ docker login -u AWS -p eyJwYXlsb2FkIjoiQ1pUVnBTSHp
FNE5OSU1IdDhxeEZ3MlNrVTJGMUdBRlAxLlk4MDhRbE5lZ3JUW
```

. . .

```
W5VK01Ja0xQVnFSN3JpaHCJ0eXB1IjoiREFUQV9LRVkifQ==
-e none https://161599702702.dkr.ecr.us-west-2.amazonaws.com
```

The results will say:

```
Login Succeeded
```

Command 3: Build your Docker image using the following command. You can skip this step if your image is already built:

```
$ cd code/banking-api
$ docker build -t azat-main-repo.
```

You might have done this already. Skip to step 4. If not, then build the app image. The build command should end with a similar-looking output:

```
. . .
Step 13/13: CMD npm start
> Running in ee5f0fb12a2f
> 91e9122e9bed
Removing intermediate container ee5f0fb12a2f
Successfully built 91e9122e9bed
```

Command 4: After the build completes, tag your image so you can push the image to this repository:

```
$ docker tag azat-main-repo:latest 161599702702.dkr.ecr.us-west-2.
amazonaws.com/azat-main-repo:latest
```

Output: there's no output.

Command 5: Run the following command to push this image to your newly created AWS repository:

```
$ docker push 161599702702.dkr.ecr.us-west-2.amazonaws.com/azat-main-
repo:latest
```

AWS relies on the `docker push` command. Here's the push output example:

```
The push refers to a repository [161599702702.dkr.ecr.us-west-2.
amazonaws.com/azat-main-repo]
9e5134c1ad7a: Pushed
e949bf24b1c4: Pushed
2b5c968a7072: Pushed
858e5e857851: Pushed
10e038bbd0ad: Pushed
ad2f0f4f7c5a: Pushed
ec6eb0ab894f: Pushed
e0380bb6c0bb: Pushed
9f8566ee5135: Pushed
latest: digest: sha256:6d1cd529ced84a6cff1eb5f6cffaed375717022b998e7
0b0d33c86db26a04c7
4 size: 2201
```

Remember the digest value (the last hash). Compare the digest with one in the repository when you look up your image in the web console in EC2 ➤ ECS ➤ Repositories ➤ azat-main-repo, as demonstrated in Figure 15-7.

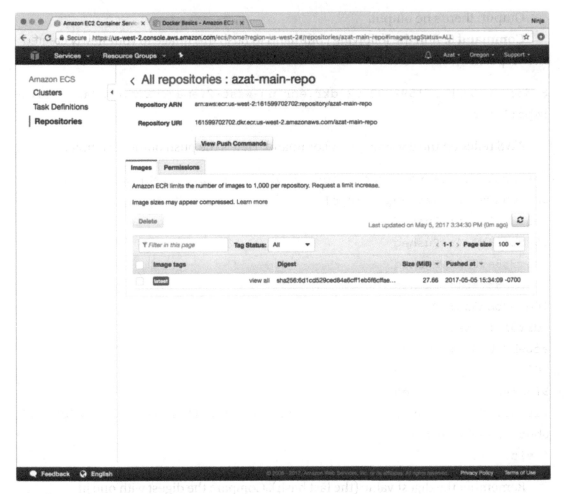

Figure 15-7. *The image uploaded to the newly created container repository is listed with the correct digest and timestamp*

For more information on the steps below, visit the ECR documentation page.

The image's in the cloud, and now is the time to set up a certain mechanism to run this image.

Create a New Task Definition

Tasks are like run commands in Docker CLI (`docker run`) but for multiple containers. Typical tasks define:

- Container images to use

- Volumes, if any

- Networks

- Environment variables

- Port mappings

Go to the Task Definitions in EC2 ECS and, as you might guess, press on the button which says *"Create new Task Definition"*, as it does in Figure 15-8.

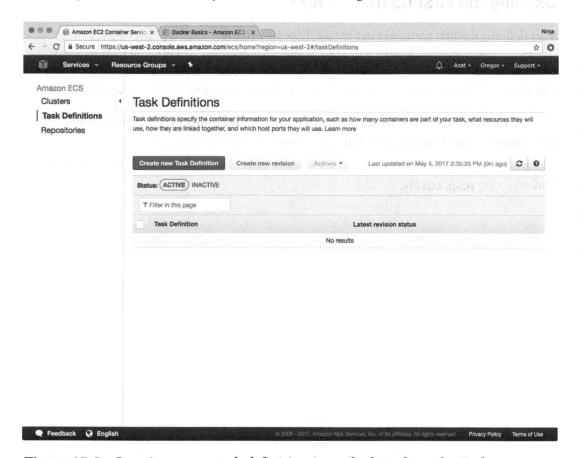

Figure 15-8. *Creating a new task definition is easily done from the Task Definitions screen*

Defining the Main Task Settings for the Example

Use the following settings for the task to make sure your project is running (because some other values might make the project nonfunctional):

- Two containers: `banking-api` (private AWS ECR) and `mongodb` (from Docker hub)

- Connect to `mongodb` via the network alias

- Map 80 (host) to 3000 (container) for `banking-api`

- Set env vars for `NODE_ENV` and `DB_URI`

Let's define the first container—Node app `banking-api`.

Defining the First Container: App

Start defining the first container in the task. Enter the name: `banking-api-container`.

Then define the image URL taken from the repository (your URL will be different), e.g.,

`161599702702.dkr.ecr.us-west-2.amazonaws.com/azat-main-repo:latest`

Define host 80 and container 3000 ports in port mappings. Name, image, and ports are shown below in Figure 15-9. The values are `banking-api-container`, `161599702702.dkr.ecr.us-west-2.amazonaws.com/azat-main-repo:latest`, and `80:3000` respectively.

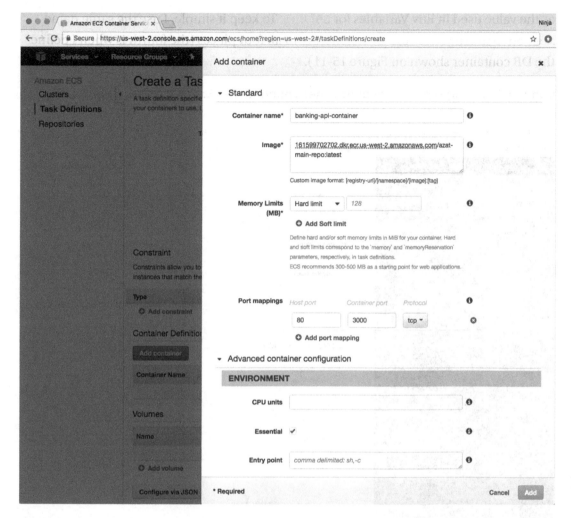

Figure 15-9. *The correct API container configurations have name, image ID, and port values*

Scroll down in the same modal view and add Env Variables (Figure 15-10):

```
DB_URI=mongodb://mongod-banking-api-prod-container:27017/db-prod
NODE_ENV=production
```

Add to Links, as shown in Figure 15-10, the name of the future MongoDB container to give this app container an access to the database container (second not defined yet container). We map the name of the DB container in this app container and the name of the DB container in ECS. The name of the DB container in this app must be the same as the value used in Env Variables for `DB_URI`. To keep it simple, I use the same name `mongod-banking-api-prod-container` in all four places (the fourth is when I define the DB container shown on Figure 15-11).

```
mongod-banking-api-prod-container:mongod-banking-api-prod-container
```

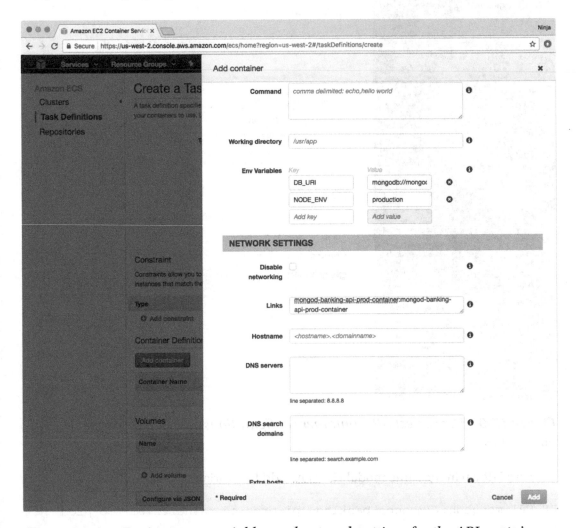

Figure 15-10. *Environment variables and network settings for the API container*

A picture's worth a thousand words. Ergo, see the screengrab below on Figure 15-10 that shows the correct values for the environment variables and the Network settings to link the database to the API.

That's it for the API container. Next we will deal with the database container settings which we must define *in the same task definition* as the API container.

Defining the Second Container: Database

Analogous to the previous container (API), define the name and URL with these values for the DB container (Figure 15-11):

- *Name*: `mongod-banking-api-prod-container`

- *Image URL*: `registry.hub.docker.com/library/mongo:latest`

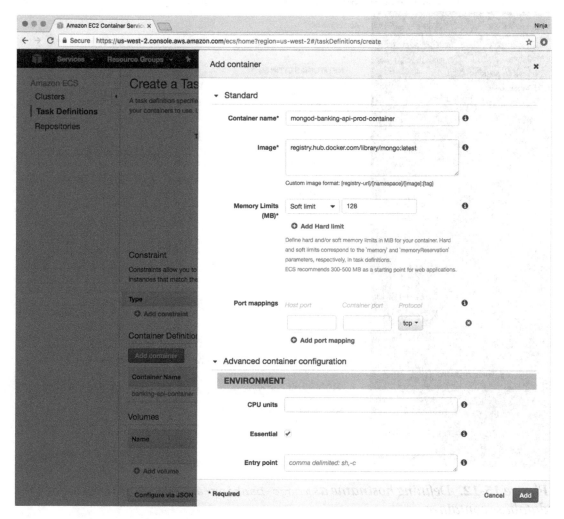

Figure 15-11. *Database container settings have name and image URL*

The next piece is very important because it allows API to connect to this database container, so pay attention closely. Scroll down to the hostname in the Network settings and enter Hostname as `mongod-banking-api-prod-container`, as shown below in Figure 15-12.

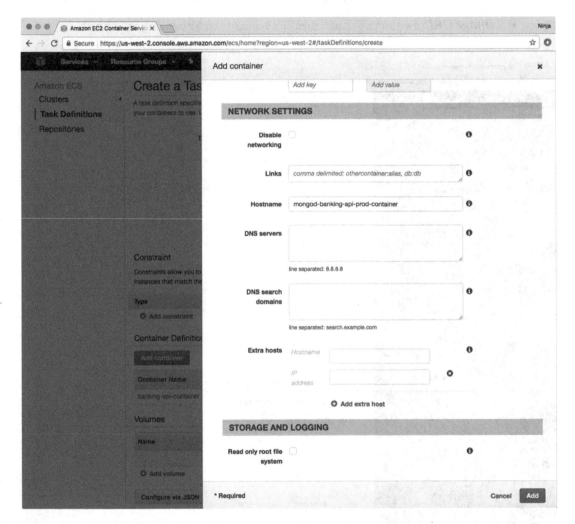

Figure 15-12. *Defining hostname as* `mongo-banking-api-prod-container` *for the database container*

After this hostname, we are done with the database container settings. Since you've added two containers to the task, everything is ready to create the task. Do it and you'll see a screen similar to the one shown below in Figure 15-13.

Figure 15-13. *The newly created task shows two containers and their respective image IDs correctly*

Alternatively, you could specify volumes for database and/or the app at the stage of the task creation. But I will leave that for the next book. Send me a $5 Starbucks gift card, if you're interested in this topic.

Creating Cluster

Cluster is the place where AWS runs containers. They use configurations similar to EC2 instances (Figure 15-14). Define the following:

- *Cluster name:* `banking-api-cluster`

- *EC2 instance type:* m4.large (for more info on EC2 type, see AWS Intro course on Node University)

- *Number of instances:* 1

- *EBS storage:* 22

- *Key pair:* None

- *VPC:* New

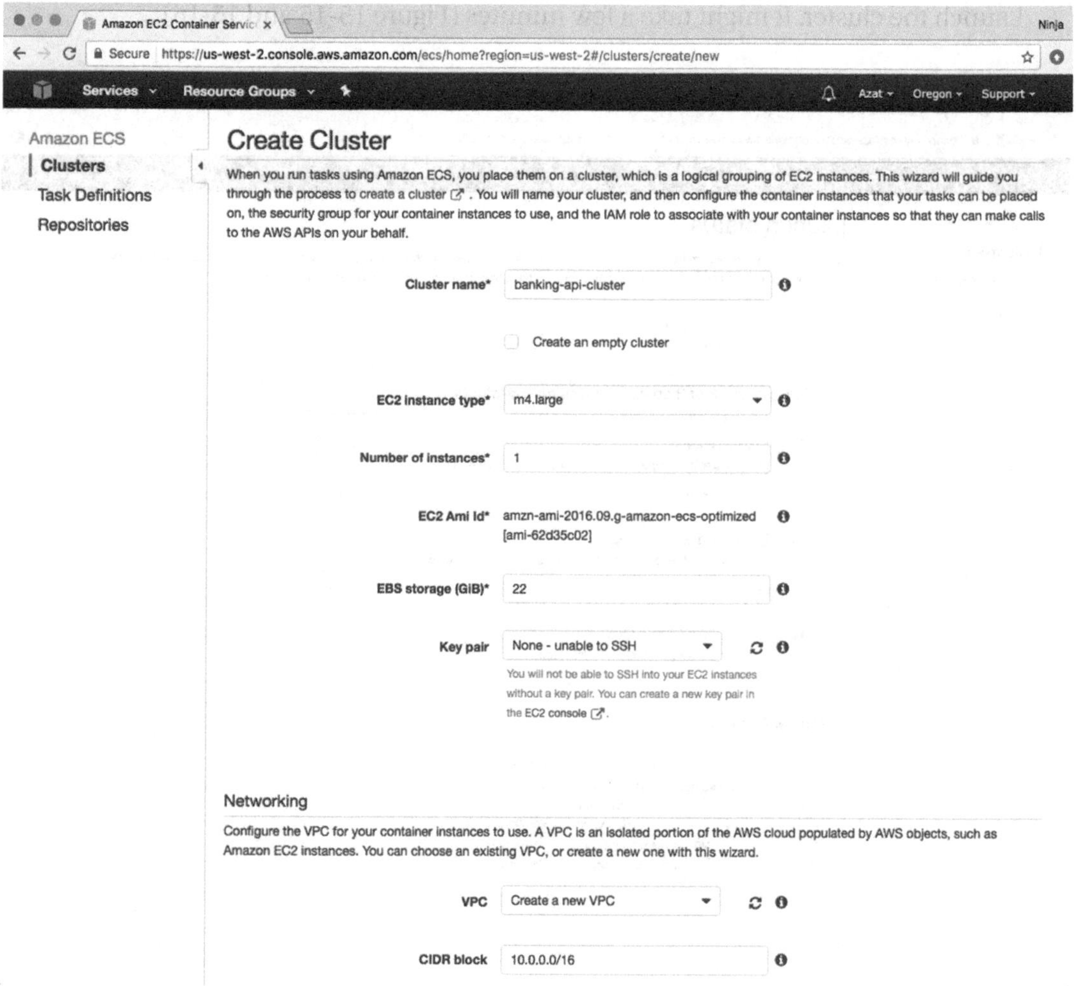

Figure 15-14. *"Create Cluster" page with settings not unlike settings of an EC2 instance*

If you are not familiar with AWS EC2, then I wrote a blog post that TK.

Launch the cluster. It might take a few minutes (Figure 15-15 and 15-16).

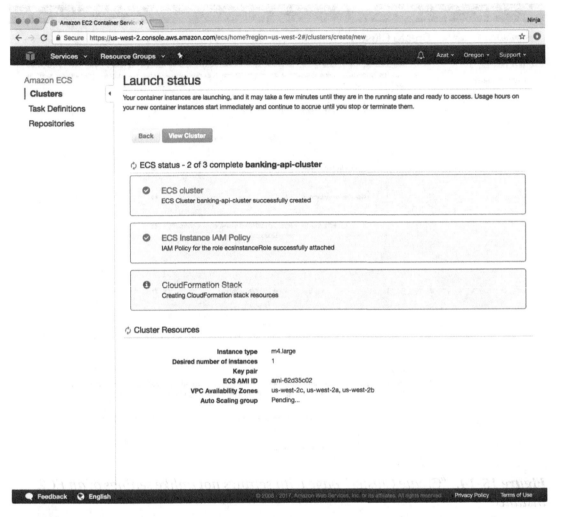

Figure 15-15. *Launching a cluster has three steps: cluster, IAM policy, and CF stack resources*

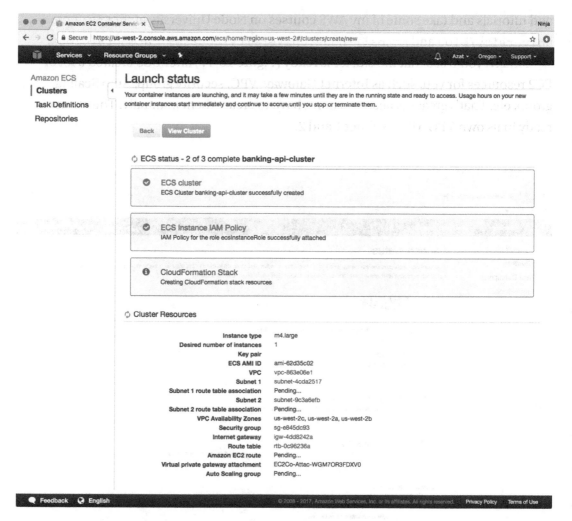

Figure 15-16. *Creating a cluster involves creating multiple AWS resources which are shown at the bottom: VPC, security group, routes, subnets, autoscaling groups, etc*

You'll see the progress as shown in Figure 15-5. Under the hood, AWS uses AWS CloudFormation which is a declarative way to create not just single resources such as Virtual Private Clouds or EC2 instances but whole stacks of dozens or more of such resources. CloudFormation (CF) is like an aircraft carrier. I talk more about CF in my course: `https://node.university/p/aws-intermediate`.

Later, you'll start seeing these resources as I captured in Figure 15-16. All of them will enable the smooth running and functioning of your containers. There are much more to AWS. I recommend learning CloudFormation, EC2 and VPCs. If you want to learn more about AWS and Node besides what's covered in this chapter, read my free blog posts and tutorials and take some of my AWS courses on Node University at: `https://node.university/blog` and `https://node.university/courses/category/Cloud`.

Finally, you'll see that the cluster is ready (Figure 15-17) after ECS created a lot of EC2 resources for you, such as Internet Gateway, VPC, security group, Auto Scaling group, etc. That's great because you don't have to create them manually. The cluster is ready in its own VPC with a subnet 1 and 2.

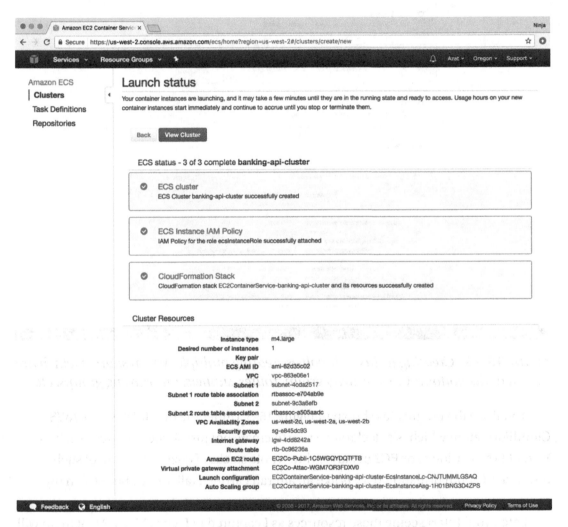

Figure 15-17. *The cluster is created when resources are created*

In my example on Figure 15-17, you can see the Availability Zones (AZs) `us-west-2c`, `us-west-2a` and `us-west-2b`. (AZ is like a data center.) That's good because in case something happens in one AZ, we will have the ability to launch or use another AZ.

We uploaded images, created task definition and launched the cluster. However, if you are thinking we were done, then you are mistaken my friend. The next step is to create a service because no app is running yet without the service.

Creating the Cloud Container Service and Verifying it

The last step is to create a service that will take the task and the cluster and make the containers in the task run in the specified cluster. That's an oversimplified explanation, because the service will do more, such as monitor health and restart containers.

Go to Create Services which is under Task Definition ➤ banking-api-task ➤ Actions ➤ Create Service. You will see this that our ECS service is ready because it's been created, as shown in my screenshot on Figure 15-18. (Amazon made a mistake by writing Elastic Container Service service with a double "service".)

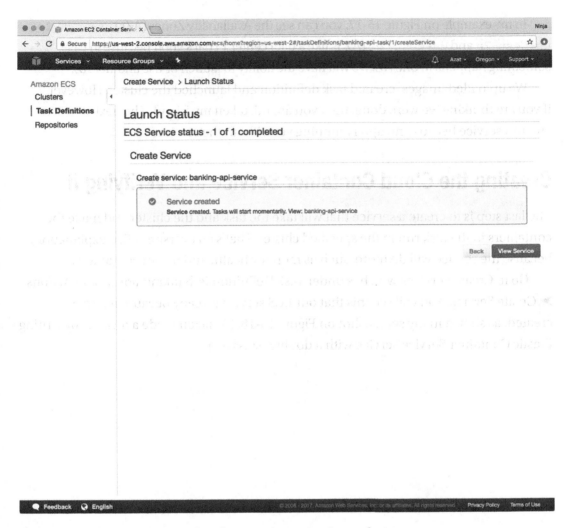

Figure 15-18. *ECS service banking-api-service is ready*

Phew. Everything should be ready by now. The containers should be *RUNNING*.
To verify it, we need to grab a public IP or public DNS. To do so, click Clusters ➤
banking-api-cluster (cluster name) ➤ ESC Instances (tab) and Container instance
as illustrated in Figure 15-19, which shows the running container instance with the
corresponding Public DNS and Public IP. We need those. Either one of them.

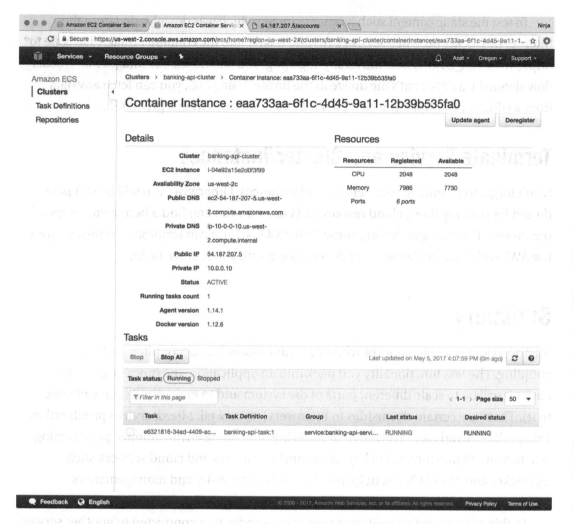

Figure 15-19. *Container instance under the cluster shows public IP and DNS name*

Copy the public IP or DNS for that cluster (which is like an EC2 instance). We will need it for testing. First, we need a dynamic content test. That's the Node API and MongoDB. To test the dynamic content (content generated by the app with the help of a database), open in a browser with {PUBLIC_DNS}/accounts. Most likely the response will be [] because the database is empty, but that's a good response. The server is working and can connect to the database from a different container.

Next, we need a static content test, which is our static asset, i.e., image, inside of the container.

To test the static content such as an `png` image which was downloaded from the Internet by Docker (`ADD` in `Dockerfile`) and baked into the container image, navigate to http://{PUBLIC_DNS}/node-university-logo.png. You should see the images that Docker downloaded via `ADD`. That's the image in the image. Using `ADD`, you can fetch any data from a URL. For example, you can fetch HTTPS certificates from a private S3.

Terminate Service and Cluster/Instances

Don't forget to terminate your service and instances. Otherwise, you will be still paying dinero for running those cloud resources. (I am sure you can find a better way to spend the money. For example, buying some DOGECOIN.) You can terminate resources from the AWS web console. Do so for ECS first. Make sure you remove tasks.

Summary

Microservices is an old concept when you think about it as decoupling and loose coupling. The less functionality you pack into an application, the more flexible and easier it will be to scale different parts of the system and to maintain it (make changes to it). There are certain downsides to microservices as well. Microservices proliferation brings all the overhead involved in monitoring, managing environments, provisioning, patches and deployments. Luckily, Node and containers and cloud services such as Docker and AWS ECS can help in reduce this complexity and management of microservices.

In this chapter you've built your own microservice that connected to another service (MongoDB) both locally and in the cloud. You used Docker by the way of making an image. What's great about this dockerization is that your project is extremely portable. It's mostly independent of OS or any other discrepancies, which often can bite a developer in the tail.

The next chapter is on serverless. It'll take the abstraction in the cloud to an even higher level than containers and microservices, because it allows to not have *any* environments at all. Node developers just supply the code to run it in the cloud.

CHAPTER 16

Serverless Node with AWS Lambda

Servers are fun until they are not. Imagine that you run a few Node services that are important but used sporadically. Maybe you have REST APIs to access and perform CRUD on tables in your noSQL DynamoDB database. You spend money on six large AWS EC2 instances, but you need them only infrequently. It'll be more cost effective to use the serverless architecture with AWS (Amazon Web Services) Lambda then EC2.

Unlike EC2, AWS Lambda doesn't have to run all the time. This way with Lambda, your company will pay only for actual use (compute) time. In other times when there's 0 traffic, it won't be charged at all! Big saving.

Imagine also that your last IT Ops person is leaving to work for a hot Artificial Intelligence Big Data Augmented Reality ICO-funded startup. Your company can't hire a replacement. Luckily, you read this book and docs, and you know that Lambda stack will require almost no maintenance because AWS manages its app environment. You can do everything yourself. The system quality might be even better than your IT Ops person could have achieved. AWS hires lots of good experts who will work on your Lambda infrastructure. All the patches, security, and scaling is taken care off by the AWS experts!

Let's learn how to get started with Lambda by building a REST API for any database table, not just one. As an example, you'll be using and working with messages, but clients can work with any table by sending a different query or payload. Later, you'll be able to create auth and validate request and response in API Gateway (not covered in this lab). You are going to use three AWS services, which I will cover in this chapter:

- DynamoDB

- Lambda

- API Gateway

© Azat Mardan 2018
A. Mardan, *Practical Node.js*, https://doi.org/10.1007/978-1-4842-3039-8_16

This chapter's project is deployed into the cloud AWS Lambda CRUD HTTP API microservice to save data in AWS DynamoDB (key value store). The API Gateway is exposing the HTTP interface. The API code is easy to implement, but the serverless setup (AWS Lambda and API Gateway) is hard. This project is broken down into digestible easy subtasks:

1. Creating a DynamoDB table

2. Creating an IAM role to access DynamoDB

3. Creating an AWS Lambda resource

4. Creating an API Gateway resource

5. Testing the RESTful API microservice

6. Cleaning up

Let's get started with the database.

Creating a DynamoDB Table

The name of the table in these examples is `messages`. Feel free to modify it in the command options as you wish. The key name is `id`, and the type is string (`S`):

```
$ aws dynamodb create-table --table-name messages \
  --attribute-definitions AttributeName=id,AttributeType=S \
  --key-schema AttributeName=id,KeyType=HASH \
  --provisioned-throughput ReadCapacityUnits=5,
  WriteCapacityUnits=5
```

You'll get back the Arn identifier `TableArn` along with other information:

```
{
  "TableDescription": {
    "TableArn": "arn:aws:dynamodb:us-west-1:161599702702:
    table/messages", "AttributeDefinitions": [
      {
        "AttributeName": "id",
        "AttributeType": "N"
      }
    ],
```

```
  "ProvisionedThroughput": {
    "NumberOfDecreasesToday": 0,
    "WriteCapacityUnits": 5,
    "ReadCapacityUnits": 5
  },
  "TableSizeBytes": 0,
  "TableName": "messages",
  "TableStatus": "CREATING",
  "KeySchema": [
    {
      "KeyType": "HASH",
      "AttributeName": "id"
    }
  ],
  "ItemCount": 0,
  "CreationDateTime": 1493219395.933
  }
}
```

You can also get this info by:

```
$ aws dynamodb describe-table --table-name messages
```

You can get the list of all tables in your selected region (which you set in `aws configure`):

```
$ aws dynamodb list-tables
```

Next on our agenda is the access role to this table.

Creating an IAM Role to Access DynamoDB

The next step is to create an identity access management role that will allow the Lambda function to access the DynamoDB database. We shall start with this JSON file, which describes a thing called *trust policy*. This policy is needed for the role. Copy this code and save into `lambda-trust- policy.json`:

```json
{
  "Version": "2012-10-17",
  "Statement": [
    {
      "Sid": "",
      "Effect": "Allow",
      "Principal": {
        "Service": [
          "lambda.amazonaws.com"
        ]
      },
      "Action": "sts:AssumeRole"
    }
  ]
}
```

Let's create an IAM role so our Lambda can access DynamoDB. Create a role with a trust policy from a file using this AWS CLI command (you installed AWS CLI, right?):

```
$ aws iam create-role --role-name LambdaServiceRole --assume-role-
policy-document file://lambda-trust-policy.json
```

If everything went fine, then the role will be created. Compare your results with next one, which has the trust policy content under AssumeRolePolicyDocument *in addition* to the identifiers of the newly created role: the role ID, name, and Arn. Here's my result. Yours will have different IDs. Write down the role Arn somewhere so you have it handy.

```json
{
  "Role": {
    "AssumeRolePolicyDocument": {
      "Version": "2012-10-17",
      "Statement": [
        {
          "Action": "sts:AssumeRole",
          "Principal": {
            "Service": [
              "lambda.amazonaws.com"
            ]
          },
```

```
        "Effect": "Allow",
        "Sid": ""
      }
    ]
  },
  "RoleId": "AROAJLHUFSSSWHS5XKZOQ",
  "CreateDate": "2017-04-26T15:22:41.432Z",
  "RoleName": "LambdaServiceRole",
  "Path": "/",
  "Arn": "arn:aws:iam::161599702702:role/LambdaServiceRole"
  }
}
```

Next, add the policies so the Lambda function can work with the database. In the following command, the role is specified by name `LambdaServiceRole`, which if you remember is the name we used to create the role in the previous command. In other words, we attach a special *managed policy* that grants our future Lambda functions (which will use this role) an access to DynamoDB. The name of this special policy is `AmazonDynamoDBFullAccess`. Not all services have managed policies. In some cases, developers will have to attach policies for read, write, etc. one by one, and these are called *inline policies*.

```
$ aws iam attach-role-policy --role-name LambdaServiceRole --policy-
arn arn:aws:iam::aws:policy/AmazonDynamo
DBFullAccess
```

No output is a good thing in this case.

Another optional managed policy, which you can use in addition to `AmazonDynamoDBFullAccess`, is `AWSLambdaBasicExecutionRole`. It has the logs (CloudWatch) write permissions:

```
{
  "Version": "2012-10-17",
  "Statement": [
    {
      "Effect": "Allow",
```

```
      "Action": [
        "logs:CreateLogGroup",
        "logs:CreateLogStream",
        "logs:PutLogEvents"
      ],
      "Resource": "*"
    }
  ]
}
```

The commands to attach more managed policies are the same—`attach-role-policy`.

Creating an AWS Lambda Resource

On a high level view, our Lambda function (file `code/ch16/serverless/index.js`) looks like this:

```
const doc = require('dynamodb-doc')
const dynamo = new doc.DynamoDB() // Connects to the DB in the same
region automatically, no need for IPs or passwords

exports.handler = (event, context, callback) => {
  switch (event.httpMethod) {
    case 'DELETE':
      // Delete item
      // Call callback with ok
    case 'GET':
      // Read items
      // Call callback with items
    case 'POST':
      // Create item
      // Call callback with ok
    case 'PUT':
      // Update item
      // Call callback with ok
```

```
      default:
        // Call callback with error
    }
}
```

The access to the database is provided via the `dynamodb-doc` library, which is instantiated into the `dynamo` object. No need for IP/domain or passwords. The IAM and AWS will do everything and provide the access to the entire DynamoDB instance, which can have multiple tables per account per region. AWS has just a single DynamoDB "instance" per region, like US West, but there are multiple regions per account.

The Lambda function, which is in this case a request handler, is very similar to the Express request handler. There's a function with three arguments: event, context, and callback. The request body is in the `event.body`. The request HTTP method is in `event.httpMethod`. It's worth mentioning that Lambda functions could be and do anything— not just be request handlers. They can do some computation or work with data. All the operations are done with these three arguments: `event`, `context`, and `callback`.

Here's the full code for the function. It checks HTTP methods and performs CRUD on DynamoDB table accordingly. The table name comes from the query string or from the request body.

```
'use strict'

console.log('Loading function')
const doc = require('dynamodb-doc')
const dynamo = new doc.DynamoDB()

// All the request info in event
// "handler" is defined on the function creation
exports.handler = (event, context, callback) => {
    // Callback to finish response
  const done = (err, res) => callback(null, {
    statusCode: err ? '400' : '200',
    body: err ? err.message : JSON.stringify(res),
    headers: {
      'Content-Type': 'application/json'
    }
  })
```

```
  // To support mock testing, accept object not just strings
if (typeof event.body === 'string') { event.body = JSON.
parse(event.body) }
switch (event.httpMethod) {
      // Table name and key are in payload
  case 'DELETE':
    dynamo.deleteItem(event.body, done)
    break
      // No payload, just a query string param
  case 'GET':
    dynamo.scan({ TableName: event.queryString
    Parameters.TableName }, done)
    break
      // Table name and key are in payload
  case 'POST':
    dynamo.putItem(event.body, done)
    break
      // Table name and key are in payload
  case 'PUT':
    dynamo.updateItem(event.body, done)
    break
  default:
    done(new Error(`Unsupported method "${event.httpMethod}"`))
  }
}
```

So either copy or type the code of the Lambda function shown prior into a file. Then archive it with ZIP into db-api.zip. Yes. It's a simple archive, and that's how we will deploy it, by archiving and uploading this archive file. No Git. Funny how Lambda packaging is so low tech, right?

Now, we can create an AWS Lambda function in the cloud from the source code, which is now only on your local machines. We will use the create-function command.

```
$ aws lambda create-function --function-name db-api \
  --runtime nodejs6.10 --role
  arn:aws:iam::161599702702:role/LambdaServiceRole \
  --handler index.handler \
```

```
--zip-file fileb://db-api.zip \
--memory-size 512 \
--timeout 10
```

Let unpack the command and its three main options:

- For the role `--role`, use your IAM role `Arn` from the IAM step.

- For the `--zip-file`, use the code for the function from the zip file you created earlier.

- For the `--handler`, use the name of the *exported* method in `index.js` for AWS to import and invoke that function.

Just to clarify, `--zip-file fileb://db-api.zip` means upload the function from this file named `db-api.zip`, which is in the same folder in which you run the command `create-function`.

Memory size and timeout are optional. By default, they are 128 and 3 correspondingly.

You can see that the Node version is 6.1. AWS takes care of installing and patching Node any other environment (Python, Java, Go, etc.).

Another important thing to notice and to know about is the function name itself, which is `db-api`. We'll use this name a lot for connecting this function to API Gateway later in this chapter.

Run the `create-function` command with your `Arn`. Also, make sure Node is at least version 6. The function name must be `db-api` or other scripts in this chapter won't work.

Results will look similar to this but with different IDs of course:

```
{
  "CodeSha256": "bEsDGu7ZUb9td3SA/eYOPCw3GsliT3q+bZsqzcrW7Xg=",
  "FunctionName": "db-api",
  "CodeSize": 778,
  "MemorySize": 512,
  "FunctionArn": "arn:aws:lambda:us-west-1:161599702702:
  function:db-api",
  "Version": "$LATEST",
  "Role": "arn:aws:iam::161599702702:role/LambdaServiceRole",
  "Timeout": 10,
```

```
"LastModified": "2017-04-26T21:20:11.408+0000",
"Handler": "index.handler",
"Runtime": "nodejs6.10",
"Description": ""
}
```

I like to test right away. To test the function, I created this data that mocks an HTTP request. It's just an object with the HTTP method set to GET and the query string with the table name parameter. I saved it in the `db-api-test.json` file so you can copy it from the book's repository or from the following snippet.

```
{
  "httpMethod": "GET",
  "queryStringParameters": {
    "TableName": "messages"
  }
}
```

You can copy this object into the AWS web console, as shown in Figure 16-1, or use CLI like a real hacker you are.

For CLI, run from your terminal or command prompt the AWS CLI command `aws lambda invoke` with parameters to execute the function in the cloud. The parameters will point to the data file with the mock HTTP request using `--payload file://db-api-test.json`:

```
$ aws lambda invoke \
  --invocation-type RequestResponse \
  --function-name db-api \
  --payload file://db-api-test.json \
  output.txt
```

It's actually pretty cool to execute a function in the cloud from the command line. It can be useful when the function performs something heavy computational. The function doesn't have to be an HTTP endpoint. It can take any data and give you the output.

The testing can be done from the AWS web console in Lambda dashboard as I mentioned before. Simply select the blue "Save and test" button once you've navigated to function's detailed view and pasted the data (Figure 16-1). Disregard the template that says Mobile Backend. I show how I tested the GET HTTP request with a query string in Figure 16-1.

Input test event   ✕

Use the editor below to enter an event to test your function with. You can edit the event again by choosing **Configure test event** in the Actions list. Note that changes to the event will only be saved locally.

Sample event template   Mobile Backend   ▾

```
1 ▾ {
2       "httpMethod": "GET",
3 ▾     "queryStringParameters": {
4           "TableName": "my-first-table"}
5 }
```

Cancel   Save   **Save and test**

Figure 16-1. *Mocking an HTTP request to our AWS Lambda in the AWS web console*

The results should be 200 (ok status) and output in the `output.txt` file. For example, I do NOT have any record yet, so my response is this:

```
{"statusCode":"200","body":"{\"Items\":[],\"Count\":0,\"ScannedCount\":0}","headers":{"Content-Type":"application/json"}}
```

The function is working and fetching from the database. You can test other HTTP methods by modifying the input. For example, to test creation of an item, use POST method and provide the proper body, which must have `TableName` and `Item` fields, just like in the Node code of our function. Structure the data in body exactly how the function expects it.

```
{
  "httpMethod": "POST",
  "queryStringParameters": {
    "TableName": "messages"
  },
  "body": {
    "TableName": "messages",
    "Item":{
      "id":"1",
      "author": "Neil Armstrong",
      "text": "That is one small step for (a) man, one giant leap for
      mankind"
    }
  }
}
```

Enough with the testing by the way of mocking the HTTP requests. The function is working, okay? It was invoked from the AWS CLI and from the AWS web console. Now we want to create a special URL that will trigger/invoke/execute our function every time there's a request.

Creating an API Gateway Resource

API Gateway will allow us to create a REST API resource (like a route, a UR,L or an endpoint). Every time someone sends a request, this resource will invoke our Lambda. You will need to do the following to create the REST resource/endpoint:

1. Create the REST API in API Gateway

2. Create a resource /db-api (as an example, it's similar to /users, /accounts)

3. Define HTTP method(s) without auth

4. Define integration to Lambda (proxy)

5. Create deployment

6. Give permissions for an API Gateway resource and method to invoke Lambda

The process is not straightforward. In fact it's prone to mistake and errors. I spend many hours tweaking and mastering all these API Gateway steps to automate them, that is, I created a magical shell script. As a result, you can use a shell script which will perform all the steps (recommended) or... send hours banging your head against the table like I did. The AWS web console can help too. It can simplify and automate *some* steps for you too if you use the right template.

The shell script is in the `create-api.sh` file. It has inline comments to help you understand what is happening. Feel free to inspect `create-api.sh`. For brevity and to avoid complicating the chapter, I won't go over it line-by-line but I'll show the file with comments.

```
APINAME=api-for-db-api
REGION=us-west-1
NAME=db-api # function name
API_PATH=db-api
# Create an API
aws apigateway create-rest-api --name "${APINAME}" --description
"Api for ${NAME}" --region ${REGION}
APIID=$(aws apigateway get-rest-apis --query
"items[?name==\`${APINAME}\`].id" --output text --region ${REGION})
echo "API ID: ${APIID}"
PARENTRESOURCEID=$(aws apigateway get-resources --rest-api-id
${APIID} --query "items[?path=='/'].id" --output text --region
${REGION})
echo "Parent resource ID: ${PARENTRESOURCEI}"
# Create a resource as a path, our function will handle many tables
(resources) but you can be more specific
aws apigateway create-resource --rest-api-id ${APIID} --parent-id
${PARENTRESOURCEID}
--path-part ${API_PATH} --region ${REGION}
RESOURCEID=$(aws apigateway get-resources --rest-api-id ${APIID}
--query "items[?path=='/db-api'].id" --output text --region ${REGION})
echo "Resource ID for path ${API_PATH}: ${APIID}"
```

```
# Add a method like GET, POST, PUT, etc.; for CRUD we need all
methods so just put ANY . Here you can set up auth as well
aws apigateway put-method --rest-api-id ${APIID} --resource-id
${RESOURCEID} --http-method ANY --authorization-type NONE --no-api-
key-required --region ${REGION}
LAMBDAARN=$(aws lambda list-functions --query "Functions[?FunctionNa
me==\`${NAME}\`].FunctionArn" --output text --region ${REGION})
echo "Lambda Arn: ${LAMBDAARN}"
# Create integration
# http-method: proxy any http method, but could be only GET, POST,
PUT, etc.
# type: proxy everything, other possible options: HTTP and AWS
# integration-http-method: must be POST for method to lambda
integration to inkove lambda
aws apigateway put-integration --rest-api-id ${APIID} \
--resource-id ${RESOURCEID} \
--http-method ANY \
--type AWS_PROXY \
--integration-http-method POST \
--uri arn:aws:apigateway:${REGION}:lambda:path/2015-03-31/functions/
${LAMBDAARN}/invocations
aws apigateway create-deployment --rest-api-id ${APIID} --stage-name
prod --region ${REGION}
APIARN=$(echo ${LAMBDAARN} | sed -e 's/lambda/execute-api/' -e "s/
function:${NAME}/${APIID}/")
echo "APIARN: $APIARN"
UUID=$(uuidgen)
# Add permissions to invoke function
# use uuid to make sure we don't get already exists error
# in source-arn, change to prod/GET or prod/POST where pattern is
stage/http-method
aws lambda add-permission \
--function-name ${NAME} \
```

```
--statement-id apigateway-db-api-any-proxy-${UUID} \
--action lambda:InvokeFunction \
--principal apigateway.amazonaws.com \
--source-arn "${APIARN}/*/*/db-api"
# This is where you can control responses
aws apigateway put-method-response \
--rest-api-id ${APIID} \
--resource-id ${RESOURCEID} \
--http-method ANY \
--status-code 200 \
--response-models "{}" \
--region ${REGION}
echo "Resource URL is https://${APIID}.execute-api.${REGION}.
amazonaws.com/prod/db-api/?TableName=messages"
echo "Testing..."
curl "https://${APIID}.execute-api.${REGION}.amazonaws.com/prod/db-
api/?TableName=messages"
```

Run my API Gateway script to create the API endpoint and integrate it with the Lambda function (if you modified the region or the function name, you'll need to change those values in the script as well):

```
$ sh create-api.sh
```

In the end, the script will make a GET request to check that everything is working. This is an example of running the automation script for the API Gateway (your IDs and Arns will be different):

```
$ sh create-api.sh
{
    "id": "sdzbvm11w6",
    "name": "api-for-db-api",
    "description": "Api for db-api",
    "createdDate": 1493242759
}
```

```
API ID: sdzbvm11w6
Parent resource ID: sdzbvm11w6
{
    "path": "/db-api",
    "pathPart": "db-api",
    "id": "yjc218",
    "parentId": "xgsraybhu2"
}
Resource ID for path db-api: sdzbvm11w6
{
    "apiKeyRequired": false,
    "httpMethod": "ANY",
    "authorizationType": "NONE"
}
Lambda Arn: arn:aws:lambda:us-west-1:161599702702:function:db-api
{
    "httpMethod": "POST",
    "passthroughBehavior": "WHEN_NO_MATCH",
    "cacheKeyParameters": [],
    "type": "AWS_PROXY",
    "uri": "arn:aws:apigateway:us-west-1:lambda:
    path/2015-03-31/functions/arn:aws:lambda:us-west-1:
    161599702702:function:db-api/invocations",
    "cacheNamespace": "yjc218"
}
{
    "id": "k6jko6",
    "createdDate": 1493242768
}
APIARN: arn:aws:execute-api:us-west-1:161599702702:sdzbvm11w6
{
    "Statement": "{\"Sid\":\"apigateway-db-api-any-proxy-9C30DEF8-
    A85B-4EBC-BBB0-8D50E6AB33E2\",\"Resource\":\"arn:aws:lambda:
    us-west-1:161599702702:function:db-api\",\"Effect\":\"Allow\",
```

```
    \"Principal\":{\"Service\":\"apigateway.amazonaws.com\"},
    \"Action\":[\"lambda:InvokeFunction\"],\"Condition\":{\"ArnLike\":
    {\"AWS:SourceArn\":\"arn:aws:execute-api:us-west-1:
    161599702702:sdzbvm11w6/*/*/db-api\"}}}"
}
{
    "responseModels": {},
    "statusCode": "200"
}
Resource URL is https://sdzbvm11w6.execute-api.us-west-1.amazonaws.
com/prod/db-api/?TableName=messages
Testing...
{"Items":[],"Count":0,"ScannedCount":0}%
```

You are all done! The resource URL is there in your terminal output. The script even tested the function for you if you look at the very last line (must be `"Items": []` unless you inserted a few records in the DB already).

Testing the RESTful API Microservice

You can manually run tests by getting the resource URL and using cURL, Postman, or any other HTTP client. For example, my GET looks like this (replace the URL with yours):

```
$ curl "https://sdzbvm11w6.execute-api.us-west-1.amazonaws.com/prod/
db-api/?TableName=messages"
```

But my POST has a body and header with a unique ID:

```
$ curl "https://sdzbvm11w6.execute-api.us-west-1.amazonaws.com/prod/
db-api/?TableName=messages" \
  -X POST \
  -H "Content-Type: application/json" \
  -d '{"TableName": "messages",
    "Item": {
      "id": "'$(uuidgen)'",
      "author": "Neil Armstrong",
```

```
    "text": "That is one small step for (a) man, one giant leap for
    mankind"
  }
}'
```

Here's an option if you don't want to copy paste your endpoint URL. Use env var to store URL and then CURL to it. Execute this once to store the env var `API_URL`:

```
APINAME=api-for-db-api
REGION=us-west-1
NAME=db-api
APIID=$(aws apigateway get-rest-apis --query "items[?name==\`${APINA
ME}\`].id" --output text --region ${REGION})
API_URL="https://${APIID}.execute-api.${REGION}.amazonaws.com/prod/
db-api/?TableName=messages"
```

Then run for GET as many times as you want:

```
$ curl $API_URL
```

And run the following to POST as many times as you want (thanks to `uuidgen`):

```
$ curl ${API_URL} \
  -X POST \
  -H "Content-Type: application/json" \
  -d '{"TableName": "messages",
    "Item": {
      "id": "'$(uuidgen)'",
      "author": "Neil Armstrong",
      "text": "That is one small step for (a) man, one giant leap for
      mankind"
    }
}'
```

The new items can be observed via an HTTP interface by making another GET request... or in the AWS web console in DynamoDB dashboard as shown below in Figure 16-2:

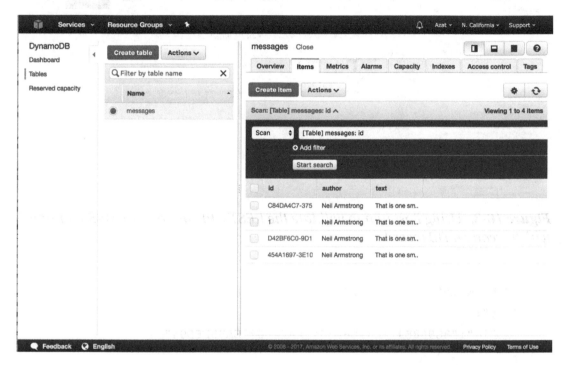

Figure 16-2. *Verifying newly created DB records in the* `messages` *table by looking at the AWS web console's DynamoDB dashboard*

You have yet another option to play with your newly created serverless REST API resource: a very popular GUI app for making HTTP requests called Postman. Here's how the POST request looks like in Postman. Remember to select POST, Raw, and JSON (`application/json`):

To delete an item with the DELETE HTTP request method, the payload must have a `Key` field of that record that we want to delete. For example:

Figure 16-3. *Using Postman to validate the REST API endpoint to AWS Lambda, which creates a DB record*

```
{
    "TableName": "messages",
    "Key":{
        "id":"8C968E41-E81B-4384-AA72-077EA85FFD04"
    }
}
```

Congratulations! You've built an event-driven REST API for an entire database, not just a single table!

Note   For auth, you can set up token-based auth on a resource and method in API Gateway. You can set up response and request rules in the API Gateway as well. Also, everything (API Gateway, Lambda, and DynamoDB) can be set up in CloudFormation instead of a CLI or web console (example of Lambda with CloudFormation: `http://bit.ly/2xMBSry`).

Cleaning Up

You can leave your function running since AWS will charge only for the usage, but I prefer to clean every AWS resource right away. Remove the API Gateway API with `delete-rest-api`. For example, here's my command (for yours, replace the REST API ID accordingly):

```
$ aws apigateway delete-rest-api --rest-api-id sdzbvm11w6
```

Delete the function by its name using `delete-function`:

```
$ aws lambda delete-function --function-name db-api
```

Finally, delete the database by its name too:

```
$ aws dynamodb delete-table --table-name messages
```

I've taught this project over 20 times, so I know the common problems that can arise. This is the troubleshooting of the common issues:

- *Internal server error:* Check your JSON input. DynamoDB requires a special format for Table Name and ID/Key.

- *Permissions:* Check the permission for API resource and method to invoke Lambda. Use the test in API Gateway to debug.

- `UnexpectedParameter: Unexpected key '0' found in params`: Check that you are sending proper format, JSON vs. string.

- `<AccessDeniedException><Message>Unable to determine service/operation name to be authorized</Message></AccessDeniedException>`: Make sure to use POST for `integration-http-method` as in the `create-api` script, because API Gateway integration can only use POST to trigger functions, even for other HTTP methods defined for this resource (like ANY).

- *Wrong IDs:* Make sure to check names and IDs if you modified the examples.

Summary

Amazon Web Services offers myriads of cloud services, and most of them use and benefit greatly from Node. Serverless architecture is one popular use case for Node. In AWS, the serverless service is AWS Lambda. It uses managed and configured Node environment to run code (among other environments such as Python, Java, and other dinosaurs). The code can be HTTP request-response services (microservices) when you add API Gateway to Lambda. That's what we did, but that's not all. Lambdas can be just code for sending notifications, doing data crunching, and performing any other tasks.

CHAPTER 17

Conclusion

Lo and behold, this is the end of the book. There was a study that showed that the majority of programmers read zero books per year.[1] So, pat yourself on the back, because you're on the road to awesomeness when it comes to building Node.js web apps.

Regarding the material covered in *Practical Node.js*, we explored real-world aspects of the Node.js stack. To do this, many things were essential, and by now you should have an awareness of how pieces fit together. For some technologies such as Pug and REST API, our coverage was quite extensive. However, most of the packages are very specific and tailored to our apps' goals, so those topics were given a brief introduction, with references for further learning. Here's a list of topics we covered:

- Node.js and npm setup and development tools

- Web apps with Express.js

- TDD with Mocha

- Pug and Handlebars

- MongoDB and Mongoskin

- Mongoose MongoDB ORM

- Session, token authentication, and OAuth with Everyauth

- REST APIs with Express and Hapi

- WebSockets with ws, Socket.IO, and DerbyJS

- Best practices for getting apps production ready

- Deployment to Heroku and AWS

- Structuring and publishing npm modules

---

[1]http://bit.ly/2xOm8V6

© Azat Mardan 2018
A. Mardan, *Practical Node.js*, https://doi.org/10.1007/978-1-4842-3039-8_17

- Node HTTP/2 Servers

- Asynchronous Code in Node

- Node Microservices with Docker and AWS ECS

- Serverless Node with AWS Lambda

Author Contact

If you enjoyed this reading, you might like my programming blog about software engineering, startups, JavaScript and Node.js: `webapplog.com`.

I speak at conferences and publish online courses. I am not active on Instagram or Snapchat but I post regularly on YouTube, Twitter, Facebook, LinkedIn and Google+. Follow me, the author of this book, on Twitter @azatmardan for tips and news about Node.js. And subscribe to me on YouTube, connect with me on LinkedIn, and friend me on Facebook. I posted all my social media links: `http://azat.co`.

Further Learning

I wrote 18 books to date. Here's just the short list of my other related books:

- *React Quickly* (Manning, 2017)

- *Pro Express.js* (Apress, 2014)

- *Full Stack JavaScript, 2nd Edition* (Apress, 2018)

- *Write Your Way to Success* (Apress, 2018)

- *Using Your Web Skills to Make Money* (Apress, 2018)

If you don't have much time to read, like most of us, then check out my podcast on iTunes, Google Play and Stitcher. It's called Node University. You can find the links at `https://nodeuniversity.simplecast.fm`.

Lastly, you can supplement your reading with videos and coding exercises at Node University: `https://node.university`.

Index

A

addListener method, 335

Amazon Web Services (AWS)
  advantages, 372
  DNS, 376
  EC2 instance, 373
  EPEL, 372
  HTTP traffic, 375–376
  Node.js, 374
  NPM, 372–374
  server.js, 374
  yum command, 373

Application programming
    interface (API), 29, 277
  array objects, 29
  math objects, 30
  string objects, 30

Asynchronous code
  async/await function, 426–429
  async module, 418–421
  promises
    axios, 422
    callback argument, 423, 426
    catch statements, 421
    error handling, 424
    fs.readFile(), 422
    myAsyncTimeoutFn function, 423
    setTimeout() method, 423

Authentication, blog, 224
  destroy(), 226
  findOne(), 225

  return keyword, 225

Authorization, 206, 220
  Express.js middleware, 206–207

AWS Lambda, 473
  API Gateway resource
    automation script, 487–489
    create-api.sh file, 485
    GET request, 487
  DynamoDB
    create table, 474–475
    IAM to access, 475–477
  resource, 478
    aws lambda invoke command, 482
    create-function command, 480–481
    dynamodb-doc library, 479
    HTTP method, 479–480
    HTTP request, 482–484
  RESTful API microservice, 489–491
  troubleshooting, 493

B

Behavior-driven
    development (BDD), 89

Blog, 218
  authentication
    destroy(), 226
    findOne(), 225
    return keyword, 225
  authorization, 220–224
  run app, 227
  session middleware, 219–220

497

© Azat Mardan 2018
A. Mardan, *Practical Node.js*, https://doi.org/10.1007/978-1-4842-3039-8